VIBRANT DEATH

Theory in the New Humanities

Series editor: Rosi Braidotti

Theory is back! The vitality of critical thinking in the world today is palpable, as is a spirit of insurgency that sustains it. Theoretical practice has exploded with renewed energy in media, society, the arts and the corporate world. New generations of critical 'studies' areas have grown alongside the classical radical epistemologies of the 1970s: gender, feminist, queer, race, postcolonial and subaltern studies, cultural studies, film, television and media studies.

This series aims to present cartographic accounts of emerging critical theories and to reflect the vitality and inspirational force of on-going theoretical debates.

Editorial board
Stacy Alaimo (University of Texas at Arlington, USA)
Simone Bignall (Flinders University, Australia)
Judith Butler (University of Berkeley, USA)
Christine Daigle (Brock University, Canada)
Rick Dolphijn (Utrecht University, The Netherlands)
Matthew Fuller (Goldsmiths, University of London, UK)
Engin Isin (Queen Mary University of London, UK, and University of London Institute in Paris, France)
Patricia MacCormack (Anglia Ruskin University, UK)
Achille Mbembe (University Witwatersrand, South Africa)
Henrietta Moore (University College London, UK)

Other titles in the series:
Posthuman Glossary, edited by Rosi Braidotti and Maria Hlavajova
Conflicting Humanities, edited by Rosi Braidotti and Paul Gilroy
General Ecology, edited by Erich Hörl with James Burton
Philosophical Posthumanism, Francesca Ferrando
The Philosophy of Matter, Rick Dolphijn
Materialist Phenomenology, Manuel DeLanda
From Deleuze and Guattari to Posthumanism, edited by Christine Daigle and Terrance H. McDonald

VIBRANT DEATH

A Posthuman Phenomenology of Mourning

Nina Lykke

BLOOMSBURY ACADEMIC
LONDON • NEW YORK • OXFORD • NEW DELHI • SYDNEY

BLOOMSBURY ACADEMIC
Bloomsbury Publishing Plc
50 Bedford Square, London, WC1B 3DP, UK
1385 Broadway, New York, NY 10018, USA
29 Earlsfort Terrace, Dublin 2, Ireland

BLOOMSBURY, BLOOMSBURY ACADEMIC and the Diana logo are trademarks of Bloomsbury Publishing Plc

First published in Great Britain 2022
This paperback edition published 2023

Copyright © Nina Lykke, 2022

Nina Lykke has asserted her right under the Copyright, Designs and Patents Act, 1988, to be identified as Author of this work.

For legal purposes the Acknowledgements on pp. x–xii, and p. 257 n. 1, 1, 6; p. 258 n. 1, 3, 7; p. 259 n. 1, 5, 8; p. 263 n.1 and p. 268 n. 1, 2 constitute an extension of this copyright page.

Cover design: Katja Aglert
Cover photo: Diatomaceous Cliff at the Island of Fur in Limfjorden, Denmark © Nina Lykke, 2021

All rights reserved. No part of this publication may be reproduced or transmitted in any form or by any means, electronic or mechanical, including photocopying, recording, or any information storage or retrieval system, without prior permission in writing from the publishers.

Bloomsbury Publishing Plc does not have any control over, or responsibility for, any third-party websites referred to or in this book. All internet addresses given in this book were correct at the time of going to press. The author and publisher regret any inconvenience caused if addresses have changed or sites have ceased to exist, but can accept no responsibility for any such changes.

A catalogue record for this book is available from the British Library.

Library of Congress Cataloging-in-Publication Data
Names: Lykke, Nina, author.
Title: Vibrant death : a posthuman phenomenology of mourning / Nina Lykke.
Description: London ; New York : Bloomsbury Academic, 2022. | Series: Theory in the new humanities | Includes bibliographical references and index.
Identifiers: LCCN 2021034006 (print) | LCCN 2021034007 (ebook) | ISBN 9781350149724 (hardback) | ISBN 9781350149731 (pdf) | ISBN 9781350149748 (ebook)
Subjects: LCSH: Death. | Posthumanism. | Phenomenology.
Classification: LCC BD444 .L95 2022 (print) | LCC BD444 (ebook) | DDC 128/.5—dc23
LC record available at https://lccn.loc.gov/2021034006
LC ebook record available at https://lccn.loc.gov/2021034007

ISBN:	HB:	978-1-3501-4972-4
	PB:	978-1-3501-8782-5
	ePDF:	978-1-3501-4973-1
	eBook:	978-1-3501-4974-8

Series: Theory in the New Humanities

Typeset by RefineCatch Limited, Bungay, Suffolk

To find out more about our authors and books visit www.bloomsbury.com and sign up for our newsletters.

For you, Mette . . .

CONTENTS

List of Illustrations	ix
Acknowledgements	x
Notes on Text and Photos	xiii

Overture
TRAVELLING TO THE WORLD OF THE DEAD – A TRIPTYCH   1

Chapter 1
QUEERING DEATH AND POSTHUMANIZING MOURNING:
INTRODUCTION   7

Interlude I
LACRIMOSO E LAMENTOSO (CRYING AND LAMENTING)   23

Chapter 2
THE EXCESSIVE MOURNER   39

Interlude II
VIBRATO BRUSCAMENTE (ABRUPTLY VIBRATING)   57

Chapter 3
THE VIBRANT CORPSE   71

Interlude III
SILENZIO APPASSIONATO (PASSIONATE SILENCE)   91

Chapter 4
IS THE WALL OF SILENCE BREACHABLE?   105

Interlude IV
ARDENTE E ONDEGGIANTE (BURNING AND UNDULATING)   131

Chapter 5
MIRACULOUS CO-BECOMINGS?   143

Interlude V
MILAGROSA (MIRACULOUS)   161

Chapter 6
PLURIVERSAL CONVERSATIONS ON IMMANENT MIRACLES   167

Interlude VI
GLISSANDO (GLIDING BETWEEN PITCHES)   187

Chapter 7
DOING POSTHUMAN AUTOPHENOMENOGRAPHY, POETICS AND DIVINATORY FIGURING   199

Interlude VII
CON ABBANDONO E DEVOZIONE (WITH SELF-ABANDON AND DEVOTION)   223

Coda
BETWEEN LOVE-DEATH AND A POSTHUMAN ETHICS OF VIBRANT DEATH   235

Notes   255
References   269
Index   279

LIST OF ILLUSTRATIONS

FUR CLIFFS (PHOTO SERIES)

© Nina Lykke 2021

1	Travelling to the World of the Dead.	1
2	To the Waters, to the Waters.	6
3	Lacrimoso e Lamentoso (Crying and Lamenting).	23
4	Vibrato Bruscamente (Abruptly Vibrating).	57
5	Silenzio Appassionato (Passionate Silence).	91
6	Ardente e Ondeggiante (Burning and Undulating).	131
7	Milagrosa (Miraculous).	161
8	Glissando (Gliding between Pitches).	187
9	Con Abbandono e Devozione (With Self-Abandon and Devotion).	223
10	What if Every Critter's Death was Vibrant?	253

ACKNOWLEDGEMENTS

This book is dedicated, first and foremost, to you, my forever beloved, Mette Bryld, to thank and honour you not only as my forever beloved, but also as the great feminist scholar, activist and writer you were. I wrote my books either to you or together with you. *Cosmodolphins* (Bryld and Lykke 2000) we wrote together. *Vibrant Death* is written to you, but also together with you. You live in me, and I live in the algae sand with which your ashes are now merged.

Vibrant Death is also dedicated to you, Camila Marambio, my spiritual-intellectual guide, amazing curator-artist, philosopher and activist, who has opened up my limited Western horizon to spiritual materialism, and to Abya Yala cosm-ontologies and philosophies. For the opening up of Abya Yala horizons to the Selk'nam people, I also warmly thank you, Hema'ny Molina Vargas, indigenous writer, activist and philosopher, president of the Corporacion Selk'nam Chile. My sincere gratitude goes to both of you, Camila and Hema'ny, who, as part of our joint work on *Decolonising Mourning* (Vargas, Marambio and Lykke 2020), taught me that writing letters to the dead makes sense for real, not only in a liminal world in-between 'real' and 'not-real'.

My warmest thanks go also to you, my dear friends, fantastic colleagues and very constructive readers, Margrit Shildrick, Marietta Radomska, Madina Tlostanova, Camila Marambio and Katja Aglert, who gave me very useful comments and responses on different parts of the manuscript.

Thanks so very, very much to you, too, my dear, dear rainbow family, Uffe Bryld, Rikke Øxner, Eigil Bryld, Naja Marie Aidt, Dorthe Staunæs, Sverre Raffnsøe, Asker Bryld Staunæs, Matilde Mørk, Sal Bryld Staunæs, Sofus Bryld Staunæs, Zakarias Bryld Aidt and Johan Heurlin Aidt. And also to you, Carl Emil Heurlin Aidt – we would so much have wanted to still have both you and Mette physically in our midst, though I am happy to know both of you now in spectral shapes. A very warm thanks to all of you for giving me free rein to include you in the autobiographical stories in the book, and in some cases to use your names explicitly. These stories are yours as well, even though they are told exclusively from my perspective. Thanks so very much for the immense trust you have placed in me; I sincerely hope that I have not in any way betrayed this trust through the ways in which I told the stories. I also want to thank those of you who, along the road, read and commented on various parts of the poetry collection and autobiographical stories. Your comments were very important to me. Thanks so much to all of you for your strong, loving and continuing encouragement and support.

Also a warm thanks to you, my dearest friends, who agreed to appear under your own names in some of the autobiographical parts of *Vibrant Death*: Lene

Jørgensen, Margrit Shildrick, Camila Marambio and Berit Starkman. I hope it comes through, in the parts where you appear, just how much your supportive friendship and interventions in my journey through mourning have meant to me.

Thanks also to everyone who participated in the mourning circles. In addition to those whom I have already mentioned above, and therefore will not mention again, I would like to thank Bente Rosenbeck, Yvonne Mørck, Lene Nielsen, Jes Bryld, Per Hedberg, Kirsten Bryld, Lars Burgaard, Tine Lykke Frandsen, Finn Lykke, Anne Bendixen, Dorrit Munk Jørgensen, Anders Jensen, Karin Birgitte Holm Sneskov and Arne Sneskov.

A warm thanks also to all of you with whom, over the years, I have shared intense memories of being intimate with death and dying, in particular Camila Marambio, Naja Marie Aidt, Eigil Bryld, Uffe Bryld, Rikke Øxner, Berit Starkman, Matilde Mørk, Tine Lykke Frandsen, Finn Lykke, Anne Bendixen, Ida Hillerup Hansen, Kirsten van der Stelt, Stine Adrian, Madina Tlostanova, Edyta Just, Marietta Radomska, Katja Aglert, Wibke Straube, Patricia MacCormack, Magdalena Górska, Malin Arnell, Gillian Einstein, Victoria Kawesa, Ejvind Frantzen, Lise Frantzen, Kristian Sørensen, Amalie Otkjær and Anne Bettina Pedersen. Without your openness and passionate willingness to share, I would not have been able to write this book.

For continued support and encouragement, I want to very warmly thank the Bloomsbury Academic *Theory in the New Humanities* series editor, Rosi Braidotti. Thanks for welcoming *Vibrant Death* to your series. It makes me really happy that this book, which for me is so very personally important, will be part of your series, Rosi. Thank you so much!

Moreover, many warm thanks for lots of inspiration and in-depth talks to the Alien Encounters group, Katja Aglert, Line Henriksen and Marietta Radomska, to the Queer Death Friends Zoom party group, Margrit Shildrick, Patricia MacCormack and Marietta Radomska, to the Queer Death Studies Network, and especially to my co-coordinators, Tara Mehrabi and Marietta Radomska, but also to you, Varpu Alasuutari and Annika Jonsson, who were also crucial for the launching of the Queer Death Studies network in 2016.

Very warm thanks to Visual Artist and Professor of Art Katja Aglert for front-page design, and for advice on the visuals – and to Opera Translator Cristopher Cowell for finally tracing the translator of the aria *What is Life to Me without Thee?* in the version sung by Kathleen Ferrier. Thanks to Musicologists Taru Leppänen and Hannu Salmi for helping me with important steps along the road towards solving the puzzle about this very elusive translation. Thanks so much also to former Royal Danish Orchestra musicians Ejvind Frantzen (hornist) and Troels Svendsen (violinist) for your efforts and advice regarding my use of musical terms.

Thanks also for great collaboration to the wider circles of collaborators, colleagues and friends in the Queer Death Studies Network, the Collective for Radical Death Studies and CIRQUE (Inter-University Centre for Queer Research) at the University of Pisa.

A very warm thanks to language editor Liz Sourbut for your always fantastic, precise and meticulous editing work.

Thanks also to the anonymous Bloomsbury peer reviewers for useful comments on the manuscript and synopsis.

Finally, a warm thanks to you, my multicoloured cat Musse. You have been lying next to me throughout the process of writing, accepting that your sleeping-assemblage overlaps with my writing-assemblage. For me, your presence during my writing was really joyful. I hope that your feline dreams were pleasant and joyful as well.

NOTES ON TEXT AND PHOTOS

Vibrant Death is built up as an entanglement of different kinds of texts. *Chapters with Arabic numbers (1–7)* consist of philosophical contemplations and autobiographical stories, the latter italicized in the text. In *Interludes with Roman numbers (I–VII)*, my poems are clustered according to their ambiance – except for *Interlude V*, which is an interview. At the end of each interlude, a textbox facilitates the transition between the interlude and the chapter following immediately after. The entrance point to *Vibrant Death* is a poetic *Overture*, and the book is ended by a contemplative *Coda*.

The photos that illustrate the journey of *Vibrant Death* through mourning are taken by me. They show the cliffs and beaches of the island of Fur, an island in a big fjord, Limfjorden, in the Northern part of Denmark. The cliffs and seabed around Fur are made by diatoms, single-cell aquatic algae, fossilized 55 million years ago. My beloved life partner's ashes are scattered in the waters outside of Fur, so, for me, it is a place of spiritual material contemplations.

Overture

TRAVELLING TO THE WORLD OF THE DEAD: A TRIPTYCH

Illustr. 1 Travelling to the World of the Dead. © Nina Lykke 2020.

I. Contralto Kathleen Ferrier Singing Orpheus

When my imagination vividly calls forth, again and again, images of my lesbian life partner's cancer death, Orpheus' lament for dead Eurydice, sung by British contralto Kathleen Ferrier,[1] resonates in my mind's ear. This trouser role of Orpheus gives both the opera and the aria a queer twist. The male character, Orpheus, became a signature role for Kathleen Ferrier at the peak of her short career as an opera singer during the late 1940s, before her premature death from breast cancer in 1953, at the age of 41.

From her youth in the late 1950s, my partner was very much attracted to opera. In particular, she was fascinated by the extremely wide-ranging registers of female voices and their powerfully fleshy articulations of passion, as well as by the queer performances of characters in trouser roles. Through my partner's guidance, I fell deeply in love with classical opera and its queer posthuman viscerality and sexiness. After my beloved's death, I turned the playing of the arias we both loved into spiritual–material moments of passionate reconnection. Orpheus' lament for dead Eurydice, sung by Kathleen Ferrier, was and is one of my favourites.

This is how the Orpheus/Eurydice story of love, death and mourning became a *leitmotif* for this book. The vibrancy of Kathleen Ferrier's deep, strong and passionate contralto voice reminds me of the voice of my dead beloved, and, like Orpheus, I could not accept the narratives of death as a final cutting apart. So, like him, I also embarked upon a journey to the world of the dead, driven by intense grief and the passionate desire to reconnect with my dead beloved. Orpheus was a musician, so he took his lyre with him to the underworld, and used his music to gain access to the closed world of the dead. My journey was guided by the writing of poetry, spiritual–material practices and philosophical analysis, and these three modes of knowledge-seeking led me to rethink and reimagine death and mourning. Like Orpheus, I was unable to return my beloved to life, but the journey brought me to understand the life/death threshold differently, and to see death as vibrancy rather than nothingness. Queerfeminist, posthuman, immanence philosophy, along with Spinoza's notion of *conatus*, the striving of all matter, dead or alive, to persevere, helped me in this process. With *Vibrant Death,* I offer you my travelogue.

II. Orpheus' Lament

Aria from C. W. Gluck's opera Orpheus and Eurydice, 1762/1774[2]

1.
What is life to me without thee?
What is left if thou art dead?
What is life, life without thee?
What is life, without my love?
What is life if thou art dead?

2.
Eurydice! Eurydice!
Ah, hear me! Make answer! Make answer!
Thy dear lord am I so faithful,
Thy faithful lord who loves thee,
who doth love thee!

3.
What is life to me without thee?
What is left if thou art dead?
What is life, life without thee?
What is life, without my love?
What is life if thou art dead?

4.
Eurydice! Eurydice!
In my dread anguish none can comfort,
none can aid me.
Earth is cruel, heaven is cold!

5.
What is life to me without thee?
What is left if thou art dead?
What is life, life without thee?
What is life without my love?
What is life, life without thee?
What is life if thou art dead,
If thou art dead,
If thou art dead?

III. Going to the Underworld . . .

I came here in a dream – to the waters, to the waters, swimming among the brown, slimy algae. Never before have there been so many algae in the water. They are sliding around my body while I swim. I feel them all over my body. I cannot see the bottom. It is a bit frightening, but still I feel at home. At home among these soft, slimy, brown tendrils of algae. Algae tendrils all over. All over. I cut my foot quite badly when I walk into the shore again. The stones are really sharp here. But I do not see the wound until I am sitting on the beach again after the swim. It is hot – and very different from last year. Drier at the top of the cliff, browner, more wildly growing algae in the water. Are there more stones as well? The pine tree that had fallen from the top of the cliff last year, but which still had green pine needles, is now totally greyish-brown. But it is still here. Other parts of the cliff have been eroded even more – and a cave which I could enter before has now completely disappeared. Everything changes here. Changes from year to year. I keep thinking about how this place is going to be my grave – my ashes are to be scattered here when I die. This is certain. Uffe and Eigil have the exact coordinates. It is a strange feeling. Thinking again and again about Virginia Woolf's suicide, walking into the river Ouse with stones in her pocket. But I am not attracted to that idea now, as I was previously. The 'come as ashes, not as flesh', which you whispered to me through the wind, while caressing my swimming body, has worked. Nevertheless, I am still passionately attracted to this place. I fell asleep, and had strange, lucid dreams that merged with waking dreams – lying in my bed, listening to the waves of the fjord. I visit the spring every year as well. The magic of the place where the spring gushes from the cliff – and where I touch its ripples with my hand. Strange are the ways in which the words of my poems echo in my head when I walk along the cliffs. I create a resonance, amplify, intensify the magic through my own words. Journeying to the underworld, and staying there forever. Words are strange – storytelling, poetry, philosophy. Miracles – are miracles happening here? Yes, and no, I do not know. What is a miracle? It cannot be willed or controlled – but you can prepare for it, this is what Camila wisely taught me. And there are miracles here. You are here, and so is Carl, now dead as well – and everyone who took part in the ash-scattering ceremony. Your older brother who confirmed his atheist beliefs that death is nothingness while we all walked to the cliff together in the twilight after the family party the evening before we scattered your ashes over these waters. I am bound to this place – I will be coming here as ashes in an urn some day, and they will all sail out and scatter my ashes over the same place. I hope that the slurping sound will be heard as well at that time. You will recognize it, and you will know that I am on my way. Who else would make this obscene slurping sound? It will perhaps be a sunny day, a warm day like it was in 2014, when we scattered your ashes. The cliffs will be clearly visible from a distance. At a distance, you cannot see their colours. They look dull and brown. It is only when you come really close that you can see the colours. At first, I could not believe that all these colours stemmed from the fossilized algae species, diatoms, which built the seabed and the cliffs here millions of years ago, but I discovered that they did. Eigil sent me an SMS with several hearts, when I wrote to him that I had been swimming with you. Perhaps he, too, believes in the spiritmattering vibrations in this place, even though he is an atheist sceptic, as were you, who gave birth to him, my forever beloved?

Illustr. 2 To the Waters, to the Waters. © Nina Lykke 2016.

Chapter 1

QUEERING DEATH AND POSTHUMANIZING MOURNING: INTRODUCTION

This is a book about death – death as vibrant; death not in opposition to life, but existing in a flat continuum intertwined with it; death as an articulation of the vitality and vibrancy characterizing all matter, whether dead or alive, inanimate or animate, non-human or human. *Vibrant Death* is about a death that is pervaded as thoroughly as life by the striving of all matter to persevere, which Spinoza (1996 [1677]) named *conatus*, and which political philosopher Jane Bennett (2010), along Spinozist lines, characterized as 'vibrant'. It is about a death that is imbued as deeply as life with the dynamic inhuman forces of matter that since Aristotle have been known as *zoe* (Braidotti 2006). It is about a death that is as strongly as life intensely affect-laden, even though Freud (1920) chose to divide their strivings, separating the forces of *thanatos* from those of *eros*; in this book, these forces are ontologized as totally intertwined. The book is about a death that is entangled as tightly as life in a cosmic dance of spirit-matter (Anzaldua 2015).

But *Vibrant Death* is also a book about mourning, and the depth of sorrow and devastation into which the cancerdeath of my beloved life partner plunged me. It is a book about hammering against the wall of silence which the death of my beloved set up between us. However, *Vibrant Death* is neither a nostalgic book about irreparable loss nor one about 'overcoming' the mourning of a beloved in a neoliberal, health-normative sense. In contrast, the aim of *Vibrant Death* is, first, to critically disrupt modern Western pathologizing of excessive mourning, and instead in an affirmative mode to resignify the position of the mourning 'I' as one of resistance, holding the potential to contemplate death differently. Second, *Vibrant Death* aims to explore these potentials, and, in particular, to look at the ways in which a queerfeminist posthuman phenomenology of mourning may enable an opening up of new horizons in terms of de-exceptionalizing and reontologizing death as part of a flat sequence of vibrant events, taking place beyond dualist divisions of life/death, spirit/matter, human/non-human, organic/inorganic, culture/nature. Third, it is the aim of *Vibrant Death* to poetically investigate and philosophically reflect upon spiritual materialist as well as vitalist materialist pathways to co-become and reconnect with my dead beloved, transformed to corpse and later to soft, fine ashes, spread in a fjord, Limfjorden, in the Northern part of Denmark, and mixed with the diatomaceous sand of the seabed there.[1]

In short, the overall aim is to pursue the onto-epistemological potentials enabled by a queering[2] and posthumanizing of the mourning 'I', and to re-evaluate the material remains of human bodies along the lines of a posthuman, immanence philosophical, vitalist and spiritualist materialism. The title *Vibrant Death* reflects this aim. It emphasizes, in particular, an inspiration from political philosopher Bennett's conceptualization of 'vibrant matter' (2010) and its reference to seventeenth-century monist philosopher Benedict de Spinoza's concept of *conatus* (1996 [1677]). I argue that, if all matter is conative, vibrant, and striving to persevere, then this must apply not only to living bodies, but also to dead ones. In this sense, the book takes Bennett's conceptual framework further. Her reflections concern assemblages of different kinds of inorganic and organic matter, but she does not explore the life/death-thresholds that are the focus of *Vibrant Death*. In this book, I use the notion of vibrancy as a lens to reflect upon the matter of which a dead body is composed, as well as to contemplate the thresholds being crossed and the decisive metamorphoses that occur when an organism dependent on an oxygen/carbon-dioxide exchange with the atmosphere takes its last breath: exhaling without inhaling.

The mourning 'I' and human material remains may seem to be a challenging and uncomfortable place from which to depart, when it comes to posthumanizing, and de-exceptionalizing the human. For obvious reasons, there are many pathways leading to problematic reconfirmations of human exceptionalism in this context. The mourning 'I', the human corpse and its bodily remains are undoubtedly arenas full of heavily human exceptionalist symbolism. However, precisely for that reason, these are also locations where it is of key importance to initiate critical posthumanizing and de-exceptionalizing work.

In a paradoxical sense, my personal entrance point helps me in my endeavours to avoid a re-exceptionalizing of (Western) concepts of the human, when dealing with the mourning 'I' and material remains of human beings. What helps me in the process of posthumanizing, de-exceptionalizing and queering death is that it is a deeply felt personal need for me, indeed, a key part of my mourning, to transgress the heavily normative gaze on the mourning 'I', the human corpse and bodily remains that unfolds in dualist Christian discourses and imaginaries, as well as in those produced by Cartesianism and modern science. I find the ways in which the mourning 'I' and human bodily remains appear in these discourses and imaginaries profoundly unsatisfying, and disturbing. In Christian discourses and imaginaries, the mourning 'I' can look forward to perhaps becoming an immortal soul (depending on the goodwill of God and Jesus, of course!); as such, this 'I' may once again meet the soul of the beloved, whose material remains in this scenario are reduced to nothing but a launching pad for a disembodied resurrection. On the other hand, in the discourses and imaginaries anchored in secular scientific and Cartesianist mechanistic materialism, death appears as a gateway into nothingness, because the subject is gone. Neither of these positions, nor those in-between,[3] are satisfying to me, because all of them are founded in a dualist split between mind and body, and share a basic contempting and instrumentalizing approach to flesh and matter. Each in their own way are also founded on a self-identity that is based upon a claim to human superiority vis-à-vis the more-than-human world. The fleshiness of the human corpse, which it shares with the dead body matter of many other mortal beings, is either cast as abject, as language philosopher Julia Kristeva (1982) pointed out, or as plain mechanics (in a Cartesian sense). Either way, it is not related to anything spiritual, enchanted or vibrant; the latter is reserved for the human subject/mind/immortal soul, and thus kept in an exceptionalized, separate and elevated–immaterial position.

My beloved died from cancer after four years of illness. I took care of her until the very end, helping her to materialize her desire to die peacefully at home instead of being subjected to the disciplinary medical regimes of a turbulent hospital ward. The dead body of my beloved lay in our house for almost thirtytwo hours before the undertaker could drive her to the morgue. So, I had time to contemplate her corpse. Kissing the ice-cold lips, forehead and cheeks of my beloved, helping the undertaker to dress her and put her in the casket, made it very palpable for me in an embodied affective sense how both the Christian, Cartesian, and secular scientific approaches to the human corpse are deeply disturbing – and insulting to the enchanted and spiritual-material fleshiness of the dead body, its vibrancy, its *conatus*, its power to affect other bodies in a Spinozean sense.[4] What was lying there in front of me was neither just a launching pad for the soul, nor simple, driverless mechanics, nor nothingness. It was something different. However, what was it? What kind of relations was it that I, as the mourning 'I', was building with it? What did it teach me? How did it change me? These were the questions I felt a strong urge to pursue, and this book is a result of my pursuit.

Writing this introduction, I am sitting in the room where my beloved died. I have shed devastated tears over her dead body in this room, but also seen how vibrant she was, even when transformed into a silent and cold corpse. I have felt my dead beloved's absence and imperceptibility intensely here, where we have lived together for almost forty years. But I have also reflected profoundly upon the meaning of terms such as 'absence' and 'loss'. Because, although my beloved is no longer here as a living embodied subject, she is still present in every pore of this house and this particular room. She is here as memories of our past shared life and as effects of her past actions. *But*, in addition to being here as a memory of the human subject she was, she is also very materially present as vibrant traces, as a fleshy posthuman materiality (dust, DNA, etc.), which even science will confirm does not disappear just like that. Forensics – a kind of material spectrology – is built upon that particular knowledge, but so is the philosophical contemplations of the phenomenality of spectrality which I shall discuss, among others based on philosopher of language Jacques Derrida (1994).

So, what does it mean that my beloved has passed away and is no longer here? The more I have immersed myself in the existential questions of my passed-away beloved's transitions, metamorphoses, and present vibrancies and whereabouts, the more complex the issue has become. Or, to put it differently, the more clearly I have come to understand that the questions of subjective presence or absence, and being corporeally alive or passed away, need to be rethought and reimagined beyond conventional onto-epistemologies and imaginaries, embedded as they are in secular science and mechanistic understandings of the body, and/or Christian soul/body dualisms. These conventional onto-epistemologies are hopelessly entangled in a contempt for flesh and matter, combined with an insensitive indifference to its vibrancies, which goes hand in hand with an equally problematic exceptionalizing of human issues, including human death. Moreover, they are normativizing – and completely missing what must be a central ontological point, from a feminist, posthuman, new-materialist point of view; namely, that mind and body cannot be separated. For all these reasons, neither Christian nor secular-scientific, mechanistic materialist discourses have been able to give me any sensible answers to the existential questions prompted by my beloved's death and my process of mourning her. In my quest to transgress the insulting contempt for the flesh of both Christianity and secular mechanistic science, I came to understand that I needed new feminist posthumanist, queering, decolonizing, materialist onto-epistemologies, a posthuman and vitalist ethics of affirmation, and materialist spiritualities and practices. In *Vibrant Death*, I explore my many questions poetically, and bring them into dialogue with philosophical frameworks which can help me make sense of them.

A Feminist Posthuman Phenomenology of the Mourning 'I'

Vibrant Death explores and reflects upon the paradoxes of my passed-away beloved's metamorphoses and present modes of existence, while unfolding a feminist posthuman phenomenology of the mourning 'I'. Western philosophy has primarily explored death from the position of enunciation of the philosopher subject. This is a subject who manifests as a bounded sovereign 'I' trying to come to terms with mortality, including hir own death – which existentialist philosopher Jean-Paul Sartre, for example, tellingly discussed under the heading 'My Death' (1958: 552ff.).[5] Throughout the history of Western philosophy, the sovereign 'I' has struggled with the thought of hir own death. In different ways, it has tried to come to terms with the predicament of death via the tools of philosophy – from Plato (2009) comforting himself and his readers with the thought that death means the release of the soul from dull bodily matter to Sartre (1958) establishing death as nothingness outside of meaningful subjective life, a zero point from which we should withdraw our attention in order to concentrate on our here-and-now subjectivity, freedom and existence. But what about the mourning 'I'? Where is it located in all of this? Does it make sense to claim that the mourning 'I' embodies a different position than the sovereign 'I' – and, if yes, how? Investigating these questions is a key concern of this book.

The short answer to the question of where the mourning 'I' is located in Western philosophy is: nowhere. Therefore, the possibility of it taking up an alternative position to the many philosophical versions of the sovereign 'I' seems to be open. A long philosophical tradition, carried by shifting authoritative voices, reflects on the relation to death of the sovereign 'I', whereas the perspectives of the mourning 'I', lamenting the death of a beloved, have been relegated to the margins of philosophy. A key line of argument of *Vibrant Death* is that this is a serious omission, because a reflection on the positioning of the mourning 'I' can generate important new perspectives. In contrast to the sovereign 'I''s struggles with, and resistance to, the thought of its own death and annihilation, the mourning 'I' is deeply attracted to death in a desiring manner. To the mourning 'I', life appears unliveable without the passed-away loved one, and the 'I''s own death, therefore, stands out as desirable – as a pathway to reconnect with the beloved. What I shall argue, against this background, is that this philosophically different point of departure may enable an alternative relational, transcorporeal, non-exceptionalizing, posthuman feminist and deeply queer approach to death, embracing it as an inevitable aspect of being a vibrant part of the more-than-human world. *Vibrant Death* is an attempt to reflect upon such an approach.

But while the mourning 'I' does not have a place in Western philosophy, the affective state of utter devastation, and the passionate desire to become one with the beloved, now turned to dust, has, in contrast, been a favourite topic of Western literature, opera, drama and visual arts. Prominently, it has been figuratively embodied by the romantic couple, where the one left behind by the other's death performs a 'love-death' [Liebestod],[6] i.e. kills himself to fulfil the desire for embodied reunification with the beloved, as in Shakespeare's *Romeo and Juliet*. The love-death motif unfolds when the heartbroken state of the 'I', mourning the death of the beloved, makes hir desire only one thing: to reconnect, while sharing death. The storyline of the myth of Orpheus and Eurydice is a popular example of the love-death motif, reappearing again and again in literature, opera, film, etc. from Virgil (BCE 37–30) and Ovid (1717 [CE 1]) via, among others, Monteverdi (1972 [1607]) and Gluck (2019 [1762]) to Camus/Moraes (1959). So, indeed, the mourning 'I' is present in Western culture. While absent from philosophy, this 'I' has been thriving in the context of literary, opera and art history studies, i.e. in cultural environments, where the stakes have been poetic/artistic, aesthetic performance, embodiment and affect rather than contemplations of death with the tools of philosophy and rational thought. In *Vibrant Death*, I challenge this compartmentalization, and explore the philosophical potentials of the mourning 'I' and its desire for love-death.

However, as the love-death motif is conventionally performed in Western canons, it is linked to romantic passions, conceived within human and heteronormative frames. So, while pinpointing that *Vibrant Death* transgresses a problematic division of labour between Philosophy and Literature/Arts, this does not imply that the book follows in the footsteps of classic Western literary and artistic traditions concerning the romantic couple and the love-death motif. I approach the death of my beloved in a different, posthumanizing, queering, immanence philosophical mode. It is in the context of this latter approach that I argue for the mourning 'I''s unexplored philosophical potentials. First, I look at what radically distinguishes the mourning 'I' from the sovereign 'I' of Western modernity; namely, its strong desire for love-death, for a merging with the dead beloved. Second, I focus on the posthumanizing, corpo-affective aspects of this merging. I reflect upon the ways in which the beloved's body becomes inhumanized as dust, earth, worms or ashes, and how, against this background, the sexually tinged fantasy of love-death becomes associated with a passionately transcorporeal, material and posthuman vibrancy, very different from the disembodied and human exceptionalizing fleshlessness of the soul in Christian discourses. It is in this sense that I propose that the position of enunciation of the mourning 'I', which I explore philosophically and poetically in *Vibrant Death*, can be used as a platform to open up new horizons towards a posthumanizing, queering, de-exceptionalizing, and decolonizing of death. The Orpheus/Eurydice myth's way of articulating the love-death motif is notable, here. In contrast to many other love-death stories, the dramatic endpoint of the storyline is not the mourner's following the dead beloved into the grave. Instead, the focus is Orpheus' quest to venture into the underworld and return dead Eurydice to life, and the dramatic effects of the initial success and ensuing failure of that quest. This underworld journey sets Orpheus/Eurydice apart from other Western versions of the romantic couple's commitment to love-death, and opens potentials for a posthumanizing reading – and also for a decolonizing approach which goes beyond the frames of Western modernity altogether.

The key poetic source for *Vibrant Death*'s poetic-philosophical explorations of the mourning 'I''s experiences of the beloved's death is my own poems, written as part of my process of mourning and lamenting my passed-away partner. Love and death are undoubtedly entangled key themes in my poems, as they are in classic literature on love-death. However, I shall also emphasize that my spiritual materialist attraction to love-death are fuelled by different desires than those relating to an immaterial meeting of souls. What drives my poetry writing and the spiritual materialist practices to be reflected upon in this book are queer and posthuman desires – desires that, informed by hopes grounded in immanence philosophy, are attuned to a search for ways to co-become with my dead beloved in her now corporeally metamorphosed states of being as dust, as ashes mixed with sand in a seabed, as spectral phenomenality.

The phenomenology of the mourning 'I' which I unfold in *Vibrant Death* is thus to be understood as relentlessly posthuman, and transcorporeally interconnected with more-than-human worlds. In line with posthuman feminist scholar Astrida Neimanis (2017: 23), I reject the claim that posthuman thought and phenomenology sit uneasily together. I follow Neimanis when she underlines that the body phenomenology of philosopher Maurice Merleau-Ponty (2003) is always already posthuman in the sense that the bodily situation and lived experience in focus not only concerns the 'subjectivized human level', but also the body in its materiality and transcorporeal relationship with the more-than-human world (Neimanis 2017: 24). This is crucial for Neimanis, when she depicts the ways in which 'we' (both humans and non-humans) experience ourselves as 'bodies of water' in a multiplicity of dimensions, among them very visceral and non-conscious levels of the body. But it is also centrally important for the mourning 'I' of *Vibrant Death*. The transcorporeal pursuit of spiritual-material processes of co-becoming with the dead beloved implies a transgression of humanist ways of mourning. It means going beyond mourning practices that stay within the limits of remembering the human subject as she was – and defying norms that whisper mourners in the ear that to keep mentally healthy they should neither relate to the phenomenality of spectral presences nor to the agencies of inhuman material remains in the here-and-now. I definitely do not reject humanist ways of mourning through remembering. However, I do not want to be confined to contemplating my dead beloved and our companionship only as fixed in a static past. So I venture into zones of the here and now, where transcorporeal relations with my dead beloved's vibrant posthuman materialities can be explored.

Entering the Book through the Orpheus/Eurydice Figuration

My own poems and autobiographical stories constitute a major source for the book's contemplations of love-death. But the story of Orpheus/Eurydice (Ovid 1717 [1 CE]) plays a role in them, too. This particular story of love-death became important to me when my partner died, as I embarked upon the journey of voicing my grief and desire to co-become and reconnect with her in queerfeminine and posthuman manners through poetry writing, spiritual-material practices and philosophizing. This inspiration came to me, I did not seek it out. I shall discuss it here because it helped me to articulate and investigate my position of mourning 'I', both poetically and philosophically.

My first encounter with the opera *Orpheus and Eurydice* (Gluck 2019 [1762]) was the aria *Orpheus' Lament,* quoted in the *Overture* to this book, as sung by British contralto Kathleen Ferrier. Ferrier's queer contralto in her trouser role as Orpheus resonated strongly with the ways in which I, who sexually identify as a queer femme, had always been attracted to the deep voice of my queermasculine lesbian partner. However, it was not only due to the opera that the story of Orpheus and Eurydice gained special significance for *Vibrant Death*. Another reason relates to certain features of the storyline, which mean that the Orpheus/Eurydice story differs from the conventional romantic articulation of the love-death motif, and resonates with the overall themes in my poetic and philosophical framing of a posthuman phenomenology of the mourning 'I'. I shall look at these features in more detail now, taking my point of departure in the way in which the story has been handed down in the poetic writing of the Roman poet Ovid (1717 [CE 1]). Let me take a look at the features that resonate with my imaginary and theoretical framings – and at the same time provide an introductory overview of the content of *Vibrant Death,* here reflected through the lens of the Orpheus/Eurydice figuration.

First, measured against the background of modern, health- and life-normative biopolitical discourses, Orpheus figures as an icon of the excessive mourner. According to modern norms for 'healthy' mourning, he is someone who mourns 'too much' and 'too long'. I explore the relationship between the positions of the mourning 'I' and the excessive mourner in *Chapter 2, The Excessive Mourner,* prefaced in poetic form by *Interlude I, Lacrimoso e Lamentoso (Crying and Lamenting).* Critically-affirmatively, I resignify the position of the excessive mourner as a state that opens up horizons of positive epistemological potential, rather than signalling the risk of a depressive disorder. To give an initial introduction to my take on the issue, with the Orpheus/Eurydice story as lens, I want in this introductory chapter to emphasize how, in Ovid's text, Orpheus is portrayed as an excessive mourner through his passionate dedication to bringing Eurydice back to life. This ambition and desire absorb all of his interest, and lead him to defy the irreversibility of death. What fuels Orpheus' complete unwillingness to accept the *im*possibility of bringing anybody back from the world of the dead is the intertwined affects of love and devastation, key affects of the excessive mourner. These affects are also what power his unwavering determination to engage in a dangerous mission to enter the underworld in order to persuade its king and queen, Hades and Persephone, to release Eurydice and let her return to the world of the living with him. In Ovid's words, Orpheus is 'Inflam'd by Love, and urg'd by deep Despair' (1717 [CE 1]: 332), and even though he has striven to come to terms with the 'realities' of Eurydice's death, he does not succeed; love is too powerful a force to be controlled:

> Long I my Loss endeavour'd to sustain,
> And strongly strove, but strove, alas, in vain:
> At length I yielded, won by mighty Love;
> Well known is that Omnipotence above!
>
> Ibid.

The entanglement of all-absorbing love and an equally overwhelming and completely uncontrollable upwelling of pain and devastation due to the loss of the beloved, which is characteristic of the excessive mourner, is also accompanied by a lack of any fear of death. Orpheus dares to undertake the dangerous journey into the underworld because he is not in any way afraid of being trapped in the world of the dead, or prevented from leaving it again. On the contrary, as part of his long supplication aimed at persuading Hades and Persephone to free Eurydice, he tells them that it is his firm desire to remain in the underworld with her, to die himself, if they cannot or do not want to let her go:

> But if the Destinies refuse my Vow,
> And no Remission of her Doom allow;
> Know, I'm determin'd to return no more;
> So both retain, or both to life restore.
>
> Ibid.: 333

So, for the excessively mourning Orpheus, his own death is a better alternative than living on without Eurydice.

Second, in addition to performing as an icon of the excessive mourner, the Orpheus/Eurydice story also resonates with another major line of thought in this book; namely, that the world of death is imbued with *conatus* and vibrancy, and that the perspective of the mourning 'I' is a fruitful entrance point to thinking through these issues. These arguments will be developed further in *Chapter 3, The Vibrant Corpse,* and explored poetically in *Interlude II, Vibrato Bruscamente (Abruptly Vibrating).* For now, I just want to emphasize how the Orpheus/Eurydice story articulates a relation between death and vibrancy. Just as Orpheus, immersed in his desire to reconnect with his beloved, does not accept that it should be impossible to access the underworld, neither does he take it for granted that the material world of the dead should be a place without affectivity. Upon his arrival in the underworld, he begins to play his lyre and sing in the hope that he can touch Hades and Persephone affectively, reminding them of their own love for one another:

> And yet a Hope within my Heart prevails,
> That here, ev'n here, he [mighty love, NL] has been known of old;
> At least, if Truth be by Tradition told;
> (...)
> You both [Hades and Persephone, NL] by Love and Love alone, were joyn'd.
> 1717 [CE 1]: 332–3

Through the love radiating from him, Orpheus does, indeed, succeed in influencing Hades and Persephone, and much more than that. Interpreted within the framework of Spinoza's casting of bodies as affect-laden and able to affect other bodies (1996 [1677]), Orpheus' walk through the underworld, singing and playing as he goes, can be read as no less than a massive awakening of a dormant affectivity and vibrancy. Hades and Persephone become moved to do something unheard of; namely, they agree to release Eurydice – on the condition that Orpheus is not allowed to look back at her while they walk out of the world of the dead. But it is not only Hades and Persephone who are moved, so are all the underworld's zombies, of whom there are many in Greek mythology. They begin to weep or otherwise respond with profound affectivity to Orpheus' lament and his plea for the release of his beloved Eurydice:

> Thus, while the Bard melodiously complains,
> And to his Lyre accords his vocal Strains,
> The very bloodless Shades Attention keep,
> And silent, seem compassionate to weep;
> [There follows a list of names of different figures from Greek mythology who, affectively moved, deviate from their usual routines of zombielike mechanical suffering, ending with the fierce Furies who also begin weeping in resonance with Hades' and Persephone's being moved to compassion, NL]
> Then first ('tis said) by sacred Verse subdu'd,
> The Furies felt their Cheeks with Tears bedew'd:
> Nor could the rigid King, or Queen of Hell,
> Th'Impulse of Pity in their Hearts repell.
> 1717 [CE 1]: 333–4

Within the framework of this book, I read Ovid's poetic description of Orpheus' mass reawakening of the dormant affectivities of the underworld as resonating with Spinoza's point about bodies affecting bodies (1996 [1677]), and, in particular, with my insistence that it must be considered as applying not only to living bodies, but to dead ones as well. Because, when Spinoza states that there is only one kind of conative matter, it follows that this matter must be the substance of which both living and dead bodies are made and, therefore, both must be conative.

Third, the Orpheus/Eurydice story, as told by Ovid, resonates with yet another theme of central importance to this book; namely, the theme of death as becoming-imperceptible, reread from the perspective of the mourning 'I'. This theme is explored in detail in *Chapter 4, Is the Wall of Silence Breachable?* and poetically articulated in *Interlude III, Silenzio Appasionato (Passionate Silence)*. In the immanence philosophical approach to death developed by immanence philosophers Gilles Deleuze and Felix Guattari (1988), and in the posthuman death theory of feminist posthumanist immanence philosopher Rosi Braidotti (2006, 2013), both of which are central to my unfolding of a figuration of vibrant death in this book, death is defined as becoming-imperceptible. This means that death is framed as a 'merging into the eternal flow of becomings', implying a 'disruption of the self' and a 'dissolution of the subject' (Braidotti 2006: 252). Braidotti emphasizes this becoming-imperceptible as the moment at which you 'become corpse' and 'coincide with your body' (ibid.: 252-3). She defines death in a vitalist, posthuman manner as the agency of 'the inhuman within us' (2013: 134), which is made up of the impersonal, dynamic forces of *zoe*. In Chapter 4, I engage in a more detailed discussion of this immanence philosophical approach to death as becoming-imperceptible. There, I focus on the implications of a shift of analytical vantage point from sovereign to mourning 'I'. This means a shift from reflecting upon the dissolution of the sovereign 'I' in anticipation of one's own death to contemplating the ways in which the becoming-imperceptible of the beloved is experienced from the perspective of the mourner. As a first step in this discussion, in this introductory overview, I call attention to the ways in which the moment of Eurydice's becoming-imperceptible is dramatically explored in Ovid's story, as it is experienced from the position of Orpheus at the instant when he violates his contract with Hades and Persephone. As he walks ahead of Eurydice towards the exit from the world of the dead, Orpheus looks back to see if everything is well with her. This is the devastating moment of Eurydice's final becoming-imperceptible (her second death), illustrated by an image rich in tactile associations: the mourning 'I', Orpheus, reaches out his arms to his beloved, but embraces only empty air:

> His longing eyes, impatient, backwards cast
> To catch a Lover's Look, but look'd his last;
> For, instant dying, she again descends,
> While he to empty Air his Arms extends.
>
> 1717 [CE 1]: 334

Through my own poems, which I present in this volume, some of them alongside images from the many dreams I have experienced throughout the years since my beloved's death, and which in innumerable ways reiterate the moment of her becoming-imperceptible, I have come to crystallize the mourning 'I''s experience of the beloved's imperceptibility into the image of bouncing against an insurmountable wall of silence – as reflected in the title of Chapter 4, *Is the Wall of Silence Breachable?*. Orpheus also hits this wall. After his fatal look back, Eurydice is finally lost, and Orpheus is denied the possibility of love-death. The forces of the world of the dead prevent him from entering again, even though he does his utmost to persuade the underworld's gatekeeper, Charon, to take him once more aboard his boat across the Styx, the river of death. In vain. This is not possible:

> Now to repass the Styx in vain he tries,
> *Charon* averse, his pressing Suit denies.
> Seven days entire, along th'infernal Shores,
> Disconsolate, the Bard *Eurydice* deplores;
>
> 1717 [CE 1]: 335

Orpheus is doomed to remain alive, separated from dead Eurydice, in a world that no longer holds any attraction for him. Ovid portrays Orpheus' gloomy life, hidden away in a deserted mountain setting, 'bleak with northern blasts' (ibid.: 335), where there is nothing left for him but profound grief.

Nevertheless, neither Orpheus' tale nor the story of *Vibrant Death* ends at the wall of imperceptibility. There is a fourth point of resonance between the two, which extends beyond this wall. As part of his excessive grief, Orpheus does not play his lyre for several years. But eventually, he begins to pluck its strings again, and, once more, his music has an impact. The mountains, his new habitat, are without shade, but now they begin to attract trees from all directions. In resonance with Orpheus' resuming his playing, an abundance of trees transplant themselves to the place:

> A Hill there was, and on that Hill a Mead,
> With Verdure thick, but destitute of Shade.
> Where, now the Muse's Son no sooner sings,
> No sooner strikes his sweet resounding Strings,
> But distant Groves the flying Sounds receive,
> And list'ning Trees their rooted Stations leave;
> Themselves transplanting, all around they grow,
> And various Shades their various Kinds bestow.
> [After this follows approximately 20 lines, which list in detail the
> abundance of different trees transplanting themselves to the area following
> the call of Orpheus' lyre.]
>
> Ibid.: 335–6

I read the shift, which occurs in the final stanza of Ovid's poem *Orpheus and Eurydice*, in line with the Spinozean dynamics of bodies affecting and being affected by other bodies. Even though Orpheus is separated from Eurydice, *conatus* can nevertheless bridge the gap between life and death, and so the experience of the wall of imperceptibility does not become the exclusive endpoint for him. This reading of Orpheus' journey through excessive mourning as eventually leading to a crumbling of the wall of imperceptibility resonates with my own unfolding of a posthuman phenomenology of the mourning 'I' in *Vibrant Death*. My poetic explorations, spiritual-material practices and philosophical contemplations lead me beyond the gloomy pounding against the wall of imperceptibility.

While the first part of Chapter 4 addresses the wall of silence, its second part engages with the possibility of making it breach and crumble. This occurs through a focus on the mourning 'I''s becoming open to encounters with the phenomenality of the dead beloved's spectral presences, for example in dreams and visions, and to co-become with her materially metamorphosing inhuman remains, now transformed into ashes mixed with algae sand in a seabed. Framed against the background of Deleuze and Guattari's reflections (1988: 149–66) on the molar (bodies as whole entities) and the molecular (bodies dissolved into molecularity), a distinction between molar mourning (oriented towards the embodied human subject who was) and molecular mourning (addressing phenomenally spectral aspects of the deceased, as well as her metamorphosing material remains), helps to make philosophical sense of the relationship as ongoing rather than being locked into a fixed and immutable past. *Chapter 5, Miraculous Co-Becomings?*, prepared poetically by *Interlude IV, Ardente e Ondeggiante (Burning and Undulating)*, takes a step further towards making sense, immanence philosophically, of the ongoingness of the relation between the mourning 'I' and the dead beloved. It speculates about the agencies of dead bodies, reframing Spinoza's questions about the doings of bodies as a question which also concerns the doings of dead bodies. Drawing on Bennett's (2010) reflections upon the material and affective thing-power of assemblages of non-human actants, which may or may not include embodied human subjects, this chapter reflects upon the agency of dead bodies, taking its point of departure in a cluster of events (happening right before and after my beloved's death) that I experienced as somehow having miraculous qualities.

While in Chapters 4 and 5 I speculatively aim to make sense of my moving beyond the wall of silence into an experience of ongoingness within immanence philosophical and vitalist materialist frameworks, *Chapter 6, Pluriversal Conversations on Immanent Miracles*, takes a step in another direction. Prepared by *Interlude V, Milagrosa (Miraculous)*, an interview with me about the miraculous events that I experienced together with my dying beloved right before she died, and followed up after her death, Chapter 6 brings the book's immanence philosophical and vitalist materialist contemplations into pluriversal conversation with spiritual materialist cosm-ontologies and philosophies. In particular, I focus on the work of indigenous, queerfeminist scholar and activist Gloria Anzaldua (1987, 2015). A pluriversal approach (Tlostanova and Mignolo 2012) implies a critical undoing of the universalizing gestures embedded in Western onto-epistemological thought. Working from a pluriversal perspective has been important for my journey through mourning. Western immanence philosophy and vitalist materialism are important for my unfolding of a figuration of vibrant death. But when it comes to making sense of the agency of dead bodies and to establishing ongoing relations with the dead, indigenous cosm-ontologies and spiritual materialist philosophies have come to make up another key entrance point for my establishment of the figuration. I draw upon Anzaldua's spiritual materialist reflections on spirit-matter in the context of her reclaiming of her Aztec ancestry from a queerfeminist and decolonizing position. I investigate diffraction patterns between spirit-matter, as framed by Anzaldua, Bennett's vitalist materialism (2010), and Braidotti's reflections upon the ways in which death as becoming-imperceptible and becoming-one-with-the-inhuman-forces-of-*zoe* enable a radically immanence philosophical, 'spiritual' (Braidotti 2006: 254f) understanding of death.

All of this implies that, through my philosophical argument and poetic explorations in this book, I come to build up a figuration of vibrant death. This figuration is based on an understanding of the relations between dead and living bodies as not merely existing in a fixed past, but to be seen instead as affective, transcorporeal, transversal connections that are ongoing, and continuously re/established in the here-and-now. One more resonance between this figuration and the Orpheus/Eurydice story can be noted against this background. I have indicated how the mid-section of Ovid's poem shows Orpheus as a figure whose powerful bodily desires, in a Spinozean sense, affect and become affected by the vibrancy of the material world of the dead. I mentioned that this part of the poem could be read as mapping out a first instance of affective transcorporeal transversality – in resonance with my analysis of the vibrancy of the corpse in Chapter 3. But, notably, the book's further reflections in Chapters 4–6 resonate also with the image of Orpheus – as he appears at the end of Ovid's poem, when his eventual return to playing the lyre brings him in tune with the agencies of the non-human world of trees. By transplanting themselves to and rooting in the area, where Orpheus is located, while playing, these trees create continuous links between the surface world and the underworld: the world of the living and the world of the dead. Their roots extend to the underworld, while trunk and crown inhabit the surface world.

Against the background of this link between the figuration of vibrant death and the Orpheus/Eurydice story, the book's *Coda, Between Love-Death and a Posthuman Ethics*, prepared by *Interlude VII, Con Abbandono e Devozione (With Self-Abandonment and Devotion)* returns to the story. Through an exploration of its wider mythical genealogies in non-modern cosm-ontologies, its framing of the life/death threshold is here related to cyclical understandings of time and embodiment. Based also on a final, pluriversal conversation between my revitalization of the Orpheus/Eurydice story and Gloria Anzaldua's spiritual activist and ethico-political revitalizing of her ancestral Aztec cosm-ontologies, I end the book by suggesting that the figuration of vibrant death resonates with a vision of a posthuman, planetary ethics – an ethics which implies a remodelling of the relationship between life and death against the background of cyclical thought. With this vision I also want to contribute to the search for pathways to engender transmutations of contemporary Anthropocene necropolitics and the pain inflicted by it. The vision implies an embracing conative endurance, as well as cyclical processes of shapeshifting and renewal within the life/death continuum. The poem, *What if Every Critter's Death Was Vibrant?*, which ends the book, offers a poetic vision of this figuration.

Reflections on Emergent Methodologies

The methodologies that I explore in *Vibrant Death* are to be seen as experimental, emergent and postqualitative (St. Pierre 2018), combining poetry, philosophy and autobiographical analysis. To be true to the process of emerging, it makes most sense to discuss the methodologies as a retrospective reflection upon the process unfolding throughout the book. Accordingly, the methodologies will be discussed in the last chapter before the Coda, namely *Chapter 7, Doing Posthuman Autophenomenography, Poetics and Divinatory Figuring*. Like the others, this chapter will also be prepared poetically by an interlude, *Interlude VI, Glissando (Gliding Between Pitches)*. However, as part of this introduction, I want to make a few remarks about my methodological approach which it might be helpful for readers to have in mind already at this stage of their reading.

My work on the book is guided by the belief that it is important to transgress the boundary between poetry/arts and philosophy, and its corollary, the division of labour between affective-sensual and intellectual knowledge-seeking and knowledge production. First of all, this approach resonates with a Deleuzean rejection of the separation of thought, affect and embodiment, a rejection to which this book is indebted. Second, my approach is in line with the basic feminist claim that the personal is political – a claim which, I think, still holds true, even though feminism has continually ramified it in many rhizomatic directions since the claim was first made. I met my beloved through feminist activism, and I want to honour our shared experiences through this reference. Third, the combined poetic and philosophical approach is overall in line with the book's aim to shift perspective from the bounded sovereign 'I' to a posthuman phenomenology of the mourning 'I'. As indicated through my references to classic Western love-death dramas, the mourning 'I' approaches death radically differently from the sovereign 'I' when lamenting the death of the beloved, intensely desiring to follow hir to the world of the dead. Bringing philosophical contemplation and poetic lamentation into close interaction is a way of taking a methodological consequence of this shift. Fourth, yet another reason why entangled poetic and philosophical investigations are important for *Vibrant Death* is related to the aim of transgressing human exceptionalism and de-exceptionalizing human death in a posthuman sense. This transgression implies a critical ethical re-evaluation and rejection of the necropolitical casting of lives defined as lying outside the sphere of the human as, by definition, disposable. I claim that entangling poetic explorations with philosophical ones, makes it become easier to break through the epistemological boundaries that philosophy has constructed around the exceptionally human position of enunciation of the sovereign 'I', insofar as poetry (and arts more generally) make up arenas which experimentally may open horizons towards more-than-human positions of enunciation and redistributions of agencies in more radical ways than it, conventionally, has been possible for philosophy. Posthuman aesthetics and poetics explore such routes.

The two-tiered methodological approach – the combination of poetic and philosophical analysis – implies that both the format and content of the book are experimental. I cross between the genres of poetry and theory/philosophy writing. Moreover, in order to establish the mourning 'I' as a lens for the analysis, I combine autobiographical poetry writing with the method of autophenomenography. The latter is a branch of autoethnography that uses phenomenological accounts of the lived experience of the researcher-subject as lens and material for the analysis (Allen-Collinson 2010; Lykke 2018). Both autoethnography and autophenomenography use the researcher's lived experience and autobiographical accounts as research material, and there are clear overlaps between the two methods. But they differ insofar as the former takes its point of departure in ethnographic methods, while the pivot for the latter is a phenomenological approach focusing on a corpo-affective, transcorporeal and relational 'orientation' and 'attentiveness' (Allen-Collinson 2010: 283). I am inspired by the autophenomenographic methodology, but I also take it in radically new – posthuman, postqualitative and poetic – directions in this book. I will, as already stated, reflect in-depths upon these directions in Chapter 7.

Interlude I

LACRIMOSO E LAMENTOSO
(CRYING AND LAMENTING)

Illustr. 3 Lacrimoso e Lamentoso (Crying and Lamenting). © Nina Lykke 2017.

LAMENTS

1.
To lament the dead is an ancient custom –
and the lament one of the oldest genres.
In modern times, however,
death is clinical,
if possible,
hidden deep in the bowels of hospitals.
We neither sing laments
nor invite mourners
to weep and wail
at funerals.
The bereaved
try to retain their composure
and cry in silence.

2.
But why not
cry out your grief to the four winds?
proclaim your pain to all the corners of the world?
let tears gush forth?
give yourself to sobbing?
open all the locks when breakers of despair
are sweeping in,
throwing you out of your depth?
pulling you towards
death by drowning?
Do you try to fight against the waves?
The undercurrent takes you anyway.

KARAOKE WITH KATHLEEN

1.
What is life to me without thee?
What is left if thou art dead?
What is life to me without thee?
What is left if thou art dead?
Orpheus' lament to deceased Eurydice,
sung by opera singer Kathleen Ferrier
who died from cancer
six decades before you.
You were 16 back then
and heard her on record.
Kathleen's queer contralto voice
lamenting Eurydice
who could not be called to life again
made an indelibly impression on you.
What is life to me without thee?
What is left if thou art dead?

2.
You taught me to love the voice of Kathleen –
dark and powerful like yours,
a voice to immerse yourself in,
a voice of deep desires.

3.
What is life to me without thee?
What is left if thou art dead?'
What is life to me without thee?
What is left if thou art dead?
I am walking up and down the room
between your deathbed
and the record player.
You are lying there,
unfathomably half-smiling,
looking at me
under eyelids a bit open,
a while ago congealed,
when you exhaled
the very last time.

4.
What is life to me without thee?
What is left if thou art dead?
Sobbing I join in:

What is life to me without thee?
What is left if thou art dead?
Crying out together with Kathleen,
forcefully releasing
Orpheus' overwhelming pain:
Eurydice, Eurydice.
Singing, sobbing, sobbing, singing,
karaoking with Kathleen.
Putting record on replay.
Orpheus shouting:
Eurydice, Eurydice.
'Do not leave me!
Do not leave me!'
Eurydice.
EURYDICE.
Walking up and down the room.
Sitting down
next to your body,
take your hand,
caress your forehead,
kiss your lips,
repeatedly.
You are cold now,
and so silent,
but I whisper
that I love you,
that I love you.
Eurydice.

5.
Keep on walking, crying, sobbing,
singing, sobbing, once again,
putting Kathleen on replay.
Sitting next to you
to kiss you
and to whisper
that I love you,
and will stay forever with you,
my flesh, your flesh,
we are one,
and perhaps I can still help you
magically to return.
Eurydice, Eurydice
What is life to me without thee?
What is left if thou art dead?'

6.
But the widow,
called to action,
has to find
an undertaker,
write a death announcement
now,
phone the doctor,
who shall certify
your death,
make you enter the statistics:
one more cancerdeath
recorded.
I am devastated,
amputated.
My beloved now and always,
my compassionate companion,
my for ever conjoined twin,
violently is your flesh
totally cut off from mine,
leaving an intolerably
aching amputation wound.

WHERE ORPHEUS FAILED

1.
Where Orpheus failed
was not in defying Hades' prohibition
against turning his head
to look back for Eurydice
as they escaped the Underworld.
Orpheus failed
when he became so absorbed
in the beauty of his own songs
that, like another Narcissus,
he could not feel the presence of
anything but himself.
This is why he had to look back
to see
if Eurydice was still
walking behind him.

2.
During the long years of your illness
I became convinced that
this was where Orpheus failed.

3.
During the long years of your illness,
I worked hard to avoid
failing where Orpheus failed.

4.
During the long years of your illness
I made every possible effort
to be a hyper-attentive
hyper-compassionate companion,
a body of support,
trying to do it right
where Orpheus failed.

5.
Truly, I could not always maintain this state of
constant hyper-attentive, embodied empathy.
Compassion fatigue overwhelmed me,
from time to time,
it forced itself between us.
One of the many days of despair

during your five-week long
stay in a hospital in Berlin,
where three open-stomach operations
drained you of all bodily strength,
I had to leave you one afternoon,
and simply go home to our apartment
to meditate in the bathtub,
drink wine alone,
do yoga,
listen to music,
relax,
forget everything around me.
But all the other 34 days in Berlin,
I was with you
at all times,
day, evening, and sometimes also at night.
I made every effort to get access
to sit at your bedside
in the intensive care unit,
when you awoke
from anaesthesia
after the operations.
I moistened your mouth,
when you were not allowed to drink.
I slept in a hospital bed next to yours,
so you could feel safer at night
when the third operation
had weakened the stamina,
you had so resiliently maintained
during the first two.
It alleviated your insomnia
that I was there.
I kept track of all your tubes and drops,
and supported you with my arms and body,
when you tried to get out of bed
to speed up the healing of the long, long wounds,
which were cut open again and again
through the repeated operations.
I cooked food for you,
healthy, tasty dishes,
and carried them with me in the metro
on the hour-long journey from
the apartment in Prenzlauerberg to the Charité hospital,
to counteract your lack of appetite,
made worse by the dull and tasteless hospital food.

The nurses taught me to adjust your oxygen apparatus,
and to give you injections of insulin.
I wrote down everything the doctors told us
on their daily rounds
to make sure we did not forget important details.
I read the news about the 'Arab Spring' aloud to you,
at times when you were too weak
to hold the newspaper in your hands
and read it yourself.

6.
I became one with your cancersick body.
For years I was
always
ready,
prepared,
alert.
Everything, everything,
I will do for you, my love.
Just tell me,
what you need.
I'll go for it,
I'll bring it,
I'll run out, and wait, and run back again,
repeatedly,
ceaselessly,
always,
by day
and by night.
My love,
I am here,
for you
for you,
my love,
for you.
I lend you my body
as your healthy prosthesis
which can help you
with everything
your own body
cannot do
anymore.
You have me here,
right here,
no matter what,

next to you,
non-stop.
Just promise me not to die!
I'll carry you
from the edge of the abyss.
I'll drag you away,
I'll struggle,
I'll heave.
I am strong,
unstoppable,
resilient,
and patient as hell.
I never give up.
You can trust me,
my love,
for ever.
Just promise me not to die!
Just promise me not to die!
Just promise me not to die!
Just promise me not to die!
Just promise me not to die!
Just promise me not to die!
Just promise me not to die!
Just promise me not to die!
Just promise me not to die!

7.
I believed we had a magical pact.
I believed in preventing your death,
if I could just manage
to avoid the failures of Orpheus.
But nothing, oh nothing,
no, nothing
was enough,
not the magical pact,
nor my belief
in Orpheus' mistakes
and my own recipe
for getting it right.
Confronted with Death,
all my efforts fell
totally
utterly
inexorably
short.

TEARS[1]

1.
You burst into tears
when listening to
Kathleen Ferrier
singing
Orpheus' lament to Eurydice,
his despairing cry
'Eurydice, Eurydice!'
You burst into tears
because of the deep wound
you knew that your death
would leave in me, your beloved.
You burst into tears
because of the abyss of grief
into which you knew that you would
cast both me,
 your children,
and grandchildren,
when you left us.
You could not bear the thought
of the unending sorrow
you could not help inflicting upon us,
whom you loved most of all.
You could not bear the thought
that there was nothing
you could do
to relieve our pain.
You heard us calling you in vain:
'Eurydice, Eurydice!'
and it filled you with
an immense sorrow
that it was not in your power
to comfort us.

2.
We cried together,
every time the cancer relapsed.
We cried together,
as long as there was hope
that it could be stopped.
We cried together
the day we got the message
that there was no hope left.

I knelt by your chair
sobbing with my head in your lap.
You caressed my head carefully.
I clutched your hands.
'Eurydice, Eurydice!'

3.
From time to time
I also cried,
without you witnessing it.
I saw your eyes full of sorrow,
mourning the loss of the life,
you loved,
mourning the relentless
decay of your body,
mourning having to leave
us, your loved ones,
with our grief
at losing you.
But you refused to be absorbed by sorrow.
'Enough! There is too much sniffelling here!'
you said,
when we had cried together
for some time.
And then I cried
instead behind your back, my love,
hid my tears from you.
Perhaps you also hid yours from me?
I sobbed and sobbed,
because I was about to lose you,
because I saw your immense sorrow,
because I could not bear the grief
that was in you, in me, between us.

4.
'Eurydice, Eurydice!'
I called out crying
in the days, weeks, months and years after your death,
throwing myself sobbing
against the accursed wall
that now separated us,
and just returned the echo of my voice,
'Eury-Eurydice!'
My hands bled
from hammering against the wall,

while tears blinded my eyes,
so I could not clearly see,
whether the wall dissolved,
and if you really walked behind me
on the way out of the land of death.

5.
Now I miss the wild crying,
the all-absorbing grief.
Tears like cloudbursts,
unlocking all the gates of heaven.
Tears like fine drops,
rolling unceasingly down my cheeks.
Tears like pouring November rain,
cutting my skin relentless as a knife.
I miss the sobbing
that bursts from the body
with strangling power,
the sobbing that cannot be suppressed,
the sobbing, rising in spasms
from deep down in the diaphragm,
bursting its way through the chest
like an avalanche turned upside-down,
the sobbing, which explodes from the throat
in gasping cries.

6.
When the crying stopped,
and the tears dried up,
I was enveloped in sadness and gloom.
You were with me
when I cried,
my sobbing called you to life
as an intensely present absence.
Now, when I no longer cry
you are really gone,
imperceptible, vanished.
But I will not let you go.
You must not leave me like this.
Stay with me!
Dwell close to me!
I want to feel you here!
So let me keep the tears!
Give the mourning back to me!
Reawaken my sobbing!

ELEGIAC DAYS

1.
I lie, curled
within a snail shell
all night.
Cautiously, I extrude my feelers,
but draw them quickly back again.

2.
Laboriously, I climb up from a black hole.
The strong sunlight hits me,
I screw up my eyes.
I cannot see anything,
and long to retreat to the soft darkness.

3.
I am sitting at the top of a lighthouse,
elevated above the earth's surface.
I look down at the people,
walking small as ants
far below me.
I brush a mosquito from my arm.
It was about to bite,
and perhaps succeeded in sucking up some blood.
So what?
I do not kill the mosquito.
Perhaps its bite will irritate my skin for days.
But it is only trying to get food.
Conatus was the name Spinoza gave
the appetite to persevere,
the resilient striving that pervades all matter.
I have no appetite.
The mosquito flew away
to suck blood somewhere else.
Again, I sit alone in my lighthouse,
staring across the evening-dark sea,
and meditating on the phenomenon
of loss of appetite
Loss of appetite!

MANIC DAYS

1.
Manic days
replace elegiac days.
I hang out with people after the conference,
go disco dancing under stroboscopic lights
with colleagues.
Young dancers gather encouragingly
around me on the dance floor,
they seem to think
that I am cool,
but strange
with my snowy white hair
and my supple yoga-body.

2.
I invent big projects,
initiate new networks,
accept invitations,
write contributions
to books and journals,
when colleagues ask me
to do so.
I participate in many, long skype meetings
with anyone
who wants my advice.
I invite many guests to my house
and cook lavish meals for them.

3.
When morning comes,
I wake in panic
at the thought of
all the things I initiated,
wishing only to be alone,
alone with you and my grief.

Interlude I: Lacrimoso e Lamentoso – **Lacrimoso,** tearful, referring to the Latin word lacrima, tear, and **Lamentoso,** lamenting, are terms used in classical music composing. They indicate that a particular piece of music should be performed in a mode, which expresses deep sorrow and devastation. Here, they resonate with the mood of the poems of *Interlude I*. The poem *Laments* prepares the scene of mourning, interpellating the ancient genre of the lament that has unfolded in different cultures to poetically voice grief. *Karaoke with Kathleen* articulates the intertwining of Orpheus' lament, as sung by opera singer Kathleen Ferrier, and the mourning 'I''s karaoke-like imitation. The Orpheus/Eurydice *leitmotif* reappears in *Where Orpheus Failed,* introducing the ways in which even compassionate care work, ultimately, cannot prevent the beloved from dying, In *Tears*, the Orpheus/Eurydice figuration articulates the shared lamenting of Death's powers to cut apart. *Elegiac Days* and *Manic Days* provide snapshots of the mourning 'I''s oscillations between sorrowful withdrawal and manic action in response to the intense feelings of loss, pervading the everyday life of the excessive mourner. The weeping and lamenting mode marks the entrance to **Chapter 2, The Excessive Mourner**, focusing on the mourner who delves into mourning.

Chapter 2

THE EXCESSIVE MOURNER

As I write this chapter, I pass January 29, during the night of which my partner died, six years ago now. The fact that I still mourn her intensely makes my grief complicated and excessive, when considered from the perspective of psychology and psychiatry. From Freud's reflections on mourning and melancholia (1917) to the powerful *Diagnostic and Statistical Manual of Mental Disorders* of the American Psychiatric Association (APA), DSM-5 (2013), it has been normatively established that it is mentally unhealthy to remain in a state of mourning. It even seems as though the pathologizing of long-term mourning is currently intensifying. In earlier editions of DSM, mourning and devastation following the death of a loved one was exempted from the conditions of loss that required attention as mental situations generating the risk of a depressive disorder. A much debated new feature of DSM-5 (2013) is that this exemption clause for grief after the death of a loved one has been removed. This removal implies that feelings of intense bereavement after such a loss per se are to be included within the spectrum of potential pathology.

The removal of this exemption clause has caused much debate among psychiatrists (Kavan and Barone 2014). For some, it is a necessary gesture to make sure that post-loss-of-a-loved-one depressions are found, diagnosed and treated. For others, it is a move which pathologizes mourning in problematic ways. What strikes me as I browse the debate is that, no matter what, there is a rather strong consensus that mourning beyond a certain limited period of time is 'complicated' and a signal of potential pathology. The time limit can be some weeks (Pies 2020), or even a year (Mayo Clinic 2020), but 'realistic' grief work is supposed to make mourning stop, and enable the mourner to regain 'an interest in life and feel[ing] hopeful again' (Carney 2018). Within such discourses, my mourning practices clearly pinpoint me as a person living in a risk zone, with depression looming threateningly on the horizon. Seen from the perspective of Freud, DSM and mainstream psychology and psychiatry, six years of mourning is excessive.

So, for sure, mainstream psychology would consider my strong desire to stay with mourning rather than trying to 'move on with life' (ibid.) to be asking for trouble. That this is the case was spelled out to me by an event which occurred some weeks after my partner's death. I will tell the story of this normative encounter with psychological definitions of mourning in order to illustrate how overall normativities regarding un/healthy mourning work at an individual, everyday level. With the story, I also want to open horizons towards normcritical resistance, when it comes to mourning practices.

A Normative Encounter[1]

After my partner's death, I was forcefully confronted with the norm that we who mourn should put the mourning behind us after a certain 'appropriate' period of time. The confrontation took place when, some weeks into my new life as a queer widow, I was contacted by a professor of psychology at a Danish university. She was carrying out a research project on the grieving behaviour of people who had lost their life partners. A nurse from the palliative team who assisted me in taking care of my partner during the last weeks of her life, had asked me if I would agree to be an informant on this project. When she asked me, I was totally immersed in taking care of my dying beloved, so I just shrugged and said 'sure' without giving it any more thought. So, a couple of weeks after my beloved's death, a big questionnaire landed in my mailbox.

The first part of the questionnaire was based on a series of multiple-choice questions. These questions made it clear between the lines what were to be seen as 'un/healthy' and 'in/appropriate' behaviours for me in my new role as widow. The questions, and the answers which could be ticked, were clearly normative, urging me to put the loss of my partner behind me. For example, according to the implicit message of the questionnaire, it was definitely better for me to go out and meet people than to sit at home and be 'depressed' or 'sad'. Interestingly, the terms 'depressed' and 'sad', which refer to two distinctly different emotional states, were collapsed into each other, and it was clear that neither of them represented a 'healthy' option. The 'healthy' option was instead to find 'new' kinds of happiness, and perhaps in due time a new partner. If I was the 'dependent' personality type, I should also try to adapt to this new situation in which I did not have a 'strong shoulder' to lean on or a partner to ask for advice. Heteronormative and gender stereotyping assumptions about me pervaded the questionnaire. Between the lines, images of the 'widow' - imagined as an elderly, heterosexual woman who has lost her husband, and who is assumed to be totally unfit to handle her life conditions without his help - were present everywhere in the phrasings of the multiple-choice questions.

The second part of the questionnaire was different, and under immediate consideration, a bit less disgusting. But after a close reading, this part, too, turned out to be extremely normative. Here, I was asked to describe, in a freely associative narrative form, the status of the 'chapters of my life' until now, and look forward towards new 'life chapters' - without my partner. In terms of the future, the questionnaire suggested that I could try to imagine three possible new life chapters, although it was 'kindly' pointed out that it was ok, too, if I could perhaps only imagine one or two new chapters, and even if it was totally impossible for me to imagine life without my partner, this was also ok. Because - as the questionnaire tolerantly told me - 'there are no right or wrong ways in which to identify or describe your future life'. However, the possibility that the category 'your future life' was perhaps not relevant to me at all, because what I desired to do was to immerse myself in an eternally extended instant of mourning and lamenting, was definitely not something the authors of the questionnaire would like to see me think about.

I found the questionnaire disgusting. But I thought that perhaps I could teach the psychology professor who had designed it something about queering the norms of mourning – about opening and deconstructing instead of closing and normatively fixing identity categories and prescribing 'healthy' and 'unhealthy' behaviours. So, I wrote a lot of comments to the questions describing how I did not fit the categories, and therefore could not answer. I also tried to phone the psychology professor to discuss the questionnaire. But after a phone call that utterly failed in its purpose, when confronted with a very evasive psychologist, clearly in the grasp of strong feelings of awkwardness and unease when talking to me, I gave up the pedagogical project of teaching her about a queering of mourning. I understood that the more energy I put into trying to make her understand that her questionnaire was hopelessly normative and useless, the more she saw in me an inappropriate research object, who talked back and in this way spoiled her opportunity to undertake a 'neutral' positivist observation of me and my 'grieving behaviours'.

Cripping, Queering and Posthumanizing Excessive Mourning

I challenged the questionnaire due to my strong urge to dwell in mourning. But in so doing, I also struggled to establish a platform for resistance to the health-normative imperatives of neoliberal biopolitics (Rose 2007). These are imperatives that prompt us, who inhabit Western modernity, to relentlessly pursue normative ideals of individual health and happiness (Ahmed 2010) – ideals requiring us to control and contain our desires to mourn. As articulated by crip and queer theory one set of strategies to resist these imperatives is linked to normcritical resignification (Butler 1993), i.e. to create new critical-affirmative meanings that move beyond stigma and pathology. Along these lines, this chapter enters into a resignification of excessive mourning. I claim that it is important to immerse oneself in mourning and to insist on slow scarring rather than quick healing. Attending to the persistence of deep mind/body wounds, inflicted through the loss of loved ones, is an individual resistance strategy, but can also be taken to more collective and public levels.[2]

In order to reflect upon resistance and resignification of excessive mourning, I call forward different theoretical approaches. First, I draw on crip theory (Sandahl 2003; McRuer 2006; Kafer 2013), interpellating a 'cripping' perspective, which signifies a critical-affirmative, political reclaiming of the stigmatizing term 'cripple', analogous to the ways in which the derogatory term 'queer' was reclaimed and resignified by the queer movement and queer theory (Butler 1993). When I take inspiration from crip theory, I focus on turning the stigma and pain related to complicated and excessive mourning into potential. Though, the point is not to romanticize or essentialize specific non-normative aspects of subjectivity and embodiment that materialize in the wounds and scarring processes of the mourning 'I'. What I suggest is that the potentials to be unleashed here can emerge from an exploration and resignification of the pathologized subject position of the excessive mourner. I want to give new meanings to this position, resignify it, as part of opening up horizons for an unfolding of a posthuman phenomenology of excessive mourning.

Alongside crip perspectives, I mobilize queer theory. Critical crip scholars (Sandahl 2003; McRuer 2006; Kafer 2013) have argued that crip and queer theory have much in common in terms of radically challenging normativities and normalizations, and resisting fixed and stabilized definitions and dichotomies related to bodies, sexualities, lifestyles etc. Resistance is strengthened by the use of verb forms: cripping and queering, stressing processes rather than essentialized situations and identities, often signalled by nouns or adjectives. However, when using cripping and queering as analytical tools, it should be noted that they are not interchangeable. Both are needed (Kafer 2013), because the critical sensibilities that go with each of the terms differ in some respects. Considered separately, cripping and queering modes and moods imply a multitude of overlapping, but also very different sensibilities. In my analysis of the position of the excessive mourner, I mobilize intersections of both perspectives. 'Cripping' addresses resistance to normativities of ablebodiedness and ablemindedness, referring to a political, critical-affirmative resignification of the normative and pejorative term 'cripple' as holding potential for mourning differently. Using queering as a tool, I generally refer to non-normativity in a broad sense (Radomska, Mehrabi and Lykke 2020: 89). But I also take a specific, femme-inist (Dahl 2012, 2014), point of departure in my embodied sensibilities as a queer femme, approaching my autobiographical material as an autophenomenography of doing queerfeminine widowhood (Lykke 2015). I define this approach along the lines of queer femme theorists (Cvetkovich 2003; Dahl 2012, 2014; Gómez-Barris 2017), who in different ways emphasize how queer, non-normative femininities can be used as critical-affirmative, corpopolitical lenses of interpretation. Moreover, I specifically stress how, for me, queerfeminine sensibilities resonate with posthuman critiques of the sovereign subject and an ethics of intercorporeality (Shildrick 2005, 2009; Weiss 2009).

Working from my autobiographical material, the story *A Normative Encounter*, the poems of *Interlude I, Lacrimoso e Lamentoso (Crying and Lamenting)* and a couple of further stories, *Sorrowful Pleasures* and *To Become a Powerless Prosthesis*, giving snapshots of the final weeks of my partner's life, this chapter focuses on two issues: time and wounds. Both are of key importance to the understanding of excessive mourning. With regard to the issue of time, which is so central to psychological and psychiatric definitions of un/healthy mourning, I explore how resignification requires us to pay attention to strange temporalities. I look at how the time-zones of excessive mourning are related to those emerging from queering and cripping modes and moods (Halberstam 2005; Freeman 2007, 2010; Kafer 2013). But I also address how the temporalities of mourning are somewhat different, requiring that cripqueer reflections on time are taken further against the background of posthumanizing and immanence philosophical frameworks. Concerning the problem of wounds, I focus on the corpo-affective, fleshy, intercorporeal and material aspects of queer femme widowhood, such as the embodied feeling of being an amputee or a conjoined twin, separated through painful resection.

Cripqueer Time

Time and temporalities play a key role in defining the excess which, in the eyes of mainstream psychiatry and psychology, can lead mourning in a pathological direction. Risk is measured in time, whether the limit of uncomplicated grief is set to a couple of weeks (e.g. Pies 2020) or 12 months (e.g. Carney 2018). Time was also brought to my attention when the questionnaire that I was asked to fill out after my partner's death urged me to think about the future in terms of future life chapters without my partner, instead of staying in a state of mourning. What I shall look at here is how time can also become central to the process of resistance and resignifying. Following one's desire to mourn far beyond the maximum acceptable time limits, and defy chrononormative ideas of 'futurity', articulated, for example, as new life chapters, can be rethought and resignified as acts of resistance. I am not arguing that resistance is an automatic or easy process. But I follow queer scholar Ann Cvetkovich, who, in an in-depth queer- and affecttheoretical analysis of her years of depression, made an argument for the ways in which 'resting in sadness without insisting that it be transformed or reconceived' (2012: 14) had healing effects for her, which could not be framed within a chrononormative time scheme, and its requirements regarding a quick and happy 'return' to productive life.

In order to dig deeper into the issue of the temporalities of mourning and to flesh out what it may mean to insist on resisting the norms that pathologize the desire to stay in a mourning mode and mood, I also draw upon cripqueer feminist scholar, Alison Kafer's reflections on crip time (2013: 25f.), and the way in which it is affiliated with queer time. Queer time has been theorized as 'time out of joint' (Freeman 2007: 159) and as 'strange temporalities' (Halberstam 2005: 1). Delving into these may liberate people who are living non-normative lives from feeling pressured by 'normative narratives of time' (ibid.: 152), such as chrononormative progress narratives, that mould expectations about the temporal trajectories of intimate life through norms of reproductive heterosexual family-building (ibid.). Through a crip lens, strange temporalities may take other shapes, though. Kafer (2013) argues that queer and crip perspectives on time both overlap and differ; for example, in relation to the issue of futurity and longevity, with the normative cultural focus on living a long life as an ultimate good thing. Kafer acknowledges a certain overlap between queer and crip time, when, in the wake of the HIV/AIDS epidemic of the 1980s and 1990s, the queering of time in a mode of resistance could be interpreted as entering 'a temporality that refuses futurity (. . .), prompted by gay men who had been forced by death and disease to rethink the cultural focus on living long lives' (ibid.: 41). However, Kafer also pinpoints how a queer critique of the norms of longevity can slip into a problematic relationship with cripped class issues. This is the case, when it is ignored how, for example, poor people with disabilities are politically prevented by cuts in welfare programmes from gaining access to resources which might ensure that they actually get the opportunity to live long lives (ibid.).

As I navigate between these different cripqueer interpretations of strange, non-normative temporalities in my search for ways to theoretically frame my feelings of unease and resistance to the normative discourses nudging me to stop mourning and instead focus on new life chapters, I find myself in a state of disidentification (Butler 1993). I identify with the cripqueer work on strange temporalities, but in somewhat different ways. Queer and crip reflections on time help me to better understand the strange time-zones I inhabit as mourning 'I'. But, still, they do not quite grasp my way of inhabiting time in strange ways. On the one hand, thinking along the lines of strange – cripqueer – temporalities sustains my urge to resist the norms requiring me to suppress my desires to keep on mourning. They help me to resignify the unease I felt when asked to respond to the questionnaire. I want to delve excessively into my mourning, despite the ways in which the DSM and other mainstream psychiatry and psychology discourses diagnose the trajectory of the excessive mourner as potentially pathological. However, on the other hand, in order to come to terms with the temporalities of mourning, which nurtured my resistance to the questionnaire's discourses on future life chapters, I also need to determine where my sensibilities and subject position as mourning 'I' differ from queer or crip modes and moods. Like Kafer, who enriches the queer discussion of strange temporalities through a crip perspective, I use the sensibilities of the mourning 'I' as an entrance point enabling me to twist cripqueer considerations of temporalities that transgress chrononormativity even further.

The Strange Temporalities of Mourning

Contemplating the strange temporalities that I inhabit as mourning 'I', first of all, I find myself led to disidentify with conventional modern secular modes and norms of mourning. These modes and norms restrict my temporal outlook in two significant ways. They encourage me to limit my passionate desire to lament and interact excessively with a ghostly past. I should avoid becoming too excessive a mourner, who turns away from chrononormative trajectories that point me towards a happily productive future. Moreover, these conventional norms urge me to foreclose any thought of reconnection with my beloved, assessing it as a sign of insanity and/or anachronistic superstition if I seriously explore such possibilities. Or, in other words: I should turn towards the present and the future, but certainly not in order to cultivate 'hallucinations' about reconnection. The desires that excessive mourners may nurture to delve into 'magical thinking' (Didion 2012) about the beloved's spectral return should definitely also be kept at bay.

To theorize the temporal restrictions with which secular modern subjects are urged to comply, let me, once more, recall Sartre's conceptualization of death as nothingness (1958), together with Freud's reflections on mourning and melancholia (1917). When Sartre defines death as nothingness, philosophically assumed to occur when the subject vanishes with the final exhalation, the logical temporal arena for the mourner to turn towards is the past. Dealing with memories of the past (material artefacts such as photos, letters or clothes, as well as immaterial ones, e.g. remembered scenes of past togetherness) is all that appears to be left for the mourning 'I'. As mourning 'I', you are supposed to stay with memories fixed to an immutable and now passé past, and accept the (positivist) reality principle, which states that the passed away beloved can only be present in the stasis of the past tense. It is, as Freud teaches us (ibid.), precisely because the logic of the reality principle implies that the passed away beloved must be seen as absent in the present, vanished for good, and not available to summon back, that it becomes equivalent to an unhealthy turning of the back on reality if the mourner shifts hir focus away from the forward-running arrow of time to stay with the static past. If you, as mourner, ignore the reality principle, then from a modern secular point of view, you are to be considered either insane, or bound up in anachronistic superstition or – basically the same thing – in excessive religious beliefs. Or, in other words: obeying the logic of the modern positivist reality principle forecloses any possibility for the mourning subject to contemplate the passed away beloved outside of chrononormative time.

Taking these views of Sartre and Freud as iconic, I claim that the modern secular mourner is supposed to obey two kinds of – slightly contradictory – temporal norms, which both derive from the positivist reality principle. One is to restrict yourself to turning to the past, and to your memories, leaving out any idea of ongoingness in the here-and-now and possibilities for future encounters. The other is not to cultivate your memories of the past for too long, but instead turn towards 'future lifechapters', as the questionnaire framed it, in a chrononormative sense. Insisting on my desire to lament and immerse myself in long-term mourning, as well as to prepare for reconnection with my dead beloved, brings me into conflict with both of these temporal norms, as well as with the positivist reality principle.

To come to terms with the ways in which my resistance to these norms can be not only critically framed, but also affirmatively grounded in new understandings of my desires to inhabit time differently, I find queer critiques of conventional ideas of longevity and normative futurity (Halberstam 2005) helpful and refreshing. Still, the queer challenge to a focus on 'future lifechapters' resonates only partially with me. Instead of setting the living of a queer life, conceived as a temporal sequence of rhizomatically evolving joyful encounters in the here-and-now as an alternative to chrononormatively inhabiting longevity and normative futurity, as mourning 'I', I need to take a different path. I need to confront conventional norms of longevity and futurity from the perspective of my desires to rest in temporalities that exist beyond any human lifetimes, circumscribed by birth and death, whether lived individually from moment to moment in a queer fashion, or heteronormatively focussed on normative longevity.

Shifting from queer to cripqueer perspectives, I also find some overlaps between my resistance to chrononormativity and critical resignifications, articulated from the position of the depressive 'I', but again with modifications. Kafer suggests a cripqueering of this position, attending to the resignifying and critically-affirmative potentials of depression in terms of the way in which it 'slows down time, making moments drag for days' (Kafer 2013: 38). When Cvetkovich, moreover, insists on 'resting in sadness' (2012: 14) to heal depression, she, too, cripqueers the depressive 'I' critically affirmatively.[3] Both Kafer's and Cvetkovich's resignifying gestures definitely speak to me. Still, I somehow need to disidentify with them, too. In contrast to the depressive 'I', whose urge to 'slow down time' and 'rest in sadness' emerges from feelings of emptiness and a lack of desire to engage, I am overwhelmed by the passionate desire to reconnect. I feel strongly attracted to all kinds of quests towards finding ways to transgress the wall of imperceptibility and silence that my partner's passing the life/death threshold has created around her. In temporal terms, I do not feel that time 'slows down' as described by Kafer, leaving me stuck in a frozen moment of a linear, forward-moving timeline. What I feel instead is that moving forward in chronological time, life chapter by life chapter to use the metaphor of the questionnaire, leaving a time-zone called the 'past' behind, immersing myself in one called the 'present', while looking forward to another one called 'future', has lost its meaning for me. Reconnection can only take place outside of and beyond this forward-moving chronological time that is tied to individual human lifetimes.

So, in sum, I see my quest as aligned with queer and crip efforts to inhabit time differently, but my conclusion is also that my desire to mourn excessively creates a need in me to delve into even stranger temporalities than the ones suggested in discussions of queer and crip temporalities. The queering and cripping efforts stay within human timeframes, while my desires as excessively mourning 'I' push me into radically posthuman directions – towards contemplations of temporalities that goes beyond the horizons of individual human lifetimes altogether.

Defying the norms, which prevent mourners from engaging too intensely with the past, I cultivate and indulge excessively in memories of my past life with my beloved. I live in the same house that we inhabited together for 37 years. This house, and most of the things in it, are phenomenally saturated with memories of our life together. I cultivate these in excessive manners, defying the so-called reality principle, when I embrace the momentary, and always unexpected spectral encounters which these things can produce. Moreover, I do not limit myself to experiencing my beloved through ongoing encounters with the past. I try also to go beyond the second set of conventional temporal norms which require a normative orientation towards 'future life chapters'. I prepare myself for miraculous encounters with my dead beloved not only in spectral encounters with the subject she was, but also in her current modes of being as ashes mixed with diatomaceous sand in the waters of Limfjorden, where her ashes are scattered. Helped by spiritual-material practices, I prepare myself for both kinds of encounters (with the spectralities and with the vibrant assemblages of which my beloved's material remains have become part). Both these kinds of encounters take place in timezones that extend beyond definitions of 'past', 'present' and 'future' in a chrononormative sense. To come to terms with these timezones, I shall in the next chapter take inspiration from Derridean hauntology (1994), and from Deleuze's definition of time as *Aion* rather than *Chronos* (Deleuze 2020: 167–72).⁴ First, however, the second part of this chapter, will dig into the other crucial dimension, characterizing excessive mourning, namely wounds.

Unscripting Christian One-Flesh Narratives

From the strange temporalities of excessive mourning, I shall turn towards corpo-affective aspects, which make up another cornerstone of this book's posthuman phenomenology of the mourning 'I'. Focusing on the poems of *Interlude I* and on two stories from the final weeks of my partner's life, *Sorrowful Pleasures* and *To Become a Powerless Prosthesis*, which I will tell in order to deepen the understanding of our corpo-affective bond, I shall highlight how the inhabiting of mourning must be understood as a fleshy affair – as a response to becoming wounded. Mourning is not only a state of mind, it is also a bodily condition and practice. I shall dig deeper into the carnality of mourning, taking my point of departure in a cluster of images in the poems of *Interlude I*, which circulates around a central figuration of my partner and me being 'one flesh'. In *Karaoke with Kathleen*, the one-flesh figuration is articulated through the poetic 'I''s experience of the loss implied in having a part of the body cut away, becoming an amputee, or of being one of a pair of conjoined twins, resected from one another. The fleshy link between my partner and me, which produces a wound when cut up, is also implied in the image of the poetic 'I' in *Where Orpheus Failed*, who is becoming-one with the cancersick body of the poem's 'you', acting as her 'healthy prosthesis', while carrying out intensive care work to try to save the life of the 'you'.

The fleshy feeling of oneness and the corresponding idea of death as a violent cutting apart resonated with my gut feelings back then. It was as though my beloved's death sliced us apart in a very carnal and embodied sense – as though we literally were 'one flesh' being cut up. But how can I make sense of this fleshy feeling of 'oneness', and of becoming cut apart? Can I reclaim the Biblical image of turning into 'one flesh' (Genesis 2020), along with the phrase 'until death do us part' of the Christian Marriage Vows (Wikipedia 2020)? What does it imply to use this Biblical and Christian imagery, which is related strictly and normatively to a heterosexual and exceptionally human bonding, a patriarchally conceived marriage between Man and Woman in a stereotyped and essentialized sense, confirmed by the spiritual intervention of the patriarchal trinity of Father, Son and Holy (phallo(go) centric) Spirit? What can I do with all these associations which I so strongly oppose and detest, both politically and theoretically? Can the one-flesh-imagery be reontologized and resignified to make sense within a radically different, cripqueer, feminist, posthuman and immanence philosophical framework?

I claim that such a reontologization and resignification is possible. My tools for the reclaiming include, first of all, that the same-sex relationship between my partner and me as such queers and unscripts the strictly heteronormative Biblical one-flesh story. In the discourse of the Bible, oneness is supposed to occur 'naturally' between Man and Woman (Genesis 2020), and definitely not in 'unnatural' relations, such as those between two women, two men, or other genderqueer constellations. However, second, alongside the obvious ways in which same-sex and genderqueer relations fundamentally clash with the Biblical bill, I shall also reontologize the experience of bodily oneness, and hence of death as a cutting apart, within an immanence philosophical framework, radically detaching the Biblical imagery from any kind of Christian dualist mind/body split. In the remaining part of this chapter, I shall elaborate upon this framework, reontologizing and resignifying both the becoming-one-flesh and the corresponding cutting-apart as making up a queer, posthuman and depatriarchalized figuration of corpo-affective companionship and intercorporeality. This figuration allows me to grasp important qualities of my relationship with my partner, including the ways in which I came to experience her death as a painful amputation.

Compassionate Companionship

To reontologize the fleshy feelings of oneness within an immanence philosophical framework, expressing the loss as a carnally painful experience of cutting apart, I shall first reflect upon my and my partner's relationship as a compassionate companionship. I have previously (Lykke 2018) defined compassionate companionship[5] as embodied relations of mutual bonding, building on an active mutual commitment to being-with and being-for each other – a commitment imbued with affect, understood along the lines of a Spinozist tradition, revitalized by immanence philosophy (Deleuze and Guattari 1988; Braidotti 2006; Massumi 2015). I understand affect and affectivity in a Spinozist sense, i.e. to be considered as linked to what bodies do rather than what they are, and how they affect and are affected within a framework of events and encounters with other bodies. Against this background, companionship is seen as being made up of a series of everyday micro events, which imply continuous sequences of embodied encounters between companions. When the companionship is a long-term relationship of love, intimacy and friendship, it can, I suggest, generate a corpo-affective attunement, an intense sensitivity to the other's body and affective condition, based on what philosopher Ralph Acampora called *symphysis* (Acampora 2006: 76). Acampora suggests *symphysis* as an embodied, Spinozist rethinking of the notion of sympathy, stressing the component of corpo-affectivity. Coining the concept of *symphysis*, Acampora underscores that it is not only a question of feeling for and caring about the other, but also implies that the subject, in a material, corpo-affective sense, is affected by and co-experiences the ways in which hir significant other/s are bodily affected. The effects of horror movies on audiences may illustrate this co-experiencing: your heart beats faster and your stomach clenches when you watch the person on screen being threatened. Translating symphysis into verb form, *symphysizing*, I stress that the bonding between companions builds upon intercorporeal, affective processes, and not upon a static relationship, defined once and for all. I suggest that close, long-term and intimate companionships of love, intimacy and friendship can create bonds that continuously materialize a mutual corpo-affective co-experiencing, i.e. the generation of vicarious experiences related to the intimate companion's experiences.

To illustrate what symphysizing means, I shall add two stories from the final weeks of my partner's life to this book's autobiographical archive. These stories reflect the period when my partner was so physically weakened by the cancer that the image of me performing as her healthy bodily prosthesis, used in the poem *Where Orpheus Failed*, takes on very literal meanings, both when the mutual symphysizing succeeds, as in the first story, *Sorrowful Pleasures*, and when it fails, as in the second story, *To Become a Powerless Prosthesis*, which points towards the existential cutting apart of death.

Sorrowful Pleasures[6]

Three weeks before you died, you got the idea that we should go on a weekend trip to Copenhagen to have dinner at Alberto K, a gourmet restaurant located on the 20th floor of the Radisson Hotel, with a view over the whole city. More than a month earlier, the hospital had given us a final prognosis: 'Between two weeks and two months!' So we both knew that the end was near. You were physically very weak and could not walk without someone helping you. You were also using an oxygen apparatus twentyfour hours a day due to a chronic lack of breath. When you suggested the weekend in Copenhagen and the dinner at Alberto K, I could not help thinking that it was impossible. However, when I understood that you meant it very seriously, and that you were really keen to do it, I first became terribly stressed. How could I make sure that you would not get too cold during the approximately two-hour drive to Copenhagen, putting you at risk of catching pneumonia, which in your extremely weakened condition could easily kill you? What if I had to change the cylinder of the oxygen apparatus in the emergency lane of the motorway, while the cold January wind filled the car, increasing the risk of pneumonia even further? Would you be able to sit in a restaurant where there might be no really comfortable chairs? Thousands of worried thoughts rushed through my head.

But in the midst of all my worries, your resilient appetite for life and pleasure, even in these gloomy times, made me enormously happy. Going for weekends like this is something we have loved to do together for many years. And now, you wanted us to do it again. Enjoy life together. Don't let cancer and death block the pleasure. Just go ahead. What could prevent us from doing this but my fear of all the things that might happen? But why let fear reign? You were not afraid.

It became an unforgettable evening. It was, of course, evident to everyone in the restaurant how ill you were. Thin as skin and bones. With a bandana around your bald crown. Supported by a cane and by my body, you walked, bowed, into the restaurant with the breathing apparatus in your nose – I carried the big oxygen cylinder in a shoulder bag. The waiters bustled about us, politely and professionally keeping up the illusion that this was a totally ordinary restaurant visit. Did we want to start with an apéritif? And so on. We ordered fish and a bottle of the finest vintage champagne, the most expensive one we have ever bought in a restaurant. The city lights beamed up around us, while we slowly enjoyed the champagne and the fish. We overlooked the Copenhagen lakes and the neighbourhood behind them, where Eigil, Naja and Zak had recently rented an apartment. I no longer remember what we talked about. But lucidly clear is the feeling of sitting up there on the 20th floor together with you, my love, while, in a growing champagne ecstasy, we observed how the different neighbourhoods of the city unfolded themselves in front of our eyes – the city in which we had both lived for many years during our childhoods and youth.

The next morning you woke up with more strength than you had had for a long time. We ate breakfast – and this meal, too, was served in the restaurant on the 20th floor. Now we got a table that faced towards the other side of the city – towards Copenhagen's main station and Vesterbro. From this table, we could almost see Uffe and Rikke's flat. 'Shouldn't we phone them and ask if they want to come over for a cup of coffee, before we drive home?' you asked. Elated at the thought that you felt so well this morning, we called them. Uffe picked up the phone, and was completely taken by surprise when he learned that we were sitting in the 20th-floor restaurant of the Radisson Hotel, overlooking the street where he and Rikke live. When he had taken leave of you after the Xmas celebration at home in Odense, I think he had never expected you to come to Copenhagen again. We all knew the gloomy prognosis we had received from the doctors in early December – 'Between two weeks and two months . . .'. And now, on January 10th, we were suddenly phoning and asking if he and Rikke would join us for coffee, in a totally everyday manner. They came over, and we sat down in the lobby bar. While we were sitting there, enjoying our coffee, you came up with one more proposal. 'Why not eat lunch together at Santos?' Santos is a great Chinese restaurant, located at Vesterbrogade, very close to Uffe and Rikke's apartment. Uffe has celebrated his birthday with us several times there. 'It's so close,' you said, 'we can easily walk over there.' Uffe, Rikke and I looked at each other, as though we all had the same reply in our heads: 'But this is impossible! Your cancersick body is so frail now. It was already so very difficult for you to walk the few steps from the hotel elevator to the lobby bar. And it's raining, and you shouldn't get wet – you could so easily catch a fatal pneumonia.' However, none of us spoke our thoughts aloud. Your illusion of being able to do such everyday things as walking to a restaurant, located only five or ten minutes' walk from where we were, and your outspoken and visible joy, keeping up this illusion, was so strong that none of us could do anything but 'go with the flow!' 'Yes, let's go to Santos and eat lunch,' Uffe said. 'Great idea!' Rikke added. 'Yes,' I said, 'let's do it. But perhaps we should rather take a taxi to get there? Because you have no real walking shoes here, only your slippers, and they'll get soaked in the rain.' 'Ok, yes,' you said, and accepted my way of keeping up the illusion that your body was still capable of performing a five-to-ten minute walk. We would call a cab so that your slippers would not get soaked in the winter rain, not because you could not walk anymore.

During the lunch at Santos, the elated mood which had captured all of us continued to unfold. You read the menu meticulously many times and ordered several dishes with strange-sounding Chinese names – many more than the very few bites you were actually able to eat. But the strange names, and the fantasies about the *exquisite dishes that hid behind them, had a very elating effect on you. We shared the delicious Chinese specialities you had ordered, and after this we said goodbye to Uffe and Rikke, and started happily on the two-hour drive back to Odense.*

To Become a Powerless Prosthesis[7]

One morning, a week before you died, you could no longer walk down the stairs from our bedroom to the living room. For several weeks, I had had to support you heavily when climbing up and down the staircase to the bedroom, morning and evening. You leaned upon me so that I could free you of part of your own body weight, which, even though you were now only skin and bones, was nevertheless too heavy for you in your weakened and cancer-starved condition. However, with my support, you had until now been able to laboriously climb up and down the stairs, one step at a time, and your resilient will and perseverance prompted you to never give up.

Since you started having trouble walking, it had been easier for you to climb down than up the stairs. When going down, it was not only the support from my body which had made it easier for you to move your feet from step to step, but also the pull of gravity. But this morning, one week before you died, the pull on your legs, generated by gravity, instead made you lose your balance. Your legs were so weak now that you could not control your feet as each in turn lost touch with the firm surface of a step as it moved to the next one immediately below. Each foot now just fell like a stone when you moved it out into the void between the steps, and the fall made your whole body waver dangerously. At the beginning of this slow, wavering and laborious journey downstairs from step to step, I succeeded in supporting you enough for your body not to completely lose its balance. But when we still had the last four or five steps to go, your knees suddenly collapsed under you, you lost your balance completely and fell, slipping down a couple of steps without me being able to do anything except somewhat mitigate the fall by helping you to sit down on the bottom step. But then you sat there, stuck.

For a long, long time after this – I think an hour or so went by – we both worked hard to get you standing on your legs in an upright position, so that we could continue our walk to your big armchair in the living room, so close, and yet so far away. But you could not get up by yourself, and your body was much too heavy for me to lift you to your feet. We tried to get you up onto a kitchen chair, which I had brought to the stair where you were sitting, stuck, in the hope that we could get you from there into a standing position. But, for a very long time, we could not even get you up onto this chair. At first, you sat on the last step of the staircase. Later, you slipped down to the floor, while we both worked hard and desperately to find ways to jointly succeed in getting you up onto the kitchen chair. I no longer remember what it was that, finally, enabled us to manage it, and from there got you to stand up so that, supported by me, you could walk the few remaining steps to your armchair. But I do very clearly remember our feelings of powerlessness and grief. Your feeling of powerlessness and grief that you were no longer capable of controlling your legs. And my feeling of powerlessness and grief that your body was much too heavy for me to be able to help you to stand up, when you did not have any strength in your legs or arms to help me lift you. Why had the cancer made your long, strong, beautiful, and until now very fit, legs powerless and useless? Why had my body been transformed from a capable to an incapable prosthesis?

Symphysizing and Amputation

I developed my definition of compassionate companionship (Lykke 2018) in order to make sense of my and my partner's embodied attunement, but also to enable me to theorize the existential corpo-affective cutting apart, which occurred beyond our control, while she was dying, and, through her dying, I was thrown into a process of becoming-widow. I consider corpo-affective symphysizing to be a crucial aspect of my definition of compassionate companionship. It is also a central point of entrance to an immanence-philosophical reontologization and unscripting of the Biblical one-flesh image, as well as the corresponding cutting-apart-through-Death image of the Christian marriage ritual. Symphysizing and the fleshy feeling of amputation are two sides of the same coin. All of my bodily sensibilities were, at the time, oriented towards my dying beloved's corpo-affective condition and towards my symphysizing being-for and being-with her as compassionate companion, and towards receiving passionately loving, caring and symphysizing attention from her. But when she took her last breath, all the symphysizing giving and taking that was circulating between us was suddenly and violently cut off, from one moment to the next, leaving me with an excruciating pain that could only momentarily be relieved by the cathartic effects of tears.

Symphysizing is to be seen as one of the cornerstones of the posthuman phenomenology of the mourning 'I', which I unfold in this book, and the carnal pain that occurs when the symphysizing bond is existentially broken by death is a central component of what, in this chapter, I approach as excessive mourning. I see symphysizing as a key to unpacking the conjoined-twins and amputation images of *Karaoke with Kathleen,* and to make sense of the poetic 'I's intense, but in the end unavailing, efforts to save her beloved from Death through prosthetic care work in *Where Orpheus Failed.* Intense endeavours to re-establish the symphysizing relationship are also a central key to the image of the poetic 'I' of *Tears,* who beats her hands until they bleed against the wall of imperceptibility behind which she experiences that her beloved has vanished, and who is absorbed in a multitude of different crying practices, trying to keep the passed away alive in the spectral form of memories. The stories in this chapter, too, *Sorrowful Pleasures* and *To Become a Powerless Prosthesis,* spell out how the intense feeling of amputation occurs against the background of the equally intense feeling of symphysizing.

Sorrowful Pleasures is an example of the ways in which symphysizing efforts and desires continued to circulate between us until the very end of my beloved's life, in a mutually enabling sense. In this story, my beloved pushes me forcefully beyond my initially strong feelings of anxiety that I will not be able to safely manage her so very frail and fatally cancersick body during our pleasure tour to

Copenhagen. At first, my beloved is much more confident in my prosthetically caring abilities to make this tour into a success than I am myself. But her queermasculine insistence and symphysizing confidence that 'of course' we can make it mobilizes my queerfeminine dedication and desire to transgress myself for her and with her. Her confident insistence reawakens my symphysizing confidence that 'of course' her frail and dying body can still endure the strain and stress of the long car ride, and 'of course' I can take her safely to Copenhagen and bring her back again to our home in Odense, no matter what. The mutually enabling symphysizing makes the tour into a success and a happy event in the midst of these gloomy times, when all of us, including my beloved herself, knew that she was very soon to die.

This story about successful and mutually enabling symphysizing is contrasted against the story of disabled symphysizing in *To Become a Powerless Prosthesis*. The latter depicts the cancerous horrors that pervaded our lives that January, which was marked by the prognosis that we had received in early December, predicting that my beloved would die within a maximum of two months. Symphysizing is still an overwhelmingly powerful dynamics between us in this story, but foregrounded here is the immense gap between my bodily capacities and the help my dying beloved needs, symbolized gloomily by the way in which her legs fail her totally on the staircase. This gap, which made me feel like a powerless prosthesis, spelled out to both of us with undeniable clarity how quickly and forcefully her rapidly approaching death, relentless as a tsunami, was sweeping away our powers of symphysizing. I suggest that it is this experience of the inexorable disabling of these powers, which my partner's death generated in me, that lies at the core of the corpo-affective feeling of amputation and the experience of excessive mourning as a painfully aching amputation wound.

A Posthuman Phenomenology of Intercorporeality and Queer Femme Widowhood

My excessive resistance to modern norms of mourning, insisting upon slow scarring rather than quick healing, has led me to immerse myself in processes of unlearning layer upon layer of arrogantly disembodied modern, secular-scientific and Christian thought. Through these processes, I have found ways to relieve the amputation pain through a revitalizing of our symphysizing in new forms, preparing for spiritual-material reconnections in terms of co-becoming with my beloved's unexpected spectral phenomenalities and the assemblages of which her inhuman remains have become part. This will be the topic of coming chapters. For now, I shall prepare for these later reflections, ending this chapter by spelling out the links between my concept of symphysizing and a more general phenomenology of intercorporeality and concorporation. I shall relate these to the case of conjoined twins, as well as to queerfeminine embodiment, both of which add important dimensions to the understanding of the figuration of the excessive mourner called forth in this chapter.

The phenomenon of conjoined twins, and the concorporation implied, has been highlighted by several critical body theorists (Shildrick 2002, 2005, 2009; Weiss 2009) as a deeply anxiety-provoking threat to ingrained modern ideas about individuality and bodily autonomy, the 'one body, one identity' paradigm of modern legal, ethical, political and social discourse (Weiss 2009: 22). In contrast to the normative idea of the autonomous and sovereign individual that lurks behind the modern construction of the concorporation of conjoined twins as anomalous and monstrous – to be surgically separated at any cost, even the risk of death of one or both twins – these body theorists focus on intercorporeality. Intercorporeality refers to our corporeal interlinkage with other bodies that is an existential condition of all life. Against this background, the phenomenon of conjoined twins is reinterpreted as a special case which spells out the general existential intercorporeality – intertwinement of all bodies – in a particular and undeniably clear way. Reading my definition of compassionate companionship and symphysizing through the lens of this body-theoretical discussion of conjoined twins, I claim that the former, like the latter, can be understood as putting the existential condition of intercorporeality on display. Like the phenomenon of conjoined twins, compassionate companionship, built on mutual symphysizing, can also be defined as profoundly questioning and transgressing the ideal of the autonomous body and the sovereign subject. Such companionships are emerging from desire, but I claim that they can materialize an intimately physical co-experiencing of the other's body which makes it relevant to think along the lines of intercorporeality, and even a kind of concorporation.[8]

For me, the resistant dedication to intercorporeality and concorporation that is implied in my relationship of compassionate companionship with my partner is deeply intertwined with my sexual identification as a queer femme and with my queerfeminine sensibilities that led me to an overwhelming attraction and desire to become one flesh with my queermasculine partner. Before I became aware of queer-femme-inism as a collective movement, and before I started to understand femme embodiment – or 'femmebodiment' (Dahl 2012) – as a claim to a specific branch of critical-affirmative feminist knowledge production, corpopolitically emerging from reflections on non-normative femininities (Cvetkovich 1995, 2003; Dahl 2012, 2014; Gómez-Barris 2017), I was politically and theoretically ambivalent about my queerfeminine desires. I have always loved to unfold them intimately together with my queermasculine beloved. I also enjoyed proudly insisting on our outspoken butch/femme relationship which, in many mainstream feminist and lesbian feminist circles, was seen as a 'politically incorrect' eroticization of oppressive, mono-normative masculinity/femininity relations. Furthermore, both politically and theoretically, I have for years fiercely defended my partner's queer masculinity against feminist claims that the practising of female masculinity did nothing more than reproduce oppression (Lykke 1993). However, the relative political and theoretical invisibility of femme positions in lesbian and queer feminism, and the general degrading of femininity in much feminist theory, also meant that for years I was blind to the potentials of queer femme knowledge production. Basically, I understood my queerfeminine desires as anachronistically mimicking patriarchally defined femininity. However, delving into queer-femme-inism has enabled me to understand and proudly resignify these desires, as well as to critically-affirmatively cultivate the archive of non-normative feminine sensibilities they reference, including that of sexual difference theory (Irigaray 1985; Cixous 1992; Braidotti 1994; Grosz 1994). This is an archive that allows me to take seriously my desire to excessively lament the death of my beloved, and to relentlessly cultivate the queer eroticism of mourning, putting the existential process of slicing apart on replay, as I do in the cluster of Orpheus/Eurydice poems in *Interlude I*.

When cross-fertilized with posthuman theories of intercorporeality and concorporation – spelled out in the cases of conjoined twins and compassionate companions – the archive of queer-femme-inism creates space for the embedding of the amputation wound and the painful sense of being cut apart in a posthuman, queer-femme-widow figuration. This is a figuration that also links up with the deeply eroticized, bodily pain of the excessively mourning 'I', bent on love-death, which I touched upon in the introductory chapter – and will return to in the *Coda*. According to Braidotti (2002: 3), a figuration is not a metaphor, but a cartography, a mapping of a subjectivity, understood as non-unitary, but also pervaded by wilful desires to become – to affect and be affected – in intercorporeal relations with others. In line with this definition, a posthuman, queer-femme-widow figuration, absorbed by the excruciating pain of the amputation wound inflicted by the beloved's final exhalation, can thus be understood as a cartography depicting the subjective inhabiting of the moment of the beloved's passing the threshold between life and death as a traumatically eroticized paradox. In this moment of intense symphysizing, when the embodied borders between 'I' and 'you', as in a shared orgasm, are completely dissolved, the 'I' is, in the same instant, violently cut off from the abruptly vanishing 'you'. It is this traumatic and paradoxical moment which I find it meaningful to capture through the figure of amputation. What happens is a dissolution into oneness, while, at the same time, a violent, totally unwanted instantiation of an externally inflicted incision is enacted that creates an insurmountable wall of imperceptibility. The amputation is to be understood as the tearing open of an intercorporeal linkage, that creates an all-absorbing corpo-affective wound and long-lasting phantom pain, emerging from the overwhelming desire to revitalize the intercorporeal bond across the insurmountable wall of imperceptibility.

Interlude II

VIBRATO BRUSCAMENTE (ABRUPTLY VIBRATING)

Illustr. 4 Vibrato Bruscamente (Abruptly Vibrating). © Nina Lykke 2018.

CANCEROUS WALKS[1]

1.
Power walking on the snowy paths of the park,
at least 12,000 steps per day
is your goal.
'My body must be strong, to go under the surgeon's knife,' you say.
And we take one more turn,
high-speed walking
from the Seahorse bridge to the playground
and back again.

2.
We walk in silence around the lake.
We look at the newly hatched swan chicks.
But Death walks between us
absorbing all words.

3.
We walk together with the children
round a deep, clear blue lake in the German Alps.
Later that summer we walk with them
along the unending beaches of the North Sea Coast.
It is vacation time – we are together.
Now it is Death who is silent
– for a while taking the count.

4.
The brown autumn leaves cover the path in the wood,
but they cannot stop you and me.
Invincible,
we fly through the wood
over the meadow
along the narrow path
between the river and the rhododendron thicket
back to the forest –
high-speed Nordic walking.
The rhythm of your supple hips,
intensely swaying in front of me.
The precise way you use the sticks
to make the soft damp autumnal
forest floor
give you impetus.
I follow you further and further,

wilder and wilder,
faster and faster,
synchronously conjoined.
One does not move without the other.
We are one with the sticks,
with the woods,
with each other.
I love you.
We do not know that this is the very last time
we will go Nordic walking in the woods together.

5.
The winter is waning,
but the rain is still cold,
when we take a walk in town.
We walk and walk –
with fierce resilience.
You struggle against
the inexorably growing fatigue.
Why is your right leg dragging?
Why is your arm trembling?
Why are you out of breath?

6.
You collapse in the bathroom.
Your legs will not obey.
Emergency call to 112.
Blood-poisoning, metastases in the brain.
Wheelchair, chemo, radiation.
'This is not happening! This is not happening!'
Tears and raindrops from the warm spring shower
merge on my cheeks,
when I leave the emergency ward at 5am.
Ungeschehenmachen,
trying to make what has happened not happen,
is a defence mechanism of the psyche, Freud says.
'This is not happening! This is not happening!'

7.
You recover somehow.
Now you can walk to the lake and back again.
To walk around the lake is too far for you.
But we walk to the lake and home again, many times.
Full of high summery hopes for longer walks in the future.

8.
You walk the 100 steps to the nearest bench in the park.
This feels a long walk for you now.
You'll have to rest,
before we take the next 20 steps
across to the bench by the rotunda.
We sit there for a long time
looking at the autumn flowers.
And then we walk the 120 steps back home.
'Thanks for the trip,' we say to each other.

9.
'Do you want to take a walk?'
'Yes, Yes!' you say impatiently.
I support you,
so you can use the impetus from my body
to get up from the armchair.
You lean on your walker,
moving your weight from one foot to the other,
as if walking.
Even though you cannot move your legs forward now,
we take the 'walk' with the walker
many, many times during the day.
No 'walk' must become the last one.
But it is winter, and you are dying.

YOU BECOME A STRANGER

1.
You wind the plastic tube of the oxygen apparatus around your hand.
The tube ends up in a knot
and much too short
every time you do it.
Many times a day I have to unwind it,
so the oxygen supply
which is vital to you now
does not stop.
I ask if it isn't better to stop
winding the tube around your hand all the time.
'Yes,' you say tonelessly with your hoarse and breathless voice,
and then you continue to wind the tube around your hand.
Why do you do this?
I do not understand it.
For the first time you are becoming a stranger to me,
slipping into another world with a different logic.
Teach me your new language!

2.
I walk to the kitchen to cook for us.
We are going to eat dinner,
once more experience food as the last bulwark
of something
that feels controllable.
You sit in your armchair in the living room.
Suddenly you call me,
you, who have never been afraid to be alone
ask me to help you move to the room behind the kitchen,
so you can sit close to me and see me,
while I cook the food.
Is it the threatening loneliness of Death
which scares you,
when you are alone in the living room?
Why did it take me so long to understand that?
And do I understand it now?

BREATHING SOUNDSCAPES

This poem was inspired by a breathing encounter between artist Malin Arnell and scholar Magdalena Górska. The encounter was invented and performed as part of Arnell's artistic dissertation 'Avhandling /Av_handling (Dissertation / Through_ action)' (2016) in a former nuclear reactor hall deep beneath the Royal Technical Academy of Stockholm, now transformed into a performance space. The encounter was also inspired by Górska's doctoral dissertation 'Breathing Matters' (2016).

1.
It is completely dark.
We are 25 metres beneath the surface of the earth
in an old nuclear reactor hall,
carved into the rock beneath the Royal Technical Academy of Stockholm,
now transformed into a scene for experimental performance art.
The artist Malin Arnell performs Dissertation/Av-handling Through Action.
It takes three days.
On the second day, at 9am
we are sitting in the pitch-dark hall,
listening to Malin and her co-performer Magda
who breathe in tandem without words:
A dramatic sequence of breathing soundscapes
shifting between panic, anxiety, calm, relaxation, excitement, joy, grief . . .
Loudspeakers amplify this breathing encounter,
project it into the enormous space.
The darkness, the grey rock walls and the amplified breathing
embrace us
– totally.
My body dissolves in darkness,
absorbed into images of your death more than two years ago.

2.
Early in the January day that will be your last
you fight your way up from the deep-deep morphine sleep,
which you have slept since the nurses visited you late last night.
Much strength and energy is needed,
as though you were climbing a steep-steep mountain to reach us.
But your stubborn wilfulness helps you succeed.
Your eyelids part, and you look at us.
Eigil has come home from Mexico during the night,
and I tell you that he, Uffe, and I are with you now.
We kiss you – and hold your hands.
I tell you once more a long story
of the coming reunion,
our ashes merging with oysters and swaying seaweed

at the bottom of the sea.
For a long time we sit quietly like this,
close-close to you.

3.
Later in the morning you become restless.
We have tried to prop you more upright
to ease your breathing as much as we can.
But it is difficult,
your body is heavy, you cannot move it yourself.
We push you and your pillows around
to make it more comfortable for you.
But, powerlessly, we feel that instead we are making things worse.

4.
Your breath quickens.
Again you suffer intensely from the clinically named 'secretion rattling'
(your lungs filled with phlegm
you are too weak to cough up yourself).
You gasp and gasp and gasp –
every breath becomes an inexorable effort.
Squeaking, wheezing, rattling, groaning, gasping breaths
explode from your throat,
as though it is being torn apart.
Your wide open eyes
plead for help,
the gap between your needs and the little we can do to ease your suffering –
overwhelming.
I put my hand behind your lower back
pushing it forward
to give your thorax more space to expand when you inhale.
'The nurses will soon come and give you more medication
to ease your inhalation,' I intone.
But I am terrified: is this the stranglehold of death?
'Ok!' you exhale the little word in a strangely deep, almost breathless,
but also very trusting voice.

5.
After the nurses' visit
you fall into a deep sleep –
again.
Your breathing calms.
The whole day and evening we sit around you.
You hold our hands, sleeping.
Every time a hand moves a bit,

you catch the next one –
without waking from your deep calm sleep.
Each of us gets to hold your hand –
many times.
When you die, 18 hours later,
your breathing is calm, peaceful and light –
almost graceful,
as a soap bubble,
being blown and then vanishing,
we see your last exhalation as a movement
under the skin of your neck.

6.
A small everyday video, recorded three months earlier:
Musse, the kitten who has invited herself to live with us
is playing in a rocking chair.
She chews energetically on a toy mouse,
her movements make the chair rock violently.
She is intirable – biting, rocking, knocking the mouse to the floor, jumping
    after it quick as lightning, and then back again to the wildly rocking chair.
I am filming the kitten with my phone.
She is in focus,
but at the edge of the image,
your hands, your morning paper and your coffee cup appear;
breakfast sounds: you tap the top of a boiled egg.
A dissonant background noise disrupts the idyllic image:
Your breathing, much too short, squeaking and groaning.
'Now, I think you have filmed enough!' you say
in a voice that is breathless and pained.
I look at the date on the video.
Three days after this recording,
your shortness of breath became acute,
and the doctors granted you a portable oxygen apparatus.
From then on, this oxygen apparatus went with you everywhere.
We turned it off again after your last exhalation.

7.
Eleven months before you died
breathing difficulty was the first symptom indicating
that the cancer had entered a new and more dangerous stage.
At first, we explained it away with 'smokers' lungs'.
We bought an inhalator for you.
But your breathing problems became worse day by day.
You were rushed to hospital with severe symptoms of blood poisoning.
Blood poisoning can generate shortness of breath.

Antibiotics controlled the blood poisoning,
but the breathing difficulties kept increasing.
Then, a biopsy of a tumour, resected from your neck
revealed that next to your liver cancer
your body had developed an aggressively metastasizing lung cancer.
A PET scan showing great black spots of cancer all over your upper body
   knocked the breath out of us.

8.
I have always loved to listen to your breathing.
Memories of your breathing fill my imagination.
Your breathing,
when I slept next to you at night,
your breathing,
when we made love,
your breathing,
when we spoke over the phone
and your dark, melodic contralto voice
caressed my ear
sending tremors of desire through my body.

9.
An 'Ok!'
exhaled almost breathlessly
in your deep dark voice –
a trusting 'Ok!'
came to be your very last word.
It was as though, when I said
'The nurses will come soon and give you medication'
you heard and understood the compassionate sub-text
that all of me cried out:
'I will do everything-everything I can for you, my love!'
I often hear the echo of this special 'Ok!' within me,
your last 'Ok!'
My mother's last words
when she died from cancer, fourty years earlier, were:
'I'm slipping away now! Don't you think I should just slip away now?'

10.
Can cancerdeath be simple and straightforward?
Just a last exhalation like the vanishing of a soap bubble?
Is belonging to the privileged urban classes
– who, according to statistics,[2] consume 90% of the world's morphine –
a prerequisite for such a cancerdeath?

11.
I wake up from my trance.
Malin and Magda's breathing encounter has come to an end.
The enormous nuclear reactor hall 25 metres beneath the surface of the earth is totally silent.
Some audience members stand up and begin to leave.
Others, like me, stay on in silent contemplation.
Nobody speaks.
The silence is overwhelming.
Everybody seems absorbed by their emotions.
The lights are turned on slowly.
Now I also walk out.
The end.
'Ok!'

YOU DON'T KNOW DEATH[3]

1.
You don't know death,
until you have moistened the mouth of your dying beloved
for the very last time;
until you have seen her passionately suck water from a cotton-wool stick,
as though it was vintage champagne;
until you have whispered to your dying beloved
that you believe in the miracle,
which you both wish for,
that you believe you will meet again
as pearls in oysters between seagrass leaves,
when your ashes,
mixed with hers,
are scattered over the sea.
You don't know death,
until you have seen your beloved's very last breath appear
like two waves on her neck
and you have listened intensely with your ear to her mouth
hoping to hear one more inhaling
which does not come,
and you hear
only the murmur of the oxygen apparatus.

I love you forever!
'What is life to me without thee?
What is left, if thou art dead?'

2.
You don't know death,
until you have pressed your lips
against the ice-cold lips of your dead beloved
in a very last kiss;
until you have dressed her dead body
for the journey into the unknown;
until you have seen her gently sleeping,
almost smiling in the willow casket
casually and elegantly lying there
in jogging trousers, slippers and silk jacket.
You don't know death until you have
inhaled the scent of raspberries
from the mouth of your dead beloved
and remembered the raspberries,
that she passionately craved from you two days before she died,

even though she could no longer swallow.
'Do you want raspberries?' you asked,
'Yes, hell, I do!'
she replied.

I love you forever!
'What is life to me without thee?
What is left, if thou art dead?'

3.
You don't know death,
until you have wandered intensely alone in the places where you walked
so many times together;
until you have seen you beloved in the skies and
heard her whisper in the wind,
'I am with you, my love, I am just here.'
You don't know death,
until, with burning desire,
you have wished that your dead beloved would come back to take you with her,
perhaps as a vampire, for whose kiss of death
you longingly expose your neck.

I love you forever!
'What is life to me without thee?
What is left, if thou art dead?'

4.
My dead beloved is not here, but where is she?
The urn with her ashes lies beside me when I sleep.
'I am with you, my love, I am right here.
Don't you believe me?'
'You are here, and you are not here.'
You have become imperceptible.
But your ashes are so fine and white and soft and present.
Do I know death now?
No!
Death is like the dream,
you cannot control it.
Every night I wait passionately to fall asleep to meet you in my dreams.
But, like death,
so dreams
always come unexpectedly.

I love you forever!
'What is life to me without thee?
What is left, if thou art dead?'

Interlude II: Vibrato Bruscamente – Vibrato, vibrating, and **Bruscamente**, abruptly, are Italian terms, borrowed from music composing to interpellate the mood of the mourning 'I', who, as explored in the poems in *Interlude II*, is abruptly jolted from caretaker to mourner by the beloved's death, but also prompted to take passionate lessons from the vibrancy of the dead body. *Cancerous Walks* contemplates the relentless deteriorating of the beloved 'you''s bodily capacities, but also her conative desire to persevere. *You Become a Stranger* reflects on the days immediately before the 'you''s death, when suddenly unfamiliar ways of acting anticipates the devastating soon-to-occur vanishing as a human subject. In *Breathing Soundscapes* and *You Don't Know Death*, the mourning 'I' retrospectively engages with the moment of the beloved's death, first, with breath as the lens and, second, through touching and being touched by the dying and dead beloved's metamorphosing flesh-and-blood body. The abruptly vibrating mode prepares for **Chapter 3**'s contemplation of **The Vibrant Corpse**, the enigmatic – vibrant and disruptive – process of becoming-corpse, experienced from the perspective the mourner.

Chapter 3

THE VIBRANT CORPSE

It is not only mourning, but also death that is regulated by strict norms, rules and principles. These are not only entangled with national health regulations and legal systems, but also closely intertwined with cultural traditions and religious beliefs. However, I saw the latter as having nothing to do with my partner and me. We both considered ourselves to be feminist atheists in terms of not believing in any of the existing monotheistic religions, framed as they are beneath the phallo(go)centric auspices of a male head-god. We were also both deeply opposed to the way in which Christianity has been normatively cast as part of national identities, especially by the political Right, both in Denmark, our country of citizenship, and in the West more generally, and we were appalled also by Christianity's role in colonialism. Furthermore, we were profoundly against the ways in which both women's reproductive rights and queer sexualities have been persecuted and suppressed in the names of phallo(go)centric religions, Christianity figuring prominently among them. Finally, I was brought up by a leftist family that was strictly atheist for scientific as well as political reasons. I have never been a member of any religious community, even though, when I was growing up in the 1950s, it was very uncommon in Denmark not to be a member of the Danish Protestant Church. Due to the anachronistic fact that Church and State were and still are not separated in this country, you are automatically enrolled, if your parents or you yourself do not make a particular effort to say no to church membership. But I was never a Church member and my beloved left in her early youth, as soon as she had become old enough to legally decide for herself.

When my beloved died, I had no inclination whatsoever to follow Christian or other conventional religious customs and norms regarding the modes of relating to a dead human body. On the contrary. But could I totally avoid these customs and norms? I knew from previous deaths in my atheist and leftist family that, living in a country where Christian Protestantism is a state-sanctioned religion, and where death has to involve the State Church in various ways, I would have to be vigilant and attentive that no Christian symbols or customs sneaked in behind my back, once the various authorities responsible for taking care of dead bodies until they are buried or cremated became involved. Active resistance was required to prevent Christian norms from making their mark on the process. In this chapter, I shall focus on the entanglement of my resistance to Christian normativities and my urge to reontologize the corpse from abject to vibrant.

Guided by the immanence philosophical approach, which makes up an overarching framework of the book, this chapter will argue for a radical shift away from mainstream, modern Western ontologies of the corpse, built on Christian and/or secular scientific understandings. The process of reontologization will follow two related tracks. First, I discuss how the approach to the human corpse in Western modernity is steeped in a deep contempt for flesh and matter, which is embedded not only in Christian, but also in secular-scientific imaginaries. The latter is moulded by Cartesian dualisms, separating the thinking 'I' from the body, which is understood in a mechanistic way. I discuss how, as a result of this contempt, the corpse is cast as abject (Kristeva 1982) and uncanny (Freud 1919). To also make this point in an autophenomenographical sense, I enlist a story, *Are Corpses Uncanny?* This autobiographical story recounts one of many incidents in my overall struggles to avoid Christian symbols or customs interfering with the trajectory of my partner's dead body, discussed in detail in an earlier autobiographical essay (Lykke 2015). Second, I frame an alternative to the conventional perception of the corpse as abject and uncanny. This alternative framing is based on the poems of *Interlude II, Vibrato Bruscamente*, and on yet another autobiographical story, *Your Countenance* – all of which, in different ways, contemplate my partner's process of passing the threshold between life and death. I argue for a rethinking of the corpse as a vibrant *zoe*-body (Braidotti 2006; Bennett 2010). Moreover, I suggest that the process of dying is to be understood as a process of becoming (Deleuze and Guattari 1988), a becoming-corpse (Lykke 2018)– i.e. a process governed by material forces, which are conative, dynamic, generative and inhuman.[1] Finally, while arguing for a continuum between life and death in an immanence philosophical sense (Braidotti 2006), I also reflect upon the incision that death enacts upon living matter, and how the radical metamorphoses involved in becoming-corpse are to be taken seriously into account.

Resisting Christian Territorializations of Dead Bodies

Passionate feelings emerging from a deep urge to continue to provide bodily care for my beloved's corpse, as I had done for her living body until she took her last breath, guided my actions in the hours and days after her death. Among other things, it was clear to me that I needed to protect my beloved's process of becoming-corpse against interference from Christian norms and claims to territorialize death, and provide proper arenas and ways to practise mourning. I was not opposed to interference per se, which, indeed, is also practically impossible. There are legal rules and principles prescribing the ways in which dead bodies must be handled; you have to follow these rules, and, to do so, you are dependent on interference and actions from different kinds of authorities (from the doctor issuing the death certificate to the Danish Ministry of Ecclesiastical Affairs that, back then, still had to give permission for a person's ashes to be scattered over the sea). However, for years, my partner and I had actively opposed the lack of separation between Church and State in Denmark, and it was our deeply felt conviction that Christian agencies, including their inherently heteropatriarchal promotion of contempt for the flesh, should be kept out of all state-regulated procedures, only to be used on a freely chosen basis by those who so wished. So, while complying with the rules, I was also bent upon having everything take place along the lines of the atheist-feminist-founded decisions which my beloved and I had made together before she died. Her body should be cremated after a non-Christian funeral ritual, and the ashes scattered over a seabed, where there are many oysters, and where my ashes could also be scattered one day.

However, to materialize these wishes would it really, along the road, be necessary to protect my beloved's body from being submitted to Christian norms and interference? Why and how would anybody want to inflict a normative Christian regime upon my beloved's body, if I, as her legally registered partner,[2] did not want or allow that? Didn't we live in a country with a constitutional right to freedom of religion, and therefore also with freedom to practise other kinds of rituals than those enrolling dead bodies in Christian contempt-for-the-flesh regimes? Hadn't new kinds of governmentality, which included deregulation, not been taking place in recent years, including in matters of religion? I remembered very well how, thirtytwo years earlier, I had tried in vain to protect my beloved – atheist and socialist feminist – grandmother's corpse from Christian interventions. Back then, I had not been allowed to prevent a representative of the Protestant Danish State Church from symbolically confirming Christian power over dead bodies by throwing a spoonful of earth on my grandmother's coffin before cremation. But wasn't the situation different now, more than three decades later?

Yes and no. When the very nice and caring municipal night nurses returned to our house in response to my call about an hour or two after my beloved's death in order to confirm that she had died, and relieve her body of catheter and other medical gadgets, it suddenly stood out uncannily clearly to me just how much Christian nudging is still taking place around dead bodies in Denmark. Unspoken Christian norms pervade our cultural imaginaries and nudge people to encounter corpses in certain ways rather than others. The encounter with these two very nice and professional nurses was the first, but certainly not last, incident, which confirmed my feeling that I needed to stay alert to protect my beloved's process of becoming-corpse from Christian interference (Lykke 2015).[3]

The two night nurses were very caring, friendly and efficient in a professionally and practically competent way. They clearly wanted to offer help – in full accordance with my wishes. Still, their sincere desire to support me included actions nudging me to take into account conventional Christian norms. First, they suggested that we light candles, and I said no, mostly because my partner as a lung cancer patient had really started to hate candles due to the polluting particles they emit. But then the nurses asked a question which made me really alert: How did I want my partner's hands arranged? Should they fold them? No, definitely not. In a friendly but I think very decisive tone, I told the nurses to leave my partner's hands precisely as she herself had put them in her moment of death. After this, I think they understood that I really wanted to do things my own way, and perhaps for that reason, they did not say anything about my partner's half-open, half-closed eyes and mouth. So my partner's countenance and posture, including that of her hands, were not manipulated. However, I have later reflected on the ways in which that explicit suggestion about rearranging the hands led me, for a moment, to start reflecting about my beloved's countenance. I remember that, for one second, the question flew through my head, whether I myself should close my partner's eyes, and then, in the next second, it became lucidly clear to me that not only my beloved's hands, but also her face, should stay precisely as she herself had formed them in her moment of death. I knew that it would be an insult to her and her very self-determined way of life to interfere. She would definitely not have liked any meddling, either with her hands, or her facial expression.

Retrospectively, the explicit suggestions about the candles and the arranging of the hands in a Christian pose, and my ensuing momentary hunch about the countenance, led me to consider the subtle, but strong, Christian discourses, narratives and values that were operative from the very beginning of my partner's new existence as corpse. I agree with poststructuralist tenets that subjects are constituted in discourse, even though, at the same time, I also consider poststructuralism's neglect of the role played by corpo-affective transcorporealities problematic.[4] On the one hand, therefore, I see it as pertinent to ask how discourse comes to matter, and recognize that the ways in which Christian normativities emerged even in my strongly atheist-feminist and anti-Christian imaginary speak volumes about the disciplining force of these narratives. On the other hand, from a posthuman perspective, I also consider it to be crucial to investigate how matter – in this case, corpse matter – comes to matter (Barad 2007). I shall return to the mattering of my dead beloved's body matter. But first, I shall take a closer look at the Christian – and also Cartesian – discourses and narratives which decisively mould encounters with dead bodies for those who happen to inhabit Western modernity. To do so, I shall begin with the story about my struggle to find a non-Christian space in which to hold the funeral ceremony for my beloved.

Are Corpses Uncanny?[5]

It proves difficult to find a place for the funeral ceremony that I would like to organize for you, together with my rainbow kin and friends. We want a non-ecclesiastical room. Immediately, it strikes me that the buildings of Odense Secular Convent for Noble Women, a beautiful historical place, located five minutes' walk from our home, would provide a great environment for the ceremony. We can walk to the place through the park that borders our garden, carrying you in your casket along the paths where we have walked so many times together. Seen from a feminist perspective, the building has an interesting history. It dates back to the 16th century, but in the 18th century, the noblewoman Karen Brahe reorganized it as a library and a school for learned women. Karen Brahe's Library is known to hold the largest and oldest Danish collection of books in the national language.⁶ *For years, local women's groups put political pressure on the city council, trying to make it restore the building as a museum dedicated to the learned women of the 18th century, and a cultural space for contemporary feminist art, performance and lecture activities. My dead beloved was the first chairwoman of the association, the Karen Brahe Society, which gathered the women's groups to work towards this goal. Today, the building has been very beautifully restored. But the city council has handed over responsibility for the restored building to the university instead of establishing a museum. Nevertheless, I feel that one of the large and beautiful old rooms in this particular building would be a perfect choice for the funeral ceremony. The present chairwoman of the Karen Brahe Society – a former student of the Centre for Gender Studies at the university – turns out to be very enthusiastic about the idea as well. But, since the university is responsible for the administration of the building, the chairwoman cannot give us permission to use it without the agreement of the rector. I tell her that, when speaking to the university rector, she should emphasize that the funeral ceremony is planned to take place on a Sunday, so we will not disturb the normal academic activities taking place in the building. We are also willing to pay a fee for the use of the rooms. Moreover, I suggest that the chairwoman reminds the rector that, before her retirement, my beloved was employed as a professor at the university for more than 30 years, and finally that, many years ago, my beloved was the first chairwoman of the Karen Brahe Society which pressured the city council to ensure the restoration of the building, from which the university now benefits. Having gone through all these arguments, the chairwoman and I feel totally sure that the rector cannot decline our request.*

But decline it is precisely what he does, the chairwoman sadly tells me some phone conversations later. We can get permission to hold a memorial ceremony for you in the building, but the rector will not allow us to take your dead body inside. The rector's argument against a funeral ceremony with the casket inside the building is that it could create a precedent. Oh, what a ridiculously incoherent argument! If we are granted permission to organize a memorial ceremony in the building, couldn't this also create a precedent? Why is it so important for the rector to keep, not your mourners, but your dead body out of the building? Is he afraid that its presence will contaminate the learned halls? And even worse: if he does not fortify himself against this attack, will you, through your dead presence in the building, in a vampire-like gesture, lure all the other university employees to become obsessed by the idea of participating in the contamination? Or does the rector perhaps fear a posthumous victory for the learned feminists of the 18th century? That suddenly, after 300 years, their work at the margins of cultural history will start to ignite the imaginations of the university's employees to such an extent that everyone will want to hold their funeral ceremony in the salons of the learned women?

*However, the rector's no is no. Disheartened, I have to accept the fact that we will need to find other solutions for the funeral ceremony. After yet more struggle, I succeed in borrowing a chapel which is not in use by the cathedral, located close to my and my partner's house, and, therefore, possible to redefine as the arena for our tricksterous, non-Christian funeral ceremony.*⁷

The Abjected Corpse in Christian and Cartesian Ontologies

I find the story of the university rector's badly argued 'no' to our plea to borrow the rooms of the learned women's historical building, now under the auspices of the university, to be an appropriate entrance point to discuss how Christian and Cartesian discourses and imaginaries cast the corpse as abject (Kristeva 1982), and uncanny (Freud 1919). I claim that the common way of constructing the corpse in Western modernity is based on the deep-seated contempt for flesh and matter that is embedded in Christian and secular-scientific dualisms, the latter immersed in Cartesianism. A blatant lack of logic haunts the rector's arguments, and I suggest that the trickster destroying his ability to argue rationally is the abject human corpse. We can hold a memorial in the building without the corpse, but he will not allow us to take the corpse inside. Why? The rector cannot articulate any rational reply to this question, and I suggest that this is precisely because the abject, as Kristeva (1982) analysed it, conjures such intense disgust that it goes beyond language. According to Kristeva, the abject is what forces 'us' (modern subjects) into uncontrolled bodily reactions such a vomiting, and being unable to maintain the distance between subject and object necessary for a linguistic symbolization. The abject is what lies beyond the limits of language. Like the uncanny as analysed by Freud (1919), but in an even more radical and 'violent' manner (Kristeva 1982: 5), the abject enacts a liminality which disrupts all the boundaries between me and not-me. The rector's lack of arguments demonstrates literally how the limits of rational thought are reached here. Dead human bodies need to be strictly controlled and kept within spaces that are pre-defined for them, but their abject liminality makes them uncontainable.

That human corpses appear as abject in modern Western imaginaries is overwhelmingly documented in literature, art, media and culture more broadly. The abjected human corpse is the stuff of which horror fiction is made. It is also the reason why mediated crime reports from forensics attract such large audiences, curious to see yellow-press visuals and 'juicy' descriptions of 'the horrible', while remaining at a physically 'safe' distance from its actual materializations. As amply, although uncritically, documented in US-based historian Christine Quigley's monograph *The Corpse* (1996), what seems to be at stake in the imaginary articulations of the figure of the human corpse resonates well with definitions of the abject and the uncanny as that which occupies an in-between space between me and not-me. This is a space that is also associated with a dichotomy between human and in/sub/non-human, and with a fall from the former to the latter position. Quigley sustains her point about the corpse's threatening liminality and in-betweenness with an abundance of examples. Let me quote just one – from a popular science book about autopsies, written by pathologist Frank González-Crussi (1993):

> Not long ago this was a child; now it is a corpse, overspread by the coldness and clamminess of corpses, yet still retaining something of the living human presence. The livid hue, the icy chillyness, and the sunken outline cannot undo

the ineffable residuum of humanity that clings to the newly dead: this is why dissectors often place a surgical towel over the cadaver's face before beginning their task. The recently departed are already unsentient husks, but their corpses may still be honoured or outraged, exalted or vilified, reverenced or debased.

Quiqley 1996: 116

What this quote demonstrates is that, first of all, not only the so-called gullible publics, who are presumed to consume yellow-press portrayals of the horrible at a safe distance, but also those who are considered to be serious scientifically educated professionals, such as pathologists (or university rectors!), approach human corpses as abjected and horror-generating. This quote also highlights how the horror is linked to the newly dead's exposure of an uncanny gap between me and not-me, conceived within a hierarchy of human elevatedness and inhuman degradation. The pathologist-author spells out the phenomenology of this gap, demonstrating how the horror is experienced as the mismatch between an 'honoured', 'exalted' and 'reverenced' human subject, now only retrospectively visible as the 'ineffable residuum' of an 'unsentient husk', and dead body-matter, fallen into the abyss of the abject as 'outraged', 'debased' and 'vilified'. Finally, the description of the need to mend this gap, in terms of putting a surgical towel over the face of the dead body, is also telling. To carry out the autopsy, it is necessary for the pathologist to concentrate on the mechanics of matter, and to do so, the latter needs to be totally separated from the residuum of the human subject, considered to be located in the countenance. The pathologist has to erase the uncanny contrast between the residuum of humanness, and base, abjected matter. The surgical towel covering the face is the tool with which this erasure is performed. The conjuring trick of face-covering reconfigures the dead human body for the pathologist-author. When the face, as bearer of the residuum of humanness, is covered, the body can perform for him without any disturbing or disgust-provoking references to the fall into the abyss, and to the human subject who used to keep this flesh from falling to the level of all other 'debased' matter. The face-covering allows the pathologist to handle the body in a Cartesian sense, i.e. as endlessly manipulable, base mechanical matter to be cut and explored, in line with the ways in which the autopsy and pathological anatomy, historically, have played a key role in the building of modern medical science through 'positive' knowledge seeking via the objectifying medical gaze (Foucault 1975). All in all, an entangled knot of dualist Cartesian thought, and its associated contempt for flesh and matter, comes to the fore in the pathologist's description, while also echoing Christian dualisms.

To look further into the latter, I shall proceed to an example from the modern European literary canon: Russian nineteenth-century writer Fyodor Dostoyevsky's exploration of the badly stinking corpse in his final, monumental novel on Christian faith and modern, nihilist-atheist doubt, *The Brothers Karamazov* (1993 [1880]), finalized only four months before the author's own death. The phenomenology of the corpse as abject and uncanny, and the fall from humanness (elevated through its relation to God) to base matter, in cahoots with the Devil, is excellently pinpointed in a scene in which an old monk, Father Zosima, considered to be extraordinarily holy, dies in a convent. All the other monks and crowds from the nearby town gather around this very holy man's dead body in an excited mood, anticipating that something elevated and miraculous will take place, because the dead bodies of very holy men are believed not to corrupt or decompose as a sign of their close relation to the divine. However, what happens is that the corpse instead starts to stink very badly in the summer heat. In the novel, the bad odours emanating from Father Zosima's dead body lead the crowds, gathered around it, to shift from passionate adoration of the extraordinary holiness of the passed-away monk to an equally strong condemnation. The smell of rotting flesh is taken as proof that the monk was in cahoots with the Devil.

Dostoyevsky's novels are polyphonic (Bakhtin 1984), in the sense that there is no narrator setting the record 'straight'. Both Christian and nihilist-atheist, modern interpretations are left as open possibilities in the text – an openness that resonates with Dostoyevsky's own oscillation between Christian beliefs and modern-secular doubt about God's existence. However, the bottom line for me in this example is the ways in which Dostoyevsky's text succeeds amazingly well in bringing out deep resonances rather than differences between the Christian and the nihilist-atheist, modern approach to bodily materialities. The body can only appear exalted as long as it is believed to be animated by something elevated outside of itself (i.e. God or, in Cartesian thought, disembodied Human Reason). When the body starts to appear 'only' as matter, i.e. when it has become corpse, and exposes its inhuman corpselike processes, for example through the emission of rotting stinks, it must become abject. For the Christian crowd, this abjectness metonymically exposes the fleshy links to the Devil and Hell. For the doubting modern nihilist-atheist, it is a troubling sign that, beyond base material existence, there is no God, nothing elevated, no higher morality, nothing spiritual, no afterlife, only void nothingness. In the novel, atheist nihilism is primarily embodied by the Karamazov brother, Ivan, but in the episode of Zosima's death, it is also momentarily taken on board by his younger brother Alyosha, who was an apprentice in the convent and adored Zosima as his mentor. The defaulting miracle disturbs Alyosha deeply, and leaves him saddened for a long time.

What interests me in both the pathologist's report and *The Brothers Karamazov* are the ways in which the cluster of dichotomies of human/inhuman, sentient/non-sentient, animate/inanimate, elevated-adorable/abject-uncanny is deeply embedded in discourses of human exceptionalism, and hierarchies, setting the human subject as superior to all kinds of matter, including its own body. What keeps the human body from appearing as debased matter is, in both examples, its attachment to the living human subject. When death occurs, the body is bound to fall into abjection – as complicit with the Devil or merely as sheer mechanical body-matter, which will decay and decompose like all other matter. The parallels between these two examples (the pathologist's account and the scene from Dostoyevsky's novel) make it stand out clearly that the dichotomies at stake resonate deeply with both Christian and Cartesian thought. Human subjectivity (in terms of the immortal soul in Christianity or rational, disembodied thought in Cartesianism) represents something elevated, while flesh is rendered base, low, machinic and/or devillish, and bound to 'fall' to the low, inhuman level of the hierarchy, when, at the moment of death, the spark of life is extinguished in the subject.

The Fall into Abjection

Notable in this context of the rendering of a hierarchy between elevated human subject and base corpse matter is Kristeva's comment that the word 'cadaver' is derived from the Latin word for 'falling', 'cadere' (1982: 3). This etymology underlines how the human subject, qualified as 'I' and as 'alive', is the key component that keeps the body from falling out of the elevated and exceptional human sphere. As soon as the subjecthood and aliveness are gone, when the 'ghost has left the machine' (Ryle 1949), the body in dualist thought is no more than base – inanimate, inhuman, insentient – matter. The quote from the pathologist, Frank González-Crussi (1993), as well as the scene from *The Brothers Karamazov*, however, also illustrate how, phenomenologically, the newly dead corpse appears as abject and uncanny in the sense of Kristeva (1982) and Freud (1919), while putting the fall on display. The human corpse, in particular the newly dead, embodies a state of liminal in-betweenness, where the borders between me/familiar (human) and not-me/not-familiar (non/inhuman) are blurred. On the one hand, the corpse memorializes the elevated human 'I' who previously inhabited this piece of flesh. On the other hand, palpably and very concretely – through a quickly accelerating accumulation of signs of inhuman fleshiness (bad smell, coldness, decomposition, etc.) – the dead body demonstrates the 'fall' into conditions generally shared with all other decomposing matter. I shall contend that it is precisely this liminality, this being in-between elevated, exceptionally human qualities and base, low, inhuman, material qualities which makes the human corpse abject and uncanny. It is, I suggest, also the liminal position between these two poles that turns the corpse into a breeding ground for ghosts, vampires and other twilight creatures, considered dubious, haunting and evil, insofar as they remind living human beings of the uncanny fall into the abyss of the abject that their bodies will inevitably undergo when they die.

In order to make clear the ways in which the human corpse in its liminal in-betweenness appears as abject, let me quote Kristeva, who talks about the corpse as 'the most sickening of wastes' (Kristeva 1982: 3), and who also emphasizes the way in which the effect of the corpse on living human beings is to throw them beyond signification:

> The corpse (or cadaver: *cadere*, to fall) (...) upsets even more violently the one who confronts it as fragile and fallacious chance. A wound with blood and pus, or the sickly, acrid smell of sweat, of decay, does not *signify* death. In the presence of signified death – a flat encephalograph, for instance – I would understand, react, or accept. No, as in true theatre, without makeup or masks, refuse and corpses *show me* what I permanently thrust aside in order to live. These body

> fluids, this defilement, this shit are what life withstands, hardly and with difficulty on the part of death. There, I am at the border of my condition as a living being. My body extricates itself as being alive, from that border.
>
> Ibid.: 3

Later in the same paragraph, Kristeva specifies that this abjection is called forth by the way in which the corpse makes all signifying activity vanish in favour of an amorphous borderless void. According to Kristeva, this is a void against which we can only protect ourselves either through a religious interpretation (the corpse as what remains after meaning has been rescued insofar as the soul has left to meet God) or through a secular-scientific explanation (the corpse as the mechanical remains after meaning, the thinking subject, has been totally annulled). Without God and/or science, we are left with the abject void with its unbearably horrible breakdown of meaning:

> In that compelling, raw, insolent thing in the morgue's full sunlight, in that thing that no longer matches and therefore no longer signifies anything, I behold the breaking down of a world that has erased its borders: fainting away. The corpse, seen without God and outside of science, is the utmost of abjection. It is death infecting life. Abject.
>
> Ibid.: 4

With the concept of the abject and its 'powers of horror', illustrated in these paragraphs by the human corpse, Kristeva (ibid.) spells out the corpo-affective moulding generated by the dualist ontologies of the life/death threshold, framed by Christianity and by mechanistic, Cartesian logics. These dualist ontologies pervade modern Western imaginaries, and the rector's negative reaction to our wish to hold the funeral ceremony in the Secular Convent for Noble Women makes perfectly sense within these logics.

The Vivified Posthuman Corpse

It is interesting to note a kind of inherent agency that is ascribed to the corpse in the rector's non-argument – an agency that runs counter, in particular, to the Cartesian view of the corpse as a piece of mechanics that can only be activated through an outside agent. Such an inherent agency apparently plays a role for the rector when he projects some kind of haunting ability onto the flesh of my dead beloved's body. Otherwise, his distinction between a funeral ceremony with the dead body present and a memorial without it would not make sense. I shall dig a bit deeper into the ways in which dualist ontologies do not prevent the corpse from being ascribed agency, not even in the more secular-scientific, Cartesian versions, to which the natural-science-educated rector presumably adheres. To do so, I shall briefly refer to a study of the ways in which the agency of human corpses has figured as a prominent theme in modernist literature and art: literary scholar

Erin Edwards' book *The Modernist Corpse* (2018). Edwards' study provides an analysis of the role of the human corpse in early twentieth-century modernist literature and visual culture in the United States. She puts focus on the ways in which the corpse, somehow anticipating posthumanism, takes on a monstrous, liminal life of its own in the aesthetic imaginary of this period, inundated by the cultural shockwaves called forward by signifying features of twentieth-century capitalist, nationalist and racist necropolitics. Edwards discusses the performativity of the corpse in modernist literature and visual culture, which has contemplated mass human death in the First World War, as well as widespread white supremacist racist violence, while also looking at the posthumanizing effects of the technological visual and sound innovations that, back then, were revolutionizing contemporary media and art.

Edwards' analysis is important in the context of this chapter. She shows brilliantly how early twentieth-century US literary and visual-culture imaginaries can be read as engaged in a quasi-posthumanist 'vivification' of the human corpse, which embeds it in a 'larger ecology' that 'implicitly critiques humanism's anthropocentric commitments' without rejecting 'the humanist aims of affirming the worth, dignity, and rights of all subjects' (ibid.: 10). Edwards suggests that the vivification of the corpse in these aesthetic imaginaries calls for a posthuman redefinition of human rights to posthuman rights that 'acknowledge the embedded relations between the human and its putative "others"', including 'infrahuman animals and "dead" matter' (ibid.). In this sense, Edwards' endeavours to read modernist literature and visual culture in a mode that de-exceptionalizes and posthumanizes the human corpse sustain my reontologizing efforts. Compellingly, she spells out how the human corpse in modernist literature can be read along the lines of immanence philosophy and posthuman thought, with a focus on its material agency. Exploring the agency of the corpse is also crucial for my argument. But when it comes to the question of specifying this agency, my argument takes off in another direction than that of Edwards.

Edwards does not question, but simply reproduces, the very human phenomenology, and its corollary sensorial apparatus, upon which Kristeva's reading of the corpse as abject is based. This stands out, when Edwards, in a highly empathizing reading of Kristeva's account for her visit to the morgue (which I quoted above), and her accompanying description of the etymological relationship between cadaver, *cadere* and fall, abruptly punctuates her otherwise conventional, third-person writing by an astonishing paragraph, engaging in a phenomenological first-person account of the corpse. Echoing Kristeva's above-quoted text on her viewing of the abjected body in the morgue (ibid.: 4), Edwards gives a vivid description of a mourning 'I''s experience of the 'fall' of the corpse of a 'known person' into abjection, epistemologically accompanied by the mourner's own fall into a wordless unknown:

> And yet for most of us, looking at the corpse is anything *but* a rational or disembodied experience. The corpse viscerally shocks us into a different state of looking. Looking becomes not the certain activity of an Enlightenment eye but

an urgently embodied experience in which several senses participate: a visceral pounding of the heart, an audible pulse in the ears, tears that cloud the clarity of vision. Looking at the corpse also marks the limits of a volitional or rationally controlled gaze. I refuse to look but I cannot help but look, my gaze compelled by something other than reason. Julia Kristeva points out that the etymology of cadaver is *cadere*, meaning to 'fall' and the processes of falling inform both the corpse and the act of looking. I feel faint when I see the corpse: I fall and the world falls away, suddenly an unstable ground from which to construct a visual perspective. The corpse is a body that falls through the cracks of the known, an extraordinary body that fails to be recorded through quotidian modes of perception.

Ibid.: 13

However much I am able to follow Edwards' (and Kristeva's) account of the enormity of the epistemological gap that the corpse of a known person produces, it is to me impossible to subscribe to the phenomenological description of a 'fall' into the groundless abyss of abjection, which Edwards, echoing Kristeva, interpellates. In the following, I shall argue that the epistemological gap and the 'fall' into abjection of the corpse should *not* be seen as inevitably interconnected. A posthuman reontologizing of the corpse, which, like Edwards, I find very important, must include a posthuman phenomenology, which does *not* impose a fall into the abject of dead body matter, because this fall will always-already have re-established the sovereign, exceptionalized human subject. My claim in this book is that a posthuman phenomenology which decisively establishes a resonance with a de-exceptionalizing onto-epistemology, shifting the experience of the corpse from abjectable to vibrant, can emerge from a close following of the mourning 'I''s bodily desires. Before I move further along this road, I shall undertake a final reflection on the phenomenology of the abjectable corpse, and the question of why and how it maintains such a strong grasp on modern perceptions.

Delaying or Undoing the Fall?

What does it take to move from a phenomenology of abjectable matter to one of vibrant matter? Is it possible? Intuitively, my answer is yes. When I retrospectively reflect upon the intense symphysizing intimacy that I experienced with my beloved's dying and dead body before the undertaker drove her casket away from our house around thirtytwo hours after she took her last breath, I feel a spontaneous urge to turn Kristeva's argument totally around. Instead of claiming that 'The corpse, seen *without* God and *outside* of science, is the utmost of abjection' (Kristeva 1982: 4 [italics mine, NL]), it was and is my deep-felt intuition that the opposite is the case. The human corpse, seen *with* God, i.e. with dualist Christian thought as lens, and *inside* of a scientific framework, defined by classic Cartesianist outlooks, which are still influential in biomedical views on the body as base mechanics, is precisely what produces the dead body as abject. Neither God nor science can protect us against the abject, which will haunt us. By contrast, I claim that they are the very agents that produce the corpse as abject, and cast the ghosts, believed to emerge from it, as always-already scary, threatening or downright evil. Or, in other words, it is the deep-seated Christian and Cartesian soul/mind-body dualisms and contempt for the flesh, embedded in the discourses and cultural imaginaries of Western modernity, that come to matter when the corpse is experienced as abject and as a breeding ground for evil and haunting agencies.

To sustain this claim, I shall make a brief detour into some of the widespread rituals, which, in the context of Western modernity, are used to facilitate encounters between newly dead humans and their more or less intimate companions and smaller or broader circles of relatives, friends etc. I shall look at such rituals through the lens of a Barad-inspired postconstructionist framework (Barad 2007; Lykke 2010), which takes into account both how discourses and imaginaries come to matter, and how matter comes to matter. The point I shall make is that the dualist ontologies in which Western modernity's understandings of human death are entangled produce a clash in those who are in attendance when a human dies. On the one hand, the mattering of matter makes itself strongly and unavoidably felt by those who experience the process of becoming-corpse as bystanders. On the other hand, the more bystanders become immersed in a phenomenological experiencing of the inhumanizing process as a fall into abjection, the more strongly they are encouraged to take measures to delay the process of falling, or in other words to keep up the human appearance of the corpse.

To elaborate upon this clash and the widespread desire to delay the inhumanizing process, let me take a quick look at some delaying technologies, which have become more and more commonly used in Christian contexts during modernity, particularly in the USA, Canada and Australia. In the previously discussed monograph on the history of the corpse, Quigley (1996) gives an empirically 'thick' (Geertz 1973) account of the history of embalming. According to Quigley, a widespread tradition of embalming dead bodies emerged in the United States in the wake of the civil war of the mid-19th century. This war gave rise to practices of conserving the bodies of soldiers who had died on the battlefield, so that they could be brought home to their families to be mourned and buried. Another technological practice of preservation which, according to Quigley, has been cultivated and developed in the USA since the 19th century, is the practice of photographing the corpse in postures that are manipulated so that the face and sometimes also the body look more 'human' – for example, through closing the eyes and applying make-up to give the impression that the deceased is just sleeping. The docu-drama *Wisconsin Death Trip* (Marsh 1999), based on a non-fiction book of the same name (Lesy 1973), gives a detailed and compelling account of the ways in which this practice, in the late 19th century USA, had become common among poor working-class people and immigrants – illustrated by a collection of photographs of dead bodies from the state of Wisconsin.

Both embalming and manipulated photography can be understood as discursive material practices of technological mediation and the preservation of iconic memories of the deceased (Schwartz 2013, 2016), organized in order to discursive-materially displace and evade the uncanny icon of a corpse putting the opposite of something 'human' on display. Or, in other words, along the lines of Quigley (1996) and Schwartz (2013, 2016), it makes sense to claim that what is at stake in these practices is an attempt to evade the uncanny feelings which the abjected corpse invokes through delaying its signs of inhumanness from becoming visible.

Neither embalming nor manipulated photography are widely practised in my home country, Denmark. Nevertheless, I recognize more modest, but still highly normative, practices intended to make the corpse look more 'human' to be part of conventional Danish mourning and funeral cultures, such as closing the eyes and binding the jaw so that the mouth is not open. These practices are no doubt to be understood as modified versions of the same urge to conserve the 'humanness' and slow down the process of becoming-inhuman of the deceased.

Looking at these practices through the lens of Karen Barad's postconstructionist (Lykke 2010: 120, 141) understanding of posthuman performativity (Barad 2003), I claim that what is performatively materializing through embalming, manipulated photography, and closing the eyes and mouth of the corpse is discourses of the deceased as still-a-human-subject. But it is also very evident that Barad's point that matter always 'kicks back' (Barad 1998: 116), i.e. actively interferes with discursive materializations, is appropriate to apply here. The discourses of the deceased as still-a-human-subject are materialized through the delaying technologies and practices. But they are struggling, as it were, against all the odds, because, at the same time, matter is so palpably and undeniably kicking back in terms of a material inhumanization, the process of becoming-corpse, implying that the deceased person's countenance and body as a whole change remarkably from hour to hour.

The question which arises for me here is what happens if the inhumanization process, instead of being sought delayed, is embraced as a lesson which the dead beloved's vibrant body teaches us about its metamorphoses and transitions? Or in other words, is it possible to shift from a human phenomenology of abjection to a posthuman one of vibrancy? Based on the experience of my beloved's death, I suggest that such a shift is possible, but it relies upon an undoing rather than a delaying of the fall into abjection. In the final section of this chapter, I shall reflect upon this process of undoing. But first I shall supplement the stories of my beloved's passing the threshold from living human subject to dead inhuman corpse, articulated in the poems of *Interlude II*, with the autobiographical narrative *Your Countenance*. This narrative tells the story of how I was confronted with the abrupt clash which experiencing my beloved's process of becoming-corpse and inhuman also produced in me. I, too, felt a strong desire to delay the process of inhumanization. But, as I have articulated in the story, I felt an even stronger desire to symphysizingly follow the lead of my beloved's process of becoming-corpse as a way to maintain our intercorporeal connection.

Your Countenance[8]

I.
You died at 4 o'clock this morning in a state of deep, morphine-induced sleep. Eigil and I were together with you. The night nurses had visited just a short time earlier. We had talked with them about your breathing – that it had become so easy now, totally different from how it had been during their visits yesterday morning, when you had been awake and gasping for breath for hours. You were suffering from severe difficulty in breathing and from what in the professional language of the nurses is called 'secretion rattling' (i.e. when the lungs are filled with phlegm that the patient is too weak to cough up herself). Now there was no rattling or rustling any more, only a fine and peaceful breathing. Almost as though you were no longer ill. The skin of your face had a new tinge of transparency, and your facial expressions were calm. It seemed as though you were in a dream world without anxiety or pain – but a world where you still had contact with ours. I was sitting next to you, gently moistening your palate, tongue and lips once in a while – the way we had been doing all day, with the help of a small piece of foam rubber soaked in water. Your mouth was open, but when you sensed the water, your lips closed desirously about the foam rubber, and you breathed a light sigh of relish; it was as though you followed my moistening move with your tongue and lips in desiring pleasure, as in a kiss with the tongue. Suddenly, you looked different. The skin of your face became even more transparent, and it was as though your mouth, until now wide open, partially closed in a smile, while your eyelids opened a bit so that we saw your dreaming eyes. But at the same time, it was also as though your countenance congealed. 'I think she's died!' Eigil said hesitantly. Then we saw two big waves under the skin of your neck where your artery was. So you had not died, we said affirmatively to each other. We tried to check your pulse. We listened to your mouth. But no more breaths came. The only sound left was the mechanical murmur of the oxygen apparatus. We kept standing with our arms around each other, looking at your smiling mouth and your almost closed eyes. We were as though in a trance – in an unbreakable circle, you, Eigil and me, in a moment that would last forever. At some point, we understood that we had to extend the circle. We turned off the oxygen apparatus and called Uffe, Rikke and Naja. We sat down around your bed. For a very long time.

II.
Your moment of death had seemed calm. You had died with eyes half-closed, and your mouth a little bit open, forming a half-smile in the very moment of your last breath. Your dead body stayed in our house for thirtytwo hours until the undertaker brought us the ecological willow casket, and drove you away in it. As those hours went by, your countenance changed, congealing more and more. But still you kept looking at us with that unfathomable, Mona Lisa smile. My gut feeling told me not to interfere with your countenance. Intuitively, I felt that it would be utterly wrong and disrespectful to interfere with your face and follow the convention, which will have it that the eyes and mouth of the deceased should be closed. Why should we follow these

conventions, invented to make the corpse look less corpse-like? Rebellious as you always were, you would definitely not have liked to have others meddling with your facial expression. Instead, your congealing half-smile – signifying the ultimate threshold between the 'I' you were, and the corpse you were becoming – could perhaps tell me, the ignorant still living one, something about the crossing of this threshold.

III.
But what happened to your countenance during those thirtytwo hours, when your dead body was still with us? What lessons in co-becoming did I learn? Can the series of photos which we took of you during these hours help me in this learning process? We took the photos in order to keep you with us, and I have regularly returned to them during the years that have now elapsed since you died. They are certainly important for my mourning through memorizing, as are all the photos of you that I have. However, these particular photos are important for something else as well – something that I still do not quite know-feel. These ultimately final photos of you in human shape show the changes over time of your countenance from the congealed half-smile of your moment of death towards something less and less 'human'-looking and more and more unfathomable. This change is recorded with unanticipated clarity in the photos, and this is ultimately puzzling, forcing me to think-feel you in new ways. In my memory, you are still the one you were. But in the world of posthumous materiality, visually performed by these photos, you are coming to embody something else. I am struggling to find poetic, and philosophical words and ways to bring me closer to your posthumous materiality – to your vibrant death.

A Posthuman Phenomenology of Vibrancy

What brought me to profoundly question the phenomenology of the corpse as abject was the experience of the moment of death of my beloved, and the days of cohabitation with her dying and dead body, which I have articulated in the poems of *Interlude II*, and in the autobiographical story above. I could not but experience and make sense of my beloved's dying and dead body as vibrant, as articulated in the poem *You Don't Know Death*. The smell of fermented raspberries coming from my dead beloved's mouth, her congealed smile and half-open eyes, her oh so very cold kiss – all of this was making my beloved alien and strange, but signalled a vibrant and enchanted otherness, which strongly attracted me and called upon me to co-become with her new way of being – as her old ways have always done. I saw the process of gradual, but relentless decomposing of my beloved's body, as articulated in the poem *Cancerous Walks*, and followed her increasingly strange ways of acting, as explored in the poem *You Become a Stranger*. The processes of becoming-other started before my beloved died and accelerated afterwards. I experienced the sequence of events constituting this process as devastatingly sad, but neither abject nor uncanny. The rotting smells that started to emerge after some time did not appear to me as frightening, nor did they push me away. When I turned off the heating and opened the windows in the room where the dead body was lying in our bed, the smell disappeared. Even the vampire, in the shape of which the lyric 'I' of *You Don't Know Death* imagines the beloved's return in the dark of night, was and is an object of intense desire and longing for me, not a frightening figure. Nothing was abject, nothing was uncanny. Before my beloved's death, I wanted to take every possible action I could think of to make her feel comfortable and to ease her suffering, as explored in the poem *Breathing Soundscapes*. After the moment of her last breath, I desired most of all to dwell together with her material remains, and make sure that her process of becoming-corpse took place in a comforting, caring, loving and respectful atmosphere.

However, in my argument for a posthuman phenomenology of the corpse as vibrant rather than abject, I must of course also retrospectively ask myself: was my attraction to my beloved's dead body an expression of the excessive mourner's human projection of subjectivity onto my beloved's bodily remains? Did I just want to delay the inhumanizing, or was something else happening – aligned with the posthuman phenomenology for which I am arguing here? I claim that both were the case, but that the urge to engage with my beloved in her new mode of becoming as vibrant corpse was by far the most insistent, because my basic atheist beliefs firmly told me that there was no human subject anymore, and to believe otherwise would be to run after an illusion. So, alongside my strong feelings and desires to be with and continue caring for my beloved's dead body, as much as I had done when she was still alive, the being with and for her as corpse also called forward important new feelings and insights. Most importantly, I experienced an overwhelming and very passionate urge to learn to symphysize and co-become with my beloved in her new enigmatic mode of being and becoming as vibrant corpse.

That this new co-becoming was something I had to learn, rather than something I immediately knew how to do, also stood out with lucid clarity, because everything was new and enigmatic. In tandem with experiencing my beloved's corpse as vibrant, it was also palpably evident that a devastating existential cut had occurred between us, when she passed the threshold between life and death. I definitely did not feel that my beloved had left, because, due to my deep-seated atheism, it is impossible for me to believe in an immaterial fiction called the 'soul', which leaves the body behind. Hence, I did not experience it as though my beloved, along the lines of such dualist beliefs, was leaving her remains, heading for an elsewhere. But, in contrast to my atheist beliefs, neither could I experience it as though she had vanished into nothingness. Intuitively, I was totally certain that 'she' was not there as the human subject she had been. But the vibrant body that I kissed, caressed, clad, and dwelt next to, was what my beloved companion was now. There was no immaterial excess to this body and its material derivatives, such as dust and DNA. My beloved had become imperceptible as subject. However, what was there in front of me was undoubtedly not nothingness. My beloved's dead body was a palpably real piece of vibrantly embodied matter, lying enigmatically before me. At the same time, the excruciatingly painful amputation wound, which I described in the previous chapter, also felt very corpo-affectively real, telling me unmisunderstandably that the conditions for my symphysizing had radically and abruptly changed with my beloved's final exhalation.

Thus, the situation was loaded with enigmas, which were absolutely not understandable or graspable in any immediately phenomenological sense. Therefore, I knew that I had to go through a spiritual-material learning process to come to terms with these enigmas. But I also knew that I had to engage in this process without help from any conventional religious or secular-scientific discourses, which axiomatically would foreclose any possibility that the dead body could be understood as vibrant in a monist sense. Neither Christian nor Cartesian imaginaries or discourses could be of help, because they would both, each in their own way, exclude in advance any coming to terms with my perception of the immanent vibrancy, which like a magnetic field drew me towards my beloved's material remains. Moreover, I also knew that my project had to be based on a posthuman, trans- and intercorporeally oriented phenomenology of vibrancy, because the only one who, in a spiritual-material sense, true to this monism, could help me to figure out how to approach these enigmas, was the source from which they emanated, namely my dead beloved's vibrant body matter itself. So, immersed in pain from the amputation wound, but also thrown into contemplation of a totally opaque and un-understandable new corpo-affective, trans- and intercorporeal relationship, I engaged in a learning process of spiritual-material co-becoming with my dead beloved in her radically changed and new material existence as vibrant corpse.

As I have articulated in *Your Countenance*, the materiality of these new and radically changed conditions, and my dead beloved's radical and continuous metamorphoses were, retrospectively, also very much brought to the fore through the photos we took of her during those hours she stayed in our house before the undertaker drove her away. It was not planned like that, but still these photos came to perform the opposite role from the type of conventional photos of corpses, that I discussed above, which is meant to making them appear as still-human-just-sleeping. Instead, our photos show the inhumanizing process in time-lapsed condensation – how vibrant *zoe*-matter really kicks back and comes to matter.

Braidotti describes death as the moment where you come to 'coincide with your body' (2006: 252–3). But what does that mean? Phenomenologically, death is an impenetrable mystery, because the subject undergoing the process is simultaneously vanishing. Therefore, we, the still living, can never get an answer to our anxious 'how was it?' We can only wait until our own moment of dying to somehow get an answer to this question. However, being so intimately close to my partner during her process of transitioning from living subject to corpse still gave me a strong feeling of the vibrant and dynamic materiality of this process, but also of its total alienness. On the one hand, I co-experienced every moment of my beloved's process of dying. On the other hand, the whole process was totally opaque. While her body was becoming-corpse, she was, as a subject, becoming-imperceptible to me. What happened was enormously dynamic and forceful, but also existentially and phenomenologically totally different from anything that could be co-experienced, based on my immediate human understanding.

Nevertheless, in all this devastating opaqueness, one thing stood out with lucid clarity. My embodied co-experiencing of the disappearance of my beloved's human subjectivity, her coming to coincide with her *zoe*-body, her becoming-corpse and existentially imperceptible, was overwhelmingly sad, amputating and devastating. But it did *not* make her body abject and uncanny. My beloved's corpse stood out to me as alien and inhuman, but extremely vibrant matter to which I felt a strong corpo-affective connectedness. The experience of a strongly embodied relation to my beloved's dying and becoming-corpse is the background for the learning process which has guided me towards new engagements with spiritmatter and with my beloved's new liveliness as *zoe*-body, to be further explored in this book. It also underpins my passionate resistance against and desire to undo both Christian and Cartesian constructions of the dead body, pervaded as they both are by contempt for the flesh. In this sense, the affective intensities that I have contemplated in this chapter co-emerged. The desires to undo the ontologies which make dead human bodies fall into abjection, and my urge to learn from my beloved's radical bodily metamorphoses into new vibrancies, were and are deeply entangled.

Interlude III

SILENZIO APPASSIONATO (PASSIONATE SILENCE)

Illustr. 5 Silenzio Appassionato (Passionate Silence). © Nina Lykke 2018.

Dreamscapes – A Triptych

I. You Vanish

1.
Five nights in a row
after your funeral ceremony,
I awaken abruptly
having slept only a short time.
The feeling
that you need my help
is overwhelming.
You are in the old chapel
at the other end of the park,
where your funeral ceremony
took place.
I must hurry –
run over there,
now, right away,
it's urgent,
no time to waste –
together with Uffe and Eigil . . .
It takes a while
until it becomes clear to me
that I have been dreaming.
The insight
that where you are now,
I cannot help you,
occupies our bedroom,
fills it with pitch black despair.
Later, I doze off again,
I see a silver medallion in front of me.
It's decorated with a geographic map.
It looks like the one
my colleagues gave me,
with a diamond marking the town,
where we work.
Blue dots of sea
spread across the map,
covering more and more,
overflowing the areas of dry land.
Soon the medallion has become totally blue.
A premonition of
the satellite photograph

with the GPS coordinates,
marking the place in Limfjorden
where, six months later,
we let your blue urn sink to the bottom?

2.
A worm wriggles out
through the skin of your stomach.
It winds its way over your body,
light against your darker complexion.
I catch the worm,
tear it away from your body,
press my fist hard around it,
afraid that it will burrow
back into your body.
I squeeze the worm
to kill it,
so it cannot threaten you.
I open my hand,
and see the totally crushed worm.

3.
I know that you are about to die.
Overwhelmed by
powerlessness
and despair,
I cry
No, no, no, no, no,
No, no, no, no, no . . .

4.
I hold my hands lovingly
around your deathly pale face,
kiss you uncountable times,
imploring you to come back.
'Come back, my love,
so we can be together here!'

5.
We sit together in a dark room
holding each other's hands.
I leave for a moment.
The door hinges squeal
in need of oil.
When I return,

the darkness is even denser than before.
I can see nothing.
But I feel
that you are gone.
I call your name,
shout it louder and louder,
shriek as loud as I can.
My voice, pushed to extremes,
bounces back from a silence,
as impenetrable as the darkness.

6.
It is dark, and we climb together
over great stones at the seaside.
You are in front of me
and fast as lightning.
I lag behind.
You jump into a hole in a dyke,
leading to an underground passage.
I try to follow you,
but it is difficult to reach the stone,
from which you set off
to get in.
You have gone a long way
when, finally, I reach the entrance.
I can hear you deep inside the passage.
I shout to you.
Suddenly, silence falls in there.
Only a weak knocking on the stone wall is heard.
The recognition that something horrible has happened to you
stabs through my mind.
Powerless, I feel,
how stones block the entrance now.
I cannot get in to help you.
The weak knocking continues a while,
then a deathly silence descends.
Anxiety and grief hit me like a karate chop to the neck.

7.
We walk entwined in a garden at night.
You disappear into the bushes.
Leaves rattle secretively –
are you inviting me
to play our hide-and-seek game
from days long gone?

Quivering desire, sucking in my diaphragm,
changes to relentless grief,
when I look to the top of the high wall
that surrounds the garden
and see nothing
but the wind playing in the foliage.

8.
We say goodbye in a desolate, pitch-dark square.
I see the contours of a car driving slowly towards us
with the headlights turned off.
You disappear into the dense darkness.
I run after you,
but you are gone.

II. Spectral Interferences

9.
We stand together in front of an old mirror
that belonged to your mother.
'We don't know enough about your mother,'
I say sadly.
You look sorrowfully at the mirror.
Its surface is black.
It can no longer return reflections.

10.
We take a walk at the seaside.
We pass by an apartment
where we lived together years ago.
I look through the windows
and see mirror images of our furniture inside.
I will show you these mirrorings,
but you cannot see them.

11.
I sail alone through strange landscapes
and wander along an asphalted road
that leads into nothingness.
Afraid, I turn around,
and walk back to houses and cultivated areas.
But at home, I find a water pipe broken in the yard.
A chaos of excessively growing plants
is covering the cobblestones at frightening speed.

A pack of wolves takes me by surprise,
as I stand down there.
They rush towards me
with open jaws and wild eyes.
I reach out towards the first wolf –
feel its warm wolf breath on my face,
and its dark, soft fur against my body.
A bird presses its beak,
sharp as a needle,
against my closed eye.
I succeed in tearing it away from me.
But when I open the eye,
a rim of blood appears on the retina.
Now a group of masked figures
intrudes into the yard.
They surround me
to execute the death sentence.
I catch hold of a couple of thorny blackberry branches
and try to hit the intruders
'This is my defense!'
I say
closing my eyes laughingly.
The executioners laugh as well.

III. Joyful Deathworlds

12.
I am walking in a foreign town
looking for you.
Suddenly, I see you
in an avenue lined with tall trees.
You walk towards me,
wearing the green silk jacket, the red sweater and the black jogging pants
in which we dressed you,
before putting you into your casket.
I embrace you intensely and say 'I've missed you.'
You take my face in your hands and kiss me.
Then we walk together through the streets.
I've been here before,
and I ask you,
which streets you know.
We also talk about the streets
you don't know:
these latter ones are those
through which

I have wandered
while you were away.
I embrace you gently,
while walking.
You are so thin, so thin,
nothing but skin and bones,
but very much alive and vital.
We walk home
entwined.
I sit down at your feet.
With my face resting in your lap,
I tell you about all the things
that have happened
while you were away.

13.
My forever beloved,
you are really with me now.
Happy and not ill
you walk around our living room.
Your hair is cut like a pageboy;
It's soft and very fine,
and you look very well.
I ask you
how you got this haircut.
You say:
'It came by itself,
when my hair started to grow again!'
We dance.
We can do anything.
We are so light, almost weightless.
We lead each other into
still new embraces
and rhythmic dances.
I feel your hair
light as feathers against my skin.
The kisses grow deeper and deeper.
We are lying together
electrified,
we melt into each other.
'I love you!'

14.
We are lying together on the deck of a boat.
The warm sun embraces our bodies.
I doze off

with sounds of
lazy waves against the boat
in my ear . . .
Something makes me jump up.
Your head is partly submerged,
and your laptop is already covered by water.
You might not have noticed
what is happening,
so I tell you.
Annoyed, you say
that it does not matter now.
I should just let go of all the worries of the living,
relax and enjoy death
together with you.
We sink.
The distance to the sunny surface of the sea
grows and grows.

Interlude III

RESURRECTION

1.
The house is evening silent.
I hear the sound of someone walking
on the gravel of the driveway.
The front door opens and closes softly.
The steps of the staircase squeak.
You come in through the door to the living room,
sit down in your armchair
next to the green table.
As though nothing much has happened, you say,
'Hello, my love, shall we have some fun?'

2.
The poet Friedrich Rückert lost his children to Scarlet Fever in 1833.
They were just three and five years old.
He wrote 428 poems about his dead children,
and later the composer Gustav Mahler set them to music.
Rückert could not stop writing about his children.
One poem after another flowed from his pen,
as the tears flowed from his eyes.

3.
In one of Rückert's poems,
the children are not dead at all.
They have just left,
run on ahead
to the sunlit hills.
They do not return home.
But in the hills, he can meet them.

4.
Perhaps, you, too, have just gone on ahead of me?
To Fur?
And now you are back to visit.
'Hello, my love, shall we have some fun?
Why don't you just come with me?'

5.
The writer Joan Didion lost her life partner.
A heart attack killed him.
Between one moment and the next, he was dead.
In her book 'A Year of Magical Thinking'
Joan Didion reflects on her yearning disbelief

in her husband's disappearance.
She cannot throw out his shoes,
she tells us,
because without them
he could not come back.

6.
'I have solemnly sworn to keep writing about your life,
so nothing can take it away from me,'
Rückert wrote to his kids.
Did Karen Blixen become a storyteller
in the hope
that gothic stories could bring back her beloved, Dennis Finch Hatton?
On the radio I recently heard about a man
who made drawing after drawing of his passed-away wife.
He could not stop.
'When I write about you, you are still alive,'
the poet Hanna Hallgren wrote about her deceased father.
At first, Naja Maja Aidt could not write about her dead son Carl.
But nine months after his death
the poems flowed from her,
and became 'Carl's book' –
a wild stream of poems about her dead son.

7.
I, too, write and write about you –
write you back to life.
You are resurrected
in writing.

FUR[1]

1.
We never walked along the coast of Limfjorden together.
No memories of shared life can be found here.
In our home in Odense, you are everywhere.
Your jackets in the closet.
Your shoes in the entrance hall.
Your computer, your desk,
your big armchair in the living room.
Your books on the bookshelf.
Your bed next to mine, upstairs.
In the back yard, the shell pattern of differently coloured cobblestones,
which we designed together.
But here at Limfjorden, everything is new.
Last year, I slept here with your blue ecological urn next to me in bed,
as I listened to the waves of the Fjord
gently breaking on the beach outside.
The next day we sailed to a quiet place
beyond the cliffs of the island of Fur,
and watched your urn disappear and dissolve beneath those waves.
You are here,
you are real –
as a body of ashes.
The sunset light is broken by dark clouds.
A fine drizzle on my bent back,
as I caress the wet beach stones.
Waves move gently over my hand.
Seaweed winds around my fingers.
You are in the rain – you are in the waves.
I am coming – my love.

2.
One more year has elapsed.
I have eloped to the Fjord one more time.
I am searching for you.
Can I find you again?
Is a *rendezvous* repeatable?
As I approach the Fjord,
heavy rain is pouring from a pitch-black sky.
But over the island of Fur
a white cloud is emerging
in the midst of the dark-grey cover.
Before I reach the island,
the rain has stopped,

and the evening sun is hovering low over the Fjord.
The sky has cleared completely now.
It is very hot,
as it was two years ago when we released your blue urn into the water.
Suddenly, a light drizzle is cooling my skin –
the air is filled with raindrops pierced by sunlight,
like falling prisms.
It keeps dripping, endlessly.
How long can it rain from a cloudless sky?
I feel like swimming.
The water folds smoothly around my body.
I am floating on my back
looking up into the sky.
You hold me,
while I swim with long, long back strokes.
I fill my backpack with oyster shells.
The beach abounds with them.
Many are fused
into double, and sometimes triple shells,
inseparable
now in death
as they were before
when inhabited by live oysters.
Then my gaze is drawn
by the blue, red, yellow, black, white stones of the cliff,
a gigantic abstract painting,
created by enormous dynamic forces,
fossil on fossil,
fiftyfive million years of vibrating geological history
condensed into a sixty-metre high cliff,
erase every meaningful distinction
between life and death.
I walk along the beach under the cliff.
I visit caves, carved out by waves,
caress the gigantic crevices
that criss-cross the walls.
A spring gushes from the cliff,
its intense murmur catches my ear,
the water running over my hands.
I climb the steep slopes,
cling to bushes of heather and leaves of grass,
creep through impassably entangling pine branches
and with cuts on arms and legs
I finally reach a path
which takes me

through forest and heathland
to the summit of the cliff.
I sit in the grass for a long, long time,
contemplating the waters of the Fjord,
There, precisely there, in the direction of the three windmills,
we let go of the line to the fishing net
with your blue urn resting on a bed of oyster shells and beach stones,
our last tie to who you were before.
There, precisely there, two years ago,
 your blue urn was swallowed by the waters of the Fjord.
Uffe has told me
about a special kind of Buddhist body meditation
which requires you to imagine yourself as dead.
I try to imagine my dead body,
and the fire that will transform it to ashes.
There, precisely there,
we will meet again –
ashes to ashes.
I am coming – my love.

> **Interlude III: Silenzio Appasionato – Silenzio**, silence, is an Italian term from music composition, indicating a full-stop in the music flow, a complete cessation of all reverberations. It corresponds to the total absence of sounds, characterizing a dead body by contrast to a living one. This soundlessness becomes a sign of the beloved's vanishing as a human subject, experienced by the mourning 'I' as the 'you' is becoming bodily silent and imperceptible. **Appassionato**, passionate in Italian, signals the excruciatingly painful intensity of the mourner's experience. The experience of passionate silence is articulated in the nightmares of the beloved 'you''s vanishing, voiced in Part One of the poem *Dreamscapes*, while Part Two and Part Three, together with the other two poems of *Interlude III*, *Resurrection* and *Fur*, open horizons towards new forms of embodied spiritual-material co-becoming with the beloved as spectrally returning, as well as metamorphosed to inhuman *zoe*-vibrancy. The mode of passionate silence prepares for **Chapter 4, Is the Wall of Silence Breachable?** rethinking the wall of silence along the lines of the immanence philosophical concept of death as becoming-imperceptible, experienced and phenomenologically analysed from the perspective of the mourning 'I', who, in a posthuman sense, grapples with and gradually learns how to make forays into co-becoming beyond this wall.

Chapter 4

IS THE WALL OF SILENCE BREACHABLE?

Silence! Silence is the most conspicuous and immediate material sign that a body has passed the threshold between life and death. A living body – human or non-human – makes sounds. When you sit next to someone who is close to death, you can hear their breath, as well as their movements. This is so, even if the one dying is a person, who is strongly sedated to avoid pain. But the onset of death means that all bodily sounds disappear. A dead body is intensely silent. Coldness is another significant material sign of death. But while it takes some hours before a dead body has lost all warmth, the deadly silence which materially signifies that the threshold between life and death has been passed imposes itself inexorably on the one sitting next to a deathbed immediately after the onset of death. The moment of death is marked by an abrupt transition from a sound-making body to a totally silent one. Life can be heard. Death is silent. When the one who is dying is someone with whom you have shared everyday spaces, these too will be marked by silence – a silence intensely signalling the absence of the one who has died. For the mourner, what is popularly known as 'dead silence' is neither a metaphor nor just a banal truism.

In this chapter, I explore this silence, and the wall it erects between the mourning 'I' and the dead beloved. But I also contemplate the possibilities of breaching that wall. The overall framework for these reflections is an immanence philosophical conceptualization of death as becoming-imperceptible. I discuss how both my experience of bouncing against a wall of impenetrable silence, and that of entering into spiritual-material modes enabling me to breach the silence, resonate with such a framework. The experiences of bouncing against, as well as breaching the wall of silence are contemplated through an analysis of the poems of *Interlude III, Silenzio Appasionato*, and an autobiographical story *Will I Meet You Here or There?* I discuss how the poems and the story are rhizomatically interrelated with each other and with my overarching experience of my beloved's becoming-imperceptible. I reflect upon the ways in which the wall of silence rose when my beloved became imperceptible, and how it started to crumble when I learned to co-become with her spectral phenomenality and material remains.

The chapter is structured as follows. First, I discuss the notion of becoming-imperceptible, as developed in the work of Deleuze and Guattari (1988), and further reflected in Braidotti's death theory (2006, 2013). Second, I suggest that this immanence philosophical conceptualization of death can be enriched by a phenomenological perspective, which takes its point of departure in the position of enunciation of the mourning 'I', rather than in the conventional philosophical one: the sovereign philosopher's 'I' who reflects upon the ontology of death in resistant anticipation of hir own passing. Third, in order to unfold what it implies to re-ontologize death from the perspective of the mourning 'I' and, at the same time, to rethink mourning in posthuman terms, I analyse significant shifts and transitions in my mourning journey. In this analysis, I use the poems and story as lenses to contemplate the transitioning between my lonely bouncing against the wall of silence and the process of learning to co-become with my beloved's metamorphosed modes of existence.

Death as Becoming-Imperceptible

Becoming-imperceptible is a central concept in the immanence philosophy of Deleuze and Guattari (1988). One aspect of becoming-imperceptible is dying. However, it should be noted that, in an immanence philosophical sense, dying is not to be understood as a final endpoint. In this ontological context, life and death are not opposites, but different modes of becoming within a continuum, governed by affect-laden, dynamic and inhuman forces.[1] Becomings in a Deleuzoguattarian ontology constitute the world as multiple, open-ended and ongoing processes of differentiation or merging, characterized by speed, movement, intensity and affectivity, and not by entities or essences. The temporalities of these processes of becoming are *Aionic*, i.e. happening at a multiplicity of speeds, and moving rhizomatically in all directions rather than chronologically along a linear, chrononormative timeline (Deleuze 2020: 167–72).[2] Accordingly, death can be seen as a moment in all these processes, but not as a final endpoint.

To elaborate upon the notion of becoming-imperceptible, Deleuze and Guattari juxtapose it with a becoming-impersonal and a becoming-indiscernible (1988: 279). They further define this threefold mode of becoming through the adjectives anorganic (imperceptible), asubjective (impersonal) and asignifying (indiscernible). As discussed by Braidotti (2006), it makes sense to apply this understanding of becoming to the process of dying. Against the background of the Deleuzoguattarian ontology of becoming-imperceptible, death is to be understood, first, as a disappearance of the well-ordered, organically structured bodily entity, which we normally consider to be 'our body'. Deleuze and Guattari define this organized body as molar. Becoming-imperceptible means that the molar body dissolves in favour of the anorganic body, or the body without organs (Deleuze and Guattari 1988: 149–66) – a body which is at one with its molecular-level intensities, a body pervaded by inhuman, dynamic and affective forces. From a Deleuzoguattarian perspective, we can understand this imperceptible/anorganic and molecular body as that with which we become one when we die. Qualified, moreover, through becoming asubjective/impersonal as well as asignifying/indiscernible, death is to be considered as a vanishing in a subjectively sign-producing sense. When we die, we become asubjective and asignifying, meaning that we will no longer be generating signs in a subjective sense.[3]

It is notable here that Deleuze and Guattari do not see becoming-imperceptible as a concept that is only related to dying. Or, in other words, because dying, in their ontology, is just a process of becoming like so many others, it stops being the decisive threshold between life and nothingness which it is, for example, in Sartrean philosophy (1958), or between life and afterlife in Christian-influenced philosophies. However, in the Deleuzoguattarian ontology, becoming-imperceptible is still conceptualized as somehow more ultimate and all-encompassing than other becomings:

> If becoming-woman is the first quantum, or molecular segment, with the becoming-animal that link up with it coming next, what are they rushing toward? Without a doubt toward becoming-imperceptible. The imperceptible is the immanent end of becoming, its cosmic formula.
> Deleuze and Guattari 1988: 279

Braidotti takes this concept of becoming-imperceptible further, into a 'posthuman death theory' (2013: 137), in which the notion of *zoe*[4] comes to play a central role in a vitalist, new-materialist sense. According to Braidotti, death is a becoming-one with *zoe*. This means that generativity and *conatus* (in a Spinozist sense, 1996 [1677]: 75) are foregrounded. When the inhuman forces of which matter in an immanence-philosophical sense is made are to be understood as generative and conative, dying in terms of becoming-one with these forces will involve a dynamic, affect-laden and vibrant process. In accordance with Deleuze and Guattari, Braidotti defines death in terms of a becoming-imperceptible, equivalent to a 'merging into [the] eternal flow of becomings' (Braidotti 2006: 252) – a framing that resonates with Deleuze and Guattari's reference to a 'cosmic formula' (1988: 279), a flow of cosmic dimensions. This merging implies a 'disruption of the self' and a 'dissolution of the subject' (Braidotti 2006: 252). Paraphrasing Lacan, Braidotti also discusses becoming-imperceptible as the moment in which 'you coincide with your body', or in other words, the moment when 'you become corpse' (Braidotti 2006: 252–3). The key point is that this becoming-corpse implies a becoming-one with the inhuman conative forces of *zoe*. Braidotti makes it clear that the becoming-one-with-*zoe* is to be decisively distinguished from a death that is materially understood as an entropic state. She firmly states that this becoming:

> could not be further removed from the notion of death as the inanimate and indifferent state of matter, the entropic state to which body is supposed to 'return'.
> 2013: 137

Instead, Braidotti defines death – and by extension dying, decomposing, decaying, and becoming-corpse – in a vitalist, new-materialist manner as the agency of 'the inhuman within us' (ibid.: 134). She underlines that the conative *zoe*-forces within us, which we as human subjects understand as 'our' life, is actually not an individual possession, but what she jokingly describes as something we inhabit as 'a timeshare' (ibid.: 253). Moreover, Braidotti emphasizes that *zoe* should not be understood as 'good' in any romantic, quasi-anthropocentric sense. Quite the contrary; she stresses that '*zoe* can be cruel: cells split and multiply in cancer as in pregnancy' (ibid.: 259). The example of the *zoe*-based vitality of cancer cells, relentlessly transgressing organ boundaries, spells out *zoe*'s indifferent, and therefore sometimes cruel, agency vis-à-vis the individual subject. Seen from the perspective of a human subject dying from cancer, there is no easily inbuilt romanticizing anthropocentrism at play when thinking about the inhuman forces of *zoe* within.

Shifting the Philosophical Position of Enunciation

In order to explore death and dying as becoming-imperceptible, becoming-inhuman and becoming-one-with-*zoe*, I am in conversation with Deleuze and Guattari, as well as Braidotti. However, I also take a somewhat different route from theirs. My spiritual-material mourning practices, and my autophenomenographic exploration of my beloved's death through poetry and autobiographical stories, have led me to consider the issue of situatedness and positions of enunciation. What does it mean to reflect on the becoming-imperceptible/inhuman/one-with-*zoe* from a position of enunciation other than that of the philosopher-subject's sovereign 'I'? If the philosopher-subject conventionally reflects upon the death of the human subject with its own anticipated death as horizon, what then happens when the sovereign 'I' of the philosopher-subject is replaced by the mourning'I'? Or in other words, can the 'I' of my poems and stories, the textual 'I' of an intimate companion and queer femme, passionately mourning and lamenting the passing of a beloved 'you', give rise to new kinds of corpo-affectively grounded reflections on death and dying as becoming-imperceptible/inhuman/one-with-*zoe*?

Notably, when discussing the aporetic problem that no one can represent or consciously contemplate one's own death other than from an anticipatory position, Braidotti comments in passing on mourning as a unique philosophical entrance point to a potentially different understanding:

> One's own death is unrepresentable and only the death of the other can possibly be contemplated by the conscious subject. Thus, we can only accede to some intuition of our mortality by projecting it onto someone else or by identification or empathic connection to another, usually a loved one. This positions 'mourning' as a very central mode of relating to the other, and obliquely also to one's own death.
>
> Braidotti 2006: 240

Braidotti does not further develop these reflections on the importance of the mourning subject for an ontology of death. But it is precisely here that my poetic-philosophical and autophenomenographic work takes its point of departure, focusing on the symphysizing mourning 'I' of a queer femme as a position from which death and dying can be contemplated differently. This does not mean that I naïvely think that the decisive existential difference between inhabiting a dying body, and sitting lovingly next to someone inhabiting such a body, can or should be neglected. As discussed in detail elsewhere (Lykke 2018), I believe that it is crucial to take this difference into account, ethically as well as onto-epistemologically. My point, though, is that the position of the symphysizing mourning 'I', working from queerfeminine sensibilities,[5] and from desires for love-death and becoming-one with the passed-away beloved can be explored phenomenologically. I claim that such an exploration can generate new philosophical insights into death and dying beyond the sovereign 'I''s anticipatory reflections, which will always in one way or another be pervaded by resistance to the thought of the coming of death. To the sovereign 'I', its own death will always somehow appear as an insult and an impending disaster, since it implies a giving up of the core values of this subject, namely sovereignty and control. This means that the sovereign 'I' will be disturbed and troubled by hir resistance, when trying to think through an ontology of death, whereas the mourning 'I' will have wider and more open horizons. While the former will resist the thought of its own vanishing, the latter will tend to desire death as unambiguously as is bodily possible.[6] To the mourning 'I', death can appear as the ultimate path to free hirself from the amputation pain, inflicted upon hir by the beloved's passing, and perhaps even in the shape of a love-death figure as that which potentially makes a passionately longed-for reconnection possible. The mourning 'I' can reflect upon death differently due to hir wish to reconnect and, like Orpheus, follow the passed-away beloved into the world of the dead. Against this background, I suggest that the immanence philosophical reflections on death and dying as becoming-imperceptible/inhuman/one-with-*zoe* will be enriched, when contemplated from the perspectives of the mourning 'I'. Therefore, based on my autophenomenographic material (my poems and stories), I explore the philosophical position of enunciation of the mourning 'I', who is guided by embodied desires for co-becoming with, and ultimately for love-death and becoming-one with, the passed-away beloved, as an alternative route to an immanence philosophically framed understanding of death.

Notably, in order to delve deeper into the question: how can the position of enunciation of the mourning 'I' contribute with new perspectives to an immanence philosophical understanding of death and dying?, it is important to emphasize that this 'I' is not a fixed, bounded, goal-oriented or unitary entity like the sovereign 'I'. The mourning 'I' differs from the sovereign 'I' insofar as it is not directed by any self-defined teleology or rationally set goals. The mourning 'I' moves in multiple, non-unitary and rhizomatic directions, governed by intuitions and emerging intensities more than by so-called rational thought. Western modernity's versions of rational, positivist thought do not work well for the mourning 'I', because it is founded on the presupposition that that which the mourner desires the most, to phenomenally and materially reconnect with the passed-away beloved, is impossible because, according to hegemonic modern narratives, material death is irreversible.

Against the background of this understanding of the mourning 'I' as a decisively multiple, non-unitary and rhizomatically moving subject, I want to underline that my journey towards reconnection has never been undertaken as a fixed, goal-oriented quest. Rather, it is and has always been governed by what in Deleuzoguattarian philosophy is described as lines of flight, efforts to deterritorialize and unlearn all the internalized prohibitions and injunctions coming out of Western modernity regarding how, why and what you can or cannot think about death, dying, the world of the dead and the afterlife. I shall pursue three such lines of flight in this chapter: dreaming, spectral encounters and spiritually-materially immersing myself in the process of co-becoming with my beloved's material remains and their new assemblages; I shall discuss the latter as an engaging in alien encounters. All three flightlines are entangled with my poetic contemplations. Through analyses of poems from *Interlude III*, and the story *Will I Meet You Here or There?*, I shall spell out how all three of them have become important to me in my journey towards breaching the wall of silence.

Dreaming of Becoming-Imperceptible

The first of the flightlines to be considered as intensities driving my mourning journey in rhizomatic directions is linked to dreamworlds, as articulated in *Dreamscapes – A Triptych*. This poem is different from all other poems in this book, insofar as it is crafted exclusively against the background of dreams that I had over a period of several years after my beloved's death. For many years, I have written down my dreams when I felt they were significant. After my beloved's death, I found comfort and pleasure in intensifying this practice, memorizing in writing all the dreams in which she appeared, or which I somehow experienced as being related to her and her death. At the beginning, I did this for no other purpose than saving the memories of these occasional, nightly moments of reconnection with my dead beloved. Basically, I saw the practice of writing down the dreams as one of the ways that would help me to keep my beloved magically alive through the act of memorizing my dream encounters with her. However, the practice became much more than just this kind of memorizing device. While it began as one mourning practice among others, this one unexpectedly came to play a decisive role in my understanding of the journey in which my desire for reconnection led me to engage. Initially, I had no plans to systematically reread the dreams. But after a couple of years, and a long way into the process of unfolding my spiritual-material practices, and committing to poetic and philosophical knowledge-seeking to sustain them, it struck me that the dreams might be interesting to read in one go. By that time, I had a huge folder with close to 100 irregularly jotted down dreams. So, I sat down and read them – and to my immense surprise, the bulging folder comprised very neatly composed clusters of dream events.

To follow a Deleuzoguattarian-inspired analytical strategy, I chose to contemplate these dream clusters as rhizomatically connected plateaus, rather than as bounded entities or linearly organized sequences. In their seminal work, *A Thousand Plateaus* (1988), Deleuze and Guattari describe the chapters of their book as plateaus, and define a plateau as 'any multiplicity connected to other multiplicities by superficial underground stems in such a way as to form or extend a rhizome' (ibid.: 22). The rhizome is the two philosophers' key image of thought in action, working not like trees or taproots, but instead like plants such as grass or strawberries that send out roots in all directions. Along these lines, Deleuze and Guattari also define a plateau as 'a continuous, self-vibrating region of intensities whose development avoids any orientation toward a culmination point or external end' (ibid.). Notably, plateaus are also to be understood as composed 'not of units but of dimensions, or rather directions in motion,' and as having 'neither beginning nor end, but always a middle (milieu) from which it grows and which it overspills' (ibid.: 21). Finally, plateaus should not be seen as singular phenomena, but rather as rhizomatically related to each other. Compellingly, the two philosophers thus describe their experiences of writing in the format of plateaus as 'hallucinatory', when they watch 'lines leave one plateau and proceed to another like columns of tiny ants' (ibid.: 22).

The Deleuzoguattarian image of interconnected plateaus and a rhizomatic production of intensities extending in all directions like ant columns, without beginning or end, appropriately grasps the ways in which the clusters of dreams in my folder unfurled before my eyes when I read them in one sitting. This is why I chose to look at them as plateaus. But with this move, I also bring the analysis of the dream clusters into resonance with my overall immanence philosophical approach. To contemplate dreaming as one of my lines of flight, I shall now comment on my plateau-oriented reading of these dreams, and the poetic editing, selection and articulation of this reading in *Dreamscapes – A Triptych*. I will start with a summary overview of my reading of the dream clusters, and then dig deeper into each plateau, while keeping their rhizomatic connections in mind.

One plateau that strongly attracted my attention articulated the mourning 'I''s devastating, lonely and reiterated experiences of the subjective vanishing of the beloved, her becoming-imperceptible in terms of becoming-anorganic/asubjective/asignifying. A second plateau that spoke to me forcefully from the dreams marked ambiguities and turning points for the 'I', while a third plateau spelled out processes of co-becoming with the spectrally returning dead beloved, leading to love-death and a shared becoming-imperceptible. The poem *Dreamscapes – A Triptych* is based on selections of dreams from each of these plateaus. It should be noted that, even though the poem is divided into three parts – *I: You Vanish, II: Spectral Interferences*, and *III: Joyful Deathworlds* – there are not only rhizomatic connections internally within each part, but they also criss-cross in-between the parts. Such a criss-crossing reading is in accordance with the classic genre of the triptych. As developed, for example, by renaissance painter Hieronymus Bosch's[7] fantastic, grotesque religious motifs, the triptych-genre interpellates the viewer to look for rhizomatic relations between three interconnected panels. In this sense, the interpellated poetic genre, and the reading-as-plateaus resonate with each other.

The mourning 'I''s devastating experience of the beloved 'you''s becoming-imperceptible, her subjective vanishing in terms of becoming-anorganic/asubjective/asignifying is articulated in *Part I: You Vanish* (Stanzas 1–8). This is an edited version of an abundance of dreams in which I re-experienced the vanishing of my beloved. When reading the dreams and clustering them as rhizomatically connected intensities, it stood out to me with lucid clarity how month after month after month, again and again and again, I had dreamt that a situation of being together with my partner changed dramatically and devastatingly into one where she was very definitely gone, leading me to awaken with an excruciating feeling of pain and irretrievable loss. In many of the dreams, her vanishing was figuratively signified through an impenetrable silence, or a silence in which only indifferent non-human sounds (such as the wind in the foliage, Stanza 7) could be heard. I somehow knew, of course, that I had occasionally had such dreams. However, the massive number of them (many more than those selected through the editing of *Dreamscapes – A Triptych*), the figurative repetition of the vanishing event, and the ensuing silence, over and over again, stood out as something new to me. It is part of the ontology of dreams that they are volatile, and easily forgotten, if one does not make an effort to memorize them, and even when one does so, they tend to slide out of conscious focus. So, rereading all of these dreams in one sitting was an intense experience, which made the vanishing theme and the figure of a wall of impenetrable silence stand out. What also stood out, however, was the significant resonance with Deleuze/Guattari's and Braidotti's conceptualizing of subjective death as becoming-imperceptible/indiscernible/impersonal. When the dying subject becomes imperceptible in this sense, what the mourner experiences is intense silence.

On the second plateau, *Part II: Spectral Interferences*, (Stanzas 9–11), the dream intensities are concentrated on ambiguities and transitions. A transition is heralded by two dreams (Stanzas 9–10) that link to the sadness of the vanishing dreams of the first plateau, as well as to the ecstatic togetherness that characterizes the dreams of my beloved's spectral return on the third plateau. The two dreams of Stanzas 9–10 thematize profoundly disturbing and sad blockings of memorizing through mirroring processes which are troubled by interference of spectral kinds of in/visibility. The blurred surface of the mirror belonging to the beloved's mother (Stanza 9) prevents the 'I' and the 'you' from getting to know her better. The mirror images of the furniture from the apartment that the 'I' and the 'you' inhabited together in earlier times (Stanza 10) cannot become a shared memory of this cohabitation, because they are only visible to the 'I'. The immense sadness evoked by the irretrievably blocked memorizing, articulated in Stanzas 9 and 10, link to the vanishing dreams of Part I. However, through the establishing of an embodied togetherness of the 'I' and the 'you', the dreams in these two stanzas also link to those of *Part III: Joyful Deathworlds* (Stanzas 12–14), which articulate a happy, physical being-together of the 'I' and the 'you', the latter now a *revenant*,[8] spectrally returning to reconnect after the two have been separated for some time by the death of the 'you'. It is this ambiguous character of the dreams in Stanzas 9–10 that lead me to interpret them as part of a plateau where the intensities are concentrated on transitions.

However, the most significant articulation of a transition is the cluster of dreams which I condensed into Stanza 11. Here, the transition is articulated through an event that marks an outspoken turning point, as well as through an amplification of ambiguities. First, the 'I' is figuratively turning around while sailing and walking alone towards nothingness through strange landscapes and along an asphalted road. The dream image of solitary sailing, and walking on dead material (asphalt) towards nothingness strikes me as articulating the 'I' sailing/walking alone towards her own death, here framed in resonance with the radical, Sartresque atheist philosophy (1958), with which, as mentioned earlier, I was brought up. However, what happens in the dream is that, in the end, the 'I' refrains from immersing herself in death as nothingness. Instead, she turns around and walks home to the house where she has lived with the beloved 'you', before the latter passed away, *but only to find this 'home' radically altered in highly ambiguous ways*. The yard, which the 'I' and the 'you' jointly designed shortly before the 'you' died, is overgrown with wild plants, due to disruption caused by a leaking pipe. Moreover, instead of performing as a safe and quiet, 'homely', place, the yard is haunted by threatening non-human/in-human/quasi-human beings (a wolf pack, a bird with a sharp beak, masked executioners), launching violent attacks on the 'I'. However, while scary, these potentially deadly intrusions are nevertheless embraced by the 'I'. Together with one of the wolves from the pack, the 'I', for example, goes through a process of eroticized becoming-animal (a stage which, according to Deleuze and Guattari, is needed as part of a becoming-imperceptible), and she laughs together with her executioners.

Philosophically, I read the turning-around dream of Stanza 11 as staging that the mourning 'I' is engaged in a radical ontological shift – a shift from an atheist Sartresque ontology to an immanence philosophical one, which reframes the 'I''s passionate search for ways to reconnect with the dead beloved. If subjective death is understood as equivalent to vanishing into a Sartresque nothingness, a reconnection with the dead beloved is unthinkable. By contrast, if death and its radical 'disruption of the self', in an immanence philosophical sense, means 'merging into the eternal flow of becomings' (Braidotti 2006: 252), then material reconnection is not only possible, but ontologically inevitable. When that which Braidotti frames as 'the inhuman within us' (2013: 134) is understood as materially entangled with all other inhuman *zoe*-matter, and the sovereign subject's illusion of a separate 'I' is hence annulled, our subjective death must, as a radical consequence, entail a reconnection with all those humans and non-humans who became one with this *zoe*-matter before us.

Against this background, I read the dream of turning around as figuring a radical shifting away from an ontology of death conceptualized as nothingness, which forecloses the possibility of reconnection. The dream can, then, be seen as figuring a leaving of the kind of ontology, which for so many years was ingrained in me due to my atheist upbringing and later beliefs, but which fell decisively short in the face of my overwhelming desire for reconnection with my dead beloved. Moreover, I interpret the troubled homecoming that follows the turning around as figuring a coming to terms with the possibilities for co-becoming and becoming-one with the metamorphosing material remains of my dead beloved, which are offered by an immanence philosophical ontology of death. Notably, however, from the beginning, the process of coming to terms is experienced in an ambivalent way. On the one hand, the 'I' is experiencing the co-becoming as scary – this is figured through her experiences of intrusions into the shared 'home' by threatening wild beings. On the other hand, the attacks and the attackers also figure as attractive and desirable: the 'I''s defence against the intruders is not wholehearted. This ambivalence is rhizomatically connected to the first plateau through the theme of death as loss and loneliness, called forward by the vanishing of the beloved. But it is also linked to the third plateau and its articulating of reconnection through spectral co-becoming.

Like the first two, the third plateau, *Part III: Joyful Deathworlds* (Stanzas 12–14), also stood out surprisingly clearly to me when I read the dreams in one sitting. On this third plateau, dreams thematizing intimate and sexually tinged re-encounters and re-connections with my beloved, who is returning after a period when she has been 'away'/'dead', stood out. Again, I somehow knew that I had had many such intensely happy erotic dreams about reconnecting with my revivified beloved, returning as a *revenant*. But it was moving and surprising to me to become aware that these dreams, too, were so numerous and significant that they could be understood as a plateau – in this case, a plateau carried by intensities, which open up new horizons beyond the wall of silence, offering possibilities for spectral encounters with my beloved, as she occasionally returns within the volatile spacetime of dreamworlds. Moreover, it was strange and thrilling to become aware that this plateau, too, lent itself to an interpretation along the lines of an immanence philosophical understanding of becoming-imperceptible – now framed as spectral encounter, relational co-becoming and shared becoming-one-with-*zoe*. Instead of the threatening attackers of the second plateau, this third plateau allows the 'I' to enter into more and more vibrant, intimately sexual and ecstatic encounters and co-becomings with the spectrally returning 'you', finally leading to a climax of dying together, figured as a love-death in the shape of a shared and peaceful drowning (Stanza 14). In an immanence philosophical sense, I read this drowning together as a dreaming enactment of a shared becoming-imperceptible, understood as a becoming-one with the inhuman forces of *zoe*, here figured as the sea, whose surface is disappearing above the 'I', while she sinks into death together with the beloved.

What Can Dreams Do?

The transition from a lonely bouncing against the wall of silence to co-becoming with the beloved was enacted in my dreams, as I have articulated it in the analysis above, but what happened in the dreams was also connected to and had effects in the so-called 'real' world. I see dreams as performative and endowed with agency, and not only as mere reflections of what is conceived of in Freudian dream theory (1900) as the individual unconscious. Following inspirations from indigenous philosophies (Anzaldua 2015; Black 2018), as well as from the surrealist movement of the 20th century (Breton 1971), the ontology of dreams upon which I base my work goes beyond the limits of a Freudian understanding, where, to some extent, even radical thinkers such as Deleuze and Guattari have also left it parked. I think that a new ontology of dreams is much needed. It is too limited to consider dreams as mere representations of the individual psyche's repressed desires. I do, indeed, understand my transitioning between lonely bouncing and passionately engaged spectral encounters and transcorporeal co-becomings with my beloved's bodily remains, and their new watery assemblages, as related to my desires. However, I understand neither these desires nor the embodied subject (me) from whom they emerge in a mere individualized psychoanalytical sense. I consider the desiring individual to be trans- and intercorporeally connected to its human and non-human others, and do not understand the subject's grown-up relations to 'objects' (human and non-human) in the 'external' world to presuppose a subject-object separation. Therefore, I do not see dreams as only impacting upon and being impacted by the individual psyche, as classic Freudian dream theory (1900) would have it. But, notably, neither do I understand them along the lines of Jungian analytical psychology (Jung 1991) as linked to static archetypal essences.

But how, then, do I understand dreams? I think it is difficult to lay out an ontology of dreams, not least because of the heavy load of psychoanalytical and analytical psychological interpretations which the question calls forward. However, I consider dreams to be too important to leave with psychoanalysis or analytical psychology. To make sense of the ways in which dreams have been crucial for me in my poetic-philosophical endeavours to reontologize death, I shall therefore suggest an ontology of dreams that resonates with the immanence philosophical perspective upon which I am drawing. Against this background, I understand dreams as dynamic enactments of affective relations between embodied agencies. I see them as highly performative, because of their way of articulating affectivity at the blurred boundaries between desiring bodies and trans- and intercorporeal zoe-bound entanglements. Moreover, since dreams work in the borderlands between mind and body, as I think rightly pointed out by Freud (1900), I also claim that it will make sense to take a Spinoza-inspired route, transposing his question about what bodies can do (1996 [1677]: 71), to also bear upon dreams. Thus, I ask what dreams can *do*, rather than what they *are*, and also approach them through such Deleuzoguattarian concepts as lines of flight, intensities and affects.

Reflecting upon my previous analysis of the three plateaus of dream events with this ontological assumptions as my guideline, I have come to understand my dreams as part of a larger assemblage of forces which have sustained and nourished my processes of transitioning. This process includes an ontological shift from a Sartresque atheist belief in death as nothingness to an immanence philosophical understanding of life/death as a continuum, embedded in the dynamic forces of *zoe*. However, this ontological shift is only part of the process. Overall, I consider the transitioning as enacting profound trans- and intercorporeally grounded changes in my relationship to my beloved and her state of subjective imperceptibility. These changes involve puncturing the wall of silence through my beloved's spectral returns as the subject she was. They also imply a crumbling of this wall as an effect of my processes of co-becoming with the new assemblages of which my beloved's metamorphosed bodily remains have become part. The changes have also been crucial for the framing of my memories, related to the spacetime that my beloved and I bodily inhabited together before her death; instead of being exclusively fixed to this past spacetime, my memories have been linked together with the instants of spectral returns and co-becoming, figured in the dreams on an ongoing basis. Finally, the changes have been of key importance for the unfolding of my spiritual-material relation to my beloved's new spacetime mattering body, composed of ashes mixed with the diatomaceous earth and sand, which make up the seabed where my beloved's ashes are scattered.[9]

Notably, even though this ontological shift is to be understood as decisive, I do not consider my transitioning as a linear move through fixed states: from my experience of my beloved's vanishing into nothingness via momentary spectral encounters with her to a co-becoming with her remains and their new assemblages. As indicated by the use of the 'plateau' as my thinking tool in the dream analysis and its poeticization in the poem *Dreamscapes – A Triptych*, and the ontology of dreams suggested above, my process of transitioning and co-becoming with my beloved's remains and their new assemblages (fleshy corpse, burnt to ashes, scattered in a seabed) is to be understood as rhizomatic – full of criss-crossing lines like those made up of the tiny little Deleuzoguattarian ants running in all kinds of directions, both within and in-between plateaus.

In the remainder of this chapter, I shall dig further into my process of transitioning as mourning 'I'. As indicated above, the transitioning did not only take place with dreams as its lines of flight. To further sustain and investigate it, I shall discuss the breaching of the wall of silence; first, through spectral encounters, and, second, through moves into spiritual-material processes of co-becoming with my beloved's material remains and their new watery assemblages, to be discussed also as alien encounters. I shall focus the discussion of spectrality with the poem *Resurrection* as lens, while the co-becoming with the assemblages of material remains will be teased out through an autobiographical story, *Will I Meet You Here or There?*, and an analysis of the poem *Fur*.

The Paradoxes of Spectral Returns

The role of spectral returns in my processes of mourning have so far been discussed in relation to dreams and their poeticization. I shall now explore them further by focusing on the poem *Resurrection*. Here, the 'you' is a spectral figure whose posthumous emergence is governed by everyday qualities of what was. My passed-away beloved returns through the front door of our house, enters the living room as though nothing has happened, and invites me to do some fun stuff with her. The lyric 'I' of *Resurrection* is also comparing notes with other mourning subjects who have lost beloved companions, whom they are trying to keep spectrally alive through poetic and artistic imagination.

One of the mourners who appears in *Resurrection* is US writer Joan Didion,[10] who framed her experiences with passed-away loved ones in two bestselling autobiographical books, *The Year of Magical Thinking* (2005), and *Blue Nights* (2012). Didion lost both her husband and her daughter within less than two years, and the books deal with her devastation following these bereavements. Among other aspects, Didion reflects upon her beloveds' embodied return, so passionately desired that so-called 'rational thought' about death's irreversibility gives way to what, in the first book, she compellingly frames as 'magical thinking'. As described by Didion, magical thinking emerges from a kind of ambiguous dual consciousness. On the one hand, she describes her outlook as grounded in a modern, science-based understanding of bodily death as final and irreversible. On the other hand, she discusses how, during the first year after her husband's sudden and unexpected death from a stroke, she keeps becoming aware of the ways in which her excessive desire for his return has prompted her to unconsciously engage in attempts to amend the world imaginarily, trying in innumerable ways to undo his traumatic death. For example, Didion pinpoints how, several months after her husband's death, she begins to understand that, despite all her rational acts of organizing the cremation, the funeral ceremony etc., and thereby publicly confirming that her husband is dead, at the same time, she keeps acting on the hidden belief that he will come back and need his clothes and shoes:

> On most surface levels I seemed rational. To the average observer I would have appeared to fully understand that death was irreversible. (...) I had done it. I had acknowledged that he was dead. (...) Yet my thinking on this point remained suspiciously fluid. (...) 'Bringing him back' had been through those months my hidden focus, a magic trick. By late summer I was beginning to see this clearly. [Though] 'seeing it clearly' did not yet allow me to give away the clothes he would need.
>
> Didion 2005: 42-4

Psychoanalysis describes the mechanism of making-undone as a psychological defence against a traumatic experience (S. Freud 1926; A. Freud [2018] 1936; Laplanche and Pontalis 1973: 566-8), i.e. a defensive reaction, which involves a 'magic' (Freud 1926: 149-50) and perhaps ritualistic way of acting, signifying an annulling or reversing of the traumatic event. Didion discusses her many acts of 'magically' trying to undo the deaths of her beloved husband and daughter partly along the lines of such individual-centred psychological thought, although she also articulates a critique against psychology and, as I did in Chapter 2, makes a plea for the right to excessive mourning (Didion 2005: 54-6). Didion's first book is based on in-depth reflections upon the ways in which her overwhelming desire to repress 'reality', drawing on what she calls a 'fund of superstition' (ibid.: 125) works during the first year after her husband's death. She articulates compellingly how she keeps catching herself in ways of thinking and acting that, from the point of view of a positivist understanding of 'reality' and death as irreversible, would seem completely irrational. For example, she discusses how she keeps her husband's clothes and shoes, and how, after a long time, she becomes aware that her most hidden and innermost motivation for doing so is that she is thereby leaving open a 'magical' horizon: that her husband may return in flesh-and-blood form – and, in an everyday fashion, be in need of his clothes and shoes (ibid.: 41, 44–6).

But is Didion's 'magical thinking' only to be understood as a psychological defence? She leaves this question open, but by the end of her first book, she recognizes that there are excess meanings at stake beyond psychology. Thus, she admits that she does not want to finish the book, because the writing of it is a way of keeping her husband alive and with her:

> I realize as I write this that I do not want to finish this account. Nor did I want to finish the year (…) I know why we try to keep the dead alive: we try to keep them alive in order to keep them with us.
>
> Ibid.: 224–5

Thus, for Didion, and for the other poets and writers interpellated in *Resurrection*, as well as for the poem's lyric 'I', what seems to be at stake is cultivations of poetic modes of reversing the deaths of beloved companions in order to keep them with us. So, I will take Didion's argument a step further, and claim that the excess – that which in different ways makes all the poets and writers interpellated in *Resurrection* transgress a positivist understanding of death as irreversible – cannot be reduced to 'magical thinking' in the sense of a psychological defence. The excess is, indeed, magical, but it should rather be understood as the poetic imagination's power and ability to aesthetically create fictive worlds which can suspend everyday reality.

However, what I shall also argue is that it is even too limited to consider this excess only as a question of poetic imagination. Didion somehow suggests that she oscillates between two 'realities' – a positivistically defined one, and one where magical thinking is real. Her everyday magical acts and thoughts do not stop just because, with the 'rational' part of her mind, she has pinpointed them as 'magical'. For example, she continues to keep her husband's shoes and clothes even after she begins to see it as a psychological defence (ibid.: 41, 44–6). Living with this dual consciousness – that her husband is dead, but that she also has to magically carry out certain acts such as keeping clothes and shoes, because he could still return – is a major theme in Didion's book.

When I read the book shortly after my own beloved's death, I was captured by a strong identification with Didion's description of her split reality, and also with her way of using poetic imagination and writing to come to terms with that split. My life, surrounded by things that were part of my and my partner's daily life before her passing, has also, since then, been occupied by all kinds of everyday magical acts and thoughts – such as not removing a particular pile of books, which my beloved had planned to read, from a small table next to her armchair in our living room. I felt, and still do feel, an identification with Didion's dual reality – her split between the magic-poetic reality and the rationally 'real' one. However, the more I have delved into the process of poetic-philosophical reontologization, in tandem with the unfolding of spiritual-material practices, which I shall discuss in more detail in Chapters 5 and 6, the more I have moved beyond Didion's split-world-thinking. In Chapter 2, I started to question the 'real' of the mourning 'I'. I shall now push this questioning further, using as my lens Derrida's analysis (1994) of the paradoxicality of the spectre. Through Derrida, I shall begin to more radically undo the understanding of after-life, which is embedded in a positivist ontology, based on a strict separation between the 'real' and the 'magical'.

According to Derrida, the spectre, also understood as a *revenant* (a ghostly returning, embodied agency) is, first of all, a paradox of simultaneous absence and embodied, carnally phenomenal presence. It is a past which re-embodies itself in the present, while still signalling its link to 'the past' from which it 'returns'. Derrida describes the spectre as follows:

> the spectre is a paradoxical incorporation, the becoming-body, a certain phenomenal and carnal form of the spirit (...), some 'thing' that remains difficult to name: neither soul nor body, and both one and the other. For it is flesh and phenomenality that give to the spirit its spectral apparition, but which disappear right away in the apparition, in the very coming of the *revenant* or the return of the spectre. There is something disappeared, departed in the apparition itself as reapparition of the departed.
>
> Ibid.: 5

This paradoxicality comes clearly through when I reread the dreams that I edited for the third part of *Dreamscapes – A Triptych*, as well as when the lyric 'I' of *Resurrection* compares notes with other writers' and artists' passionate interpellations of dead beloveds. These dreams, as well as the poetic worlding practices to which *Resurrection* refers, position centre stage a paradoxical return from the past: the embodied subject as she/he/they was before she/he/they passed away is envisioned as a *revenant*, as someone who has been away (dead), and is now coming back as an apparition, which recalls a phenomenal, sensually traceable body. The figure of the *revenant* and its paradox of phenomenal absence and presence, stands out in all these poetic worldings: my beloved returning in the dreams of the third part of *Dreamscapes – A Triptych*, and unexpectedly walking up the stairs and entering our living room to suggest that we do something fun in *Resurrection*; Didion's passed away husband in need of clothes and shoes; nineteenth-century German poet Rückert's[11] dead children running ahead of their father to play in the hills (Rückert 1833–4; Mahler 1901–4); Swedish poet Hanna Hallgren[12] (2014) writing in order to keep feeling her dead father's presence; Danish writer and poet Naja Marie Aidt[13] (2019), at first completely blocked in her writing by the trauma triggered by her son Carl's death, because language has lost its meaning and function for her, but beginning to feel his presence very strongly the day she starts writing *Carl's Book* (ibid.: 33–4), and ending up pouring out poetic text in order to keep him alive.

The paradox lies in the phenomenal return. A return implies having been away, or, in other words, a hiatus between the passing away and the coming back – a hiatus which was so very clearly articulated in some of the dreams that I edited into the third part of *Dreamscapes – A Triptych*. When I bring Derrida's thoughts on this paradox to bear on my reflections regarding the ir/reversibility of the life/death threshold, the potential for an ontological blurring of the borders between 'real' and 'magical' thinking about a beloved's passing this threshold stand out. I shall thus suggest that what is at stake, as soon as we start talking about the phenomenality of spectres, is a fundamental challenge to the positivist understanding of the 'real'. In Chapter 2, I questioned the 'real' from the perspective of the excessive mourner's following hir desires to contemplate the passed-away beloved outside of chrononormative time, instead of complying with forward-running linear time, which leaves the dead embodied subject in a sealed and unchangeable past. Now I shall elaborate upon these reflections. My claim is that the Derrida-inspired analysis of spectral returns, and their paradoxical transgression of the borders between the phenomenal absence and presence of a passed-away beloved, takes me even further away from a conventional modern Western understanding of mourning. Against this background, I suggest the possibility of a phenomenology which is not only posthuman, but also posthumous in the sense that it is prepared to take seriously into account the mourning 'I''s queer experiences of spectral encounters with the passed-away beloved.

It is important here to also note Derrida's ironic comments on the transgressions of a positivist ontology that are at stake when we recognize the spectral. Derrida ridicules the compartmentalisation of positivist thought, which puts fact/reality into one box and fiction/magic/hallucination into another. In his reading of Shakespeare's *Hamlet*,[14] Derrida thus refers to the ways in which it is impossible for so-called 'scholars' to communicate with ghosts. Discussing the encounters with the ghost-father in *Hamlet*, and the suggestion that the sceptical 'scholar' Horatio should be the one to start a dialogue with the apparition, Derrida underlines that 'there has never been a scholar who really, and as scholar, deals with ghosts' (1994: 12). According to Derrida, scholars are too much immersed in dichotomous assumptions about the 'real'/'not-real' distinction to be prepared for encounters with ghosts. Scholars make a:

> sharp distinction between the real and the unreal, the actual and the inactual, the living and the non-living, being and non-being ('to be or not to be', in the conventional reading), in the opposition between what is present and what is not, for example in the form of objectivity. Beyond this opposition, there is, for the scholar, only the hypothesis of a school of thought, theatrical fiction, literature, and speculation.
>
> Ibid.: 12

Or, in other words, for the scholar, ghosts are illusions or figures of fiction, and therefore not recognized as potential interlocutors.

Derrida's ironic definition of the scholar's total lack of potential when it comes to skills in dealing with ghosts is a good platform for a further elaboration of the ways in which the mourning 'I''s contemplative horizon and position of enunciation differ from that of the sovereign modern philosopher's 'I'. I claim that the latter, to some extent, coincides with Derrida's figure of the scholar insofar as both take it as a basic assumption that ghosts are not to be seen as 'real' interlocutors. In contrast, my experience as a mourning 'I' has made me open to spectral encounters in rather different ways. I desire such encounters passionately, even though the atheist, modern scholar in me keeps telling me that they are 'unreal' or, as Didion (2005) framed it, expressions of 'magical thinking', existing in a 'ghetto', circumscribed by and set apart from 'real' rational thought. I claim that this kind of openness towards broader contemplations of 'reality' beyond positivist reductionism is part of what constitute the potentialities of my philosophical-poetic position of enunciation as mourning 'I', when I enter into processes of reontologizing death, dying, mourning and afterlife in this book.

From this position, however, I also notice a limitation in the Derridean approach to spectrality, and his concept of hauntology (ibid.: 10), which theorizes the ways in which temporal pasts can act in the present. I consider hauntology, in a Derridean sense, to be a useful framework for thinking about the ways in which the past should not be seen as a static entity, which through a chrononormative logic is temporally locked away from the present. With the concept of hauntology, Derrida makes the important point that the past is to be taken seriously into account as phenomenally acting in the here and now. However, the Derridean notion implies that spectres and the agencies of spectral pasts are first and foremost conceived as threatening; they return from the past to 'haunt' – i.e. potentially harm – the living, for example demanding that crimes and violent acts in the past should not be forgotten, but avenged in the present. In a Derridean ethics, this makes it important to learn to live well with spectres (Shildrick 2020). I recognize the political and ethical importance of using a hauntological framework to think about politically and socially oppressive, unjust and violent pasts in this way. However, working from the position of enunciation of the mourning 'I', who passionately desires spectral encounters with dead beloveds, I also think a more nuanced approach to spectral returns is necessary. I shall suggest that hauntology in the Derridean sense should be complemented by contemplations of the ethical, political and onto-epistemological implications of the passionately desired spectral embrace – be it on an individual, or on a more collective level (Vargas, Marambio and Lykke 2020). In my personal story of mourning, the desiring embracing of the spectral has been part of breaching the wall of silence.

Will I Meet You Here or There?

From the spectral embrace, I shall now turn to another line of flight, and a quite different, but just as vibrant and conative, mode of breaching the wall of silence. I shall go further into the issue of co-becoming with my beloved's material remains and the assemblages of which they are part. To do so, I shall take my point of departure in the autobiographical story *Will I Meet You Here or There?*, which thematizes a shift in my rhizomatic search for ways to reconnect spiritually-materially with my beloved. In retrospect, I see this shift as entangled with the transitioning processes discussed as moves in-between the plateaus of *Dreamscapes – A Triptych*.

...And now to the story:
Exactly one year after we – rainbow kin and friends – had lowered your ashes into Limfjorden beyond the cliffs of the island of Fur, I drove the 230 km to the island and cliffs alone in order to be together with you on the day when you would have turned seventyeight.

Fur, in the big Danish fjord Limfjorden is special due to its cliffs and a seabed that is made up of fossilized diatoms, a single-celled aquatic algae encased in a shell of many colours. The diatoms making up seabed and cliffs fossilized fiftyfive million years ago, when a subtropical sea covered the area. In the Ice Age, 10,000 years ago, the seabed was pressed up by the ice, which resulted in up to sixty-metre-high cliffs, rising out of the flat land and waters in many corners of the fjord. The island of Fur is one of the places where such cliffs, made of the many-coloured diatoms, are to be found.

The evening before my planned trip to Fur that first year after your death, I was very much in doubt. Should I drive to Limfjorden and Fur, or should I rather stay at home to be with you on your birthday in the house in Odense, which we have shared for so many years? Where was it most likely that you would meet me? Would I find you here in our house, where everything holds memories about you and where the material and spectral traces of your embodied existence for so many years abound? Here, in our living rooms, where everything is pervaded by memories of our co-habitation. We have danced in these rooms. We have laughed, quarrelled, made love, shared everything here. We have spent time together with children and grandchildren of many different ages and phases of life in these rooms. I have taken care of you here, and given you comfort, while you were about to die from your cancer. I experienced my life's deepest moments of grief and bereavement when you died here. I have been intensely alone in these rooms since your death. But I have also had joyful moments calling you spectrally forward through my writings here. We have lived together for almost forty years in these rooms. We have accreted with the rooms and with each other in a way that will inhabit me as a plastic memory as long as I live. These rooms are you and me, our children, grandchildren, cats and friends. We are these rooms, this house is our shared body.

So, indeed, wouldn't it be a journey away from you, if I drove the 230 km up to Limfjorden to celebrate your birthday? What would be the point of a journey to a place where I was never together with you while you were alive? A journey to a place where I was together with rainbow kin and friends, when we scattered your ashes, and where I slept with your ashes next to me in the blue ecological urn, a place where one day my ashes are going to be scattered to mix with yours, BUT at the same time a place where I have never been together with your living body. Should I rather stay at home, and hope for a spectral encounter with you here, or should I drive to Fur, where your ashes are scattered? Where would it be most likely that I would meet you? This became a big dilemma for me the evening before my trip to Fur on the first anniversary of our ashes-scattering ceremony. The trip had been planned for weeks, but now I was in great doubt.

I told my wise, long-term friend, Lene, about my doubts, when she came to pick up my cat, Musse, whom she had promised to take care of while I was away. Having listened quietly to my detailed account of the dilemma, Lene, who is a practicing psychologist, looked at me, and said: 'What do you think your beloved would have advised you to do?' And in the very moment when Lene said this, all doubts vanished, and I became totally sure about what I wanted to do. I should go. You, my love, were always so good at cutting through to the key issue, when I or you were oscillating back and forth in relation to a dilemma. 'Now we can't spend more time on this oscillation back and forth. Now we must come to a decision no matter what!' This was always your approach in such moments. Sometimes you even suggested that we should draw lots, when we were going to make difficult decisions. When the result then pointed us in a specific direction, you said that we should pay attention to our immediate response: did we feel it was a pity that the lot had marked out this particular direction, or did it feel the right thing to do? If we felt that it was fine to go in this direction, we should just do that, but if we felt that it was a pity to follow the advice of the lot, we should do the opposite. The important thing, you said, was that the lot-drawing pushed us beyond indecision and blocked agency into an either-or, which would force us to choose and give our actions certain directions rather than others.

Lene's question called forward a memory of your strong antipathy against feeling confined in a state of indecision, and it also immediately stood out to me with unmisunderstandable clarity that what you would reply – not without an ironic expression on your face – was: 'What the hell are you doubting about? Now you've taken my ashes all the way to Limfjorden and scattered them a year ago, and now you don't even bother to come and visit me there!!!!!' This sentence, which blazed through my mind like lightning from a cloudless sky when Lene asked her wise question, made me laugh – a redeeming laughter. I told Lene that I was totally sure what you would have answered. She laughed as well, and my decision was made. The next morning, I packed the car and drove to Limfjorden, filled with expectations that I would meet you there in a new way.

At Limfjorden and Fur, there are absolutely no memories of your living body or the subject you were. In contrast, your body, now metamorphosed into ashes mixed with diatomaceous sand and earth, is very much physically present. Perhaps, I thought, I will find some new ways there of breaching the wall of silence that arose around you when you died? Is this the message that the changes in your countenance, caught in the photos of your dead body, which we took before the undertaker drove you away, tried to make me understand?

Since I took the decision to follow your spectral call and go to Fur on your seventy-eighth birthday, which coincided with the first anniversary of the scattering of your ashes, I have gone there every summer. I have become deeply committed to the assemblage of ashes, sea, cliff, caves, springs bubbling out of the cliffs, waves, wind, island, diatomaceous sand, living algae, oyster shells, coloured stones, wild honeysuckle, raspberries, pine trees, ants, singing birds, shrieking seagulls, sunbathing seals, etc. – the assemblage of which your ashes are a part, and which my ashes will one day blend into as well.

Between Spectral Embraces and Alien Encounters

Together with the poem *Fur*, the autobiographical story *Will I Meet You Here or There?* thematizes a shift. On the one hand, the mourning 'I' is attracted to a world of spectral embraces and encounters with the beloved as the embodied subject she once was, occurring in a spacetime saturated with memories from before her becoming-imperceptible. On the other hand, a world of co-becoming with the beloved's metamorphosed material remains is opened up, located in a new space (the cliff-seabed-beach assemblage at Fur, of which my beloved's ashes have become a part) and in *Aionic* time beyond a linear chrononormative time's before-and-after thinking. This shift is sustained by the difference between the two places: the house in Odense that my beloved and I shared for almost forty years, and the beaches, seabed and cliffs of the island of Fur. The house embodies our past life together and makes up a rich arena for spectral encounters with my beloved, whose actions and material traces (as dust, things associated with memories, effects of her previous actions, pictures, etc.) are present everywhere. In contrast to our house, Fur is a place that we never visited together when my beloved was still a living embodied subject. Fur holds no memories or material traces of any earlier co-presence, but, nevertheless, the assemblages that meet the 'I' there are proliferating with an abundance of vibrant, inhuman agencies which suck me in, just as much as the house does. I suggest that a reflection on the shift between these two iconically different spacetimes, the house in Odense and Fur, articulated in both *Will I Meet You Here or There?* and the poem *Fur*, can take further the understanding of the plateaus of transitioning beyond bouncing against the wall of silence, occurring in Parts II and III of *Dreamscapes – A Triptych* and in *Resurrection*.

As I have explained, the transitioning process is to be understood as emerging from a rhizomatic assemblage of dreams, intuitions, affects, philosophical and poetic reflections, wilful searches for new relations to my beloved's remains unfolding in self-organized spiritual-material practices, and, finally, feelings of somehow being called out by my dead beloved. What I would like to underline at this stage of the analysis is that I see this calling as dual. On the one hand, it resonates with experiences of my beloved's spectral presence, which was prompted in *Will I Meet You Here or There?* by my friend Lene's wise question. On the other hand, the calling is entangled with my experience of my beloved's material remains, now embedded in the assemblage of seabed, diatomaceous sand etc. at Fur. I see my responses to the dual calling from these two agencies as that which together has enabled me to breach the wall of silence, and has taught me to experience my beloved's becoming-imperceptible in new, dynamic ways. But I also claim that my response was sustained and enabled by the ontological turn from my atheist beliefs in death as nothingness to an immanence philosophical understanding of death's vibrancy. Finally, I consider the breaching as an event in a Deleuzean sense, i.e. as an actualization of certain, virtually present, immanent potentials. To push the analysis of these potentials further, I shall look at the difference between their materialization as spectral encounters and as alien ones. For my lens I shall use the difference between the I–you relationship of *Resurrection* and that of *Will I Meet You Here or There?* and *Fur*.

What makes *Will I Meet You Here or There?* and *Fur* different from *Resurrection* is that the former do not cast the spectrally embodied human 'you', returning as an apparition from the past, as the only phenomenal and spatiotemporal mattering of the dead beloved who attracts the desiring attention of the 'I'. Instead, they explore a self-reflexive refocusing of the attention of the mourning 'I' from an exclusionary concentration on a spectral 'you', shaped as the human subject who was, to a focus on a totally different – alien – kind of 'you'. This is a 'you' who, instead of enacting a spectral return, takes on a new, inhuman shape, ready for completely different encounters in what Deleuze theorizes as *Aionic* time. This is the time of the instant, which, as opposed to the chrononormatively limited now, is not located on a chronological timeline of past, present and future (Deleuze 2020: 167–72). The ways in which the alien 'you' is enacting its vitally material attraction, sucking the 'I' into its embraces, resonates for me so much with Deleuze's description of the time of *Aion*, characterized by the instantaneousness of multiple, intense becomings in all directions beyond any chrononormative chronologies.

In an immanence philosophical sense, the emergence of this new, alien 'you' is to be understood as prompted both by the spectral agency of my beloved as the subject she was, but, in particular, by immanent agencies of the new assemblages, i.e. by something which, in contrast to the spectre, does not relate to a past, but exists unambiguously in the instant of a totally new and alien encounter. The autobiographical fact that I never visited Fur together with my partner, and that neither of us had any relations to the place until my beloved started to buy oysters from the area shortly before she died, sustains my ability to unfold a relationship with Fur as an assemblage of inhuman forces, and as a figuration of a spacetime for new encounters in a *zoe*-based and *Aionic* sense. In resonance with these efforts to relate to the Fur assemblage – the cliffs of the island, the waters, my beloved's ashes, now mixed with diatomaceous sand at the bottom of the waters beyond the cliffs – I try, in a spiritual-material sense, to make my annual visit to the island materialize as an alien encounter.

What do I mean by 'alien' here? When death from an immanence philosophical perspective means that the subject vanishes, it is implied that the mourning 'I' must give up human ways of communicating – for the simple reason that they are rendered impossible by the imperceptibility of the passed-away subject. No channels of interaction, defined within the framework of ontologies celebrating exceptionally human channels of communication, work in relation to the world of the dead. Dualist Christian thought has, indeed, tried to bridge the gap between the living and the dead by focusing on the immortal soul and the possibility for the mourning 'I' to comfort himself while looking forward to renewed communication in a heavenly afterlife. However, within an immanence philosophical framework, pathways to transgressing the wall of imperceptibility must be sought in body, matter and trans- and intercorporeal assemblages, and *not* in a 'soul', conceived as the fiction of an immaterial entity, forever detached from matter. Moreover, what is ultimately at stake must be conceptualized as an encounter with the inhuman/*zoe* other, which radically evades any kind of exceptionalizing anthropomorphization. I interpellate the conceptual framework of an alien encounter here to indicate a move towards co-becoming beyond human horizons, including those of spectral apparitions whose embrace, despite their fundamental way of challenging the sovereign, rational, human 'I' of Western modernity, still bears the hallmarks of a human past.

Fur is a contemplation of an alien encounter in this sense. Leaving behind her desire for the beloved's spectral resurrection as the embodied subject she was in the house in Odense, the mourning 'I' immerses herself in the 'you''s new, inhuman and alien world of *zoe*-based assemblages of ashes/diatomaceous-sand/cliffs/sea. The posthuman, alien I–you relationship in *Fur* is set in motion through the spatial contrast between 'home' (Stanza 1) and 'the coast of Limfjorden/Fur' (Stanza 2). The former is cast as an arena for the beloved's spectral presence, related to memories of the previous human–human relationship between the 'I' and the 'you'. In contrast, the latter is only associated with an intimate relationship to the beloved's ashes, and it is therefore open to the exploration of a new relationship. Along these lines, Stanza 2 of the poem is a poetic exploration of the 'I's corpo-affective and spiritual-material relation to the Fur assemblage of sand/sea/cliff/fossilized algae, of which the ashes have become part. The lyric 'I' sensitizes herself to the assemblage, immersing herself corpo-affectively and sensually in the waters, cliffs and flora. As the poem unfolds, the 'I' becomes embraced more and more profoundly by land- and seascapes, pervaded by their vibrant agency, touching upon the miraculous (e.g. 'how long can it rain from a cloudless sky?', Stanza 2). The poem's trans- and intercorporeal merging peaks when, at the end of Stanza 2, the 'I' anticipates her own becoming-ashes and her ultimate becoming-one with the assemblage of 'you'/ashes/seabed/sand/algae-fossils/watery environment.

The poem articulates the process of co-becoming and the ways in which it is imaginatively related to the lyric 'I''s sexually toned submitting herself to the land- and seascapes of the Fur assemblage, while being guided by an attraction, ultimately, to become-one with it herself. In this sense, the poem establishes the relationship between the lyric 'I', the 'you' and the Fur Formation as radically posthuman and alien: the assemblage of seabed, island, cliffs and fossilized diatoms, with which the ashes of the beloved are now completely merged, are imagined as radically different from the embodied human subject that she was, and the 'I's embeddedness in this assemblage is radically different from the previous human-human-relationship. The point of view and position of enunciation of *Fur* is located with the mourning 'I' and her co-becoming with the inhuman assemblages, cast as 'you'. Notably, though, the alien agencies of the latter are marked out all the way through. The lyric 'I' is drawn and pushed by the inhuman and alien forces of these assemblages, rather than acting according to the wilful choices of a sovereign human subject. This being drawn, rather than acting wilfully, resonates with an *un*-exceptionalizing and *de*-individualizing of the poetic 'I'.

Between Molar and Molecular Mourning

To finalize my contemplations on the wall of silence, and the ways in which it became breachable and started to crumble, I shall wrap up how the immanence philosophical understanding of death as becoming-imperceptible and becoming-one-with-*zoe* resonates overall with my autophenomenographic analysis of the mourning 'I's transitioning, as it unfolds in this chapter. More precisely, I will provide a summarizing reading of the transitioning with the Deleuzoguattarian distinction between the molar and the molecular as lens. This move allows me to conceptualize a key difference between the plateau of lonely bouncing against the wall of silence, and those of the spectral and alien encounters beyond it.

As briefly mentioned already, the molar is that which is a complete entity from a macro-perspective, e.g. a full human body with organs. The molecular, in contrast, is that which performs at the microlevel of molecules and particles, e.g. the body as intensity, vibrancy and movement, which Deleuze and Guattari conceptualize as a body without organs (Deleuze and Guattari 1988: 149–66). According to Deleuze and Guattari, all becomings are always already molecular in the sense that they are neither about imitating or identifying with some kind of entity, e.g. a human subject, nor related to any formal proportions, e.g. a full embodiment of this subject. Becomings are instead related to the establishing of connections at the levels of particles in movement:

> Starting from the forms one has, the subject one is, the organs one has, or the functions one fulfills, becoming is to extract particles between which one establishes the relations of movement and rest, speed and slowness that are *closest* to what one is becoming, and through which one becomes.
>
> Deleuze and Guattari 1988: 272

Basically, then, becoming implies a yielding of the embodied subject as molar, i.e. as a subjectivized entity, endowed with a body that is proportional in terms of being a well-ordered collection of organs with specific functions, in favour of entering into totally fluid states where only shifting assemblages of intensely moving molecules and particles count. Becoming-imperceptible – and dying – is, as discussed, one of these states, but a significant one insofar as it is defined as 'the immanent end of becoming, its cosmic formula' (ibid.: 279), i.e. as a going-molecular in an ultimate sense.

As I look at the transitionings of the mourning 'I' with this distinction between the molar and the molecular in mind, I suggest that the shift between lonely bouncing, on the one hand, and engagement in spectral embraces and alien encounters with the dead beloved, who has ultimately gone-molecular, on the other, can be understood as a move from molar to molecular mourning. Molar mourning is thus to be seen as referring to practices that are carried by memories of the passed-away beloved as the entitized human subject she was, entangled with resistances to the process of inhumanization – and ultimate molecularization – which is taking place as the beloved becomes-imperceptible/one-with-*zoe*. These resistances take many forms. In the previous chapter, I discussed how resistance to the inhumanization process of the corpse is conventionally embedded, for example, in traditions of embalming, staged photography, the closing of the eyes and binding of jaw, etc. I also pinpointed how I rejected these kinds of conventional practices myself. Nonetheless, I want to underline that this does not mean that I claim to be able to skip resistance to the inhumanization and becoming-molecular of my beloved just like that. On the contrary, her molecularization and my so-very-painful experiences of amputation, of having my conjoined twin cut off from my body, are totally entangled. In innumerable ways, this amputation wound and the phantom pains emerging from it made and still make me try to passionately keep 'intact', i.e. molar, the memories of my relationship with my beloved as the embodied human entity she was. I cultivate these memories through our shared house, family, friends, cat, artefacts, photos, music, books, etc. – and this abundance of memories is closely related to molarity. It would be an illusion if I pretended that, in spite of my commitment to new posthuman – and molecular – mourning practices, I am not simultaneously also deeply immersed in desire for my flesh-and-blood, queermasculine beloved as the molar human entity she was.

I also want to underline that I do not see molar mourning per se as a bad activity that should be policed or exorcized. I claim a right to all kinds of excessive mourning, even molar ones. However, the immanence philosophical approach has made me aware that molar mourning and painful, lonely bouncing against the wall of silence are perhaps two sides of the same coin. In other words, I suggest that resistance towards accepting the process of inhumanization which the dead beloved's going-molecular and becoming-imperceptible/one-with-*zoe* may constitute is precisely that which blocks the opening up of new horizons in the direction of less painful mourning practices. It is my thesis that such a block is kept up when the mourner is confined in desire to remain in a fixed and immutable past, in molar memories of that which was. Remaining in such a perception of the past means clinging to something that cannot exist in the present, because the beloved as molar entity, embodied human subject with identity and proportions, has vanished forever. Therefore, clinging to this perception, and the chrononormative timeline on which it is based, will keep the mourning 'I' suspended in the devastating feeling of amputation, and overwhelming loss and lack. I claim that it is this devastating feeling of loss and lack – the impossibility of fulfilling the desire to be with the beloved in a molar sense, i.e. as the embodied human subject she was – which produces the experience of bouncing against the wall of silence. In this sense, molar mourning practices can become potentially destructive for the mourner. If such practices stand alone, without being mixed with other, more vital and affirmative, mourning activities, molar mourning locks the mourner into a nostalgic longing along a linear chronology, which, at the same time, is cast and experienced as irreversible. However, I should also underline that I might have stayed in these molar mourning practices, had I not gone to Fur on the anniversary of our scattering of my beloved's ashes there, prompted by the spectral and alien calling of my beloved and my friend Lene's wise question (as described in *Will I Meet You Here or There*?).

In contrast to molar mourning, what I shall define as molecular mourning can no doubt be embedded in many different lines of flight and processes of becoming. As described in this chapter, the process of becoming a molecular mourner has been actualized for me through spectral embraces and alien encounters. Since the molecularity of these two kinds of actualizations are different, I shall take a final look at them one by one.

As discussed in my autophenomenographic analysis of the second and third parts of *Dreamscapes – A Triptych*, and *Resurrection*, as well as through my reference to the spectral aspects of my beloved's calling me in *Will I Meet You Here or There?*, the spectral embrace is a materialization of an affirmative I–you relationship, which is to be understood, first of all, as radically different from a meeting of two molar subjects/bodies. Spectres and *revenants* – as I have discussed them through a Derridean lens – are to be understood as phenomenal, but not in a molar sense. In popular belief, spectres are known for their ability to walk through walls and overcome other barriers that are considered insurmountable for molar bodies that can only act in space, circumscribed by Newtonian physics. I think that the extra-human abilities of spectres can be considered as popular wisdom's way of articulating the concept that spectral phenomenality is molecular in a Deleuzoguattarian sense, rather than molar. The molecularity of spectres means that you have to learn to undo your own molar subjectivity and embodiment in order to intra-act with them, and I think such an undoing is precisely what is articulated in Parts II and III of *Dreamscapes – A Triptych, Resurrection* and *Will I Meet You Here or There?* In all three texts, the poetic 'I' makes herself open to embraces with a 'you' who is explicitly marked out as a *revenant*, a spectral apparition of a sleeping or waking dream, or summoned by a calling (such as the one that was prompted by my friend Lene's question in *Will I Meet You Here or There?*). The ways in which these texts explicitly mark the 'you' as spectrally returning makes the portrayed encounter between the mourning 'I' and 'you' different from an act of memorizing, enacted as part of a molar mourning process. It should be noted that the spectral apparition of the 'you' in these texts somewhat resembles the entity appearing in molar processes of memorizing, i.e. the embodied human subject which the beloved was. However, the elusiveness of the spectre, as well as the strange temporalities it interpellates, make it overwhelmingly clear to the mourner that its phenomenality is very different from the molar entity that was. When, for example, I look at photos of my partner, it is a molar object, my beloved at a certain, frozen moment in the past, that lies before my eyes. The figure in the photo is not in any way elusive; it is congealed and static, and I can keep it in front of me as long as I want. But I cannot transgress the experience of an insurmountable temporal distance between that past frozen moment, captured in the photo, and me, as a viewing subject in the now. In contrast, the spectral apparition, whether experienced through sleeping or waking dreams, or as a calling like the one my friend Lene's question prompted me to hear, is completely elusive – it can disappear at any moment. But, at the same time, it is directly intra-acting phenomenally with me in the *Aionic* time of the instant. If I can undo my own molarity and desire for a molar relation as that which was, the spectre is there, and we can enjoy the instant of togetherness.

Molecular mourning, using the spectral embrace as its line of flight, keeps up an I–you relationship which, although decisively different, still has a certain resemblance to the molar one, based on the congealed memories of what was. In contrast, the other kind of molecular mourning to which I am referring, namely the one working along the flightline of an alien encounter, extends beyond any kind of resemblance to a human–human relationship. The alien encounter and co-becoming with the metamorphosed, material remains of my beloved and their new assemblages as algae sand, cliffs and seabed is radically different from a human–human relationship, and this means that an even more radical process of becoming-molecular is required of the mourning 'I'. While the spectral embrace momentarily reassembles the molecules of the 'you' in a quasi-imitation of her former molar embodiment, allowing the 'I' the instantaneous pleasure of a togetherness which, although elusive and molecular, still bears a resemblance to the relationship that was, the actualization of the alien encounter demands that the mourning 'I' dissolves all of her desire to reiterate that which was. This co-becoming with the new assemblages means starting from scratch on totally uncharted, inhuman grounds, completely detached from what was, and de-exceptionalized in a human sense. To co-become with the alien assemblages of the Fur Formation, the mourning 'I' will have to prepare to become alien herself. She has to enable herself to try to become as imperceptible, inhumanized and molecular, as radically dissolved as a molar human being, as is the new 'you'. She has to engage in attempts to unlearn molarity in order to become open to all kinds of metamorphoses together with the new 'you'. The ultimate striving for this radical openness is what I define as molecular mourning with an alien line of flight.

I want to underline that the shift from molar to molecular mourning, which I have reflected upon here, and the process of molecularization of mourning, which also implies a posthumanizing and de-exceptionalizing of human dimensions, is not to be understood as an easy or controlled process, occurring once and for all. Phenomenologically, it is a deeply affect-laden process, and also to be understood as totally open-ended and full of oscillations between molar/human and molecular/posthuman mourning. Notably, alongside a deep and pleasurable engagement with the spectral and the new alien assemblages, I am also still deeply committed to molar memories. I continue to dream about my beloved's vanishing as the human subject I knew, and always awaken with a feeling of immense and irreparable sadness, because, once more, I have been bouncing against the wall of silence. However, unlearning molarity and preparing myself for spectral and alien encounters, has for me also become a question of establishing a vital ethics of affirmation and a material spirituality, both of which I think are politically much needed.

Interlude IV

ARDENTE E ONDEGGIANTE (BURNING AND UNDULATING)

Illustr. 6 Ardente e Ondeggiante (Burning and Undulating). © Nina Lykke 2017.

WHAT REMAINS

1.
I remember the day
when your hair was to be cut off.
You had decided
it should be done
in one go.
A daily dose of radiation against your skull
to decrease the brain metastases
left your pillow covered in black straws
every morning when you got out of bed.
'Better be shaven bald once and for all
than lose my hair slowly
from day to day,'
you said.
Your dark helmet of hair,
your soft, fine hair,
which so many times
has electrified my naked body.
Your shiny dark hair
which made people
think that you were much younger
than me,
even though you were twelve years older.
The hairdresser
arrived with her clippers.
You and she went into the bathroom.
I stayed in the living room
in indecision –
I would not fill the moment
with a sentimentality,
which I knew
you would hate.
'The hair will grow again,
this is only a temporary thing,
you are not dying!
A bald skull is butchy!'
So many incantations.
It happened fast as lightning.
Cut, sweep the floor, put the hair in a garbage bag.
Only a tiny, tiny tuft
avoided the broom.
I found it on the bathroom floor,
and saved it carefully.

Your hair never recovered to the stage,
where it really started to return.
When you died it was one cm long.
But I keep the tiny tuft
which I found on the bathroom floor
that day
when your hair was cut off.

2.
Eigil brought me
two dark brown pearls
to put in your casket.
Fire turned them to white ashes
together with your dead body.
Your blue urn with the white ashes
was lowered into the sea,
where the oysters breed.
Precisely one year after
the day of your death
two light grey pearls came back.
Uffe found them
in an oyster shell.
I keep those two
light grey pearls.

3.
Dark hair,
white ashes,
two dark brown pearls,
metamorphosing
into two light grey pearls,
I carry all of them –
a symbol
that you live
in me.

A PACT

1.
We let go of the line – our last tie to who you were before . . .
With a gurgling, slobbering slurping, the obscenity of which I know you would
    have loved,
the water swallows your blue ecological urn
to be dissolved at the seabed.
Swaddled in a sea-blue fishing net on a bed of oyster shells and beach stones,
you sink to the bottom of Limfjorden
outside of the cliffs of Fur,
close to the habitats of oysters.
The birth of Venus from the womb of the cliffs
in a reverse shot.
Roses gently rocking on the waves.
Somebody spots the head of a seal, enjoying the warm sun.
Naja reads from her story about a devil-may-care Karen Blixen.
We sing 'You are so beautiful and gorgeous.'

'I am coming, my love!'

2.
Seven months earlier . . .
'Don't you think you can take it away, the lu[ng]ca[ncer]?' you say in your
    broken voice.
'The miracle will happen. It disappears tonight,' we tell each other.
'We will go to the oysters together.'
Later you add to our story:
'The wrong disappears, and the right returns.'
It is as though you want once more to confirm that you, too, really believe in
    the miracle.
Your hand moves, electrifying, all over my naked body
I cover your warm body with my kisses.
'You may touch them,' you say,
and I let my fingertips run gently through the long scar fissures
which, since the many operations the previous winter,
crisscross each other on your stomach.
At the foot of your soft mound of Venus
denuded by chemo like the top of your head
my swift tongue laps up salt water from your oyster mouth.
We are reborn as oysters,
forever rocking among seagrass on the bed of the sea.

'I am coming, my love!'

3.
Six months earlier...
We sit together at the white table in the room behind the kitchen.
The darkness of January, brain metastases, slow-motion conversation:
'I'm sorry, it takes so long to gather my thoughts now,' you say.
We sign the necessary papers.
Death has its norms and regulations.
The Ministry of Ecclesiastical Affairs must give its blessing
to allow our ashes to be scattered across the sea.
It is hard work to avoid the embrace of the State Church.
That evening, we eat oysters and celebrate the pact in champagne.

'I am coming, my love!'

4.
Five months earlier...
We carry you in the willow casket from our home
through the Fairy Tale Park to the old chapel
which, thanks to a friendly priest
and a lot of negotiations,
we have been allowed to borrow from the cathedral next door
to conduct our queerfeminist and non-Christian ritual of transition.
Sharp sunlight breaks suddenly through grey January clouds,
as we walk towards the bushes of the rotunda at the centre of the park.
A group of young jugglers and a dancing dog are approaching from the opposite direction.
The jugglers turn away, embarrassed and awkward, when they see our funeral procession.
But the dog keeps dancing happily.
Should laughter yield to mourning?
Or does mourning need laughter?
Mother Trickster becomes impatient. 'Giguggen, Gigaggen!' she shouts. 'Come on!'
The wind rattles the heavy door of the chapel so strongly that it flies open,
as we, standing around your casket, are performing the oyster-pearl ritual:
'Fire to fire, air to air, water to water, earth to earth, body to body.'

'I am coming, my love!'

5.
Four months earlier...
From the kitchen window
I see a fire in the park.
It is midnight.
Soaring flames illuminate the pitch-black space.
I call the fire brigade.

The fire engine cannot find its way.
I guide it over the telephone.
But it takes almost an hour until the fire is extinguished.
The next day I observe how the leaves on branches several metres above the fire
    have been fried dark brown.
All summer, the spot is black and bare of grass.
I wish so ardently to receive signs from you.
Is this a sign?
God appeared to Moses as a burning bush,
we were told in school.
But I never believed that story.

'I am coming, my love!'

6.
Six months after...
It's January again,
It's a year since you died.
I mourn, thinking about your ashes,
scattered in Limfjorden six months ago.
I read Virginia Woolf's farewell letter to Leonard,
which she wrote on March 28, 1941.
You were three years old back then,
and I was not born until eight years later.
I imagine following Virginia –
determined to seek death and ignoring Leonard's protests,
she writes: 'Nothing anyone says can persuade me.'
She left the letter on her writing block in her garden lodge,
then walked the half mile to the River Ouse.
Here she filled her pockets with stones
and waded out into the river until the current took her.
Were you afraid, Virginia, when the river took control of your body?
Did you feel regret, when it was too late?
Or were you happy to feel the force of the water transform
the dead weight of depression to euphoric lightness?
I am not trying to escape depression, as you were, Virginia.
But I admire your feminist wilfulness,
and thank you for the tip.
Your stones make my mourning easier to carry.

'I am coming, my love!'

7.
Here and now...
I read Virginia Woolf's farewell letter once more,
But I write instead:

'No one but you, my love, can persuade me.'
You live in me,
hard and shining as the mother of pearl,
soft and sensitive as oyster flesh.
as an impatient whisper in my ear:
'So, come, my love,
learn the new language.
The language of fire.
Come to me as ashes,
not as flesh.
Flesh to ashes.
Ashes to pearls.
This is the pact.
Don't forget!'
'I am coming my love!
My ashes shall merge with yours!'

SIGNS?

1.
The evening after we had received
the final fatal prognosis,
I asked you to give me something
I could keep with me
after you had passed away.
You gave me the Polish wood carved figure
of a poor woman with a strong face,
marked by deep grief and precarity,
which had attracted your eye
at a market in Warsaw,
where you lived for many months
as a young exchange student.
Now the figure
lies next to me in our double bed.

2.
A multicoloured kitten
moved in with us
a few months before you died.
The kitten's greed for life –
and your immense sorrow
that you had to leave it,
created strange diffraction patterns.

3.
At your funeral ceremony
we heard the wind
rattling the door of the chapel,
but when we looked outside
everything was calm.

4.
Later, the same winter,
a fierce fire broke out,
just across the river.
I stood in the kitchen and looked at
the glow, which illuminated
the midnight park.
It sucked my gaze in,
while ghostly shadows
danced
invitingly on the kitchen wall.
Now I have a small piece of solidified metal,

which was lying for a long time
in the place
where the fire had raged,
until I picked it up
and put it on my kitchen table
among my stones from Fur.

5.
During summer a light drizzling rain,
sunlit raindrop prisms,
caressed my desiring body.
They fell and fell from the cloudless sunset sky
over Limfjorden.

6.
A plant on the windowsill,
given to you as a gift
many years ago,
started to flower excessively
after you died.
You always took special care of this plant,
even when other houseplants did not make it.
But it has never had so many flowers as now.

7.
Two brown pearls were put in your casket.
Two grey pearls returned from the sea
precisely one year after you died.

8.
A song came to me,
as I drove
the long way to Limfjorden
to meet you –
as I drove the car alone,
our car,
that you'd so much loved to drive:

9.
'You can have my Polish figure
when I die.
Since I always loved it dearly
I now give it so you nearly
will be able still to touch me,
when I die.'

10.
'You can have my little kitten,
when I die.
When I now am soon to leave you
she will soothe, where I bereave you.
You can have my little kitten,
when I die.'

11.
'I will speak with windy voices,
when I die.
Breezes softly in your ear sing,
roaring storms you're also hearing.
I will speak with windy voices,
when I die.'

12.
'In the fire, we'll be dancing,
when I die.
Flames us totally embraces,
embers wildly interlaces.
So, in fire, we'll be dancing,
when I die.'

13.
'Raindrops shall caress your body,
when I die.
Through the drops I will excite you,
and their kisses shall ignite you.
Raindrops shall caress your body,
when I die.'

14.
'And my plant will flourish lushly,
when I die.
Lavish flowers, it produces,
and its fragrance you seduces.
And my plant will flourish lushly,
when I die.'

15.
'I shall send a pair of grey pearls,
when I die.
I shall use an oyster sending
them, before the year is ending

I shall send a pair of grey pearls,
when I die.'

16.
From body, air, fire, water, earth, body
we come.
To body, air, fire, water, earth, body
we return.
The circle is connected
'The wrong disappears,
the right returns.'
I come
to you
as ashes,
not as body.
We will meet among algae and oysters at the bottom of the sea.

Interlude IV: Ardente e Ondeggiante – **Ardente**, Italian for burning, is in classic music composing indicating music to be performed with a fiery glow, while **Ondeggiante**, means undulating, moving in waves, and refers to a musical phrasing which intends to awaken a feeling of undulation. The two terms are invoked to articulate an oscillation between passionate intensities related to fire, and to waves on the sea. Both elements are central to the posthumous metamorphoses of my beloved's dead body, which was burnt to ashes, and after that scattered over the waters of Limfjorden. But, together with this reference to cremation and ashes scattering over the sea, fire and water are also more generally indexing the whole cluster of elements which made up key components of the funeral ceremony which together with rainbow kin and friends, I arranged for my dead beloved. It was built up around fire, air, water, earth and bodily matter, which all of them also have become central to the materialist spirituality which I developed. I explore this spirituality in the poems of *Interlude IV*, *What Remains*, *A Pact*, and *Signs?*, preparing for **Chapter 5**'s contemplations of **Miraculous Co-Becomings?** with the assemblage of seabed, ashes, sand, sea critters such as algae and oysters, with which the waters of Limfjorden abound.

Chapter 5

MIRACULOUS CO-BECOMINGS?

Do miracles happen?[1] If so, how can we understand them? In this and the next chapter, I will circle around these questions, but give no definitive answers. Like dreams and spectres, miracles are elusive phenomena. They evade the sovereign subject's efforts to control and conceptualize them in unambiguous positivist terms. They can neither be willed into existence, nor confined to universal definitions. I want to reflect upon an onto-epistemology and ethics of the miraculous, while acknowledging that the miraculous is entangled with the lines of flight (dreaming, spectral and alien encounters) to which my excessive mourning has committed me, and fully shares the elusiveness of these flightlines.

However, while being fully prepared to take into account the elusiveness of miracles, I still also recognize that the question of the miraculous is slippery in more ways than one. I want to take my spiritual-material intuitions, and poetic knowledge seeking, seriously into account. But I am also keen not to cheat myself in a superficial New Age manner, creating comforting fata morganas out of my desire for reconnection. Moreover, I am painfully aware of the ways in which a focus on the miraculous can easily allow dualist beliefs in divine and human exceptionalizing interventions to slip in through the back door. Even though I was brought up as an incarnated atheist, and as an adult continued to commit myself to atheism, for my whole life I have been entangled in Western imaginaries, which are pervaded by Christian values, thought figures, and narratives which, therefore, might sneak in unacknowledged. Finally, as well as taking all these *caveats* into account, I also need to address my atheist doubts seriously, which prompt me to scrutinize how, philosophically, I can sustain my intuitions and poetic understandings of the miraculous events I experienced as part of my process of mourning, and have articulated in the poems of *Interlude IV*, *Ardente e Ondeggiante*.

The bottom line, though, is that I take the risk. I embark upon the slippery slope in order to reclaim the miraculous for a materialist spirituality, and a spiritualist materialism. I want to contribute to a de-territorializing, and to a disruption of the ways in which monotheistic religions, among them Christianity, have monopolized and colonized the miraculous, confining it within authoritarian, elitist, and dualist belief systems. Moreover, this and the next chapter's forays into the miraculous are also part of my questioning of the limitations of modern secular scientific imaginaries and atheist philosophies of death as nothingness, which relegate the miraculous to the realm of so-called 'premodern', 'primitive' superstition and/or madness. My aim is to transgress both the dualist Christian understanding of the miraculous, and the positivist, secular-scientific rejections of it. Overall, the chapter's attempt to understand the miraculous differently is embedded in my ethico-political commitment to a queering, posthumanizing, and decolonizing of questions about the so-called 'afterlife', which for so long have been left in the hands of spokespersons for dualist religions or discarded as nothingness.

For me, it is of key importance for the discussion I am going to unfold that I am in doubt about the ontology of miracles, as much as I am unsure about how to ontologize the lines of flight through dreams, spectral and alien encounters addressed in the last chapter. Nonetheless, my intuitions give me an unambiguous certainty. Intuitively, I am as certain about the rhizomatic cluster of miraculous events that I experienced both before and after the death of my beloved, as I am about my dreams, and my spectral and alien encounters. In this sense, I do not doubt the miraculous qualities of the experiences I poetically articulate in the poems of *Interlude IV*, and in the story *A Miraculous Event?* which I will tell in this chapter. This is qualities which I further elaborate in the interview presented in *Interlude V, Milagrosa*, located between this and the next chapter. Furthermore, intuitively, I have no doubts at all about the transcorporeal, vibrantly material agencies, extending far beyond my powers as a human subject, in which the cluster of miracles that occurred as part of my excessive mourning entangled me. I have already hinted at these powers through the previous chapter's focus on the agencies of dreams, spectres, and the Fur assemblages. Now I shall take a step further into the discussion of these agencies. A key focus of this chapter and the next is a scrutiny of the question of whether, and if so how, it is possible to make philosophical sense of the miraculous events of which I became part.

I approach the miraculous co-becomings articulated in my poems and stories in a way that links immanence philosophical, vitalist new-materialist thought with indigenous-inspired non-modern or a-modern approaches to spiritmatter. Linking these approaches, I subscribe to a pluriversal (Tlostanova and Mignolo 2012) onto-epistemology, i.e. one that does not universalize modern Western outlooks. Moreover, as far as terminologies are concerned, let me also mention that I use the terms non-modern and a-modern in line with Bruno Latour (1993), in order to avoid the linear progress narrative embedded in the concepts modern/*pre*modern. I endorse Latour's point that 'we' (so-called 'moderns'), in fact have never been 'modern' in the sense that our strictly and scientifically sustained purifications of categorical divisions between nature/culture, subject/object, mind/matter, and natural/supernatural perhaps worked pragmatically in some (often rather violently oppressive) ways, yet still only came about through vast reductions in complexity; these purified divisions were never really fit to provide the full and universal picture they promised to deliver. Finally, when speaking of spiritmatter, I refer to the mattering of spirit, understood as a vital immanent force. In so doing, I draw inspiration from the work of decolonial and posthuman feminist theorist Felicia Amaya Schaeffer's (2018) analysis of convergences between queerfeminist and decolonial scholar Gloria Anzaldua's indigenous-centred philosophy (1987, 2015) and feminist posthumanism.

To discuss the potentially miraculous effects of the transcorporeally acting assemblages of which my beloved's ashes have become a part, this chapter starts with a Spinoza-inspired question: What can dead bodies do? Building on my reflections on the vibrant corpse (Chapter 3), and its metamorphoses (Chapter 4), I allow this question to guide me through an analysis of the story *A Miraculous Event?* and the poem *What Remains*. Taking seriously my methodology of being true to my intuitions, but also sustaining them philosophically, I try to make sense of a key miracle, which is described in these two texts. I also scrutinize my intuition that my contemplations of this miracle somehow led me to interpellate Jung's notion of synchronicity (2008 [1955]) – a notion which I only reluctantly invite into my text and reflections. My reluctance stems from the problems that I see in adhering to Jung's concept; in particular, because I consider it to be embedded in a too human-centred mysticism. However, by entering into a critical conversation with Jung's concept, this chapter provides a reinterpretation of the phenomenon of synchronicity against the background of Bennett's reflections on vibrant matter, thing-power, and affect (2010: 2–17).

In Chapter 6, I follow up with a pluriversal reflection on the miraculous, diffracting the Bennett-inspired approach with a series of other approaches. More precisely, I summon a sounding board to help me create a cartography and frame an onto-epistemology and ethics of the miraculous, which can account for the rhizome of miracles, also articulated in the poems *Signs?* and *A Pact*. In so doing, I fulfil two requirements which I consider to be both philosophically and ethically crucial. On the one hand, the framing must allow the upholding of an understanding that casts miracles as fundamentally elusive and incomprehensible phenomena. On the other hand, the framing should ensure that the reductionist traps of positivism are evaded. These are the traps that require a rejection of phenomenal agencies and reality effects which cannot be verified by positivist procedures. In this sense, the argument of the chapter follows up on Chapter 4's reflections on the onto-epistemologies of flightlines, related to dreams and spectral and alien encounters. To fulfil these requirements, the sounding board, summoned in Chapter 6, is composed such that it can facilitate conversations between immanence philosophical, vitalist materialist, posthumanist frameworks, and indigenous, spiritualist materialist, and decolonizing ones. Towards the end of that chapter, I revisit the rhizomatic cluster of miraculous events articulated in my poems and stories, in order to contemplate their alignment with the suggested onto-epistemological framings, and to link the discussion of an ethics of the miraculous specifically to a posthuman phenomenology of mourning.

The Agency of Dead Human Bodies and Their Inhuman Remains

In Chapter 4, I discussed the shifting of the position of enunciation from sovereign to mourning 'I'. Now, I shall take a look at a further shift – a shift in the distribution of agency, away from the human subject to vibrant, transcorporeal assemblages. In the previous chapter, I twisted the Spinozean question – what can bodies do? (1996 [1677]: 71) – in order to apply it to dreams. Now I shall give it yet another twist, and ask: what can dead human bodies and their inhuman remains do?

To enter into a reflection of this question is simultaneously straightforward and complicated. It is straightforward when I take a point of departure in Spinoza's monistic thought, and the ways in which it has been further developed by Deleuzean philosophy. If there is only one dynamic and vital substance, one conative striving of all matter to persevere (ibid.: 75), then, as discussed earlier in the book, we must see life and death as a flat continuum. This implies that the body's *conatus* must be understood as cross-cutting the life/death threshold, i.e. applying to living bodies as well as to dying, dead and decaying ones, human as well as non-human. Or, in other words, when the human corpse is no longer seen as just a piece of mechanics, left by the soul or by the Cartesian ghost in the machine (Ryle 1949), and considered instead from within an immanence philosophical frame as an inhuman material vibrancy, the corporeal remains of this dead body must be understood as pervaded by *conatus* just as much as the living body that was there before. From this perspective, the inhuman remains must be conceived of as capable of doing, in a Spinozean sense – as endowed with the ability to affect and be affected – just as the living body used to be.

This is the straightforward, immanence philosophical answer to the question 'what can dead human bodies and their inhuman remains do?' However, seen from the perspective of the mourning 'I', to answer like this seems comforting, but too easy. Since my beloved's death, the question of the *conatus* of the dead human body, its inhuman remains and their transcorporeal assemblages has been very much on my agenda. My becoming as a philosopher-poet of the mourning 'I' has made me painstakingly aware of all the complications that this question opens up, even though the answer might at first glance seem straightforward. In addition to being thrown into a mess of complications, the process has taught me that there is not much help to be got, either from Spinoza or Deleuze, when it comes to the specifics of dead bodies' doings. Bennett's reflections on the agencies of thing-power and assemblages, understood as conative – vibrant – matter (2010), and Braidotti's posthuman death theory (2013), which I discussed in Chapter 4, are the closest I have come to finding useful frameworks for thinking about these specifics. But, still, when it comes to the questions of the specific agencies and vibrancies of dead bodies, neither Braidotti nor Bennett are very outspoken. Braidotti is primarily focused on the doings of living, embodied subjects, including those who want to self-style[2] their own death (2006: 249–50) rather than on grappling with the question of the agencies of dead bodies. Bennett reflects in-depth on the vibrancies of non-human assemblages and things, and on the ways in which embodied human subjects have to learn to understand themselves not as sovereign, but as vitally material parts of these assemblages (2010: 14). But she only touches in passing upon the question of how dead bodies may actually act as entangled parts of these assemblages.

Bennett's rich account of many different kinds of organic and inorganic, conative – vibrant – matter only addresses one corpse explicitly and specifically, namely a dead rat (ibid.: 4). The corpse of this rat is part of a garbage assemblage, which Bennett interestingly uses to define her notion of thing-power, i.e. things' power to act (ibid.: 2–17), and to discuss the affective agencies of vital non-human actants (Latour 1996: 373). However, the rat's transgression of the life/death threshold is only mentioned in passing. Bennett describes how the rat corpse – together with other organic and inorganic parts of the garbage assemblage (a plastic glove, a plastic bottle cap, a mat of oak pollen and a stick of wood) – strongly and suddenly catches her attention, while she is walking along a street and sees these items in a gutter (2010: 4). She enrols this assemblage in her text in order to address the impersonal, but forceful affectivity of vibrantly material thing-power. The assemblage of these things, she tells the reader, made a strong affective impression on her, forcefully demonstrating that so-called 'waste' does not vanish, but instead keeps on acting, even when it lands in the gutter.

A key point for Bennett is to state that the organic/inorganic distinction is not important for an understanding of the agency and affectivity of thing-power. In this argument, the rat counts as an organic thing in line both with other organic things (pollen, stick of wood) and inorganic ones (glove, bottle cap). The rat's metamorphosing from alive to dead, though, does not matter in Bennett's account. Still, almost inadvertently and parenthetically, Bennett does give the rat's passing a moment of special attention. She speculates about its death through a reference to the violent human agency that may have caused it: the act of a successful rat poisoner. She also displays a kind of ambivalence which bears something of a resemblance to that which, in Chapter 3, I discussed as a common response to human corpses – making them oscillate between being abject and not-dead-at-all-only-sleeping. Bennett notes that the rat corpse repels her, but in an almost quasi-anthropomorphizing way, in a parenthesis (2010: 4), she also poses the casual question: perhaps the rat was not dead at all, but only sleeping?

As it is Bennett's intention here to radically erase hierarchies and blur the boundaries between dead/living, organic/inorganic, animate/inanimate, human/inhuman matter, and to underline that 'inferior' gutter existences are just as conative, agentic and materially vital as is the embodied human subject, whose intense affective attention they irresistibly attract, she certainly achieves her goal. However, I would have liked to hear more about the dead rat. How/why did it attract more intense, if only momentary, attention from the vitally material human subject (Bennett) than the other parts of the assemblage? Did the rat's doings change when it passed the life/death threshold, and if so, how? Did it challenge new hierarchies and blur other boundaries when it became a corpse? Why these reflections on the acts of the potential poisoner? Why did the rat corpse, in a quasi-anthropomorphic way, start to oscillate between being 'dead' and 'perhaps-only-sleeping' in front of the vitally affected human subject? Why did it appear as so abject to her? Did its ratness and its corpseness intra-act,[3] and did this intra-action make the overwhelmingly abject thing-power, which thanks to Freud (1909) and Deleuze and Guattari (1988: 233) we know may emanate from rats, become even more intense to the human subject becoming-affected than it would have been, had the rat 'only' been sleeping? Questions abound for those who, like me, want to understand the vibrancies of dead bodies and their power to affect everything and everybody, the living, the dead, the undead, and the non/living.

To open the discussion of questions related to the vibrant doings of dead bodies and their remains, I take these vitalist materialist and immanence philosophical frameworks as my frame of reference. But I also need to take them further. So, I shall diffract[4] them with the posthuman phenomenology that I have developed through my poetic and autophenomenographic explorations of intuitions, emerging from my spiritual-material unfolding of mourning practices. To set the scene for this diffraction and the chapter's exploration of the agency of dead human bodies, their inhuman remains, and transcorporeal assemblages, I shall start with a cartographic exploration of different modes of doing of dead bodies. I shall do this through an analysis of the story *A Miraculous Event?* and the poem *What Remains*. More precisely, I shall bring Bennett's notion of affective and vibrant thing-power (2010: 2–17), which refers to the agency of non-human assemblages, into conversation with my reflections on the doings of dead human bodies, their inhuman remains and transcorporeal assemblages. The analysis will be a launchpad for raising open-ended questions regarding the potential powers of these assemblages to generate miracles. But let me first tell the story that articulates the most outspokenly phenomenal miracle which was part of the rhizomatic cluster of miraculous events that I unexpectedly experienced through my process of mourning and learning to co-become with my dying and dead beloved, and her inhuman remains.

A Miraculous Event?

On the first anniversary of my beloved's death, a strange thing happened. In remembrance of my beloved, our son, Uffe had bought oysters from Limfjorden, where six months earlier we had scattered his mother's, my beloved's, ashes. In one of these oysters, he found two grey pearls. Oyster pearls are extremely rare. My beloved and I have eaten many oysters in our lifetime, but never ever found a single pearl. However, Uffe found two in one oyster on this very special occasion! He gave me the two pearls as a present with the words that in some way they symbolically represented my beloved and me. That the two grey pearls landed on Uffe's plate was in itself an event which touched upon the miraculous. However, the miraculous qualities stood out even more, because these two grey pearls matched two brown ones, which also had a symbolic meaning. They had been provided by Eigil, our other son, one year earlier as part of the gift giving involved in our self-invented funeral ritual. This ritual built upon a mythlike story which my beloved and I had jointly imagined shortly before her death, following a sudden and out-of-the-blue moment of shared intuitive insight that a miracle would make the cancer disappear from her body and allow us to bodily reconnect (memorialized in Stanza 2 of A Pact*). This myth was a story about meeting again as grains of ashes-sand in a place with many oyster beds, where perhaps an oyster would use both of us to grow pearls. The two brown pearls, symbolizing my beloved and me, had been put into her casket. We did this as a* symbolic act meant to pave the way for our future reconnection as ashes-sand at the bottom of the sea. This act was also designed to be a public and ritual confirmation of the pact my beloved and I had made (and involved our rainbow family in) right before her death – a pact which involved a promise that our ashes should be scattered in the same place. Against this backdrop, it was difficult not to intuitively experience it as part of a rhizomatic cluster of related miraculous events, when, one year after my beloved's death and cremation – which involved the two brown pearls being burnt to ashes insofar as they were in the casket – two grey pearls, carried inside an oyster, came back from Limfjorden, where the ashes had been scattered. In between, I had been struck by the miraculous qualities of a rhizomatic cluster of other events – all somehow related to my own and my rainbow family's process of mourning, and to my beloved's material transitioning from living to dead flesh, cremated to ashes, scattered over the sea (Limfjorden) beyond the island of Fur, and mixed with sand in the seabed, made of fiftyfive-million-year-old, fossilized diatom algae. I have memorialized all these events in the poems Signs? and A Pact. I was awestruck by the ways in which all of these events offered themselves to me as strange and totally unexpected, but transcorporeally and intensely affectively mattering, coincidences. But of all these events, the returning pearls was by far the strangest. It was the only one that could not make sense as anything but a miracle, totally in resonance with the miraculous moment of shared intuition that my beloved and I had had before she died. It was the one thing which, even in my moments of greatest doubt, could not but reconvince me with its miraculous phenomenality.

Desiring to acknowledge the miraculous qualities of what had happened here, I asked a jewellery artist, Trine Trier,[5] whose art is inspired by the sea, to make me a necklace, which iconically embodies this rhizomatic cluster of miracles. Trine and I composed the necklace together – with three parts. The two oyster pearls were enclosed in a small tube; some grains of my beloved's ashes were put inside a silver medallion; finally, another small tube was filled with a tiny tuft of my beloved's hair that I had kept since the day she decided to become shaven-headed, when she was losing her hair due to radiation therapy, administered to diminish the wildly growing cancerous metastases in her brain, as described in the poem What Remains.

What Can Vibrant Dead Bodies Do?

I shall begin the discussion of the agency of dead human bodies, their inhuman remains and assemblages, by taking a look at the three parts of my necklace. With Bennett's notion of thing-power, the affective agency of things, as my overall framework, I shall reflect upon the different modes of affective thing-agency they embody.

First, *the tuft of hair*: it acts as a relic. Relics belong to a category of things that, conventionally, are intensely associated with thing-power, albeit most often in divine or exceptionally human meanings, and, undoubtedly, *not* in a vitalist materialist posthuman sense. Nevertheless, I shall start my cartography here, since, with my necklace, I have consciously recalibrated the relic phenomenon to make it part of my self-invented spiritual-material practices. These are practices which, throughout, I have unfolded in conversation with vitalist materialist and immanence philosophical, feminist and posthuman frameworks. Bennett (2010), Braidotti (2006, 2013) and Deleuze and Guattari (1988) were, indeed, my key philosophical sounding boards, when I initiated these practices – sometimes collectively together with rainbow kin and friends, and sometimes by myself – during the months immediately before and after my beloved's death. My funeral speech, as well as the funeral rituals we invented (Lykke 2015), were pervaded by these lines of thought.

Along the lines of Bennett's reflections on thing-power, and my desire to bring it into conversation with the doings of dead bodies, I argue that relics are interesting because, conventionally, they are defined as things that are pervaded by vibrant powers to affect, due to their corporeal relation to the body of someone who has turned into a corpse. The word relic comes from the Latin word *reliquiae*, meaning 'remains'. A relic is conventionally a body part or a material object which has belonged to, or in another way had an intimate bodily relation with, a now deceased person, whose life and deeds are collectively commemorated and/or sacralised as having iconic significance in religious or cultural ways. Relics are supposed to be endowed with performative affective power. Or, in other words, they *act* (Kazan and Higham 2019). If they do not perform vibrant actions, they lose their status as relics. Many Christian relics, such as the famous Veil of Veronica, which is said to have been used to wipe sweat and blood off Jesus' face while he was carrying the cross towards Golgotha, are believed to have healing powers. The alleged performative powers of relics are also used politically – for example, to prove the past existence of a holy person and, through such material 'proof' for congregations of believers, to legitimate the religious authority of the church or monastery in possession of the relic. Religious relics act due to being pervaded by divine power. However, the sustaining of religious authority and power is not the only function of relics. They can also perform in more secular ways. Locks of the famous 19th-century German romantic composer Beethoven's hair make up an example of secular relics, believed to put those in possession of such a lock in touch with the composer's artistic genius. Some of Beethoven's locks have been kept until today. Their performative powers are apparently believed to be fully intact – at least, in 2019, one such lock was sold at the renowned auction house of Sotheby's in London for 35,000 British pounds (Pentreath 2019). Mid-twentieth-century rock'n'roll icon Elvis Presley's guitar is another example of a secular relic. It was sold at auction in 2020 for US$1.32 million (Beifuss 2020).

The actions of these kinds of religious or cultural relics are inscribed in dualist schemes, referring to either divine powers or the powers of artistic genius and/or individual human uniqueness. In this sense, they are to be distinguished from the immanent vibrancy and affectivity related to what Bennett (2010) calls thing-power, and what I, taking inspiration from Braidotti, also see as the generative forces of *zoe* (2006). As I understand it, it is the latter kind of affective powers – an immanent vibrancy – that are at work in my relic. However, even though the difference between my relic and conventional ones is thus significant, it is still perhaps less dichotomous than it seems at first sight. At least, I note that the belief in the performative powers of relics has emerged from very ancient traditions, much broader and more diverse than the ways in which the meanings of the phenomenon have been territorialized by specific Christian and Western humanist-romantic traditions, and reserved for the celebration of divine powers or artistic genius. With these examples, I also want to pinpoint the ways in which the modern world, allegedly founded on so-called rational thought, is pervaded by all kinds of beliefs in the affective power of relics.

Still, my hair relic is also different from those discussed above insofar as it is not part of a collective framework. In contrast to the Veil of Veronica, the locks of Beethoven's hair, or Elvis Presley's guitar, it is private, individual, and personal. But, as such, my relic no doubt resonates with an abundance of similar personal relics, playing deeply affective roles for all kinds of mourners – a lock of hair from a dead beloved, a ring that belonged to a much-missed mother, the favourite teddy bear of a passed-away child, etc. Such personal everyday relics, used as part of individual mourning practices, are widespread, and I do not claim that my hair relic is any different or more special than those of other mourners. It means everything to me, but will appear banal in the eyes of people who did not have a close relationship with my partner.

However, within the framework of a reflection on the agency of dead bodies, and their powers to act through things, it is worthwhile to pay attention to both collective and individual relics. Individual relics share with the collective ones a specific way of establishing material connections with the deceased. In line with recent relic theory (Kazan and Higham 2019: 145), I consider both kinds of relics to work through the forging of metonymical relations of bodily contiguity and intimate touch between the relic-remain and the material body of the subject that was. In other words, I claim that the performative powers and agency of relics are based on a metonymical relation of transcorporeal touch within an assemblage of highly affect-laden actants.[6]

This argument is built on linguistic theory, where the metonym is a trope, which is contrasted against the metaphor. While the metaphor creates relations of comparison and resemblance between signified and signifier, the metonym shapes one of contiguity and touch (Jakobson 1987: 307). In the sentence 'I drink a glass', the word 'glass' is a metonym, because it refers to the content of the glass (e.g. wine), and does so against the background that the wine and the glass are touching each other. Combined with an ontology of signs as materially performative (Barad 2003), the metonym stands out as interesting in a posthuman sense, and also as particularly relevant to a reflection on the agency of relics and the thing-power of dead bodies. The performativity of the metonym can be understood as forging material, transcorporeal relations of touch and intimate, bodily contiguity that work as a kind of affective relay, leading the dead body of the subject that was (my beloved, Jesus, Beethoven, Elvis Presley) to intensely affect the living subject who has entered into communication with the relic as mourner, worshipper, fan, etc.

More specifically, my hair relic opens up a possibility for me to palpably, albeit spectrally, to get in touch with the past intimate life of my partner and me.

Performing as a metonym, it creates the basis for a kind of haptic visualization,[7] bringing me in touch with my beloved's body, both before and after she lost her hair to cancer treatment. The tuft of hair brings me tangibly in touch with the scene that marks a threshold between the before and after states, articulated in the poem *What Remains*. In a phenomenal, haptic sense, the tuft of hair materializes my memory of the day when my beloved called a person to cut off the rest of her beautiful silky, dark hair, which she was in the process of totally losing due to radiation therapy. This was the day when I picked up the tuft from the bathroom floor. The materialized memory has a highly performative effect on me – it affects me passionately. It facilitates spectral encounters with my beloved to wear the necklace, and through it to keep my beloved's hair close to my body, spectrally revitalizing the many intimate situations when I felt her hair caressing my body. The hair relic functions as a relay for spectral aspects of my molecular mourning. But it is also linked to my molar mourning, prompting me to memorize a bygone past.

Now, I shall turn to the second component of my necklace, *the teaspoonful of my beloved's ashes*. These are enclosed in a silver medallion whose metallic materiality establishes a mutual transfer between the temperature of the ashes and my body whenever I wear the necklace. Like the tuft of hair, the ashes, too, establish a metonymical relation of contiguity and touch, but in ways that push me more radically beyond molar human mourning. The tuft of hair can momentarily connect me with my beloved in a spectral embrace, but a key function of its relic-like qualities are, still, to memorize the molar human past, my beloved's body as it was when she was alive. The ashes in the medallion work in a far more complex way. It is also establishing a metonymical relation of contiguity and touch, but in addition to forge links between temporalities of past and present, it is first and foremost establishing metonymical links across different modes of human and inhuman existence. A key aspect of the metonymical work, carried out by the medallion is to create a haptic relationship between me as human subject, still embodied in a molar body of living flesh, and my beloved's now molecular and vibrantly inhuman state of *zoe*-based existence as part of the Fur assemblage and Limfjorden. Or, in other words, an important function of the medallion is to establish a multiple metonymical relation to the molecular instantaneousness of the *Aionic* time of co-becoming.

Let me spell out the complex work of the medallion in more detail. First of all, the ashes contained in the medallion have a metonymical relationship to the great bulk of my beloved's ashes, which were scattered in Limfjorden six years ago, and became part of the assemblage of seabed and algae sand beyond the cliffs of Fur. When I wear the necklace, the medallion embeds me phenomenally in this assemblage. Second, since my own ashes are going to be scattered in the same place, mixed with the last part of those of my beloved, the medallion also connects me metonymically to my own death, my final becoming-imperceptible and becoming-one with the Fur assemblage, Limfjorden, and my beloved, thus fulfilling the pact about reconnection that we made before she died (as articulated in the poem *A Pact*). In contrast to the tuft of hair, which, first and foremost, relates to spectral moments of revitalization of a past and to molar mourning, the ashes are decisively linked to a molecular mourning in the *Aionic* time of co-becoming with my beloved's inhuman remains. However, to further emphasize the complexity of the medallion's work, a third point also needs to be made. In addition to forge metonymical relations between human and inhuman modes of existence and link to *Aionic* time, the medallion is also working in line with the tuft of hair in terms of fostering metonymical links between past and present. The ashes in the medallion, thus, link me haptically to the scenic memories of that specific day when we scattered the majority of my beloved's ashes, as well as to my annual visits to the cliffs of Fur. Finally, and precisely like the tuft of hair, the ashes are also metonymically establishing a material bond with the living body that was. This final function is linked to the ways in which the ashes make up a metamorphosed stage of the body that was, generated by the processes of dying and the ensuing cremation. So, in sum, the medallion carries out very complex work, which affects me deeply in all of these different ways. Wearing it as part of the necklace is part of both my molar and my molecular mourning.

Finally, the third component of my necklace: *the two oyster pearls*. These pearls are clearly more difficult to locate in the vibrantly material assemblages related to my beloved's body and its remains than the tuft of hair or the medallion of ashes. They have never been directly in touch with the body that was, so is it pertinent to ascribe thing-power, related to my beloved's remains, to these two pearls? What kind of inhuman assemblages and transcorporeal agencies, if any, are at play here? What is it that leads these two pearls to affect me so deeply – even more deeply than the tuft of hair and the ashes? I experience the 'return' of the two pearls as miraculous, but what does that mean? In the remaining part of this chapter, I will approach this question from different angles, but without trying to give any final answers, staying instead with the elusiveness of miracles.

While it was growing, the oyster from which the pearls came was part of the Fur/Limfjorden assemblage, where my beloved's ashes are scattered. So, some kind of metonymical relation of contiguity and touch, albeit mediated by the waters of the fjord, can be noted between the pearls and my beloved's ashes. But this can be said about all organic and inorganic elements of these waters. For example, it also applies to all the components of my extensive collection of shells and stones from these waters. Still, compared to this collection, which is also very dear to my heart, I experience the pearls as embodying something in excess – something that phenomenally links me transcorporeally and affectively even more closely to the assemblage of which my beloved's remains have become part than these other items; something that aligns the two oyster pearls with the hair and the ashes in terms of their intensively affective thing-power – and which even make their power to affect me exceed that of the hair or the ashes. This excess stems from the intuition that the two pearls, 'returning' from the sea exactly one year after my beloved's death, resonate with the two brown pearls that we put into the casket to be cremated together with my beloved's corpse. Moreover, the miraculous excess is linked to a related intuition: that the resonance between the two sets of pearls could not be just a projection on my part, because the emergence of the oyster pearls on my rainbow son's plate was so completely unexpected and in no way to be anticipated. But, still, can it really make sense to see the two sets of pearls as related, and if so, how?

I am confident about the miraculously tinged intuition of the resonance between the two sets of pearls. However, reflecting on this intuition also alerts me to the dangers of the slippery slopes which lead down from the notion of the miraculous towards dualist and human exceptionalizing thinking – and how it does this in a more radical way than either the hair or the ashes. While the hair and the ashes are directly materially related to my beloved's body, and to the affective powers in which this bodily relation entangles me as an effect of our long, intimate bodily companionship, the two oyster pearls are not. So, what is it that enables them to affect me as much as – and in some ways even more than – the hair and the ashes? Have I – in line with Catholics believing in the healing powers of Veronica's Veil or the romantic music lovers expecting that a lock of Beethoven's hair will bring them directly in touch with the composer's artistic genius – allowed a dualist understanding to enter through the back door to interfere with my efforts to unfold a vitalist materialist and posthuman phenomenology of mourning? I will dig into this question in the following sections.

Synchronicity – A Detour into Jung's Human-Centred Vitalism

One of the methodological rules that has guided me in writing this book is that I want to see where my poetic and spiritual-material intuitions as a mourning 'I' lead me, while at the same time also critically scrutinize whether and how my poetic and spiritual forays may contribute to an immanence philosophical understanding of death, dying, mourning. To be true to this methodology, I shall now – reluctantly! – make a detour to Jung's book *Synchronicity* (2008 [1955]).[8] As mentioned, I am critical of Jung's human-centred and mystically tinged theories. *But* I am also intuitively struck by the way in which some of his observations regarding the phenomenon that he conceptualized as synchronicity, i.e. an a-causal but significant coincidence, resonates amazingly well with the miraculous excess which for me is related to the two pearls that 'returned' from the sea, as articulated in *What Remains* and *A Miraculous Event?* Moreover, the notion of synchronicity seems to be well attuned to the rhizome of other miraculous events, I experienced, such as those described in the poems *Signs?* and *A Pact*. Jung's work has been rejected and largely ignored by different critically materialist and leftist schools of thought – due to his mysticism and also because of his troubling relations to Nazism (Braidotti 2002: 130). I share this critique in many ways, and add that he was also tapping into human exceptionalism. All this made me quite reluctant to follow my methodology of being true to my intuitions in this particular case. Nevertheless, to be consistent in my methodological choices, the next sections of the chapter will dig critically into the question of whether or not it is possible, from an immanence philosophical perspective, to rethink the phenomenon that Jung conceptualized as synchronicity.

Let me start the digging by noting that Deleuze and Guattari's scattered remarks on Jung actually make it seem as though, in some respects, they find him 'profounder' (1988: 241) than Freud. This is because the former resists the latter's Oedipal narrative as the foundation for the human psyche, and probably also because Jung, in his own mystical way, taps into a-modern spiritual traditions from which Deleuze, too, drew inspiration, albeit differently (Ramey 2012). Deleuze and Guattari also stress that Jung's approach to the imaginary role of animals in the psychic life of humans (1988: 235-6) is slightly less human-centred than Freud's, even though in the end Jung, too, reduces animals to symbols for something (quasi-)human. In Jung's theoretical universe, animals do not articulate oedipal figures and conflicts, but instead they carry archetypal meanings (1988: 259), and this cedes authority to universal myths of the collective human unconscious rather than suggesting the immanence of vibrant matter. Still, when assessing Jung's approaches from an immanence philosophical and vitalist materialist point of view, it is notable that early twentieth-century embryologist Hans Driesch'[9] concept of entelechy (a 'non-mechanical agent responsible for the phenomena of life', Driesch 1914: 34) was important for Jung's approach to synchronicity (Jung 2008 [1955]: 30; Addison 2009). Driesch' philosophy actually plays a significant role as an intermediate stage on Bennett's path towards outlining a vitalist materialism (2010: 69-76), so could Jung in this light perhaps be considered as a quasi-vitalist materialist in line with Driesch? Finally, Jung's longstanding collaboration with the Austrian quantum physicist Wolfgang Pauli[10] should also be noted in this context, and his efforts to link the phenomenon of synchronicity to theories of quantum correlations, which do not obey the laws of Newtonian physics (Limar 2011). This layer of quantum physics in Jung's reflection, too, can perhaps testify to his attempts to move beyond his otherwise foundational essentializing and dualist focus on universal archetypes and a kind of authoritative, transcendent world soul, the collective human unconscious. Nonetheless, the bottom line is that the latter is predominant, and Jung's theories do not emerge as viable for a critical analysis focused on immanence, flows of intensities, change, and becoming. Still, I shall compare notes with the Jungian analysis of synchronicity in order to dig deeper into my intuitions that the miraculous excesses that I experienced as linked to the 'returning pearls' and to the rhizome of other events that co-shaped my process of mourning, somehow resonate with the phenomena for which Jung coined this term. I shall scrutinize Jung's account of synchronicity, related to experiences of unexpected, a-causal, but somehow meaningful coincidence and ask if this phenomenon can be rethought beyond the Jungian conceptual framework with its dualist and human exceptionalizing ontology.

To do so, I first of all take my point of departure in Jung's own surprise about the phenomenon of synchronicity. He, as it were, stumbled over it – in his patients and in himself, and was completely astonished. He also explicitly emphasized that he did not really have an explanation for the phenomenon (2008 [1955]: 6). Indeed, he actually found it so much out of synch with any reasonable scientific expectations he might have, that he was perhaps as reluctant as me to deal with it. At least, he waited 20 years before publishing anything about it (ibid.: 5). This story of deep hesitancy, which Jung openly presents in the preface to his first book-length discussion of synchronicity (ibid.), indicates that the phenomena which he clusters under this label certainly did not enter into his conceptual framework because they fitted the bill well. In contrast, synchronicity seems to have imposed itself on Jung – and throughout the book he clearly indicates that he struggled hard to give it a theoretical and scientifically supported foundation. Against this background, I suggest that it may make sense to look for another – immanent and posthuman – direction for theorizing the phenomenon, rather than the transcendent and human-centred one that Jung himself took. I ask: can Jung's observations regarding what he describes as a principle of a-causal synchronicity become a stepping-stone in my efforts to make immanence philosophically and vitalist materialist sense of events of miraculous coincidence which I intuitively experienced as part of my mourning?

Let me first see what Jung says about the phenomenon of synchronicity. For Jung, a relation of a-causal synchronicity is 'a psychophysical parallelism' (ibid.: 124), established through a 'simultaneous occurrence of two meaningfully but not causally connected events' (ibid.: 36). Basically, one of these events is 'a certain psychic state', while the other is 'one or more external events which appear as meaningful parallels to the momentary subjective state – and, in certain cases, vice versa' (ibid.: 36). To illustrate the phenomenon, Jung gives, among others, the example of a young woman – one of his patients – who had a dream about a golden scarab. While she was in the consultation room telling Jung about this dream, he heard something like a 'gentle tapping' on the window behind him. He turned around, opened the window, and to his surprise, he saw that it was a rare scarabaeidae beetle that had made the noise (ibid.: 31) – a beetle which is the closest kin to the North African scarab to be found at the more Northern latitudes, where he and his patient were located. The beetle flew in, Jung caught it in his hand, and showed it to the patient who, if we believe him, was as astonished as he was himself. According to Jung, the significant coincidence between the scarab in the patient's report of her dream and the real-life beetle at the window seems to have convinced the young woman to give up her strict 'Cartesian', and rationalistic, 'animus'-dominated outlook (ibid.: 33), and to become more open to the emotional 'anima' dimensions of life. The scarab in the dream is to Jung an archetypal symbol of renewal. Jung tells us that the patient was stuck in the middle of a process of transformation, and the scarab dream was opening up new horizons towards her embracing of emotionality. But it still seemed as though a final push was needed, and this is what the beetle tapping against the window accomplished, Jung argues. More precisely, he says, it seemed as though this totally unexpected and coincidental, but significantly resonating, external event of the beetle being at the window at the very moment when the young woman was describing her scarab dream became a decisive turning point in her process of transformation.

From a feminist point of view, this is, first of all, a problematic story about the ways in which Jung, in line with Freud and other analysts, time and again have nudged young women into giving up their 'masculine' ambitions to embrace appropriate 'feminine' behaviours, understood along essentializing, gender-binary lines. Second, it is also a story about a problematic, human-centred, and essentializing view of the psyche: Jung's concepts of the archetype and the collective unconscious – the beetle/scarab as a universal, archetypal symbol of human renewal. However, what interests me in the context of my attempts to outline an immanence philosophically grounded and vitalist materialist onto-epistemology of the miraculous, related to unexpected agencies of transcorporeal assemblages, is not so much the therapeutic outcomes or Jung's interpretations of them. Instead, I want to note that the corpo-affective and transcorporeal qualities of the event, which Jung conceptualizes as synchronicity, appear strikingly comparable to those qualities characterizing the events in which I became enrolled as mourning 'I', and which peaked with the 'return' of the two oyster pearls. Against this background, I argue that Jung's analysis, read against the grain, can be the stepping-stone I suggested above – i.e. used as an event to compare notes with, as I work out my own way towards a vitalist materialist onto-epistemology of the miraculous, understood as a totally unexpected, coincidental event, shaped by immanent agencies of transcorporeal assemblages.

Seen from a human point of view, the beetle's tapping against the window is unexpected, unwilled, uncontrolled, and could have gone unnoticed. But, still, the tapping triggers an assemblage of multiple actants (beetle, Jung, patient, her report on the scarab dream, the therapeutic conversation, the window, the consultation room) to coalesce and produce an intensely affective event of a multitude of immanent co-becomings. The material fact that Jung actually notices the beetle, acts upon its tapping against the window, and makes the patient aware of it as well, becomes entangled with another material fact, the temporal coincidence between the beetle's tapping and the ongoing therapeutic conversation, which was related to the young woman's scarab dream. The result of these transcorporeally coalescing, human and non-human forces is a unique event, full of strong intensities and affects. For the involved humans, it raises questions about 'hidden meanings', prompted by the unlikeliness, uniqueness, and unexpectedness of the coincidence between (*a*) an intense meaning-making process: the patient's dream report, and the analytical situation, (*b*) the beetle at the window and (*c*) the complete lack of graspable causal connections between these temporally linked elements.

Platforms dedicated to the search for 'hidden meanings' and 'signs' in such highly affectively charged and unlikely events are multiple. This is where discussions of divine intervention would take off, as well as, in Jung's case, conversations about a-causal, but highly symbolic archetypal links between inner psychic states and outer occurrences. However, I take a radically different route. I do not search for 'meaning' in external, transcendent agencies – God or the collective archetypal unconscious world soul. Instead, I ask if, and if so how, it can make sense to understand Jung's event, as well as the equally causally ungraspable, but apparently 'meaning'-ful coincidences that I experienced, as miraculous in a sense that resonates with an immanence philosophical and vitalist materialist framework. Moreover, I ask if, and if so how, my reflections on metonymical agencies, discussed in relation to my hair relic and my beloved's ashes, can be helpful in terms of carving out such a framework for understanding the miraculous.

Immanent Miracles?

From Jung's perspective, as already discussed, a relation of a-causal synchronicity establishes a correlation between an inner, psychological, event and an outer one, but without any observable causal connections between the two. The correlation is instead established through a combination of temporal coincidence between the outer and the inner event, and a link between them that is experienced as carrying a deeply affect-laden significance. In my case involving the two 'returning' pearls, the inner event can be interpreted as my own and my rainbow family's state of intensified mourning on the first anniversary of my beloved's death. The significantly correlating outer event would be the extremely rare emergence of two pearls inside an oyster on the plate of my rainbow son, exactly one year after his mother's death and after a funeral ritual that included two brown pearls, affectively infused with symbolic meaning. Interpreted within a classical Jungian framework, this coincidence would qualify as so significant and unique that it would count as a model case of a-causal synchronicity, and I would have to look for an archetypal figure related to pearls and oysters.

However, instead of looking for transcendent meanings, embedded in archetypal figures, I want to discuss whether it makes sense to understand this incident as an immanent miracle to be defined as a transcorporeal assemblage of multiple human and non-human actants coalescing to produce an intensely affective event[11] involving a multitude of immanent co-becomings. Against the backdrop of such an understanding, a key cluster of actants can be untangled. One of these is the assemblage of waterflows, oysters, and sand in Limfjorden, which led some grains of sand to enter a growing oyster, prompting it to generate two pearls. Another actant is the fishermen who harvested the oyster without knowing its contents, and sent it to the market, where my rainbow son bought it for the dinner of remembrance which he and his wife had arranged on the anniversary of my partner's, his mother's, death. A third actant is the affective state of intensified mourning which the anniversary of my beloved's death invoked in me as well as in my rainbow family. A fourth actant is the funeral ritual which we – my rainbow family and I – had invented the year before, and which included the two brown pearls that were placed in the casket to be cremated together with my beloved's corpse. A fifth actant is the ways in which, before her death, my partner and I co-experienced a miraculous moment, articulated in *A Pact* and *A Miraculous Event?*, and also commented upon in the interview in the Interlude *Milagrosa*, following this chapter. This actant includes the shared intuition about her bodily healing and our spiritual-material reconnection – an intuition which triggered our story about going together to the oysters at the bottom of Limfjorden. Involved in this latter actant is also the pact that my beloved and I entered into, which included my rainbow sons promising in due time to scatter my ashes in the same place as hers. A sixth actant is the metamorphosed remains of my beloved, transformed from fleshy corpse to ashes through cremation, mixed with water, sand, seabed, and sea creatures (oysters, algae etc), when scattered over Limfjorden beyond the cliffs of Fur. A seventh actant is the thick cluster of metonymical relations of contiguity and touch forged between all these actants (oyster pearls, brown pearls, Fur assemblage and waters of Limfjorden, my beloved's ashes, my and my rainbow family's mourning practices, etc).

I suggest that what happens is that all of these actants coalesce as an assemblage, and become meaning-making as a rhizome of metonymical relations, when their different processes of co-becoming are aligned and actualised as an event, the dinner of remembrance of my beloved on the anniversary of her death, where the two oyster pearls appeared. The event makes the two oyster pearls known to the human actors, while they also forge a highly corpo-affective link with the metamorphosed corpse assemblage (cremated corpse and brown pearls, now mixed as ashes, and scattered over Limfjorden, thereby becoming entangled with the water, sea creatures, and seabed there). The oyster pearls create this link through their metonymical relationship of contiguity and touch with the same waters where the cremated corpse and the brown pearls are now located. The oyster that grew the two grey pearls was, as mentioned, harvested in the waters of Limfjorden.

From a phenomenological perspective, the moment of surprise when the oyster pearls appear can be experienced as miraculous due to the ways in which the unique, unexpected, and unlikely appearance of these pearls, through the agency of metonymical meaning-making processes, immediately becomes deeply entangled with the rest of the assemblage of co-becoming actants (the two brown pearls, the funeral ritual, the scattering of the ashes in the fjord, etc.). The uniqueness, unexpectedness, and unlikeliness, as well as the existence of a thick cluster of metonymical relations, constitute a parallel to the event involving the scarab dream and the beetle tapping on the window that Jung described. However, instead of considering the miraculous qualities of the two events through the lens of Jung's human-centred vitalism, or other transcendent explanations, I suggest that the experience of miraculous excess, generated by this kind of extraordinary event, can be seen as immanent effects of the co-becoming of human/non-human actants, coalescing into assemblages, which give rise to the shaping of thick and heavily affect-laden clusters of metonymical links.

In the next chapter, I shall sustain this suggestion, and ground it further within a speculative outline of an immanence philosophical and vitalist materialist understanding. I shall also establish a pluriversal conversation on the issue, bringing a-modern onto-epistemologies and cosmologies into the conversation.

Interlude V

MILAGROSA (MIRACULOUS)

Illustr. 7 Milagrosa (Miraculous). © Nina Lykke 2018.

An Interview about the Miraculous

Interviewer: Camila Marambio[1]
Interviewee: Nina Lykke

Towards the end of my process of writing the poetry collection, included as Interludes in *Vibrant Death*, my friend Camila Marambio, Chilean curator, artist and nomadic researcher, interviewed me. One of her questions focused on the miraculous events that I had articulated in the poems *What Remains, A Pact* and *Signs?*. The interview was very important for me in terms of helping me to confirm my intuitions about the miraculous events happening to me and my beloved both before and after her death – and for starting to unlearn the effects of my upbringing within modern Western onto-epistemologies, which has left me prone to not fully recognize miracles as phenomena which do happen 'for real'. Camila prompted me to also enter into a process of relearning other ways of thinking about miracles, taking a point of departure in Gloria Anzaldua's new mestiza philosophy (1987, 2015) and other indigenous-centred onto-epistemologies. The process of unlearning and relearning is deeply relational. With Camila's permission, I therefore present a transcript of the interview under the title *Milagrosa*, honouring Camila's border thinking and bilingualism by using the Spanish word for miraculous as title. The interview took place in July 2017 in the old garden of an art museum, close to one of the bays of the North Sea, where the island Funen, on which I live, is located.

C   Would you describe a miracle?

N   (Pause for reflection.) Yes, certainly. The two oyster pearls coming back from the sea was a miracle.

C   What defines it as miraculous?

N   That it's incomprehensible from the point of view of the tools of the scientific worldview, the 'normal' and normative epistemic tools of the scientific worldview. I was educated within this worldview. Its tools were part of the educational system I went through. I'm not a natural scientist, but I learned the standard epistemic tools early to distinguish what is real and what is not, according to the scientific worldview . . . and seen through lenses of this worldview, the return of the pearls is incomprehensible, and this is one of the things that makes it miraculous: the incomprehensibility. I'm not saying that it's just totally incomprehensible, but incomprehensible from the point of view of the tools that I have, and that a lot of other people also have, who, like me, were educated in the scientific worldview, and have learned to distinguish certain kinds of reality. This is, of course, related to a positivist notion of reality which, in other respects, I'm very critical of. But still, I have a perception which tells me that, ok, this is a table, and it doesn't suddenly jump over there, unless there's a magician underneath the table doing a trick (laughing). So, the incomprehensibility of the event of the returning pearls is one thing which defines it as miraculous. Another thing is its wonder quality. Wonder quality ... is to be understood as a bit like love, love in the sense of 'Woww, everything just changes your world!'

C It's interesting, because I have another set of questions at this point, which are about love. But before I move on, could you perhaps comment a bit more on this incomprehensibility – and its relation to improbability, and to measurement. What is the probability percentagewise that two pearls would come in an oyster? And what can and cannot be proven? And since we're talking about miracles, I'll also ask you: do you think that a miracle just happens, or that you wish or will it to happen, or that you even construct it?

N No, I definitely do not will it to happen, or construct it, because then it's not a miracle. If you will or construct it, it's definitely not a miracle. That's why I've said many times that I didn't want to fool myself, because I think if I had constructed it – and if in the back of mind I had had the suspicion that I had called it or constructed it, then it wouldn't be a miracle. So, in that sense, I would definitely not define it as constructed or willed, because then it wouldn't be a miracle. Then it could be a great and fantastic experience, and all that stuff, but it wouldn't be a miracle.

C So can you then hope for a miracle? Wait for a miracle? Go in search of a miracle?

N I think you can hope for it. Yes, you can hope for it. And what was the next – hope, search? What was the next? It was a very good question ... Hope, search – what was the third?

C Is the miracle then something that you don't wish for, and you don't will into being?

N Well, wish for it, you can, and wait for it, as well – can you wait for a miracle? was the third thing you asked about before, and, yes, you can wait for it.

C But you don't will it to happen?

N I can wish for it to happen, and wait for it to happen, but I can't will it to happen.

C And you don't construct it?

N No, for sure not. But you asked about searching for it as well ... And I think you can search for it, because I think that's what I'm doing, when I go to Fur and Limfjorden, where my beloved's ashes are scattered. Going there, I'm searching for the miracle, so I can hope for it, and I can search for it, and I can wish and wait for it, but I can't will it, and I can't construct it. I would, indeed, love to be able to construct it (laughing), because then I could experience it more often, but it wouldn't work, because to construct it would be to deny and block the miraculous qualities. If constructed, it would just be a product of my own projections. Yeah.

C So by searching for it, by going to Limfjorden, you're making yourself available to the miracle, you're putting yourself in its line of sight, maybe, or its line of appearance?

N Yes, Yes. But I think one more quality is important. I mentioned wonder, but one more important thing is the unexpected. To be a miracle, I think it also has to be unexpected. That's important as well, because otherwise . . .

C That it's unexpected makes it unpredictable – and improbable?

N Yes. Yes. If a miracle happens, it's unexpected, and that's also why, in my poem *Fur*, in the second stanza, related to the second time I went to Limfjorden, I ask if it's possible to repeat a *rendezvous*? The miraculous is related to the unexpected. I can't go to Fur, and just do the same things as I did the year before. I have to be open for the totally new and unexpected, and to really make sure that it's not just becoming a habit, because if it became just a habit . . .

C Then there would be no room for miracles?

N No. Then it wouldn't work . . . So, therefore, I've thought a lot about how I shall organize my stay on Fur this year. To not just repeat what I did last year there . . .

C I also want to ask you about the story you tell in the poem *A Pact*, that you and your beloved wished for the miracle and even fictionalized it, giving it a characteristic. What, within your understanding of the miracle and of that episode, and the frustration that that miracle, in particular, didn't play out in the way . . .

N (Interrupts) But it did happen! The miracle did happen!

C Ok, saying what?

N Because the whole thing about the miraculous event, and the story and the ritual we built up around it, I do believe in all of it, it happened, and . . . (Starting to cry) This is . . . (Crying passionately and freely) . . . From the conversations I've had with my beloved on this, which weren't conversations, rational conversations, like the one we're having now, because you can't talk in this way with people who are really close to death, drugged with morphine, and prednisolone, and with severe brain damage, due to the cancer metastasizing wildly in the brain; she was completely lucid, but she couldn't talk, or think in ordinary ways. Did you ever take prednisolone when you had cancer?

C Yes.

N So you know about its effects. And my beloved got an enormous dose of prednisolone to relieve the oedema around the brain metastases, which were the ones that killed her, so of course in this situation with the prednisolone, the morphine and the brain metastases, everything, then you don't have a quick, rational back-and-forth conversation like the one we're having here. . . but it just came to us one day, this shared experience of something miraculous happening, and it didn't come only once; it came three times, and we talked about it, and ... I'm sure (crying passionately and freely) – and that's what makes me cry now – I'm sure that she felt it, too. She was a very, very rational and atheist person, even more so than me, but I'm totally sure that this belief in the miracle was something we shared (crying, voice quiet and faltering). It was not only my hunch that it happened, she felt it, too. (Regaining strength in the voice, but still crying.) This is ... something that I totally, totally know. So the miracle did happen. It was a shared experience, and we started the story-telling about it together ... I took the story further by organizing the funeral ritual together with family and friends after my beloved's death, by putting two brown pearls in the casket, and by arranging for the scattering of her ashes, finding the place rich in oysterbeds, to scatter them. (Voice faltering.) All that became part of the miracle story, too. And then a year after the oyster pearls returned from the sea... and I believe as much in this miraculous return as Catholics believe in the ...

C   The immaculate conception?

N   No. No. No.

C   Ahh, when you eat the body of Christ, and drink the blood during the Holy Communion?

N   Yes. When they do this Christian Holy Communion ritual: 'This is the body of Christ, etc.' The transubstantiation, which I don't believe in at all. But this miracle that happened to my beloved and me, and the promise about reconnection on the bottom of the sea that it called forward, I believe in that. (Voice faltering.) And the reason that I'm crying now is that I'm pretty, pretty sure from the way she talked about it, – from what she said about it – that she felt it and believed in it, too. I know for sure that we shaped this together (crying).

C   So you shaped the miracle?

N   Yes, we shaped the miracle together, yes, but NOT in the sense of 'constructing it'. What we – my beloved and I, and later my rainbow family and I – shaped was the story about reconnection, the funeral ritual and the spreading of the ashes ceremony, but that was after the miracle had occurred between my beloved and me; afterwards, we could take it further, but the miracle was unexpected.

C   But the miracle you're referring to now, is that still the miracle of the pearls coming back?

N   No, no. Now I'm talking about the initial miracle, that happened before my beloved died.

C   ... the spark?

N   Yes, the spark, which was a thing that came to us both. The pearls coming back was another miracle, or a part of the initial miracle, a sort of sequel ... But the spark, the initial miracle... I know precisely what happened. I was helping my beloved – by that time I had to help her with everything – so I was helping her to walk to the toilet. I was supporting her in walking, and it was very, very difficult for her to walk, so we walked very slowly, and we were close to the yellow chair in the living room, next to the living room door, and then... (voice faltering), and then we both felt it, and said to each other 'the miracle will occur, the wrong will go out and the right will come in'. It was something that came to us both, when we were next to that chair; it was just a small exchange of words, but it was with us both, and a bit later she asked me to take out the lung cancer, and we started to develop the story about going to the oysters together, and I made love to her along the lines of the story... This whole sequence was the initial miracle, and all these moments felt so different: in these moments she was neither the stranger (which I've written about in the poem *You Become a Stranger*) nor her old self; she was different, and I was different, too, and I'm so sure that we really both felt the miraculous unfold, and believed it...

> **Interlude V: Milagrosa** – is Spanish for miraculous. As *Interlude V* is different from the others, its mode is indicated, not through a term from music composition, but through a word chosen to honour Abya Yala's *mestiza* traditions of spiritual materialism. These are traditions to which the interview making up this interlude brought me closer. The Spanish word for miracles (used here with a feminine ending), also paves the way for **Chapter 6's Pluriversal Conversations on Immanent Miracles**, in which decolonial queerfeminist scholar, activist and poet Gloria Anzaldua's spiritualist materialist philosophy figures prominently. Genealogically, Anzaldua's philosophy revitalizes the spiritualist materialism embedded in these traditions. In so doing, she uses language that consciously mixes Spanish and English as an expression of her *mestizaje*, borderland identity.

Chapter 6

PLURIVERSAL CONVERSATIONS ON IMMANENT MIRACLES

The interview presented in *Interlude V, Milagrosa*, which my friend, artist, curator, and scholar Camila Marambio, conducted with me, became pivotal for my decision to not only poeticize my intuitions about the miraculous, but also to give them a prominent place in my philosophical contemplations in this book. In particular, the moment during the interview when, unexpectedly and surprisingly to myself, I started to cry, marked a turning point for me. As strange as it may sound, I was not crying out of sadness. Rather, I wept due to a peculiar feeling of joy – a joy that suddenly pervaded me when the insight struck me with the force of a lightning bolt that the miraculous experience I had had together with my beloved before she died, together with the rhizomatic cluster of further miraculous events, was truly and unambiguously real. Being prompted by Camila to define – and in a digitally repeatable form retell – that crucial moment of a shared experience of the miraculous, from which the funeral rituals and my later spiritual-material practices grew, helped me to understand that I had been living with a kind of dual consciousness. I had memorized this miraculous event with my beloved as something which, despite its phenomenality, and its spiritual and poetic importance, nonetheless only existed for me in a dreamlike, liminal world in-between the 'real' and the 'not real'. On the one hand, in trusting my intuitions, which had strongly confirmed the miraculous qualities of the event, I had articulated it in poems, stories, and spiritual-material rituals. But, on the other hand, I was not at all prepared for Camila's questions. The way in which she prompted me into a philosophical contemplation of the miraculous, and to a conceptual framing of my experience, took me by surprise. But it also made it clear to me how – despite years of engagement with feminist technoscience critiques, including critiques of positivist onto-epistemologies – my limited understanding of 'the real' had blocked me from thinking freely about phenomena such as miracles, whose existence is a priori foreclosed in a rationalistic modern outlook. Within the framework of modern thought, miracles are defined as being in excess; they are relegated to the margins as 'pre-modern', 'primitive', and/or referencing symptoms of 'madness', or at best pushed into the realm of the poetic imagination, understood as separate from 'reality'. The interview unlocked other ways of thinking about the miraculous for me, which resonated with my intuitions, and enabled me to better understand the ways in which poetic and philosophical knowledge-seeking are entangled. It was this joyful unlocking that made me cry.

In this chapter, I will follow up on the insights, gained in the interview, that brought me to understand how modern epistemologies of ignorance, at first, had prevented me from fully recognizing my intuitions about the miraculous. The chapter will speculate further on the issue of immanent miracles, while engaging in a process of unlearning the hierarchies implied in modern Western epistemic habits, which are a priori cast as superior to so-called 'premodern' and 'primitive' ones when it comes to claims about 'the real' and its excessive outsides, universalized as a decisive 'real'/'not-real'-divide. I will summon a sounding board of helpers in order to establish a pluriversal conversation about miracles. My helpers will bring to the fore a diversity of non-hierarchically ordered perspectives. They are *not* chosen because all of them are necessarily interested in immanent miracles, or would endorse attempts to give them a philosophical or cosm-ontological[1] grounding. I have selected my helpers because I hope that they can give me pluriversal pieces of advice in my speculations about immanent miracles. They share commitments to non-dualist and vitalist materialist or spiritualist materialist onto-epistemological approaches and worlding practices. But they do this from differently situated perspectives – in a geopolitical, corpo-political, and temporal sense. One group of helpers are called to my sounding board from locations within the kind of contemporary radical posthumanist philosophies upon which I have drawn in previous chapters. Another group of helpers will open up horizons towards a-modern and indigenous-based onto-epistemologies and cosm-ontologies. In this sense, I am critically following up on the insights that Camila helped me to gain about the ways in which my horizon for a contemplation of miracles was limited by ingrained epistemic habits, knowledge hierarchies, and universals, of a kind that characterize Western modernity, even including much of the contemporary, radically critical posthumanist scholarship emerging from locations within this framework.

To establish a conversation in and with my sounding board, I shall use a pluriversal approach as defined by decolonial scholars Madina Tlostanova and Walter Mignolo (Tlostanova and Mignolo 2009, 2012; Tlostanova 2015). This will enable the sounding board members to help me speculate about immanent miracles, while I situate myself in and commit to the process of learning to avoid the traps of modern Western knowledge hierarchies and their universal claims about 'real'/'not-real' distinctions. Pluriversality implies serious efforts to unlearn the universalizing modes of modern epistemic habits, while taking a point of departure in a pluritopic hermeneutics (Ibid.). This is a methodology which, from a de-universalizing perspective, 'questions the position and the homogeneity of the understanding subject', while moving towards a relational and 'interactive' knowledge building, that carefully reflects 'the very process of constructing the space that is being known' (Tlostanova and Mignolo 2009: 18). In contrast to cultural relativist approaches and mere neoliberal celebrations of multicultural thought, this interactive and pluritopically situated construction of the space to be understood serves to make visible the power of modern Western knowledge hierarchies and their inherent erasure mechanisms, which make other (a-modern and non-Western) knowledges invisible and nourish white Western epistemologies of ignorance:

> The pluritopic approach does not accentuate relativism or cultural diversity. It stresses instead the social, political and ontological dimensions of any theorizing and any understanding, questioning the Western locus of enunciation masked as universal and out-of-concrete-space. It strives to (re)construct, more specifically, the difference in the loci of enunciation and the politics of knowing beyond cultural relativism. We should not also forget the ethical dimension of pluritopic hermeneutics, which stresses the constant realization that other truths also exist and have the right to exist, but their visibility is reduced by the continuing power asymmetry, which is based on coloniality of knowledge, power, being and gender.
> Ibid.: 18

Following Tlostanova's and Mignolo's critique of cultural relativism, I want to underline that my argument about wishing to establish a pluriversal conversation with and within my sounding board does not imply that I intend to simply line up different approaches to immanent miracles for the sake of diversity. In line with a pluritopic methodology, I consider it necessary to carefully situate the different interventions, the power relations between them, and their specific ways of framing ideas about the miraculous. Moreover, I shall focus on the ways in which, as convener of the conversation, I am located in relation to these interventions. In particular, I need to make it clear how the conversation with and within my sounding board has shaped my process of unlearning the epistemic habit of Western modernity to universalize a positivist understanding of the distinction between the 'real' and the 'not real' – an understanding that dismisses miracles as belonging to the latter category, foreclosing any possibility that a reflection on them might be taken seriously.

In addition to framing a cross-cutting and non-hierarchical conversation about immanent miracles with a pluritopic hermeneutics as my thinking technology, I also suggest that the differently situated speculations that I will establish together with my sounding board can be understood through the optical metaphor of diffraction. This is a metaphor which, through Haraway (1992) and Barad (2007, 2014), has earned a prominent place in feminist theorizing about emerging methodologies. I interpellate diffraction, in particular, because I see a lot of resonance with my own efforts when Barad (2014) uses this methodology to unfold a situated conversation between decolonial feminisms (Anzaldua 1987; Minh-ha 1988) and her own feminist reading of quantum physics (Barad 2007). Recalling a conversation she had with Anzaldua in 1991 (2014: 172), Barad reads quantum physics' analyses of spacetimemattering and the way in which it works through interference patterns in conversation with Minh-ha's[2] and Anzaldua's decolonial feminist explorations of non-hierarchical differing as an undoing of intersecting power hierarchies. She presents this as a diffractive reading. This means that the analysis crosses in-between the two kinds of knowledge-building and understandings – Barad's own feminist readings of quantum physics and Minh-ha's and Anzaldua's decolonial reflections on difference and differing. This crossing creates resonances, Barad argues, while at the same time emphasizing that this should not and does not imply a reduction to sameness. The establishing of resonances between the two kinds of understanding in Barad's text is instead to be seen as a process of 'cutting together/apart'. By this, she means a process that can also be explained as 'differentiating-entangling' and 'iterative (re)configuring' (Barad 2014: 168), i.e. a process that makes mattering meanings intra-act, while maintaining their irreducible differences. Like pluritopic hermeneutics (Tlostanova and Mignolo 2009, Tlostanova 2015), Barad's way of using diffraction here seems apt for establishing non-hierarchical affinity relations between differently situated theoretical bodies, rather than letting one (the modern Western one) territorialize the field, while erasing all traces of the others. Together with Tlostanova's and Mignolo's reflections on pluriversality and pluritopic hermeneutics, Barad's diffractive cutting together/apart will also guide me as I gather my sounding board to help me speculate on immanent miracles, and convene a conversation on this issue between its differently located participants.

Before I set the conversation in motion, let me also underline that what I stated in the introduction to the previous chapter does, indeed, apply to this one as well. I neither can nor wish to pursue the Western epistemic habit of looking for final answers. Derrida's (1994: 12) observation in resonance with Shakespeare, that spectres are not inclined to make appearances for scholars, applies to miracles, too, I think. If you try to nail them down by means of conventional modern scholarship, asking for exhaustive, rational explanations, they will hide behind impenetrable walls of silence – as does death. Together with my sounding board, therefore, I will speculate and pose questions about possible entrance points to immanent understandings of miracles, but I will leave the answers open.

Miracles as Effects of Vital Mourning Assemblages?

Let me start the search for ways to further ground my speculations on immanent miracles by briefly summarizing a key problem: in order to reach an immanent and material understanding of miracles, narratives of transcendence will have to be disrupted. A central difficulty that must be confronted here is that miracles readily attract transcendent explanations. In Chapter 5, I discussed how miracles may claim to exist due to the workings of divine powers or as an effect of exceptional human agencies, such as artistic genius or Jung's archetypal world soul. To effectively set an agenda of disruption of such transcendent and dualist approaches, I shall once more call Bennett (2010) to my sounding board. She does not per se discuss the issue of miracles. Nonetheless, in the last chapter she has already assisted me in my initial efforts to establish a platform for thinking about the miraculous without recourse to narratives of transcendence. Now I summon her again to help me to briefly compare notes between a mechanistic-materialist path to disruption and a vitalist-materialist one, and make it clear why I opt for the latter.

If the task I had set myself was only to disrupt narratives of transcendence, I could have taken a point of departure in a Freudian approach, i.e. a more mechanistic-materialist psychoanalytical pathway to understanding miraculous experiences. From such a perspective, it could be argued that the shaping of the metonymical links between the two sets of pearls that I discussed in the previous chapter is a purely subjective affair – an individual psychological projection from inside to outside (Freud 1901: 287–8). This argument would be in line with standard Freudian critiques of Jung's mystically tinged attempts to think beyond the individual psyche along the lines of a collective unconscious or world soul. However, the Freudian mechanistic materialism, which focuses on the individual psyche, does not resonate either with my intuitions or with the vitalist-materialist and posthuman framework of this book. Explaining the metonymical links that were pinpointed in the last chapter through the notion of projections would limit my analytical focus to the agencies of a human subject's desire for a lost and lacking beloved. But such an explanation would completely ignore the vitality, affectivity, and transcorporeal agencies of the assemblages with which the embodied mourning 'I' is co-becoming. This is why I turn to Bennett instead of summoning Freud, and a notion of projection to disrupt the narratives of transcendence.

However, while selecting an immanence philosophical and vitalist materialist contemplation of the miraculous instead of a mechanistic materialist one, I do not deny that the affective forging of thick clusters of metonymical links between the oyster pearls and the larger assemblage (including the mourning 'I', the funeral ritual, the cremated body of my beloved, the brown pearls, the waters of Limfjorden, etc.) can be seen as an effect of the mourning process in which I and my rainbow kin were immersed. But instead of focusing on projections from the human subject to objects in the 'outside' world, I suggest that the process of vibrant becoming-a-mourning-assemblage, and as such shaping thick clusters of metonymical relations, is happening along similar lines as the coalescing of the vital garbage assemblage of dead rat, glove, bottle cap, oak pollen, and stick of wood that Bennett encountered and in which she became immersed (2010: 4). When Bennett theorizes this assemblage and the ways in which it caught her attention, she highlights that a vitalist materialist ontology should neither position the embodied and meaning-making human subject outside of the assemblage as a sovereign observer of detached objects, nor locate agency only within this observing subject. According to Bennett, agency instead emerges from the transcorporeal human/non-human assemblage, which encompasses both the vital thing-power of the non-human actants and the human subject's total and inevitable entanglement in the shared conative process of co-becoming of all actants (2010: 14). Or, in other words, the human subject's corpo-affective meaning-making and shaping of metonyms become an entangled part of the overall process of actants coalescing and co-becoming (Bennett 2010: 14). Bringing this line of thought to bear on my contemplation of immanent miracles, it becomes clear that the mourning 'I' is not the only agency in the assemblage. Therefore, it would be reductive to understand the miraculous excess which I intuitively experienced as emerging from the 'returning' pearls as a mere projection of my human feelings of loss and my desire for reconnection onto a world of non-human (organic and inorganic) things in mechanical motion. Thus, summoning Bennett rather than Freud guides me to speculatively suggest that the miracles, I experienced, can be understood as effects of the vitally material, vibrantly meaning-making mourning assemblages.

Miracles as Markers of the Limitations of Human Knowledge?

To proceed with my speculative forays, aimed at opening up horizons for new questions about the onto-epistemologies of immanent miracles, I shall also summon Spinoza. He is called forth because of his prominent role in the immanence philosophical and vitalist materialist framework in which this book is embedded. But he is also specifically invited to my sounding board because of the chapter on miracles – an otherwise rare topic in modern philosophy – that he wrote as part of his theological political treatise (2007 [1670]). Basically, Spinoza's focus is to demystify the divine miracles described in the Bible, effectively aligning them with an understanding of nature as governed by natural laws. According to Spinoza, miracles occur as a by-product of the limitations of the state of the art of the observer's knowledge:

> From these premises therefore – that in nature nothing happens which does not follow from its laws (...), the term 'miracles' can be understood only with respect to human beliefs, and (...) it signifies nothing other than a phenomenon whose natural cause cannot be explained on the pattern of some other familiar thing or at least cannot be so explained by the narrator or reporter of the miracle.
>
> Ibid.: 84

Spinoza's treatise is evidently modern in an anti-authoritarian, critical sense, opposing the use by Christian and Jewish institutions of claims about divine intervention in the shape of supernatural occurrences to legitimate their powers. However, interpreted in line with a Deleuzean reading, Spinoza's rejection of supernatural miracles in favour of a belief in the laws of nature can perhaps be read, not as a rejection of miracles per se, but as a more open-ended statement. Despite Spinoza's explicit rejection of supernatural miracles, his statement may perhaps implicitly sustain an argument for immanent ones – if we use a Deleuzean lens. Deleuze, thus, reads Spinoza's concept of nature as equating to the plane of immanence:

> One Nature for all bodies, one Nature for all individuals, a Nature that is itself an individual varying in an infinite number of ways. What is involved is no longer the affirmation of a single substance, but rather the laying out of a *common plane of immanence* on which all bodies, all minds, and all individuals are situated.
>
> 1988: 122

Against this background of Deleuze's reading of Spinoza's concept of nature as a plane of immanence, the latter's way of anchoring miracles firmly in nature (2007 [1670]: 84) could thus be understood as linking them to this plane that is radically vital, profoundly unpredictable, and impossible to fully grasp from a limited human perspective. Along these lines, immanent miracles could perhaps be speculatively understood as events that emerge in accordance with matter's rhizomatic and conative spacetimemattering, but which in their vibrant complexity, intense fluidity, and changeability are incomprehensible to the human reporter. Read through the lens of Deleuze, Spinoza's argument on miracles as markers of epistemic limitations of the human subject allows me to speculate that the miraculous excesses that I experienced as part of my mourning might be produced immanently, but in ways that – currently and perhaps forever – it will be impossible to grasp from a limited human perspective.

To the latter part of this statement, I would like to add a clarification. The distinction between a focus on current epistemic limitations and a forever-impossible-to-comprehend corresponds, to some extent, with that between a transhumanist (Boström 2005) and a critical posthumanist (Braidotti 2013, 2018; Ferrando 2019) perspective.[3] Ethically, I prefer the humble approach of the latter. Transhumanist thought is based on a belief in unlimited human knowledge-building and a corresponding unlimited (techno)scientific development, at least in principle. In contrast, a critical posthumanist approach rejects the human exceptionalizing progress narrative, which implies that (techno)scientific knowledge-seeking will, in due time, enable us to understand everything that we do not know today. From a transhumanist perspective, epistemic limitations such as those discussed above would be acknowledged, but considered temporary – i.e. seen as that which 'cannot yet' be explained. Seen from the perspective of the worldwide ecological and social crises generated by the entanglement of capitalist extractivism, colonialism, and modern technoscience, I think it is ethically important to deconstruct the *hubris* of the sovereign subject and its belief in the unlimited powers of human knowledge-seeking. Therefore, I shall remove the 'not yet' from the equation, and speculate that immanent miracles could be understood as material occurrences, which will perhaps forever remain incomprehensible from a human perspective, even though their emergence might be fully in accordance with the immanent, vitally material workings of matter, and not in need of any kind of transcendent explanation. Or, put differently: giving up a positivist onto-epistemology and its implication that we live in a mechanically predictable, controllable, and in principle transparent world, governed by immutable laws, and instead opting for a vitalist, immanence philosophical understanding of worlding as rhizomatic, conative spacetimemattering, the world becomes radically open-ended. Taking such an open-ended and vibrantly processual world as my ontological point of departure, I speculate that unpredictable things such as 'returning' pearls, unexpectedly coalescing assemblages, and thickly clustering metonymical relations can occur, even though we (humans) may not ever be able to find a 'natural' explanation. We do not have to resort to divine intervention or other kinds of transcendent agencies to make sense of such events.

Still, 'miraculously returning pearls' do not seem to fit very well into mainstream modern onto-epistemologies. Moreover, beyond Spinoza, the issue of miracles does not seem to figure centrally on the agendas of vitalist materialists or immanence philosophers. So, to further substantiate my speculative claim about immanent miracles, I shall summon more helpers to my sounding board.

Diffracting Modern and A-modern Approaches to Miracles?

The next helper to be summoned is chosen because it may enable me to speculate about miracles in ways that exceed the frames of contemporary Western philosophy, while also being helpful for creating pluriversal conversations and diffracting interference patterns with the philosophies of immanence and vitalist materialism upon which my argument has been built so far. More precisely, I shall take a closer look at the genealogies of the concept of the actant. In particular, I will consider the a-modern aspects of these genealogies, recalling Latour's argument (1993: 47) (highlighted in the previous chapter) that the term 'a-modern' may help us to avoid categorizations along the lines of a linear historical movement from 'premodern' to 'modern'.

In this and the previous chapter, I have so far used the term actant in line with Bennett's reflections on thing-power (2010). Bennett's inspiration here is the ways in which the term came to work as an influential impetus to recognize and study the intra-actions of human and non-human agencies emerging from actor-network theory (Callon 1986; Latour 1996). However, the genealogy of the concept of actant is much more complex than this. Here, I want to note and revitalize an important, but rarely discussed, genealogy. The actor-network theorists did not invent the terms actants and actors in order to analyse human/non-human co-productions. Rather, they adopted them from one of the foundational works of structuralism, the linguist Algirdas Julien Greimas' *Structural Semantics* (1974). However, the genealogical links go even further back than Greimas. When he was developing the term actant, he did so against the background of Russian formalist Vladimir Propp's comprehensive study of the morphology of Russian folktales (Propp 1971 [1928]). Genealogically, Propp's study, undertaken in the 1920s, is a crucial stepping-stone for structuralism. But what happens if we trace the genealogies of Propp's work back to the folktales? Based on a very large body of Russian folktales (Afanasjew 1985), Propp showed that their narrative structure can be understood as built upon a limited number of functions (such as protagonist, helper, adversary, conveyor, receiver) – and, importantly, that these functions in each particular tale could be embodied by both human and non-human, both natural and supernatural actors. According to Propp's study, it was the agency of these functions or actors, and *not* that of human characters per se, which, through their actions, generated the tale's plot, and storyline. Or, in other words, in contrast to modern fiction, the folktales did not locate agency with humans alone.

I bring in this genealogy not to discuss narratology, but to interpellate a link between the concept of the actant (so influential for structuralism as well as actor-network theory), posthuman thought and the a-modern ontologies reflected in Russian and broader European bodies of folktales. The tales emerged from ancient oral folk traditions but, as a result of widespread efforts, in particular as part of Romantic and nationalist movements in nineteenth- and twentieth-century Europe, including Russia, they were collected and presented in written collections. These written collections are where the folktales are now to be found. But their genealogies extend back much further than the written versions of these collections. I want to speculatively revitalize these ancient a-modern genealogies in order to let them become a sounding board for the ways in which I have so far in this and the previous chapter, in a Bennett- and Latour-inspired sense, used the concept of actant in my speculations about immanent miracles. Through a revitalization of this genealogy back to the oral traditions, I aim to establish a link with the a-modern ontologies reflected in the folktales. That is, ontologies implying that assemblages of humans and all kinds of non-humans (brooms, animals, plants, mountains, winds, waves, tricksters, monsters, elves, etc.) act and intra-act – and do so without distinguishing between the effects of actions carried out by humans or by non-humans. Allowing the notion of actant to forge this link to the worlding practices of the folktales, I intend to speculatively create resonances with these kinds of a-modern onto-epistemologies. I want to make them vibrate, when I use the term actant to frame coalescing agencies of unruly, transcorporeal assemblages, immanently exerting unpredictable thing-power, which may appear as miraculous to entangled human subjects.

It should be stressed that the enormous body of Russian and broader European folktales was heavily transformed through the processes of establishing written collections for bourgeois entertainment. As part of these processes, the tales became tinged by Christianity – in ways which are somewhat comparable to what happened to indigenous myths and tales from other parts of the world in the wake of colonization and forced Christianization. However, still, it is also worthwhile noticing how the distribution of agency in the folktales cross-cuts any distinctions between the categories of human and non-human, natural and supernatural, as conceptualized by Propp (1971 [1928]) (and Greimas 1974) through the notions of actor/function/actant. This is a useful reminder that Christian and Cartesian ways of ascribing agency only to God and divinely ensouled or 'rationally' embrained humans make up only a small island in an enormous sea of cosm-ontologies which understand the world along much more bio- and geo-egalitarian lines than does modern Western thought.

When I diffract this a-modern onto-epistemological genealogy of the notion of the actant with my Bennett- and Latour-inspired use of that concept, the aim is to enrich my speculative sounding board in pluriversal ways (Tlostanova and Mignolo 2012). With my act of diffraction, and my interpellation of the genealogies of the notion of actant to vibrate when I use the term, I want to forge a pluriversal link. This implies that the a-modern cosm-ontologies of the folktales that emerged from peasant cultures of the European middle ages, and probably further back, should be seriously considered along the lines of the current strands of posthuman thought, upon which I have been drawing in this book until now. I suggest that links to ways of thinking which accept a pluriversal, onto-epistemological egalitarianism, as well as the relevance of a-modern approaches, are important for speculations about immanent miracles – for moving such speculations away from being considered as the effects of madness or 'primitive' superstition.

Spiritual Activism – A Decolonial, Queerfeminist Entrance Point to Miracles?

While contemplating the conceptual genealogies of the actant, I hope to have made it clear that pluriversal thinking may be helpful for my efforts to make sense of miracles without recourse to divine or exceptionally human interventions. Through yet another summoning act, I shall now take a further step along this road. I summon decolonial and queerfeminist philosopher Gloria Anzaldua (1987, 2015), whose work on spiritual activism and a cosm-ontology, framed as a cosmic-scale interconnectedness of everything (human, and non-human), and based on an embodied, spiritual-material vitalism, is also encouraging me to take a pluriversal approach to the miraculous. In Anzaldua's indigenous-inspired, spiritual onto-epistemology of vital cosmic interconnectedness, miracles do happen – and they do not figure as anomalies in the same way as they do when considered through modern Western lenses. Instead of universalizing Western rationalistic frames, relegating miracles to the 'premodern' margins, Anzaldua sees the possibility of miraculous events as an integral part of contemporary everyday life.

To illustrate Anzaldua's way of approaching the miraculous, I want to refer to her description of an exchange of embraces and conversations with a large cypress tree growing close to the ocean in her Californian neighbourhood (Monterey) (Anzaldua 2015: 23, 67, 231). This cypress tree gives Anzaldua strength, healing, and inspiration, she tells us, and, in return, she offers votive gifts of thanks ('*milagritos*', 'small miracles', the diminutive of the Spanish word '*milagro*', miracle). For Anzaldua, the tree embodies the interconnectedness of everything, condensed into the image of the Virgen de Guadalupe.[4] According to Anzaldua, the genealogy of this Virgin Mary figure connects it, not to elitist versions of Catholicism, but rather to a folk Catholicism with genealogical links to Aztec and earlier Mesoamerican spiritualities. The Virgen de Guadalupe is thus closely related to the goddess Coatlalopeuh, who emerged from the Aztec earth and fertility goddess, Coatlicue. The latter is a goddess who plays an important role in Anzaldua's reclaiming of her Aztec ancestry (1987: 49). The miraculous, spiritual-material, transspecies communication which Anzaldua conducts with the tree is thus one of the ways in which she articulates her ancestral (Aztec) heritage and shamanistic consciousness. But it also embodies her *mestiza* upbringing, her political border consciousness, and her feelings of belonging to cultural in-between spaces in the borderlands between Mexico and the United States. Moreover, the intra-action with the tree confirms Anzaldua in her queer identity and her links to political communities and activism, as well as to her feelings of cosmic and planetary interconnectedness beyond national, gendered, racial, and species borders and divisions. She defines the complex entanglements embodied by the tree as related to a 'new tribalism':

> El árbol de la vida (the tree of life) symbolizes my 'story' of the new tribalism. Roots represent ancestral/racial origins and biological attributes; branches and leaves represent the characteristics, communities, and cultures that surround us, that we've adopted, and we're in intimate conversation with. Onto the trunk de mi árbol de la vida I graft a new tribalism. This new tribalism, like other new Chicano/Latino narratives, recognizes that we are responsible participants in the ecosystems (complete set of interrelationships between a network of living organisms and their physical habitats) in whose web we're individual strands.
> Anzaldua 2015: 67

Against the background of these descriptions, I interpret the tree as a spiritmattering metonym which, for Anzaldua, miraculously condenses the interconnectedness of everything in the universe beyond all borders, divisions, and dualisms. Anzaldua immerses herself in this spiritmattering cosmic interconnectedness when she embraces the tree, stretches out on its protruding roots or sits with her back against its trunk to become one with it (2015: 67). For Anzaldua, attending to the deeply embodied feeling of interconnectedness reflects what she defines as spiritual activism. She understands such an activism as an intersectional (ecopolitical, decolonial, anti-racist, and queerfeminist) practice of resistance and struggle for political change, and for social and environmental justice. This is a practice that is fuelled by experiences of spiritual material miracles, growing out of everyday life events such as the bodily embracing of and communication with the tree.

There is an affinity between Anzaldua's ontology and the universe of the folktales. Both direct me towards a world where spiritmattering agencies are not reserved for humans or monotheistic, patriarchal gods; instead, such agencies are perceived to exist everywhere. Anzaldua's ontology and the universe of the folktales suggest that it is the interconnections of these agencies that allow miracles to happen as an integrated part of everyday life. However, while the world of the folktales has been subdued by the linear trajectory of modern Western narratives of progress and marginalized as remnants of a 'premodern' and 'outdated' belief system, Anzaldua insists that an ontology of transcorporeal agencies that may generate miracles is part of the contemporary world. This is why Anzaldua figures as a prominent member of my sounding board, emphasizing how crucial its pluriversal composition is.

Diffracting Vitalist Materialist and Spiritual Materialist Approaches to Miracles?

So far, my sounding board has helped me to speculatively frame different approaches to immanent miracles. Through the conversations with Bennett and

Spinoza/Deleuze, a vitalist materialist entrance point has become visible, while a spiritual materialist one is emerging from the dialogue with Anzaldua, backed by the ontologies which can be traced in the folktales. But, in order to establish a pluriversal discussion, it is also necessary to shape an interactive relation between the different framings. So, how do the vitalist materialist and spiritual materialist frameworks talk to each other?

To address this question, I summon yet another helper, decolonial feminist scholar Felicia Amaya Schaeffer (2018), who made an in-depth analysis of Anzaldua's spiritualist materialism. In addition to this, Schaeffer is also important in my context because she, like me, wants to put Anzaldua and feminist posthumanism in dialogue with each other:

> My other goal is to spark a dialogue between Chicanx/Latinx decolonial theory in the flesh and feminist debates on experiential epistemologies and ontologies in the field of new materialism, [and] to push both fields into what I call Anzaldua's cosmic spirit-mattering, a Native-based scientific practice and philosophy that bridges indigenous cosmologies with a dazzling range of disciplines and knowledges that span alchemy, shamanism, psychology, Western and Native folklore, and science and technology studies.
>
> Schaeffer 2018: 1008

The convergence between my own and Schaeffer's projects is an important reason for inviting her to my sounding board. But I am also aware that my entrance point to a conversation between feminist posthumanism and spiritualist materialism is differently situated than Schaeffer's. I must carefully scrutinize the epistemologies of ignorance in which my location as a white Western academic have entangled me. Quoting decolonial feminist scholar Zoe Todd (2016), Schaeffer thus, as a *caveat* to me and other Western posthumanists, problematizes the colonial gesture implied in the ways in which Anzaldua, and indigenous cosmologies more generally, have not been properly credited by posthuman theory:

> As Zoey Todd reminds us, Western theories of the nonhuman and the ontological turn rely on Native ideas without crediting 'indigenous thinkers for their millennia of engagement with sentient environments, with cosmologies that enmesh people into complex relationships between themselves and *all* relations, and with climates and atmospheres as important points of organization and action' (Todd 2016: 6–7).
>
> Schaeffer 2018: 1014

I take the critical point, which Schaeffer – aligned with Todd – is making here. Following the insight I gained from Camila Marambio's interview with me, I also endorse the implication that feminist posthumanism, including its vitalist materialist and immanence philosophical branches, on which my argument in this book has been built so far, should engage in unlearning and relearning processes, while committing to pluriversal conversations. So, while I find it important to tease out potential grounds for a conversation on miracles between spiritualist and vitalist materialisms, I also want to do my best to avoid repeating colonial gestures. While looking for convergences, therefore, I also take Schaeffer's pinpointing of certain important divergences and power relations into account.

However, first, let me underline that, in line with Schaeffer (2018) and Barad (2014), I do see many convergences. Camila's interview with me brought me to understand how deeply spiritualist materialism challenges the key ontological foundations of so-called rational modern thought, such as its distinction between 'real' and 'not-real'. However, notably, vitalist materialism and immanence philosophy are likewise profoundly critical of the ontological foundations of Western modernity. So, convergences between the vitalist materialist and spiritualist materialist perspectives, articulated in my sounding board, can be clearly traced. They share a critique of the ways in which modern technoscientific imaginaries reduce the material world to inert matter in mechanical motion, and interpret any thought of vital non-human agencies as being caught in a blind alley of the 'not-real'. In this sense, both strands of thought would also, at least indirectly, be critical of the foreclosure of speculations on immanent miracles in modern rationalistic thought. When it comes to the question of effectively undermining modern onto-epistemologies that make 'real'/'not-real' distinctions against the background of Cartesian and Newtonian understandings of the world as machine, and define non-human agency as caused exclusively by external pushing or pulling forces, I would probably also gain approval from all sides of my sounding board, when enlisting Barad's framing of agential realism (2007)[5] and her posthumanist feminist reading of quantum physics as an ally.

Second, however, beyond the outspoken convergences between the different materialisms that I have invited into my sounding board, there are also frictions and divergences. In addition to the previously mentioned lack of full acknowledgement of indigenous philosophy's contributions to posthuman theory, Schaeffer also pinpoints specific frictions emerging from the questions of soul, ensoulment, spirit, and spirituality. She emphasizes the ways in which Bennett's rejection of 'ensoulment', and hence 'spirituality', 'clashes' with Anzaldua's shamanistic onto-epistemology, and criticizes Bennett for conflating 'spirituality and religion' (Schaefer 2018: 1015). Since the question of 'soul and spirit' is linked to that of agencies insofar as, for those believing in them, souls and spirits are supposed to be endowed with the ability to act, it is of key importance to my framing of immanent miracles to dig more deeply here. So I will try to tease out what impact Schaeffer's critique of Bennett can have for my speculations. Does it make sense to engage Bennett and Anzaldua in pluriversal conversations via my sounding board?

I have emphasized that I do not want to give final answers. Nevertheless, to pose the question of miracles requires a speculative reflection on the source of the agencies producing them, and here notions of 'soul' and 'spirit' keep knocking on the door. This is due to the ways in which miracles have been associated in powerful Christian traditions with divine communication with 'true' – in a Christian sense, ensouled – human believers. Framed along the lines of Bennett's vitalist materialism, my speculative question about the source of the agency potentially producing immanent miracles could be articulated like this: can these potentially miracle-producing agencies be speculatively understood as effects of matter's own vitality? Or does the way in which I suggest that we think about these agencies imply that, through the back door, matter once more becomes pervaded by what Bennett with Kant[6] calls 'an alien principle (soul)' (2010: 66)? In her definition of a vitalist materialism, Bennett is very keen on philosophically closing the back door to any kind of ensoulment of matter. So, basically, my speculations on miracles would run aground within Bennett's framework, if I do not make certain to keep the back door to ensoulment closed. Bennett seems to be as eager to keep clear of ensoulment as Spinoza (2007 [1670]) is to exorcize beliefs in supernatural miracles, and to redefine those described in the Bible as the results of natural phenomena. I endorse Spinoza's modern urge to philosophically de-authorize religious institutions, which legitimize their oppressive powers through recourse to supernatural miracles, performed by a monotheistically defined divinity. Likewise, I can follow Bennett in her feminist posthumanist urge to theoretically and politically undermine the conservative and Christian fundamentalist policies of so-called 'soul vitalists' (2010: 87). Soul vitalists see life, the vital principle, as delinked from matter, which is conceived as inert and mechanical, and instead as connected to the divine, to an exceptionally human ensoulment and to a hierarchy among ensouled humans. This is a vitalism which is deployed by right-wing Christian fundamentalists to claim the ensoulment of the human embryo in order to legitimize anti-abortion campaigns. More generally, this kind of soul vitalism can also philosophically be used to legitimize capitalist extractivist ways of exploiting and instrumentalizing non-human matter in the name of human exceptional superiority.

I find Bennett's critical discussion of the soul vitalism of the Christian fundamentalist right in the USA (Bennett 2010: 86–9) politically and theoretically important and in resonance with my critique of normative Christian dualist thought in this book. *But* I also listen carefully when Schaeffer makes the point that Bennett's total rejection of ensoulment 'clashes', in problematic ways, with Anzaldua's onto-epistemology. Illustrated through Bennett's rejection of ensoulment, but also through a lack of in-depth reflections on spirit helpers, traced in Haraway (2016: 88),[7] Schaeffer (2018: 1011–16) argues that feminist posthumanism and new materialism tend towards upholding too-limited positions on the world's immanent vitality and cosmic interconnectedness. According to Schaeffer (2018: 1014), these limitations are caused by a lack of knowledge and understanding of the kind of ensoulment and spirituality which is theorized by Anzaldua (and indigenous philosophies more broadly) as spiritmatter(ing).[8] But the limitations perhaps also stem from a certain resistance to the idea of a spirited world altogether: 'Why is it easier for Haraway (and moderns) to cross into a world of orchids than to travel with indigenous communities, including the Inuit, in their virtual journeys with spirit guides?' Schaeffer critically asks (ibid.: 1014). I think that what Schaeffer is touching upon here is closely related to the kind of modern resistances that also led me to locate the miracles I experienced with my dying beloved within a liminal space in-between the 'real' and the 'not real', until Camila Marambio pushed me to think differently. Against this background, I want to dig more deeply into the ways in which Anzaldua's and Schaeffer's way of theorizing spiritmattering is decisively different from the Western Christian-tinged understandings of soul, spirit, ensoulment, and spirituality, which critical moderns from Spinoza to secular feminists and new materialists like Bennett, Haraway and me have been so keen to reject that we perhaps have overlooked the potentials of other kinds of non-Christian ontological approaches to spiritmattering.

To distinguish spiritmattering from ensoulment in a Christian sense, it is important to consider how the notion of soul has been heavily colonized as Christian missionaries, following closely in the footsteps of other modern Western conquerors, have worked for centuries to 'harvest souls' in indigenous lands (Gernet 1994: 40).[9] Against this background, it is politically and theoretically crucial to decolonize the notion of soul, and this implies being specific about the very different meanings of ensoulment to which Schaeffer is referring, when pinpointing the limitations of modern feminist posthumanist minds. Even though I can only make such specifications crudely, due to my limited Western perspective, I shall try, knowing full well that these differences are also of key importance for my speculations on miracles. I do not claim to be able to understand more than fragments of Anzaldua's shamanistic understanding of spiritmattering, and take one more of Todd's critical points, when she underlines that, although an indigenous scholar herself, she humbly acknowledges that she, for example, only understands 'an infinitesimal bit of the concept of Sila' (a complex Inuit concept incorporating climate, weather, and breath) (Todd 2016: 5). Being the white Western academic into which my biography has shaped me, I am aware that I probably understand even less than an 'infinitesimal bit', when it comes to Anzaldua's approach to spiritmattering. However, I hope that Schaeffer (2018) and Todd (2016) might agree with me that maintaining modern Western epistemologies of ignorance is even more problematic than admitting a lack of knowledge, while still trying to make some sense of a concept, based on the little knowledge you have. So, the following reflections on Christian and indigenous philosophical understandings of 'soul/spirit' should be understood as written from a humble position.

With this *caveat* in mind, I will elaborate on Schaeffer's argument and claim that there are decisive differences between Anzaldua's notions of soul/spirit and the notion of soul that Bennett with Kant rejects as an 'alien principle' not to be mobilized as a 'supplement' to matter in order to define its agency (Schaeffer 2018: 1015). First, 'soul' in a Christian sense is defined in relation to a monotheistic god, i.e. a bounded divine entity. As a mirror of this entity, the soul is also imagined as unitary. In contrast, the spirit/soul world in a non-monotheistic context must be understood as being as multiple as the pantheon of gods, half-gods, tricksters, spirit-helpers etc. which a-modern tales and myths line up in abundance no matter where on Earth these stories have emerged. Second, in the dominant Christian imaginary, which is embedded in an ontology that has installed a dichotomous separation between divine/soul/mind and matter, the entitized and unitary soul is also imagined as disembodied and immaterial, again mirroring the divine entity. Conversely, a non-dualist ontology will allow the spirit/soul world to exist in many different and shifting relations to bodies; for example, being linked to them, shape-shifting together with them, or detaching itself from them to travel in space and time. Third, in imaginaries grounded in ontologies that dichotomously separate culture from nature, human from non-human, which Christianity and modernity do in conjunction with each other, soul is imagined as strictly and exceptionally related to the human/culture side of the divide. In contrast to this, a-modern and indigenous ontologies, which do not dichotomously separate human/culture and non-human/nature, will understand spirit/soul as trickster-like, diversified, and boundary-crossing in this respect, too. Spirit/soul will be understood as manifold and performing in a manner that is not bounded by all the divides of human/non-human, mind/matter, and culture/nature which count as hierarchical and decisive boundaries in a dualist ontology.

The notion of ensoulment and the kind of soul vitalism that Bennett rejects as non-compatible with her branch of vitalist materialism is evidently the Christian-tinged one. If Anzaldua's notion of spirit/soul can be understood along the lines of my crude sketch of a non-dualistic, unbounded spiritual multiplicity, then it is completely different from what Bennett discusses under the rubric of 'soul' and 'ensoulment'. Anzaldua does not imply that there is one soul-like force that exists outside of the material World. When she embraces ensoulment along the lines of her ancestral Aztec cosm-ontologies, 'soul/spirit' is not dichotomously delinked from body-, earth- and cosmos-matter. In contrast, when Anzaldua, for example, embraces the Virgen de Guadelupe tree, body-matter (Anzaldua's body) and tree-matter (the cypress tree) are both ensouled in an en-fleshed and en-vegetated[10] sense. Moreover, Anzaldua and cypress become each other; Anzaldua becomes cypress tree, and the tree becomes human flesh.

Against this background, when I consider the crucial question of whether or not Anzaldua and Bennett can reasonably be summoned into a meaningful pluriversal conversation, my answer is that such a conversation does, indeed, make sense. When I look at Anzaldua's multiple and cosmic spiritmattering and Bennett's affectively vibrant matter – together with Rosi Braidotti's *zoe*, discussed earlier in the book – I see their different pieces of advice as diffractable, and able to work, pluriversally, in resonance with each other. All of them can contribute to my speculations about an ontology that makes immanent miracles thinkable as phenomena emerging from coalescing spirited and affect-laden, vibrantly mattering, immanent forces. The spiritual material cosmic interconnectedness of everything in Anzaldua's ontology, Bennett's vitalist materialist claim about matter's immanent conativity and affectivity, and Braidotti's Deleuze-inspired conceptualization of the inhuman forces of *zoe* are pluriversally grounded in differing philosophical outlooks: an indigenous (Aztec)-inspired spiritual materialist cosm-ontology and alternative monist and immanence philosophical strands of Western philosophy. But these different frameworks for understanding the world's vital and spiritual mattering – and its related powers to generate immanent miracles – must also be seen as meaningfully diffractable in Barad's sense (2014). Even though I and other Western scholars must pay careful self-critical attention to limiting epistemic habits and epistemologies of ignorance coming out of Western modernity and Enlightenment, I believe that pluriversal conversations between these different approaches can work productively. This is due to the ways in which they all critically-affirmatively differentiate themselves from the dualisms of mainstream modern Western thought, which is moulded by a Christian understanding of a unitary, divine soul dichotomously and hierarchically delinked from matter, and/or by a Cartesian divide between a thinking human mind and mechanically functioning, inert matter.

Miraculous and Ethical Entanglements of the Mourning 'I'

With my sounding board as helpers, I have now established a pluriversal cluster of diffractable approaches to immanent miracles. These approaches are speculative in the sense that they do not give final answers. But I hope to have made it clear that each of the approaches is aligned with onto-epistemologies within the frameworks of which they can claim to make philosophical sense in terms of a 'could-be', the formula par excellence for speculation within the range of the plausible (Bellacasa 2017: 59).[11] Immanent miracles could be imagined as being generated in this way. Along the lines of such a could-be, I shall round off my speculations by trying out one possible way of making the different approaches momentarily coalesce into a tentative answer to the question that I posed in the introduction to the previous chapter: 'do miracles happen?' Putting emphasis on the could-be, I will now tentatively reply as follows.

Yes, immanent miracles may happen. But if/when they occur, they do *not* do so because of the intervention of divine or exceptional human powers. Miracles are instead to be seen as effects of the world's immanent material vitality and spiritmattering, and the interconnectedness of everything, which constantly produces all kinds of unexpected and unpredictable, affective intensities, interference patterns, and metonymically meaning-making assemblages. Miracles – just as much as mutating viruses or excessively growing cancer cells – are immanent effects of the wild and messy processes that make up the world. If/when miracles appear to humans, they do so as effects of occurring affective intensities and spiritmatterings in human/non-human assemblages. Miraculous events do not happen due to projections on the part of sovereign human observers, or because of interventions from divine master minds. Miracles, as they appear to humans, are immanent effects of corpo-affective co-becomings of entangled vitally and spiritually material human/non-human actants. These co-becomings are to be understood as events which the human actor may sense as miraculous and wondrous because they occur unexpectedly, and incomprehensibly from a human perspective, but also because they actualize assemblages that include intense affectivities, spiritmatterings, and thick clusters of metonymical relations. As a human, I can only guess how these events might appear to the non-human actors within the assemblages. But most likely they appear in totally different ways, when experienced from other situated perspectives than human ones.

If this tentative, speculative – in no way definitive – answer to the question of miracles stands up as plausible, i.e. as meeting the criteria of a speculative, could-be philosophical explanation, their occurrence is, in a way, also to be understood as a common thing – a part of everyday life in a vitally and spiritually mattering and vibrating conative world of cosmic interconnectedness. Anzaldua and the ancient tellers of folktales would confirm this, I think. But if miracles are common in this sense, it is perhaps not at all strange that I experienced a rhizomatically unfolding cluster of all kinds of miracles as part of my mourning. As articulated in the poems of *Interludes III* and *IV*, and in the story *Will I Meet You Here or There*, the miracles I experienced were numerous, multiple, and diverse. They involved all the elements: water, fire, air, and earth, along with a fifth one: body. They ranged from pearls returning from the sea to a fire outside my kitchen window, from a heavy chapel door flying open on a day without wind to a gorgeously flowering plant that had never produced so many flowers before, from the unexpected, but significant, arrival of a multicoloured kitten to my being held by my beloved when swimming in the waters surrounding Fur – to mention just a very few. This multitude of miracles somehow reflects their everydaylikeness, which Anzaldua also underlines.

However, even if I accept that miracles are an immanent and common part of the world's vitally and spiritually mattering immanent way of working, why did I suddenly experience so many of them? Why had I not experienced such an abundance of miracles before I entered into the process of excessive mourning? I think the answer to these questions lies in the ways in which my state of mourning led me to spontaneously unfold the sensibilities and sensitivities necessary to sense, experience, become aware of, and act response-ably[12] (with the ability to respond in a situated, sensitive, and ethical way, Haraway 2008: 88–9) to the vital and spiritual material agencies of the more-than-human world of animals, plants, sea, winds etc. I shall therefore end this chapter by speculating upon the conditions for the emergence of such sensibilities and sensitivities.

For Anzaldua, the unfolding of sensibilities and sensitivities to spiritual material agencies is related to shamanism, and shamanistic learning processes. Along the lines of her ancestral traditions, Anzaldua names the sensibilities and sensitivities upon which she herself draws as *naguala*. She explains '*naguala*' as an ability to unfold a dual shamanic vision (2015: 32–3), implying a becoming sensitive to the ways in which the spirit world of interconnectedness unfolds from the world's surfaces of separate-looking things – when, for example, the Virgen de Guadalupe, alias the Aztec goddess Coatlicue, emerges from a cypress tree in a neighbourhood of Monterrey, and materializes a cosmic connectedness. As I interpret Anzaldua's text, the sensibilities and sensitivities on which the shamanistic *naguala* consciousness ('*conocimiento*', 2015: 40) are corpo-affectively grounded, are immanent. This means that there are no authoritarian or elitist requirements or moral hierarchies at stake in their emergence. The cultivation of sensibilities and sensitivities can come to the fore and unfold in an everyday, do-it-yourself manner.

However, importantly for people brought up with a modern mechanistic perception of the cosmos, and with dualist and hierarchical understandings of culture/nature, mind/body, soul-spirit-divine/matter, human/non-human, it requires a willingness to enter into the kind of in-depth unlearning and relearning processes that Tlostanova and Mignolo (2012) have theorized. Modern subjects like me would need to unlearn the de-enchantment (Bennett 2001) of the world on which the onto-epistemologies of Western modernity are based, and relearn to sense its immanent and material vitality, and its spiritmattering. This would include a retraining of sensibilities and a relearning of the abilities to be sensitive and response-able to the ways in which we, as vitally material and spiritmattering bodies, are entangled with the world. We would, as modern subjects, have to relearn how to understand ourselves as integrated parts of the world's complex sympoietic,[13] symanimagenic[14] and cosmically interconnected assemblages, rather than as separate sovereign subjects in control of a world of inert objects in mechanical motion. We would have to learn to become-one with this vitally and spiritually mattering world, while sensing the affectivity, spirituality, and interconnectedness of everything. Such unlearning and relearning processes are crucial for an unfolding of the kind of decolonial spiritual activism for which Anzaldua argues.

For my own part, as white Western subject, I do not claim, just like that, to be able to enter shamanistic processes such as those described by Anzaldua. It would be an act of cultural appropriation and disrespect for long-learned and diversified shamanistic traditions, which I only know superficially, to make such a claim. However, I suggest that there are other, less sophisticated, but spontaneously occurring paths to become, at least crudely, susceptible and sensitive to the world's cosmic liveliness, including its miraculous events. My contemplations in this book have led me to suggest that excessive mourning may generate such a susceptibility and sensitivity. In particular, I think that delving into excessive mourning against the background of a longstanding queer femme, intensely symphysizing companionship with my beloved, has launched me into this kind of susceptibility. My strong desire to reconnect and, in a vitally and spiritually mattering sense, to co-become with her inhuman, but likewise vitally and spiritually mattering, remains and their new assemblages (algae, sand, etc.), has awakened sensibilities and generated new sensitivities in me. To a great extent, this has occurred spontaneously, not as something that I willed or planned. Nonetheless, the process of entering into molecular mourning, and co-becoming with the inhuman remains of my beloved and their new assemblages, was no doubt important for my unlearning and relearning. This process led me towards an unlearning of molar human mourning as the only possible mourning practice, and to a relearning of new spiritual material ways of mourning molecularly, while extending my strong skills in queer femme symphysizing with my beloved to her inhuman remains and their new assemblages.

Against the background of these reflections, I want, in a more general sense, to speculatively suggest that excessive states of mourning and symphysizing desires for love-death can facilitate processes of unlearning the unethical habits of the sovereign modern subject, and its unhelpful onto-epistemological approaches that blind it to the world's vitally and spiritually mattering, transcorporeal and affective interconnectedness. Mourning, practised in a posthuman and non-exceptionalizing, molecular sense, has the potential, I argue, to unfold into a platform for disrupting and unlearning the habits and onto-epistemologies which make the sovereign modern subject insensitive and blind to immanent miracles. The ethical potential of excessive, molecular mourning is thus to be seen in its ability to perhaps facilitate unlearning and relearning processes, leading the mourning 'I' to unfold new posthuman sensibilities. These are sensibilities which may implicate the mourner in processes of becoming-sensitive and becoming-response-able to the world's unruly and immanent vitality, vibrancy, spiritmattering and interfering cosmic and planetary interconnectednesses, which at times are becoming-intense, to such a degree, that miraculous events shape up.

Interlude VI

GLISSANDO (GLIDING BETWEEN PITCHES)

Illustr. 8 Glissando (Gliding between Pitches). © Nina Lykke 2015.

MOURNING CIRCLES

1.
Many are the kinship circles
that spring to life
in times of mourning.

2.
A son sits at a table
with his dying mother and the widow-soon-to-be.
They tell him the prognosis,
and take his hands
united in unfathomable sorrow.
Another son
comes rushing back from Mexico.
The dying mother climbs laboriously
out of her deep morphine sleep
to greet him home one last time.
A snapshot from his cell phone
shows mother and son hand in hand.

3.
A son and two old friends arrive
the moment they are called to help
the widow-soon-to-be,
who recognizes
that her dying beloved
needs more than one prosthetic extra body
during her final days.

4.
A brother comes to see his dying sister,
bringing her an old and yellowed photo
of him and her,
from the time when they were kids.

5.
A rainbow daughter,
since long divorced from the partner
who first introduced her to the family circle,
but still belonging closely to it,
arrives to say a last goodbye.
For a long, long time
she sits next to
her dying

rainbow mother
whom she has known since she was very young.
Shared tears of grief flow,
when she and the widow-soon-to-be
embrace each other in the hallway,
before she travels back
to where she lives.

6.
So they flock around the deathbed,
sitting there for many hours,
taking turns in holding hands,
and from time to time,
they moisten the lips and mouth
of their beloved
partner, mother, rainbow mother …
In the kitchen, another rainbow circle member is making
a delicious coq au vin
to strengthen the resilience of the mourners.
They watch and care, alternately, for the dying,
taking breaks to eat,
and then return to watch again,
till Death arrives.
After that they sit together, lingering,
around the bed of the deceased.

7.
Three grandchildren stand in silence,
looking at their dead grandmother.
Another grandchild draws a mandala wheel
as a gift for the deceased.
Yet, another rainbow circle member phones a female undertaker.

8.
Then they gather around the table in the living room,
a multiple rainbow kinship body,
united in bereavement,
planning a funeral ceremony together,
which will widen the mourning circle even further.

9.
Yet more mourners take part in the rituals
of fire, air, water, earth, and body,
celebrating all kinds of friend- and kinship bonds,
bringing many gifts to the deceased

with a strong collective wish
that they may be useful for her,
when she now transitions
into the unknown.

10.
A sister brings a huge bouquet of tulips
to her dead sister's casket,
and commemorates,
the much beloved and admired elder sister's
magic powers
to fill their childhood games
of a long gone past
with pleasurable horrors.

11.
A widow kisses her dead beloved's casket passionately
covering the lid with many, many dark-red roses.
When the female undertaker drives the hearse away,
the widow follows it,
as long as she can,
blowing thousands of kisses from her fingers:
'My love, my love, we'll meet again!'
A sister puts her arm around the widow,
standing now abandoned,
still waving to the disappearing car.

12.
Two brothers embrace each other, sobbing,
when the hearse leaves with their dead grandmother.
With their arms full of flowers,
two other brothers run home,
so that the January garden, now in full bloom,
can welcome the multiple group of mourners
returning from the funeral ceremony
as one great body,
made up of many rainbow kin- and friendship circles.

DEATH'S METAMORPHOSES

1.
Your moment of death seemed calm and peaceful.
But exhaling without inhaling again
made you different,
pushed you over a threshold
between the 'I' you had been
and the corpse you were becoming.
Before you were animate
like me,
in need of oxygen, and warm-blooded
as other mammalian beings.
Now you do not need oxygen anymore.
So what have you become?

Tell me, oh, tell me, about your new world, my love.
Teach me, oh teach me to attune!

2.
The fire of cremation
transformed you to white, soft ashes,
three-four kilo ashes.
We got you back from the undertaker
in a blue ecological urn,
made of a material which dissolves in water.
Eigil carried the package with the urn back to me in Odense.
A woman in the train
took him to task
because he had occupied the seat next to his
with the package.
'This is my mother,' he answered quietly.
I slept with the urn next to me
every night
until we sailed out
and lowered it into Limfjorden
outside of the cliffs of Fur.

Tell me, oh, tell me, about your new world, my love.
Teach me, oh teach me to attune!

3.
When the blue walls of the urn dissolved,
your ashes spread on a seabed of sand
made from diatoms,

single cell algae,
fossilized fiftyfive million years ago,
when a warm subtropical sea
covered the area
which later turned into the island of Fur.
You are now surrounded
by a wild abundance
of living and dead materials,
floating in this underwater world:
Currently living algae,
nourishment for oysters,
settling on stones,
performing sex-transing,
while giving birth to
larvae,
dancing,
among seagrass and floating shells of dead oysters,
embrace particles of your ashes
mixed with algae sand.

Tell me, oh, tell me, about your new world, my love.
Teach me, oh teach me to attune!

4.
Indigenous people in Australia
dance funeral dances
in ancestral land,
stirring up the dust,
inhaling it,
letting it penetrate all pores
of their skin,
to incorporate and stay attuned
with the dead ancestors.
I swim in the fjord,
walk on the beach
collect stones and shells
visit the caves,
which the water has carved out in the cliffs,
pay avidly attention to all the signs
from your enchanted underwater world.

5.
But
when the enchantment vanishes,
I curse the reappearing wall of imperceptibility,

trying eagerly to re-immerse myself in stories of your wondrous world, while I wait for a return of the miraculous.

Tell me, oh, tell me, about your new world, my love.
Teach me, oh teach me to attune!

AFTER-LIFE

1.
Tears filled my eyes
and wrenching sobs
started in my chest and stomach
when I first read your paper
on microchimerism,[1]
Margrit![2]
I read it on an early-morning bus,
travelling to work in Sweden
after my beloved's death.
Your paper,
Margrit,
touched me deeply,
making me give in
to silent sobbing,
a paradoxical skill
I have cultivated to perfection
after my beloved's death.
Hiding
behind big sunglasses,
staring intently
out of the window
as we passed a big lake,
strongly reflecting the cool Swedish spring sun,
I wept and wept,
because
what jolted through my body
as a lightening strike
while reading,
was that your paper,
Margrit,
sustained
my intuition
that my dead beloved has not vanished
into nothingness.
Reading about cellular chimeras
with unique genetic make-ups
of more than one individual,
appearing in
pregnancy,
blood transfusion,
and organ transplant
but perhaps even more widespread,
as a transcorporeal rule,

and delving into your biophilosohical
interpretations, Margrit,
of the huge challenge
that these minuscule chimeras pose
to the modernist beliefs in
bounded individuals,
safely demarcated from
each other,
sustained the knowledge of my guts
that my beloved's body,
violently amputated,
from my flesh,
is not dead.
But instead,
as a swarm of small chimeras,
she lives on,
rhizomatically
well dispersed in tissues everywhere,
so transcorporeal bonds
of the queerest kinds of kinship
reconnect me with her,
transforming the aching phantom pains,
healing the amputation wounds.

2.
Uffe found a book on death and time,[3]
suggesting that we read it jointly,
hoping it would help us,
navigating in the void,
opened by the death
of his mother, my beloved.
Reading avidly about the Chukchi people
living in Chukotka, the Chukchi peninsula
in Siberian North East,
awakened my intense desire
to convert to their beliefs
in rebirth
of dead ancestors,
continuously returning,
through the bodies of
the currently living,
while open-endedly allowing
difference to unfold,
transmigrating smoothlessly,
climbing in and out of bodies,
crossing borders

between sexes, species, and genetic lineages
without any need for moral ladders
of award and punishment.

3.
Avidly consuming
microchimerist
philosophy
&
Chukchi
cosmology,
I now immerse myself
in hot dreams
about my beloved's
chimeric
post-humous
existence,
and
smooth
return
in ever new
embodied figurations.

4.
I know you
live
in kin,
in rainbowkin and oddkin,
in friends,
in house and yard and garden,
in plants and trees,
in our multi-coloured cat,
but first of all in me.
You live in all of us
as we have lived in you,
as tiny small chimeras.
We died with you,
you live with us.
I love us all
for being you,
for being us
not you-You,
and not us-Us,
but you-and-us
in post-individual
difference,
and planetary kinship.

5.
But
do Chukchi cosmologies
and
biophilosophical reflections on microchimerism,
really resonate?
Is it possible to make the two
enter into mutually enriching
pluritopic, multi-sited conversations?
Do I have divinatory powers
to read the signs,
to figure out the diagrams
and trace the queer connections?
Or will my attempts to follow up these lines of flight
towards strange configurations
result in acts of improper cultural appropriation of Chukchi beliefs,
while my endeavours
to understand the agency of cellular chimeras bounce against my lack of bioscientific training?
I run the risk,
and claim the links!

> **Interlude VI: Glissando** – In music composition, **Glissando,** Italian for 'gliding', indicates that the voice or instrument, meant to perform the glissando, must glide quickly from one pitch to another, for example, from a high to a low one, or vice versa. The effect of such a gliding can be dramatic – perceived as a jump between very different registers, while still binding these together. The poems of *Interlude VI* introduce different kinds of dramatic glidings, enacted by Death. In *Mourning Circles*, the death of the beloved makes compassionate companions, rainbow kin, kin and friends glide into a sudden void, but the mourners also support the dying and each other, bonding together in close circles. In *Death's Metamorphoses*, the glidings happen through the dramatic transformations which Death makes the body undergo from flesh to ashes, scattered over the sea. In *After-Life*, the glidings are onto-epistemological: the mourning 'I' glides passionately in between very different contemplations of the big unknown, Death. The focus on dramatic glidings are setting the stage for **Chapter 7, Doing Posthuman Autophenomenography, Poetics and Divinatory Figuring**, and its reflections on the experimental methodologies of *Vibrant Death* – methodologies which embrace significant glidings between different kinds of knowledge seeking: through poetry, autobiographical analysis, and philosophy.

Chapter 7

DOING POSTHUMAN AUTOPHENOMENOGRAPHY, POETICS AND DIVINATORY FIGURING

I did not plan to write this book. The book came to me. It started with passionate poetic laments of my beloved's passing. I needed to cry my devastation out loud – very loud. So loud that the concentration on voicing and wording could perhaps absorb some of the bodily pain of the amputation wound that I felt so strongly when death cut my beloved apart from me. Sobbing, crying, weeping, howling – grieving is a deeply embodied process, and the ancient genre of the lament reflects the profound bodily need to voice grief in visceral and fleshy ways. However, the fleshy need to lament was entangled with other, just as passionate and embodied desires. I felt a strong urge to try to bridge the existential gap that my beloved's becoming-imperceptible had opened up between us. I needed to reach beyond the wall of silence, to reconfirm the promise of spiritually mattering reconnection that was embedded in the storytelling practice we had initiated with the miracle and the story about going to the oysters, seaweed, and algae together as ashes. This reaching out comprised the unfolding of spiritual material practices, from the funeral ritual to the scattering of my beloved's ashes beyond the cliffs of Fur, and my annual return to that place in order to immerse myself in it. But a crucial aspect of this reaching out was also to write, read and contemplate.

First of all, I started to write poems and stories out of a strong need to explore in detail the experiences, sensations and thoughts I had had during my beloved's process of dying, and my intuitions and responses to the further transitioning of her remains. I wanted to keep in mind exactly what had happened to me, to her, to our symphysizing companionship. I wanted to be sure that I did not overlook any signs that could teach me something about ways to undo the cutting apart that her death had imposed upon us, and to breach the wall of silence that her becoming-imperceptible had raised between us. Second, I avidly sought out and read any literature and philosophy that I felt could help me to contemplate, understand and sustain my open-ended search for new ontologies of death, dying and afterlife that avoided the traps of Christian and Cartesian dualisms. This reading was also guided by an urge to critically-affirmatively move beyond the atheist beliefs I was brought up with and educated to believe in – an atheism that was built upon a mechanistic-materialist understanding of death as an entrance to nothingness in the sense described by Sartre (1958). Third, it became very important for me to deepen my contemplations and diversify my searches for new ontologies of death and dying through sharing my intuitions and thoughts with other mourners, as well as with communities of scholars, artists, activists and practitioners who were also looking for different figurations, and alternative ways to think-feel-imagine death, dying, afterlife and the life/death threshold. I began writing this book due to all of these entangled needs, and my methodologies emerged from these multiply situated points of departure.

In this chapter, I shall retrospectively reflect upon this process of emergence, and discuss how clusters of methodologies, unfolding along the way, helped me to accomplish my aims with the book. I find it appropriate to do this retrospectively because, in a radical sense, my methodologies are to be understood under the rubric of postqualitative and emergent approaches (St. Pierre 2018). They have been shaped through the process of knowledge-seeking. They have not, in a positivist sense, relied upon pre-prepared models, which have afterwards been applied to or imposed upon the material. When methodologies unfold in this way, as part of the knowledge-seeking process, *sensu strictu*, they cannot be described in advance, but only contemplated in retrospect.

However, as mentioned in the introductory chapter, I do have methodological inspirations. I shall account for them as part of this chapter's retrospective reflection on the overall process of emergence. First, I shall discuss my use of autophenomenography (Allen-Collinson 2009, 2010, 2011; Lykke 2018), combined with creative writing as a method of inquiry (Richardson 2000; Lykke 2010, 2014), which allows for the experimental unfolding of a poetic and narrative form of knowledge-seeking – a knowledge-seeking which I also felt a need to embed in aesthetic gestures that I will discuss as posthumanizing and queering. Second, I shall characterize the methodological approaches of *Vibrant Death* through the lens of two radically postqualitative and experimental methods: divining (Ramey 2012, 2016; MacLure 2021) and figuring (Braidotti 1994; Haraway 2004; Lykke 2010; Thiele 2021), as they have both been interpreted in an immanence philosophical sense. I shall give an account of these overall methodological inspirations, too. Through the lens of an analysis of the poem *After-Life* from *Interlude VI*, I shall reflect upon the ways in which these methodologies have governed my way of linking the book's philosophical and poetic search for knowledge. The analysis of the methodologies at work and reflected in the poem will be addressed as a synecdoche or hologram, which stands in for the whole book as *pars pro toto* (part for whole).[1] The aim of this analysis is to make visible how the entangled effects of the inspirational methodologies mentioned above work in *Vibrant Death*. I will illuminate how they have allowed me to approach the great unknown, Death, through strange configurations of genres and theoretical frameworks. In addition, the analysis will suggest that death can be seen as post-individual and distributed – and that framing it in this way radically alters the conditions for mourning.

Autophenomenography, Poetic and Narrative Writing

My first motivation for writing *Vibrant Death* was the need and desire, through poems and autobiographical stories, to explore my experiences, sensations thoughts, intuitions and responses to my beloved's dying, death, transitionings and afterlife in order to trace signs that could help me to make the wall of silence crumble. Therefore, the methods of autophenomenography (Gruppetta 2004; Allen-Collinson 2009, 2010, 2011), in combination with the use of creative writing as a method of inquiry (Richardson 2000; Lykke 2010, 2014), stood out as appropriate inspirations. In earlier work on death, dying and mourning (Lykke 2018, 2019a–b; Vargas, Marambio and Lykke 2020), I have – together with co-authors – experimented with merging these approaches. In a methodological sense, *Vibrant Death* is a further development of this earlier work, combining poetic modes of writing and autobiographical storytelling with autophenomenographical analysis. In line with the autophenomenographic method, it has been a key issue for me to explore my experiences phenomenologically, while, at the same time, also reconfiguring the phenomenological approach in a queering, posthumanizing and decolonizing way. This process of reconfiguring is intertwined with the poetic-narrative-philosophical exploration of my queerfeminine, symphysizing relationship with the inhuman remains of my beloved and their new assemblages, and interlinked also with my exploring of indigenous-inspired starting points for rethinking spiritmatter(ing).

Autophenomenography (Gruppetta 2004; Allen-Collinson 2009, 2010, 2011; Lykke 2018) is defined as autoethnography with a phenomenological perspective. This implies that the researcher's own experiences are used as research material, as in autoethnography. But instead of culture and place, the prioritized focus is embodiment, bodily situations, corpo-affectivity and relations. As the method of autophenomenography was first being developed (Gruppetta 2004; Allen-Collinson 2009, 2010, 2011), the experiences to be explored were closely conceptualized and understood along the lines of the existentialist-phenomenological body philosophy of Maurice Merleau-Ponty (2001). This implied a focus on human consciousness, orientations and intentionalities. However, a starting point for me is that it is also of key importance in phenomenological analysis to take into account that we as human subjects experience phenomena in deeply corporeal, prelinguistic and affective ways. This implies that bodies often respond before thought. Accordingly, the autophenomenographic researcher should also try to find ways to approach hir own responses at these deeper levels. As Neimanis (2017: 23–4) has argued, this opens up horizons towards a posthuman take on phenomenology, which has been important for my efforts in *Vibrant Death*.

The phenomenological method aims to provide what the ethnographer Clifford Geertz called 'thick descriptions' (1973) of phenomena as they are lived and experienced in actual situations through specific embodied orientations in time and space. Such descriptions position bodies, senses and affects centrally, and call for open-minded accounts with a first-person and 'hereness' character. Working from this kind of phenomenological point of departure, feminist sports scientist Jacquelyn Allen-Collinson argues that autophenomenographic writing can provide 'a powerful lens through which to explore the subjective, richly-textured, lived bodily experience', related specifically to embodiment and affect (2010: 280). She also emphasizes that, in order to do so, a 'thick participation' (Samudra 2008) in the phenomenon to be analysed is crucial (Allen-Collinson 2011: 53). Moreover, in a critical vein, Allen-Collinson stresses the need to provide phenomenological theory and methodology – and hence autophenomenographical studies – with a feminist edge. For her, this implies a focus on intersectional situatedness, and an attention to relationality, which gives priority to intercorporeality and somatic modes of being attentive to the embodied presence of others. I endorse Allen-Collinson's feminist efforts, but I want to take the method even further, aiming for a posthuman autophenomenography. Embedding the methodology in a posthuman context, I shall underline the necessity of also paying attention to transcorporeal relations with the more-than-human world. Such relations have been of key importance for me, insofar as *Vibrant Death* explores my symphysizing transcorporeal co-becoming with the inhuman remains of my dead beloved and their new assemblages.

Writing as a method of inquiry (Richardson 2000; Lykke 2014) – another key methodological inspiration – implies an experimental merging of academic and creative writing modes, and creatively and seriously taking into account the agency of language. As the work of Allen-Collinson (2010, 2011) clearly demonstrates, a form of writing that involves a focus on the literary technique of show-don't-tell[2] (i.e. on 'showing' through scenes, actions and sense details, rather than on 'telling' through explanations) is important in the production of autophenomenographic research material, as it is in ethnographic fieldwork more generally. My methodological inspirations in autophenomenography and writing as a method of inquiry can thus be seen as intertwined. Still, I want to emphasize a difference between my postqualitative, experimental poetic-philosophical summoning of these methodologies and the ways in which they have been defined and used as part of qualitative social research. It is important in my approach that the artistic, *in casu*, poetic and narrative modes of knowledge-seeking and the philosophical analysis are seen as entangled, but equally weighted. One is not meant to be treated as a prosthetic support for the other. The poetic/narrative articulations and the philosophical contemplations are intended to complement each other in a non-hierarchical way. I discuss some of the poems in the philosophical analyses, but not all of them, and the poetic interludes run throughout the book in parallel with the philosophical chapters, converging with them, but materializing their own lines of insights, which are not meant to function as mere illustrations of my philosophical contemplations. The poetic and narrative mode is appropriate for digging deeply into intuitions, sensations, sensibilities and corpo-affectivities, and seeking poetic truths (Lykke 2010; Leavy 2016). The philosophical mode, meanwhile, is well suited to linking thoughts in unexpected ways, and making intellectually plausible and sustainable arguments. For my project, both modes have been crucial, demonstrating Deleuze's point that thinking, feeling and corpo-affective sensing are inextricably intertwined (Deleuze and Guattari 1994). With this general reference to poetic and narrative modes of knowledge-seeking as equally weighted with the philosophical ones, I have described the overall characteristics of my approach. But what about the specifics of my creative – poetic and narrative – writing strategies? How do they resonate with my efforts to unfold a posthuman phenomenology of mourning? I shall take a look at these questions now.

My crossing between different poetic, narrative and philosophical-theoretical genres and modes of knowledge-seeking is indebted to strong currents in parts of feminism to transgress boundaries between genres: such as radical women of colour feminism (Moraga and Anzaldua 1981); Gloria Anzaldua's corpo-political 'autohistorias' (2015: 138) and multi-genre texts (1987, 2015); Audre Lorde's 'biomythography', and work, that also spans a multiplicity of genres (Lorde 1980, 1982, 1984); Donna Haraway's thinking about alternative worlding practices through speculative fabulation, cyborg writing, and feminist science fiction (1991, 2016); Hélène Cixous' poetic experiments with body writing and écriture feminine (1992) – to mention just a few classic examples.

Furthermore, my poetics is framed in resonance with a posthuman aesthetics, profiled through a blurring of boundaries between bodies and artwork/poetic text, and through a redistribution of agency from the poetic/artistic 'I' to the material world and transcorporeal relations. As traced by Ferrando (2016), specifically in relation to the visual and digital arts, this is an aesthetics that has also important feminist genealogies in radical artistic movements such as surrealism and body-art. It is beyond the scope of this book to engage in a more comprehensive discussion of these artistic genealogies. But it should be noted that, as summarized by Ferrando (2016: 5–6), main themes in these traditions are: critical problematizations of boundaries such as flesh/text, inside/outside, dream/reality, subject/object and human/non-human, as well as an affirmative playing with mergers of these previously divided phenomena. Aesthetically, I consider my poetry writing to resonate with this kind of poetic/artistic dissolution of boundaries, redistribution of agencies and undoing of the humanist subject positions of classical (romantic) lyrics. Along these lines, it has been my ambition that the poetic gestures which can be traced in my poems and the philosophically reflected move from molar, human mourning to posthuman, molecular modes, should be seen as working in tandem. It has been an important part of my methodology all the way through to align the poetic, the narrative and the philosophically contemplative modes. However, in order to fully answer the question: how can posthuman endeavours be carried by an activity which is so much associated with humanist traditions, such as poetry writing?, I shall dig deeper into the specifics of my poetic writing practices in the following sections.

The Posthuman Potentials of Metonymical Writing

The specific entanglements of my poetic and philosophical modes of working are multiple. Here, I first of all will draw attention to the ways in which my poetic efforts are carried by a predominantly metonymical, rather than metaphorical, writing style. As discussed in Chapter 5, the metonym is a trope that explores touch and contiguity rather than looking for resemblances and comparisons, as the metaphor does (Jakobson 1987). Much immanence philosophical and new materialist critique of representationalism has focused on the metaphor (e.g. Braidotti 2011: 10–13). But, beyond the specific Lacanian reading of the tropes of metaphor/metonym as the mechanisms of condensation/displacement (1957) the metonym and metonymical writing styles have been understudied. I shall take a closer look at the latter, and make the argument that they do, indeed, hold the potential to explore immanence and the unfolding of posthuman aesthetics.

The theoretical and empirical differences between metonymical and metaphorical poetic styles have been delineated in sophisticated ways by the Russian linguist Roman Jakobson (1987).[3] Jakobson made a detailed examination of how a metonymical writing style works through associations by contiguity, while the metaphorical style, in contrast, constructs poetic worlds through resorting to comparisons, which are interpellated to 'explain' the occurrence through something from another sphere. While the metaphorical writing style thus installs a boundary between the poetic world and explanatory schemes outside of it, the metonymical style will instead work from a poetic field of immanence, allowing sensual touching and contiguity within it to lead the way from one element to the next in the poetic worlding practice.

The metonymical style is not per se related to a posthuman poetics. According to Jakobson (1987), who wrote about metonymy in the first decades of the twentieth century before posthuman thought became an explicit '-ism', a metonymical style is suitable for, among others, realist narrative fiction. For example, it can be a tool for poetic explorations of the human subject's sensuous experiences, cast within the framework of psychological realism. Such a use is in line with a humanist aesthetics – and resonates with a conventional phenomenological approach, which would take an exclusively human point of departure. However, I bring Jakobson's argument about the potentials of metonymical writing into a posthumanist context, and suggest that it also fits well here. To sustain the argument, I want to draw attention once more to Neimanis' (2017) reflections on posthuman phenomenology and her claim that the body phenomenology of Merleau-Ponty (2003) always already has been posthuman insofar as the bodily situation from which it departs thoroughly exceeds subjectivized human levels (Neimanis 2017: 24). Along these lines, I argue that a poetic style, based on metonymical writing, can be suitable for moving poetic text into the realms of a posthuman aesthetics in terms of exploring the poeticizing of this excess. Moreover, I claim a parallel between the posthuman phenomenology of mourning, which I have explored from an immanence philosophical perspective, and my efforts, through a predominantly metonymical writing style, to poeticize my transcorporeal relations to my beloved's inhuman remains and the basic bodily processes of death, dying and mourning. The relations and processes that I explore in my poems can be considered as somewhat equivalent to those discussed by Neimanis (ibid.), when she unfolds her posthuman phenomenology of the ways in which we (humans and non-humans) share a situatedness as and in bodies of water.

To sustain this argument, I will draw attention to the ways in which my poetic writing has been governed by efforts to approach death as a carnal, visceral and very material event, and mourning as difficult and serious bodywork. The first clusters of poems (*Interludes I–II*) work from a kind of posthuman bodily basics (walking, crying, breathing, the embodied materiality of dying, etc.), which, in terms of exceeding mere subjectivized human levels, demonstrate affinities with Neimanis' focus. These basic processes refer to material entanglements which are shared between humans and many different kinds of non-human critters. A poetic focus on these processes therefore contributes to an unexceptionalizing of the human aspect of dying. Later poem clusters (*Interludes III–IV*) are concerned with the fundamental material effects of the beloved's death on the mourning 'I', such as the experience of silence, as well as on my beloved's phenomenal afterlife and the mourning 'I's transcorporeal co-becomings with her inhuman remains and assemblages, again referring to basic human/non-human entanglements. Across thematic differences, it is thus a bottom line that a majority of these poems poeticize posthuman dimensions of death, dying and mourning, and working through metonymical processes fits well in here. Most of the poems thus move associatively from a central, material and more-than-human phenomenon to images related to it through contiguity and touch. In *Breathing Soundscapes*, for example, different configurations of breath and breathing bring one stanza and image in touch with the next. Poems working predominantly through metaphorical comparisons are exceptions. One of the few examples is the first poem, *Laments* in *Interlude I*. This poem is markedly different from the others, comparing as it does lamenting and being taken by undercurrents. The different approach of this poem is related to its programmatic function: to provide an overall introduction to the genre of the lament, which is crucial for my poetics, as I shall discuss a bit later in this chapter.

The Love-Death of the Poetic Subject

Alongside metonymical writing, another related aspect of my poetic methodology, tapping into the realms of a posthuman aesthetics, consists of my efforts to poetically reconfigure both the speaking position of the lyrical 'I' and the distribution of agencies in the poetic worlds I build. Even though my poems are shaped by the passions and affects of a mourning 'I', I see them as part of an aesthetic trend which, in a posthuman vein, runs counter to classic Western romantic lyrics and their celebration of exceptionally human emotions. Classic humanist lyrics, pivoting on Western romantic aesthetics, aim for a 'mimesis of feeling' (Culler 2017: 9), implying that the lyrical 'I' is delving into its 'inner' universe of exceptionally human feelings, called forth by its encounters with the outside world – indulging in what has mockingly been called 'the egotistical sublime' (Broglio 2019; Keats 2002). My commitment to molecular rather than molar mourning, however, prompts me to attempt to deflate this position. Instead, I have searched for poetic speaking positions that can articulate the move, so crucial for me, towards co-becoming/becoming-one with my metamorphosed beloved's inhuman, spiritmattering remains and assemblages. These are speaking positions which, as briefly summarized in the words of literary and animal studies scholar Ron Broglio, open up towards 'a nonhuman phenomenology of wonder beyond fact, reason, and mimetic description' (2019: 7).

In accordance with these contemplations of a posthuman take on poetics, the book's sequence of interludes and poems is ordered as a set of moves towards redistributed agency and deflated speaking positions. The 'egotistical sublime' (Broglio 2019: 6; Keats 2002: 60) is, so to speak, substituted by the love-death of the lyrical subject. From Interlude to Interlude – and from poems such as *Karaoke with Kathleen* (*Interlude I*) to *Signs?* (*Interlude IV*) – it is possible, thematically, to trace a movement towards less and less agency on the part of the mourning 'I' and more and more agency on the part of the beloved's inhuman remains and the Fur assemblage which attract the 'I's desires to co-become and merge, in the end through love-death. In the initial poem clusters (*Interludes I* and *II*), agency is located in the doings of human bodies (mine and my beloved's), as well as in the overwhelming, inhuman powers driving the process of dying, and decomposing, which overrule and wipe out all human efforts to counteract them. In later poems (*Interludes III* and *IV*), the agencies are distributed between the embodied mourning 'I' (acting on her desire to co-become), the beloved's various phenomenal, spectral appearances, and her inhuman remains along with their new assemblages. The intensities of the non-human agencies become stronger and stronger, moving for example, from holding the swimming 'I' in *Fur*, to potentially emitting cascades of miraculous signs in *Signs?* Against this background, I find it appropriate to state that the sequence of interludes and poems thematically articulates a centrifugal movement, spinning away from human agency.

Moreover, this movement towards diminishing the significance and effects of human agency is not only occurring at the thematic level. A somewhat parallel move is also taking place at the level of poetic enunciation. The speaking position of the poetic 'I' in classic Western lyrics is conventionally implied to be human, and endowed with powers to infuse the lyrical worlding practice (the building of the poem's universe through images, contemplations, invocations, pleas, promises, etc.) with human intentions. However, in my story, from interlude to interlude, this position is questioned and becomes emptied out, the more the agencies at the thematic level are redistributed, and relocated from human to inhuman powers. The 'I' in *Fur*, for example, is in no sense in control of the unfolding events, but is drawn into them by the powers of the landscape's different configurations, which, towards the end, lead her to imagine her own annihilation as a fleshy body. In *Signs?*, the speaking position of the 'I' is fully taken over by the spectral voice of the beloved's inhuman assemblages in the miraculously emerging song, stanzas 7–13, which is a centrepiece of the poem. The taking over of the speaking position by a fictional speaker who is not identical with the poetic 'I', is not linked to a posthuman aesthetics (Vendler 2002) per se. But, notably, such a link is forged when the fictional speaker, as is the case in *Signs?*, is marked out as an inhuman agency. The song thus reverses the relationship between lyrical subject and object/addressee, transforming the poetic human 'I' into the 'you' being addressed by someone or something whose position of enunciation is not specifically defined, and who cannot be located on either side of the human/non-human divide.

With two further poems still to come in *Interlude VII*, following this chapter, the emptying out of the position of enunciation of the poetic 'I', understood as human agency, is pushed in the same posthumanizing direction. In one of the poems, *Algae Chant*, the boundaries between the human 'I' and algal 'we' are radically blurred at the level of poetic enunciation. In the poem, the theme of love-death through drowning in the waters of Limfjorden, prepared in earlier poems, merges with an eco-critical theme, algal death due to oxygen depletion caused by water pollution as an effect of over-intensive farming. In the poem, the position of enunciation oscillates, and eventually blurs and erases all boundaries, between human 'I' and collective algal 'we'. In the second poem, *A Liver Tumour's Tale*, a cancerous liver stored in a flask at a medical museum in Berlin takes on the role of teacher, teaching a confused human 'I' to unlearn her epistemologies of ignorance when it comes to cancerdeath and the necropowers generating it, from the perspective of a more-than-human planetary ethics.

A Queer Posthuman Aesthetics of Lamenting

The carnal materiality which, throughout the book, has guided my poetic efforts is yet another feature which may resonate well with a posthuman poetics, and this applies also to the ways in which I inscribe my poetry within the genre of the lament – as programmatically interpellated in the first poem of *Interlude I*. This is a genre that, considered from the perspective of its long cultural historical genealogies, must be seen as emerging from very ancient oral traditions, rather than being understood only with reference to the more polished and humanistically sublimated genre of the elegy (Weisman 2010).[4] By summoning the lament, I reclaim the right to mourn in a physically uninhibited sense, i.e. to mourning as a fleshy activity which includes sobbing and shouting out one's pain, throwing oneself to the ground, hammering one's fists against the wall etc. Or, in other words, to mourn in forms that are tabooed as much too bodily excessive for modern Western contexts. But passionate crying and lamenting can be cathartic, and I want to reclaim these deeply embodied modes of expression. When I have given poetry readings, including to academic audiences, people have often cried a lot. At first, it surprised me that my words had such power to touch – especially because academic audiences, in particular, are not supposed or expected to display corpo-affectivities in this way. However, I came to understand that the catharsis I was seeking for myself with my poetics in terms of digging corpo-affectively deeply into the darkest and saddest moments of my grieving, and seeking out the strongest images and words to make poetic text from my very fleshily felt desire to abandon myself in sobbing, was a catharsis that was desired and needed by other people, too. I understood that my poetic wordings of my experiences of being violently cut apart from my beloved, in a very fleshy and amputation-like sense, brought my audiences into contact with their own aching amputation wounds, their own very corpo-affective processes of grieving the passing away of loved ones.

The viscerality, carnality and materiality which I see as one of the guiding principles for my posthuman poetics, is also, through my drawing upon the genre of the lament, entangled with my queerfeminine desires, and aesthetic sensibilities. This, again, forges a link with the role that classical opera has played in my process of mourning, in particular *Orpheus' Lament* from the opera *Orpheus and Eurydice* (Gluck 2021 [1762/1774]), quoted in my *Overture* to this book, and echoed in several of my poems. These connections led me to suggest that classical opera – despite its affiliation with societal elites from kings and nobility in the seventeenth and eighteenth centuries to nation and bourgeoisie in the nineteenth and twentieth centuries – can be read in posthumanizing and queering ways, and that *Orpheus and Eurydice* fits this bill very well.

Several queer scholars before me (McClary 1991; Blackmer and Smith 1995; Abel 1996; Rosenberg 2000) have in different ways made the point that classical opera abounds with strange (gender)queer elements. It is, therefore, not a new observation that classical opera can be counted one of the rich archives for queer erotohistoriography, pinpointed by Freeman (2010) as far as literature, film, video and the visual arts are concerned. However, I want to focus on an entanglement of queering and posthumanizing aspects. Along these lines, I have already, in the introductory chapter, accounted for my (gender)queering and posthumanizing approach to Ovid's myth of Orpheus and Eurydice, on which the libretto for Gluck's opera (2021 [1762/1774]) is (partly) based.[5] In the context of this chapter's discussion of poetics, however, I want to emphasize another aspect of the entanglement of queering and posthumanizing dimensions of my use of the Orpheus/Eurydice figuration. I shall thus take a look at classical opera as an artform in which the intertwining of words, voices, bodies, carnality, viscerality and corpo-affectivity make up a key component, implying that opera can be read as both queer and posthuman body art. In opera, it is the dramatic encounter between fleshily different voices that is the absolute focus of the performance, while elements such as plot, characters and morality, which are so important, for example, in classical drama, play a secondary role. As queer scholar Sam Abel points out in his in-depth investigation of the queer carnality and sexuality of opera, opera librettos are very often characterized by 'horrendous character inconsistencies, plot disjunctures, and motivational absurdities' (1996: 11). But, as Abel notes, this is not aesthetically important – it actually 'melts into insignificance in the sweep of emotional intensity' (ibid.). What primarily attracts audiences to opera is the interplay of voices, which, staged as dramatic encounters, articulate deep corpo-affective and often highly sexually charged intensities, which engage audiences in excessively 'visceral' ways (ibid.: 6), even though, as Abel notes, there is a strict taboo around this, and 'most opera books have left intact that wall of silence around opera's physical nature' (ibid.: 4).

To push Abel's line of argument further with regard to the profoundly sexual viscerality of opera, I want briefly to compare the genre to naturalistic theatre and suggest that the former works in a way that is exactly opposite to the latter. In contrast to naturalistic theatre, opera is 'embarrassingly excessive' (ibid.: 16), shamelessly exposing its framing and staging, whereas its voicing of corpo-affective intensities can be understood as naturalistic in a sense that far exceeds and transgresses any of the mimetic ambitions or efforts of naturalistic theatre. Operatic sensuality is not mimetic! I agree with Abel when he states that:

> An opera performance is a sexual act. I do not mean that opera is metaphorical or vicarious sex, an intellectual reenactment or contemplation of pleasurable sensations. There is nothing vicarious about opera's sensuality. It is real, physical erotic stimulation of the audience by the performance.
>
> Ibid.: 82

Opera brings the audience into direct, intimate and excessively fleshy contact with the innermost bodily sensuality and vulnerabilities of the singer and hir intensely vibrating vocal cords, and it is in this direct fleshiness that opera taps decisively into the more-than-human aspects of human bodies.

When opera is at its best, the singers become-voices-in-dramatic-physically-intimate-interplay rather than actors who enact roles vis-à-vis each other. Alongside the genderqueer dimensions of the Orpheus figure, cast as a trouser role, my use of *Orpheus' Lament* as leitmotif in several of my poems is referring to these so very carnal and posthuman aspects of opera. To sing 'karaoke' with Kathleen Ferrier as Orpheus lamenting dead Eurydice (as articulated in *Karaoke with Kathleen* in *Interlude I*) was and is an important and viscerally queerfeminine as well as posthuman part of my mourning. It was and is a way of giving my deep desires to become-one with my dead beloved a momentary cathartic outlet as a becoming-voice-together-with-Kathleen-Ferrier in a complex queerfeminine symphysizing and posthuman sense. On the one hand, Ferrier's contralto attracts and responds to my queerfeminine desires, while also establishing a metonymical link to sexually tinged memories of my partner's deep, queermasculine voice. On the other hand, my identification with Orpheus keeps arousing my desire to return to the amputation wound to lament *and* reconnect in a posthuman sense, i.e. through love-death to become-one with my beloved's inhuman remains and new assemblages. My use of the Orpheus/Eurydice figure in *Vibrant Death* is to be understood, in this way, as aesthetically and philosophically entangled with my efforts to unfold a posthuman phenomenology of mourning, explored through my queerfeminine desires and sensibilities.

As an addition to these reflections on my summoning of a queer and posthuman aesthetics of visceral lamentation through the book's multi-faceted references to classical opera, *Orpheus and Eurydice* in particular, I also want to make a note of my poetic interpellation of the language of classical music composition to indicate the moods and modes into which the poetic interludes invite readers. The idea for these indications stems from my public poetry readings. While reading poems to an audience, you indicate a mood and mode with your aural performance. This aspect of my poems is also present when I write them insofar as, like many other poets, I read my poems aloud to myself when composing them to determine whether they work aesthetically. This aural element disappears when the poems are printed in a book. But through my interest in classical opera's queer and posthuman corpo-affectivity and visceral effects on audiences,[6] I also became fascinated by the highly diversified and elaborate list of terms that historically have emerged out of classical music composition as composers' tools to indicate to conductors, musicians and singers how notes are meant to be played and sung. Against this background, it struck me that a recycling of this language of musical expressions could, to some extent, compensate for the disappearance of the aural dimensions of my poems. Contemplating the aesthetics of opera, I also came to think about the ways in which this particular linguistic tool, much more than the notes per se, resonates with the posthuman dimensions that I have traced in the corpo-affective fleshiness of opera. These musical expressions perform as a language of the flesh, and I came to see the long, detailed lists of musical terms (Stainer and Barrett 1898; Wikipedia 2021)[7] emerging out of classical music composition as a remarkable language, which, at its best and most precise, acts metonymically rather than metaphorically. First and foremost, these terms enable readers to get in touch with corpo-affective intensities, rather than acting as metaphors for specific, named feelings. It is clearly these intensities, and not specifically delimited feelings, which establish the communication between the composer and the musicians and singers who are to perform the music. This is why I felt that using this language as an invitation to readers could somewhat make up for the lack of an aural level of signification.

Divining and Figuring

So far, this chapter has concentrated on the methodologies embedded in *Vibrant Death*'s poetic and autophenomenographic knowledge-seeking. It has also discussed how these methodologies have worked in tandem with the cluster of needs, passions and desires that led me to write the book. Now, I shall reflect upon the methodologies that have been at work in the book's overall process of linking poetic, autophenomenographic and philosophical searches for new queering, posthumanizing and decolonizing understandings of death, dying and mourning. Contemplated in retrospect, two radically postqualitative methodologies – divining and figuring – stand out here, both of which have been interpreted in an immanence philosophical sense. First, I shall summarize the two methodologies and their relation to immanence philosophy. Second, I want to make their working modes visible through an analysis of the poem *After-Life* (from *Interlude VI*). On the one hand, I shall analyse the poem thematically as a contemplation of distributed death, i.e. death beyond the bounded body of the individual. On the other hand, I shall use the analysis to carry out a methodological reflection on the poem, which will also address the emerging and experimental approaches that characterize my overall ways of working in the whole book. More precisely, I shall meta-reflect upon the ways in which the methodologies of divining and figuring overall perform in *Vibrant Death*, using the poem and my analysis of it as a kind of synecdoche or hologram, reflecting in a condensed form the over-arching working mode of the book. In this way, I will try to avoid separating methodologies from analysis, while still making their work visible.

Let me start the initial summarizing with divining, and a reference to a recent article by postqualitative researcher Maggie MacLure (2021). Within the framework of Deleuze-inspired, pedagogical research, and drawing upon in-depth work of Deleuze-scholar Joshua Ramey (2012, 2016) on the 'half-submerged presence of occult and esoteric thought in the work of Deleuze', MacLure spells out how divination can work as a 'speculative method' (2021: 502). According to MacLure (ibid.), the methodology works through a discerning of 'stranger affinities' (ibid.), which, as pointed out by Ramey, make events ramify and intensify, while 'extending their implications to unusual and unforeseeable conclusions, carrying lines of sense farther than they are intended to reach' (2012: 174). Moreover, divination is linked to becoming a sign-reader in an immanent sense – what Deleuze, in his analysis of Proust, talks about as entering into a relation of 'apprenticeship to signs' (2000: 4). The apprenticeship to which Deleuze is referring is one that requires a long-standing and intense learning process, and an embodied attunement to the events being investigated. This kind of apprenticeship is embedded in an immanent approach insofar as it does not turn to transcendent and external explanations.

In order to briefly account for the methodology, I will summon MacLure (2021), who uses a striking and illuminating case from her own pedagogical research, a classroom ethnography. To illustrate the methodology of divining, MacLure discusses how, instead of employing explanations in a conventional social science sense, this study ended up, as its analytical key, to use a diagrammatic resonance between phenomena, which, from a conventional social research perspective, it seemed utterly strange to link. The classroom ethnography focused on a child, Hannah, who always remained silent when her name was called out during registration, and who, through her act of silence, alarmed both teachers and researchers, drawing them into a 'vortex of explanatory insufficiency' (MacLure 2021: 508). To come to terms with Hannah's inexplicable silence, MacLure turns conventional ways of constructing explanations in social research upside down. Instead of attempting to make sense of Hannah's 'strange' behaviour by using existing tools from pedagogical, social or psychological theory, MacLure uses a diagrammatic composition in the shape of a triptych as her analytical entrance point. Silent Hannah is juxtaposed with two other figures who also cause a stir through their silence. One is the scrivener Bartleby in US writer Herman Melville's short novel of the same name from 1853, who responds to all his employer's instructions with 'I would prefer not to …' (2016 [1853]: 25). The other figure is taken from a musicvideo by the indie band Radiohead's 'Just' (2021), showing a man lying in the street, causing an enormous commotion through his refusal to tell the people crowding around him why he will not get up. Through this strange and unanticipated juxtaposition, MacLure makes sense of that which cannot be made sense of. She refrains from 'explaining' in a conventional sense, and from looking for pedagogical 'solutions' to the classroom 'problem' posed by silent

Hannah. Instead, she pinpoints a resonance through the diagrammatic composition: the juxtaposition of three very different figures: Hannah, Bartleby and the man lying in the street in the Radiohead video, who all create a gigantic stir when, through silence, they signal their refusal to comply with demands to make themselves transparent to their surroundings. This is a resonance which, MacLure tells us, she as a researcher has immanently sensed through a patient, intense and meticulous search for significant signs. According to MacLure, the tracing of this resonance takes place in an immanent way, because the process is not to be understood through a returning to pre-existing theoretical paradigms. MacLure defines the composing of resonance through the researcher's immanent sign-reading, and her bringing-together of signs accordingly, as an example of an act of divination in an immanence philosophical sense. This is an act which, on the one hand, includes an aleatory element (the unforeseen, the unexpected), but, on the other hand, is guided by an immanently structuring principle: *in casu*, the diagrammatic composition whose virtual potential is actualized by the researcher. I see this kind of divinatory – but also scholarly meticulous – process of tracing, compiling and actualizing unexpected links between all kinds of material signs through patient and intense attunement, in my case to the great unknown, Death, as having been intensely at work for me while I was writing *Vibrant Death*.

I shall now turn to figuring – another speculative methododology that has inspired my work in this book. Figuring is related to the notion of figuration (Braidotti 1994, 2011; Haraway 2004; Lykke 2010). In posthumanist feminist theorizing, this concept has been used to indicate an ethico-political mode of working, which engages critically with the here and now while simultaneously opening up opportunities for an affirmative imagining of an elsewhere/otherwise. As pointed out by Thiele (2021), the methodology of figuring, shaping figurations, is to be understood as a 'speculative, relational technique', linked to processes of setting this kind of multi-layered, critical-affirmative knowledge-seeking in motion. It is a speculative methodology in the sense that it does not stay with a mimetic representation of the here and now, and relational insofar as the overall search addresses 'complex relationality as a primary condition(ing) of planetary existence' (ibid.: 229). Instead of searching for a static form of knowledge about something 'out there', the shaping of feminist figurations, as stressed by Braidotti (1994), is deeply entangled with subjective and embodied becomings of feminist researcher subjects, and their engagement in the shaping of 'political fictions' (ibid. 2002: 7). Figurations are to be understood as created in balancing acts between a critique of lived social realities and affirmative, visionary movements towards other kinds of worlding practices. To speak with Haraway, these alternative worlding efforts can be defined as practices that imply a 'permanent refusal of innocence and self-satisfaction with one's reasons and the invitation to speculate, imagine, feel, build something better' (2008: 92).

Together with divination, figuring in this critical-affirmative sense has also been important for my work on *Vibrant Death*. On the one hand, I have made a point of establishing a critical edge to the ways in which Christian and Cartesian dualisms, as well as neoliberal biopolitics and health and happiness normativities, mould modern Western imaginaries of death, dying and mourning. But, entangled with this critique, I have also been affirmatively engaged in processes of queering, posthumanizing and decolonizing, carried along by a personal quest to find paths towards new ontologies of death, dying and mourning. Bringing the methodologies of divining and figuring into conversation, I would describe my overall approach in *Vibrant Death* as an intense divinatory search for signs that can help me to critically-affirmatively figure out my dead beloved's current whereabouts and her metamorphosed form of relational, planetary existence, as well as pathways to my co-becoming and eventually becoming-one with her new inhuman assemblages.

After this brief introduction to divining and figuring, I shall now turn to the analysis of the poem *After-life,* in order to illustrate how the two methodologies can work together in practice. I shall also reflect upon the ways in which they have worked for me throughout the book in terms of helping me to link together autophenomenography, poetry writing and philosophical contemplations. However, in addition to synechdochally making visible the methodologies that have been at work throughout, with this analysis I shall also take one more step in my reflections upon the current material whereabouts of my beloved – her so-called 'afterlife', i.e. her ways of living on as part of a planetary kinship. To ensure that these two different purposes stand out clearly and distinctly, I shall first analyse the poem thematically, with a focus on the latter question. After that, I shall tease out how the analysis reflects my overall process of divining and figuring.

Rethinking an Embodied After-Life

The poem *After-Life* reflects another of the paths that I tried out in my search for sustainable, material, non-dualist answers to the question of my dead beloved's present whereabouts and modes of being. It differs somewhat from the ones I have primarily walked in the book until now. So far, I have tried to open up the question through reflections on spectral and alien encounters, and a co-becoming with my partner's transitioning and corpo-affective becoming-one with the sea where we scattered her ashes. The poem *Death's Metamorphoses* in *Interlude VI* recalls my beloved's transitioning process. However, an intersecting part of the exploration of my beloved's current whereabouts, which I have not yet discussed, involves the queer kinship circles interpellated in the poem *Mourning Circles* in *Interlude VI*, and in particular the narrower circle of rainbow kin: my partner's children, grandchildren and great-grandchildren, and their partners and rainbow children, i.e. the family circle that conventionally represents a deceased person's embodied afterlife. As a rainbow family, we have always been critical of normative heteropatriarchal constructions of family ties through genetics and lineage. But, since I also subscribe to new materialist ontologies, it is not satisfying for me to remain within a critical social constructionist framework, and simply cast the ways in which familial ties work in rainbow contexts along the lines of the formula 'families of choice' (Weston 1991; Weeks, Heaphy and Donovan 2001). The focus on 'choice' has accomplished an important task as a platform concerned with political demands for equal rights for rainbow families. However, the problem of a bracketed biology, which has haunted constructionism generally, pops up here as well, leaving open the question of material embodiment. For me, the question of material ties arose when I so desperately desired to find paths to knowledge about my dead beloved's embodied whereabouts. On the one hand, I wanted to critically surpass heteropatriarchal explanations along the conventionally intertwined lines of genetics and lineage. But, on the other hand, I also needed to philosophically ground this part of my search for knowledge about my beloved's life after death in an affirmative, corpo-material way. The poem *After-Life* articulates my speculative forays towards rethinking this question.

After-Life focuses on two related reading events that occurred in the wake of my beloved's death. It articulates how intra-active readings of two rather different, but unexpectedly converging, sources gave rise to reflections upon my beloved's corporeal afterlife in my rainbow kin, but also as part of a much larger planetary kinship. To make explicit the understanding of a corporeal afterlife that I developed as a consequence of these reading events, I shall dig deeper into these sources. One source is the bioethicist and feminist philosopher Margrit Shildrick's posthumanist-phenomenological and biophilosophical-speculative readings of the phenomenon, microchimerism (Shildrick 2016). As articulated in the first stanza of *After-Life*, I was deeply moved when I became acquainted with Shildrick's research on microchimerism a few months after my partner's death. The other source, referenced in the second stanza of *After-Life*, is the philosophy of so-called soul transmigration and afterlife of the North East Siberian Chukchi people (Rytkheu 2000; Willerslev 2013) – a transmigration which, in line with the discussion of the notions, 'soul' and 'spirit', in Chapter 6, I prefer to refer to as a spiritmattering transmigration, a transmigration or shape-shifting that involves shifting spiritual matterings. This source was also brought to my attention in the months following my beloved's death when one of my rainbow sons suggested that we should jointly read and discuss an edited volume on death and time (Refslund Christensen and Willerslev 2013) to try to come to terms with our loss and the void it had created, not only for me, but also very much for my rainbow kin. The volume included a chapter on the rebirth beliefs of the Chukchi, which prompted us to dig deeper into the topic (Jochelson 1908; Mills and Slobodin 1994; Rytkheu 2000; Willerslev 2007, 2013).

As articulated in *After-Life*, these two reading events were not only about becoming inspired in a theoretical sense. It is more appropriate to say that I metabolized the texts in an embodied thinking-feeling-imagining manner, transforming the reading into relational and deeply corpo-affective events (Massumi 2015). These corpo-affective readings shaped my understandings of the texts and led me to intuitively experience convergences between them. Both resonated intensely with my desire to learn how to co-become with my dead beloved in her new whereabouts and modes of being, and to understand her afterlife in my rainbow kin. But how could I move from this intuitively experienced convergence to the construction of philosophically sustainable links?

Let me first take a closer look at Shildrick's biophilosophical readings of microchimerism (Shildrick 2016). Reflecting on this biological phenomenon,

Shildrick pinpoints how, at a cellular level, self/other distinctions might be blurred in ways that modern Western thought, fixated on the belief in the sovereign individual self, tends to overlook. Microchimerism posits that cells with the unique genetic make-up of more than one individual are found in pregnancy, as well as in connection with transcorporeal events such as organ transplantation and blood transfusion. But, according to Shildrick (2016), some biomedical scientists suggest that the phenomenon is more widespread, and perhaps rather 'the rule than the exception' (ibid.: 106), thus opening up new horizons towards a rethinking of the sovereign individual in favour of post-individual communities.[8] The circumstances of the reading event prompted me to bring the phenomenon of microchimerism to bear on the question of life/death.

Shildrick guided me to see the biophilosophical implications for a deconstruction of Western notions of the sovereign self, and a radical reontologizing of self/other boundaries. Another posthuman feminist study of biophilosophical implications of the intense biological exchanges between mother and foetus during pregnancy and lactation, which also comments on microchimerism, lead me to think about the phenomenon also in relation to this broader context of extensive exchanges and the maternal generosity involved (Hird 2007). However, what jumped out at me while reading Shildrick's reflections in particular, was the thought that, if we are generally chimerically mixed at micro-cellular levels, then the death of the individual body can no longer be considered absolute or final in a mechanistic Cartesian sense. When individual bodies can be seen as distributed across more than one subject, new horizons open up for a rethinking of the so-called afterlife, the life after death of the individual. As long as material death is understood as a single event, related only to the individually bounded body, any afterlife is literally to be seen as an 'after'. It is then conventionally related to posthumous life in the memories of those who knew the deceased subject, and/or, in Christian thought, to the immaterial performance of the immortal soul, which has left the body behind. However, what happens if we stop conceptualizing death as absolute, final and bound to the individual? With inspiration from Shildrick's biophilosophical reflections on microchimerism, we can start to understand the cells of the deceased as living on, distributed among the chimeric cells of biological children as well as other human or non-human beings with whom an exchange of tissue has occurred. What if we follow even further Shildrick's speculations that microchimerism might be 'ubiquitous' (2016: 100), implying that we all embody an abundance of previous tissue exchanges? In this case, the 'after' in 'afterlife', *sensu strictu*, dissolves, together with any notion of a life/death dichotomy.

For me, the dissolving 'after' suggests that my beloved, although she became a corpse and, after cremation, ashes, lives on not only as ashes transformed into algae sand at the bottom of Limfjorden, but also as chimeric cells, spread out across the tissues of my rainbow kin, and perhaps much more widely than that. This insight underpinned my gut feeling of intensifying relations with my rainbow kin and all the human and non-human beings with whom my beloved in one way or another might have exchanged tissue. From this perspective, all these relations were to be understood as arenas for corpo-affective reconnection, for new kinds of co-becoming with my beloved. I was also brought to contemplate that my beloved might even live on as chimeric cells in my body.

I shall now turn to the Chukchi beliefs about rebirth (Willerslev 2013), which, as I eventually became aware, also seem to resonate widely with those of many other indigenous peoples of the circumpolar regions of the Northern Hemisphere and North America (Mills and Slobodin 1994). However, when committing myself to discussions of Chukchi and other indigenous cosm-ontologies and philosophies, I am aware that I am entering a minefield which, as articulated in the last stanza of *After-Life*, means that I could easily slip into modes of cultural appropriation. I have already discussed this problem in Chapter 6 in relation to my summoning of Anzaldua's references to shamanist traditions (1987, 2015). But it intensifies when it comes to Chukchi philosophies and cosm-ontologies, which, to a large degree, I have accessed through white Western eyes, my own as well as those of white Western anthropologists who have published accounts of these rebirth beliefs against the background of their fieldwork.[9] White anthropological and philosophical interpretations have inflicted violence and produced excess meanings, which cannot be deciphered from modern Western vantage points (Bird Rose 2004; Tlostanova and Mignolo 2009; Povinelli 2016; Vargas, Marambio and Lykke 2020). In this context, it is important, as also discussed in Chapter 6, to avoid constructing discursive hierarchies. So, in order to explore the two reading events (on Chukchi cosm-ontologies and biophilosophical readings of microchimerism), I am once again attempting to use a pluritopic decolonial approach (Tlostanova and Mignolo 2009; Tlostanova 2015), inviting the reader to mutually enriching conversations between differently situated knowledge formations without ontologically privileging one over the other, and, in particular, not privileging Western science and philosophy over indigenous knowledges, philosophies and cosm-ontologies.

With these words of caution, I shall summarize some of the main features of Chukchi rebirth beliefs, as described by Willerslev (2013) and more broadly contextualized by Mills and Slobodin's analyses of the cosm-ontologies of the indigenous peoples of the circumpolar regions of the Northern Hemisphere and North America (1994). At the heart of these beliefs are cosm-ontologies that cast both humans and the animal species predominantly hunted by the people in question as embedded in life/death circles of eternal passing away and 'returning', i.e. shape-shifting and spiritmattering in a new body. There is no reward/punishment structure in these circles; they are flat, non-hierarchical and without moral evaluation (Willerslev 2013). In this sense, they form a contrast to the so-called 'ethicized' eschatologies of 'world religions', such as Christianity or Buddhism (Mills and Slobodin 1994: 16–18), where souls move upwards or downwards in tandem with posthumous evaluations of their moral behaviours. In Chukchi and other cosmologies of the circumpolar regions of the Northern Hemisphere and North America, what happens when people die is that the spirit tries to find an appropriate new body – for example, materializing in a foetus to be reborn. It should be noted that this materializing and embodying move on the part of the ancestor is not to be seen as a mere duplication. Willerslev (2013: 82) stresses that rebirth is to be understood as a 'return of difference', which he interprets along the lines of Deleuzean philosophy. The subject who comes to embody the ancestor not only becomes one with key aspects of this ancestor, but is also free to unfold as a different individual. Moreover, there is not necessarily a one-to-one relationship between the rematerializing ancestor and one particular individual. Different aspects of an ancestor can materialize and be distributed between several currently living persons, and one person can 'carry' aspects of several ancestors. Furthermore, transmigration does not necessarily happen along the lines of kin belonging to the same bloodline, and the crossing of gender and species boundaries is regularly reported as well. In Chukchi cosmologies, the crossing of species boundaries resonates deeply with this people's belief in intimate kinship between humans and whales, which comes clearly through as part of the mythic Chukchi heritage that is an outspoken theme in the works of a contemporary Chukchi writer such as Yury Rytkheu (2000) and film director Alexei Vakhrushev (2018). In these ways, the constant flow of transmigrations in-between the worlds of the dead and that of the living seem to be understood as flexible and open-ended. Devoid of ethical punishment/reward systems, these transmigrations are also embedded in a practical, everyday mode of being, not dependent on any form of filtering by hierarchies of religious authorities or dogmas. Instead, dreams seem to play an important role in terms of announcing the desire of ancestors to shape-shift and spiritually materialize in a certain individual. The latter might learn that the ancestor is coming to inhabit hir through a dream.

What first caught my attention in Willerslev's accounts of the Chukchi rebirth beliefs was that he read them in a context of 'dealing with grief', emphasizing that the Chukchi make the mourning of dead kin easier with their focus on 'continuity rather than finality' (Willerslev 2013: 79). Because I was reading Shildrick at about the same time, I was struck by the ways in which this focus on continuity resonated strangely with the ways in which her biophilosophical reading of the phenomenon of microchimerism intuitively sparked a converging image of continuity for me: my dead beloved's chimeric cells as still very much alive and kicking in her children, grandchildren and great-grandchildren and perhaps elsewhere (as articulated in Stanza 1 of *After-Life*). When I began to contemplate these intuitions in more depth, I became drawn to the convergences between Shildrick's biophilosophical deconstruction of the notion of the bounded individual in favour of an understanding of it as chimerically distributed, and Chukchi transmigration philosophies and cosm-ontologies; as interpreted by Willerslev (2013), the latter cast individuals as composite beings, materializing and embodying ancestors, while also shape-shifting and not being mere repetitions. I was also struck by the convergences between Chukchi beliefs and microchimerism discourses insofar as both resonated so well with my desire to challenge dualist Christian and secular scientific perceptions of death. Like the microchimerism discourses, the Chukchi accounts suggested that death is not final, but rather is implicated in a continuity, coming about due to the individual becoming dispersed instead of seen as bounded off like a sovereign, modern Western subject, who is imagined to inhabit a closed, individualized body.

The readings of Shildrick's biophilosophical interpretations of microchimerism and Willerslev's reading of Chukchi philosophies and cosm-ontologies seemed appropriate for involving a pluritopic hermeneutic framework (Tlostanova and Mignolo 2009; Tlostanova 2015) for my speculations about my dead beloved's afterlife, even though I primarily had access to the Chukchi perspective through Willerslev. From two different angles, my thinking-feeling-imagining quest to trace what and where my beloved is now was given food for thought. Both converged in a figuring of my rainbow kin, as well as much wider human and non-human kinship relations, as making up one more key site for material co-becoming and reconnecting – alongside the ones I unfold in spectral and alien encounters with my beloved, and in transcorporeal relations to her ashes and the seabed where they are scattered. I have come to see all these different key sites for reconnection as working in tandem with each other.

Working through Strange and Significant Con-Figurations

I have now untangled the sources of the poem *After-Life*, and suggested pathways towards a material rethinking of an embodied afterlife. However, as already mentioned, an additional aim of this untangling is to provide a foundation for a final methodological reflection on the ways in which, in the poem, but also throughout *Vibrant Death*, I have worked through strange configurations. Or, more precisely, the poem *After-Life* and my analysis of it should also illuminate how divining and figuring, understood in an immanence philosophical sense, have been important tools for me when I have linked different theoretical frameworks, and different genres of writing, with an autophenomenographically based analysis of death, dying, mourning and afterlife. So how have divining and figuring been at work in *After-Life* and in the above analysis of it – as well as throughout *Vibrant Death*?

In line with the definition that, following MacLure (2021), Ramey (2012, 2016) and Deleuze (2000), I gave of divining, I describe my approach – in *After-Life*, in the analysis of the poem, as well as in *Vibrant Death* as a whole – as carried by a passionate desire for signs and sign-reading. To answer the burning questions about my dead beloved's material metamorphoses and current whereabouts – and to do so beyond dualist Christian and Cartesian narratives as well as beyond an atheism grounded in mechanistic materialism – I have become an avid reader of signs. I know of course that my questions do not have any straightforward answers, so turning to speculative methodologies – such as divining and figuring – has therefore seemed an obvious choice. Death stands out as the great unknown, and even though the corpo-affectively symphysizing mourning 'I''s desiring, but humbly attuning, entrance points to it seem more promising than those chosen by the self-centred sovereign 'I', intense learning processes are still required in trying to understand the material signs emitted from this unknown. To become an adept sign-reader in the immanent sense that Deleuze discusses in his book on Proust (2000), and which MacLure (2021) and Ramey (2012) associate with divination as an immanent methodology, is not easily achieved. To be able to tune in to intensities, and to sense unexpected, unusual and unforeseeable links, and figure out 'stranger affinities' (MacLure 2021: 502), is dependent on meticulous and patient processes of attunement and symphysizing. However, as indicated in Chapter 6, I think that my desires for reconnection and my queerfeminine sensibilities have guided me towards learning new kinds of attunement, including those that are required in order to use the methodology of divining.

In *After-Life*, the intensities to which I respond, and which set the process of sign-seeking in motion, are the two reading events. Both of these resonate with my desire to find poetically, spiritually-materially, and philosophically plausible ways of thinking about my dead beloved's current whereabouts and afterlife beyond Christian and Cartesian narratives, and beyond a mechanistic-materialist atheism's rejections of any idea of life after death. I did not plan either of the two reading events in advance. Neither did I know that Shildrick's paper on microchimerism (2016) would be among the conference papers I received shortly after my beloved's death. Nor was I aware that my rainbow son would suggest a joint reading of the book (Refslund Christensen and Willerslev 2013) containing a chapter on Chukchi transmigration beliefs. In this sense, both texts came to me unbidden. There was clearly an aleatory moment involved, but also an immanently structuring guidance, which, in accordance with MacLure's example of a divinatory analysis (2021), can be described as a diagrammatic composition. I became attracted to the two texts because they both resonated so strongly with my desire to find plausible pathways to think-feel-imagine answers to the questions about the afterlife and whereabouts of my dead beloved. But, before accepting each of them as signs of such plausibility, I meticulously thought through my responses and readings of both. The linking of the texts was not totally random either. In a divinatory mode, I was guided by a diagrammatic resonance between ideas of an afterlife through chimeric cells, and through transmigrating shape-shifting spiritmattering, both of which transgress the ideas of bounded individuals whose death is considered final. It was this diagrammatic resonance that first led me to link the texts. This is a link that was later sustained also by reflections on the methodologies of pluritopic hermeneutics (Tlostanova and Mignolo 2009; Tlostanova 2015) and diffraction (Barad 2014) which I discussed in Chapter 6, and which I think work well together with the divinatory approach, I am outlining here.

In sum, it is the way of working that I just described which I see as being in line with the methodology of divination suggested by MacLure (2021), and Ramey (2012, 2016) with reference also to Deleuze (2000) and an immanence philosophical framework more broadly. I follow material and immanently emerging signs that my desires and poetic-spiritual intuitions bring me to trace, while, at the same time, working meticulously to philosophically sustain the plausibilities of the links that I am forging. This methodology of divining has worked for me in different ways throughout the book. This is why I argue that its specific way of working in relation to the poem *After-Life* and the analysis of it should be seen as a *synecdoche* or hologram for the whole book. I have thus experienced the same kind of intense, avidly sign-absorbing reading events described in the poem in relation to other texts, which became philosophical and theoretical signposts for my work, such as Anzaldua (1987, 2015), Deleuze and Guattari (1988), Braidotti (2006, 2013), Tlostanova and Mignolo (2009, 2012), Bennett (2010), Cvetkovich (2012), Kafer (2013) and Neimanis (2017). While these texts helped me with the contemplation of philosophical and theoretical plausibilities, I was, however, just as eagerly tracing signs of my dead beloved's new whereabouts and material existence through my poems, autobiographical stories and spiritual practices. The divinatory process consisted of bringing all these signs together in sensible and plausible ways – along the lines of the 'could-be' that characterizes speculative realist methodologies (Bellacasa 2017).

Figuring, the shaping of figurations, has worked in tandem with this process of divining. To make this visible, I shall once again use *After-Life*, and my analysis of it, as an illustration. The figuring process taking place here builds on the process of divining. The critical-affirmative, poetic-philosophical act of bringing together biophilosophical readings of the microchimerism phenomenon with Chukchi cosm-ontologies and philosophies through the process of divining gives rise to a figuring process – a shaping of figurations. The bringing together sustains a critical undoing of all the foundations for an absolute distinction between life, death and afterlife, and gives rise to a figuration of post-individual embodiment. This is a figuration which implies that the individual's material life, and hence death, are cast as radically distributed and multiple rather than confined to a bounded body, and this state of distribution means that the 'after' in the notion of afterlife loses its meaning in an absolute chronological sense. Within the framework of this kind of post-individual way of figuring life/death, there is no 'after'. My rainbow kin, as well as all the other beings with whom my dead beloved might have exchanged tissue, and therefore within whom spiritmattering related to her may be happening, thus become sites where explorations of co-becomings and queer reconnections are potentially possible beyond biological and blood-related lineages, and beyond chrononormative understandings of 'before' and 'after'.

This kind of shaping of figurations through divining has not only been part of my contemplation of *After-Life*, but also runs throughout *Vibrant Death*. Together with divining, figuring is thus to be understood as an integrated part of the posthuman phenomenology of mourning that I unfold in the book, insofar as its overall aim has been to shape a critical-affirmative reontologization of death as vibrant. I hope to have shown that this figuring of death as vibrant is a multiple undertaking, comprising both a critique of the here and now, and an affirmative envisioning of an elsewhere/otherwise. To underline the multiplicity of the figuration of vibrant death, let me briefly summarize both its critical and affirmative aspects.

Critically addressing the here and now, I have shaped the figuration of death as vibrant by encompassing the following dimensions: challenging restrictive modern Western norms of mourning, constructed through health-normative biopolitics; confronting the Christian and Cartesian narratives casting the corpse as abject; struggling to breach the wall of silence and to make the amputation wounds inflicted by the death of the beloved begin to scar over, instead of continuing to bleed; disrupting and decolonizing the epistemologies of ignorance that prompt modern Western subjects to file away any idea of miracles under the rubric of now-superseded 'primitive and premodern' belief systems.

In addition to this 'staying with the trouble' (Haraway 2016), in terms of critically confronting the ways in which death, dying and mourning are predominantly ontologized, imagined and normatively regulated in the here and now of Western modernity, figuring in an affirmative visionary sense has also been an important part of the multiple undertaking of this book. In line with my divinatory methodology, I have followed the lead of significant – albeit often excessively strange and unexpected – signs, links and combinations, trying to foster and nurture the figuration of death as vibrant in multiple ways: allowing myself to dwell in excessive mourning and in my capacity as an excessive mourner opening up new horizons; making space for explorations of the corpse in its strange and inhuman vibrancy; letting my desire for co-becoming lead me towards molecular, posthuman mourning in *Aionic* time beyond the wall of silence, rather than staying with molar human efforts to cling to a past, conceived as a static, untouchable and unchangeable entity; unlearning modern Western epistemologies of ignorance, freeing my sensibilities from the constraints of reductivist rationalism and allowing myself to unfold my sensitivities towards the world's inhuman liveliness and miraculous possibilities for spiritmattering co-becoming. The multiple figuration of vibrant death includes all of this, and the figuration of death as distributed and multiple explored in *After-Life* is a part of this whole.

Interlude VII

CON ABBANDONO E DEVOZIONE
(WITH SELF-ABANDON AND DEVOTION)

Illustr. 9 Con Abbandono e Devozione (With Self-Abandon and Devotion).
© Nina Lykke 2019.

ALGAE CHANT[1]

1.
Living algae
in the waters,
soft and hairy,
like a cat fur.
Oh, I love you,
Algae,
my desire
is to pat you,
and to co-become with you.
Algae, Algae,
wise old critter,
can you teach me
how to photosynthesize?
Be a creature
in-between?
Peeing as an animal,
and grow branches, leaves, and fruits?

2.
Eating oysters
spiced with algae,
salty fluids
in my mouth.
Cool, clear water,
darkish night sky,
mango moon,
and algae juice.
Algae juice
on sticky fingers,
swimming naked in the sea,
splashing, splashing,
furish algae
touching bodies;
seaweed strokes
caress our skin.
Kisses growing even deeper,
swimming, swimming,
farer, farer,
from the shore.
You are leading,
mango moonlight,
touch my
shiny algae fur.

3.
Swimming, swimming,
water cooling,
naked bodies
getting colder
and more stiff.
Having trouble
with my breathing.
Gasping, gasping,
scary depths.
Dizzy, dizzy,
undercurrents,
where to go?
Dizzy, dizzy,
water, water,
all around me,
dizzy, dizzy,
in the waves.
Cannot see you!
Gone, gone!
Mango moon ray,
take me with you,
take me with you,
do not leave me,
pierce my heart,
my mango moon ray,
make me sink,
until the blackness
swallows you
as well as me.
Merging
with the waterworld,
and staying there forever.

4.
Brownish water,
dying algae,
children screaming
'Oooch, it is poison!'
Dying in a hell of sulphur,
sulphur death
in white surroundings.
Innocence:
'It was not me!
No, I did not
cause this dying,

me a white
and guiltless farmer,
who just want to do my best!
Could I ever do such harm?
For the oxygen depletion,
algae are the ones to blame!'

5.
'Farmer, farmer,
stop this nonsense!
You are over-feeding us!
Give us pleasure!
Do not gorge us!
Use your brains,
and be attentive!
Try to watch us,
and attune!
We are old
and very wise!
We can teach you
many lessons
about kinship,
time,
and
sympoiesis,
if you listen
carefully!
Otherwise,
just go
to hell,
just go to hell
      and die!'

6.
Algae time,
Aionic time,
no beginning and no end,
just unending co-becomings
and a multiplicity of instants
in a cosmic spiral dance.
Time's arrow,
moving
from simplicity
to complexity?
Who said evolution?

Just forget it!
Let us, Algae,
complex and resilient,
teach you to unlearn
your modern human *hubris*.

7.
Ancestral Algae wisdom!
In the beginning there were Algae . . .
And so there were
before and after
your beginning . . .

A LIVER TUMOUR'S TALE[2]

1.
A human liver with a gigantic tumour
about twenty centimeters in diameter –
massive areas of whitish cancer tissue
have almost supplanted the lightbrown liver flesh.
A cancerous liver,
since 1961
stored as specimen
in a transparent glass flask
at the medical museum
of the Charité hospital
in Berlin.

2.
I visited the museum
right after your
many hours long
liver cancer operation
at the hospital
in the icecold winter
of 2011.
The previous year
an eight centimeter big liver tumour
had been removed
from your liver.
We hoped that the cancer
was stopped,
but it relapsed
within less than twelve months.
Five new malignant tumours,
spreading all over
your right liver lobe
were resected
by doctors at Charité.

3.
The big liver tumour
from 1961
violently caught my gaze,
when I walked through
the exhibition halls
of the museum,
one day

during the five weeks long
time of waiting
for you
to recover enough
to take the long car-ride
with me
back home
to Denmark.

4.
I tried to keep the big tumour
out of my field of vision.
I did not want to see it.
But the whitish tumour mass
cut its way to my retina
in the second
which elapsed
before I could escape
to less terror-inducing
specimen showcases
of the museum.

5.
Now several years after your death
I return to Berlin.
With irresistible force,
the big liver tumour
pulls me once more
to the medical museum.
The powers of horror
of the enormous whitish mass
with only a small rim
of healthy light brown liver tissue around it
interpellate me relentlessly.
But I wander for hours through the streets of Berlin
to find the museum,
even though its whereabouts
are clearly marked on all maps.
I walk and walk.
As in a nightmare
which will not end
the spell of the big tumour
which has transformed
most of the light brown liver tissue
into this scary whitish mass,

attracts and repulses me,
relentlessly.

6.
What does this tumour want to tell me?

7.
Finally there,
for a long, long time
I contemplate the showcase
where the liver tumour
looks back at me from its
glass flask.
I imagine the poor middle-aged guy
who in 1961 –
the year when the Berlin Wall was built –
died from liver cancer at Charité,
back then located in the city's Eastern zone.
His tumour,
now for years on display here,
is bigger than yours ever were.
But both of you are dead by now,
through an odd kinship tie
linked to each other,
and to the many poor people,
who back then as well as now,
unheeded,
die from liver cancer
in Africa and Asia.

8.
Long forgotten studies of
'geopathologies',
to which I turn
avidly wanting to know more
about the sad kinship
of liver cancerous bodies,
teach me that –
when the man from East Berlin died in 1961 –
liver cancer was the cause of
90%
of all cancer deaths among Bantu people
in Southern Africa,
but made up only
1%

of cancer deaths
in the Western part of Europe,
located so it, probably,
could be still observed
from the windows of the wards of Charité,
just over there,
at the opposit side of the river Spree.
When the Berlin Wall was built
soon after,
all the windows of the Charité
turning Westwards,
were walled up.
After this 'the West' could no longer be observed
by the patients dying
in the cancer ward of Charité.

9.
Tracing the kinship ties
which the big liver tumour in the museum
prompt me to look for,
I am confronted
with the dangers
of living in the wrong place.
Thus,
I learn
that
liver cancer
first and foremost
hits the poor
in Africa and Asia,
growing well,
as this cancer does
in hepatitis scars,
or being richly nourished by
aflatoxin,
a toxic component of *Aspergillus* molds,
found in poorly stored grain and vegetables,
or proliferating due to
opisthorchiasis,
an infectious liver disease,
caused by fish parasites,
meticulously registered
by WHO
as 'neglected tropical disease'.

10.
But you
who grew up in the West,
where liver cancer is so rare,
still
attracted
this disease.
Why?
As your oddkin in East Berlin
whose liver tissue,
transformed into
an enormous
cancerous tumour,
which killed him in 1961,
you also lived for years
behind the 'Iron Curtain'
as an exchange student
studying Slavonic languages,
in the 1960s.
In those years of your youth,
you shared
a bad food supply,
with all those ordinary people in Eastern Europe,
who did not belong to the Communist elite.
Had you,
as one of your surgeons once suggested,
when pressed for an explanation of your cancer,
perhaps, back then, contracted an unacknowledged hepatitis,
later to become cancerous?

11.
'Noone knows,
and noone cares,
even though
the liver tumours,
resected from your beloved's body,
are probably still stored
in the biobanks of the hospitals
which operated her.
But liver cancer was and is
too rare among wealthy Western people
to really attract medical attention'
so the wise, old tumour in the glass flask
told me
in its dark and vibrant voice!

Interlude VII: Con Abbandono e Devozione – In music composing, the Italian terms **Con Abbandono** and **Con Devozione** indicate that the musician or singer should perform with self-abandon and in a passionately devoted and enamoured manner, i.e. performatively enact a becoming-one with hir instrument or voice. Here, the terms indicate the mood and mode of the poems of *Interlude VII*, insofar as both dissolve the conventionally human speaking position of the poetic 'I'. The position of enunciation of *Algae Chant* morphs from a human 'I' into an ancestral algae 'we' with hot, but deadly embraces in-between. In *A Liver Tumour's Tale* the agency of the poem is from the beginning located in the liver tumour, and not in the confused human 'I'. As the poem unfolds, the tumour takes over the speaking position of a teacher, teaching the poetic 'I' to unlearn epistemologies of ignorance and commit to more-than-human planetary ethics. This emphasis of a mood, combining devoted dedication with human self-abandonment prepares for the **Coda: Between Love-Death and a Posthuman Ethics of Vibrant Death**, focusing on the wider ethical potentials of posthuman mourning.

Coda

BETWEEN LOVE-DEATH AND A POSTHUMAN ETHICS OF VIBRANT DEATH

I began this book with a focus on the myth of Orpheus and Eurydice, which actualized themes of excessive mourning and love-death, both of which are central to my process of becoming a queer femme lesbian widow, and to the posthuman phenomenology of mourning that I develop in *Vibrant Death*. These two themes are closely linked. Love-death and going-to-the-underworld-and-staying-there-forever in the shape of a becoming-one with my beloved's new assemblages of ashes, algae, sand, seabed etc. are contemplated as the horizon of the excessive mourner's desires. I have orchestrated the two themes in the *Overture*, as well as in many of the poems and stories throughout the book. For example, they emerge in the image of drowning together in *Dreamscapes – A Triptych (Interlude III)*, and are taken further into a becoming-algae in *Algae Chant (Interlude VII)*. The latter poeticizes the fulfilling of the promise that was part of the pact initiated by the miraculous event that my beloved and I experienced right before she died (*A Pact, Interlude IV*). Now, as the book is coming to an end, I shall revisit the theme of love-death, and the excessive mourner's move towards becoming-one with the beloved's new assemblages. I shall also widen the scope to ethical and political horizons that I have come to consider as a result of my journey through mourning and rethinking death as vibrant.

I shall contemplate the ways in which the becoming-one-with implies a becoming-other and, through an autobiographical story, *Shapeshifting in Pandemic Times*, reflect upon the ways in which becoming-other can also be understood as a form of shapeshifting. Moreover, I shall suggest that the rhizomatic trajectory of posthuman mourning, moving through love-death, becoming-other and shapeshifting, which the book has explored, opens up horizons towards an affirmative, posthuman ethics of vibrant death, and a vitalist materialist politics of planetary commitment. I scale up[1] from my personal story to such wider horizons through revisiting the Orpheus/Eurydice myth and the way in which its story of shapeshifting at the threshold of life and death is embedded in a-modern cosm-ontologies of cyclicity. These are cosm-ontologies that resonate with the ones that were also discussed in Chapter 6's pluriversal conversations on miracles. Taking guidance from Anzaldua's linking of an embodied personal spirituality with broader spiritual material, political activism that takes the personal to a political and collective level (1987, 2015), I suggest a figuration of vibrant death and indicate its ethical and political implications. In the poem, *What If Every Critter's Death Was Vibrant?*, that ends the book, I offer a poetic vision of this figuration.

Shapeshifting in Pandemic Times

I. I have longed to die . . .

I have longed to die since my beloved died, several years ago now. I have written poems and philosophical reflections about the love-death of the mourning 'I', who is becoming-one with her dead beloved and her new assemblages. I have fantasized about different ways to die, imagining Virginia Woolf's suicide by walking into the river Ouse with her pockets filled with stones as well as my friend Berit's story about her recent experience of almost dying from blood poisoning, experiencing a sliding away towards death, while her dead beloved life partner came to hold her. I have concentrated intensely on the threshold between life and death – this threshold that is so decisive, even though, along the lines of Braidotti's immanence philosophical, posthuman death theory (2006, 2013), I consider life and death, ontologically, to be a flat continuum of inhuman zoe dynamics. However, continuum or not, death is also a threshold. My beloved's moment of death taught me about the decisiveness of that threshold. Her final exhalation was a radically transformative moment, transmuting a human subject into inhuman otherness. I have speculated intensely on the wall of silence which separates the mourning 'I' from the dead beloved. What is behind it? I know that until I go there myself, I must stay with speculations and intuitions. My beloved is gone as the subject she was. She is something radically different now – an instantaneous spectral presence, a vibrant, inhuman zoe existence, ashes mixed with algae sand, as well as minute chimera living on in other bodies . . . I have longed intensely to co-become with her new assemblages. I have imagined how, through my own death, I will become-one with the algae sand with which her ashes are mixed. I have longed for this merging: 'Going to the underworld and staying there forever!,' as I wrote in the Overture to Vibrant Death.

II. 'Gorgeous villa available near Bergamo . . .

The desire to 'Go to the underworld . . .' has been with me for all these years. However, during the winter of the pandemic year 2020, something changed.

In addition to poems and autobiographical stories, I have worked on a collection of fictional short stories about seeking a quick and easy death – focusing on protagonists who make plans for what, along the lines of Braidotti (2006: 249–50), could be defined as ideas for a self-styling of their own death. At the beginning of the Covid-19 pandemic in 2020, I got the idea for yet another fiction piece for this collection. This one was a story about a lesbian widow driving to Northern Italy in early 2020 – to revisit memories from vacation trips with her beloved in earlier times, but in particular for another reason, which is gradually revealed in the story. In February–March 2020, tourists were escaping from Northern Italy in panic due to the severe Covid-19 outbreak with its epicentre in the region at that time. An easy way to self-style your own death, if you were privileged enough to be able to go on a tourist trip, would, therefore, be to take the opposite route from all the other tourists. While researching material for the short story, I discovered that Northern Italian tourist websites were still advertising luxurious mountain villas with gorgeous views over Alps and lakes – now to be rented for almost nothing. Villas which, indeed, I would not have been able to afford earlier, were now available at enormous discounts! These ads made me think of the post-Watergate poster featuring former US President Nixon: 'Would you buy a used car from this man?' I entitled my short story 'Gorgeous villa available near Bergamo' and started it with the words: 'Would you rent a villa in the Italian Alps in March 2020?' The theme of the story was self-styled dying à la 19th-century romantic Russian composer, Tchaikovsky, who is said to have committed suicide by drinking a glass of water that he knew was contaminated with cholera bacteria.

III. Pandemic Paradoxes

While preparing to write my short story, I indulged in fantasies of a self-styled death from Covid-19, which would make up a central part of the storyline. At the same time, I was taking a lot of care to strictly obey the regulations and follow the restrictions and recommendations which the Danish government and health authorities were implementing as part of a national lockdown to prevent the spread of the virus. At some point, these two activities – the fantasizing and my meticulous efforts to follow all the rules and recommendations to avoid becoming infected by the coronavirus – started to appear a bit paradoxical to me. It struck me that my body was doing the exact opposite of what I was fantasizing about for my pretty much auto fictional piece of writing. On the one hand, my imagination was following my first-person narrator, alone in a rented villa in the Italian Alps close to the town of Bergamo (the epicentre of the epicentre), lying in her bed beside a window with gorgeous mountain views, hallucinating during a high fever that her dead beloved was coming to hold her . . . On the other hand, in 'real' life, I was strictly self-isolating at home in Denmark, ordering food online and making sure that no one but myself and my beloved cat was allowed into my house, taking all possible precautions to keep my private space, myself and my cat absolutely coronavirus-free. When I became aware of the paradox, the irony of the situation caused me to burst into laughter. The chasm between my fantasies and my bodily actions was just so huge! So, I started to contemplate what was happening here. Throughout the years since my beloved's death, I have noticed to my surprise that my state of excessive mourning somehow made me unable to feel anxiety and fear. So why was I now so anxiously self-isolating to avoid the coronavirus? And why, at the same time, was I so eagerly engaging in preparations to write a short story with clear auto-fictional components about a lesbian widow's privileged, self-styled Covid-19 death in Northern Italy?

One reason that my body was responding so differently from my imagination is no doubt that a Covid-19 death is not smooth or easy, but physically painful and frightening. My body responded to this – and, indeed, the protagonist of my short story would also have to deal with that. While lying in her bed in the imagined rented villa in Bergamo, she would probably be preoccupied with very different things than looking at gorgeous mountain views, and indulging in feverish dreams about her dead beloved's arrival to hold her in her arms. The TV made it absolutely clear that, in serious cases, Covid-19 and the pneumonia that often accompanies it, can affect the lung tissue so badly that the patient eventually becomes unable to breathe, and perhaps ends up dying from suffocation – one of the really scary and horrible ways to die. Surely, my conative body did not want that! But further contemplating the contradiction between my bodily responses to the 'real-life' pandemic and the embodied fantasies upon which I was drawing while preparing my fictional piece, it struck me that, perhaps, there were more things at stake than just the rational pragmatics that I had to be careful with myself, because my age and other issues put me at heightened risk of falling ill with Covid-19. Could my paradoxical way of acting perhaps also have something to do with the ways in which my relationship to my dead beloved had been changing and evolving to include ever-new dimensions?

IV. Vertigo

As I have contemplated it, while writing Vibrant Death, *the process of mourning has eventually changed the relationship between my dead beloved and me. It has become amplified and diversified – and, in the years since my beloved died, it has unfolded in new directions; my co-becoming with the algae sand in Limfjorden materializes one of these. Another direction, though, is that I have incorporated my beloved, or, to put it differently, she has somehow come to posthumously inhabit me; 'You live in me / hard and shining as the mother of pearl, soft and sensitive as oyster flesh / as an impatient whisper in my ear', as I write for example in the poem* A Pact, *Stanza 7 (Interlude IV). With the phrase, 'You live in me', I articulate a feeling that I sometimes get very strongly, as though my beloved is acting through/in me.*

My recognition of my beloved's posthumous coming to bodily inhabit me has been a gradual process. I have felt her presence in my gestures and certain modes of speaking and acting since her death. Still, as with the miraculous experiences, for a long time, I did not fully recognize this as 'real' in a phenomenal sense. Then, a startling dream made me start to think more explicitly about my dead beloved's bodily presence within me. This was a dream that in a phenomenally bodily sense put my incorporation of her very outspoken fear of heights on display. I need to mention that I have never in my previous life experienced any traces of this kind of vertigo. I have always been able to do things such as standing at the top of the Eiffel Tower in Paris, looking straight down without fear, while my beloved always felt a powerful vertigo in such situations. I can still today move to the edge of towers or cliffs without problems. Therefore, I was stunned when I had the following dream:

Vertigo Dream

I am driving a car, with my beloved sitting next to me. I drive up a very steep road, which, after an abrupt turn to the left, takes us to a kind of pier, which is at least 100 metres high and stretches out unendingly above a stormy sea. The asphalted road, which continues along the top of this pier, is no wider than the car, and even at the turn, where I abruptly stop the car when I catch sight of the pier, the road is so narrow that it is impossible to turn around and drive back the way we have come. I am caught by an intense panic, and jump out of the car to lie down flat on the road behind it, paralysed, unable to move my body in any direction – just totally overwhelmed by an intense bodily feeling of vertigo.

V. Shapeshifting

The vertigo dream became for me a sign that my processes of symphysizing had somehow led me to posthumously incorporate aspects of my dead beloved's corpo-affectivity, in this case: her fear of heights, and that some kind of reciprocal shapeshifting was taking place between us. Was she co-becoming with me as the embodied subject she had been, while I was co-becoming with her in her new embodiment as ashes mixed with algae sand? Still, I somehow continued to push this recognition back to the liminal space in my consciousness, where I deal with phenomena which I judge to exist in-between 'real' and 'not-real'. However, I was reminded forcefully of the phenomenality of the symphysizing shapeshifting which the vertigo dream had made me consider, when, during the first Covid-19 lock-down in 2020, I started to contemplate the gap between the embodied fantasies about going to Northern Italy which nourished my auto-fictional short story writing, and my bodily responses to the Covid-19 restrictions. I intuitively made a link back to the vertigo dream, because it was also so significantly marked by discrepancy between my bodily responses and my self-perception. This intuitive linking led me to ask myself whether my radically changed relationship to the thought of my own death, which my meticulous self-isolation to avoid Covid-19 had demonstrated to me, was an effect of the process of symphysizing and gradual posthumous incorporation of my beloved as the subject she had been, and the reciprocal shapeshifting which seemed to be going on between us.

My beloved would, indeed, have loved to live longer than she did. She enjoyed the bodily pleasures of living so very much and, as I articulated in the poem Tears (Interlude I), one of the things that made her immensely sad when she learnt that she was unavoidably about to die from her cancer was that she would lose the bodily *pleasure of living. That I could not help her to reverse the process of dying, and regain her ability to live and enjoy these pleasures, was one of the things that made me feel extremely sad and powerless. Maybe the physical traces of my strong symphysizing during the last years of my beloved's life with her wish to live on in spite of the rapidly progressing cancer was, perhaps, what was now, in the early 2020, making my body engage in such meticulous self-isolation to protect myself against coronavirus infection? I started to ask myself if my symphysizing relationship with my beloved had led me to incorporate not only her bodily fear of heights, but also her intensely strong embodied desire to reverse the process of dying in order to live on? I am sure that she would have taken a great deal of care not to be infected by Covid-19...*

Embracing the Dead and the Desire to Live on

With this story about shapeshifting and my changing approach to death, I want to open up horizons for a contemplation of a posthuman ethics and politics of vibrant death and mourning. But let me, first of all, ascertain that the story makes it clear that my relationship with my dead beloved is still fluid and embedded in activities of reciprocal shapeshifting and change, even now, several years after her death. Mourning the dead stands out as a process which is trickster-like, and continues to be so. In this sense, the story resonates with the Derridean claim (1994) that our relationship with the dead is ongoing and evolving. Derrida would frame the ongoingness of the relationship between the living and the dead as hauntological (ibid.:10). As discussed in Chapter 4, I would prefer to complement Derrida's notion with a more affirmative framing than the one with which the terms haunting and hauntology are associated. I suggested a framing that could also include passionately desired spectral embraces and reciprocal intra-actions. However, what I share with Derrida is that I, too, consider the relations between the living and the dead to be ongoing, continuously evolving in phenomenally unpredictable ways. In this sense, the posthuman ethics of vibrant death and mourning that I propose here converges with a Derridean ethics of radical and unconditional hospitality in its rejection of linear temporalities that lock the dead up in an immutable and fixed past, instead of radically welcoming them and being prepared for open-ended intra-actions with them in the here and now (Shildrick 2020: 179).

Second, the story underlines that conative and affective bodies cannot be controlled, and that this also goes for the body we are used to calling 'our own'. Conative matter is trickster-like. 'Your' body might act in ways that surprise you and challenge your self-perception. Even though you are deeply in mourning, desiring to die to become-one with your beloved, your fleshy body itself may want you to persevere and live on. Following Spinoza's *Ethics* (1996 [1677]), I want to embrace the conative desire to live on as a key aspect of the posthuman ethics of vibrant death to which my contemplations in this book have brought me. Therefore, I follow the lead of the story's anchoring of this desire in my shapeshifting and evolving relationship with my dead beloved, and emphasize that it occurs alongside, rather than in contrast to, my desire for love-death. In the ongoing, evolving and shapeshifting relationship between my dead beloved and me, there is room for diversity and continuous change. Within the framework of a posthuman ethics of vibrant death and mourning, the mourner's apparently contradictory desires both to die and to live on should not be considered mutually exclusive.

Third, notwithstanding the ambivalences that may or may not be involved when it comes to my desires to live/die, the story of shapeshifting, which involves my adopting a very strict coronavirus-protection regime, is, I think, also a reflection of my symphysizing taking over of my beloved's strong and deeply ingrained concerns to prioritize bodily health and wellbeing (her own as well as mine), which were much greater than mine. I began to symphysize with this concern of hers years ago. But her four years of cancer gave it a very special meaning, engaging both of us very seriously in efforts to try to reverse the process of dying and decaying which the illness relentlessly and, in the end, irreversibly, set in motion in her body. I feel sure that the incorporation of my beloved's embodied efforts to counteract the cancer (as articulated among others in the poem *Cancerous Walks, Interlude II*) is at least part of the background for my symphysizing shapeshifting now, several years later, into someone who takes self-isolation during the Covid-19 pandemic so over-seriously that it has appeared paradoxical to me to be so very passionately preoccupied with love-death at the same time.

I want to honour and pay my respects to my beloved's strong will to try to dance with the cancer in order to counteract its dragging her towards death. However, this said, I should also make it clear that this desire to honour my beloved's efforts to self-style a conative dance with the cancer does not imply that the posthuman ethics and politics of vibrant death for which I am arguing imply an embrace of the widespread modern rhetoric of a 'war' against disease, be it cancer or Covid-19. I endorse neither this rhetoric, nor the celebration of the figure of a patient who 'struggles' like a 'heroic soldier' fighting against an 'enemy'. As I have discussed in detail elsewhere (Lykke 2019b; Lykke and Marambio 2020), this rhetoric is founded in the modern cult of the sovereign 'I' and a biopolitics that presupposes a nature/culture divide, casting 'nature' as matter to be controlled by detached human subjects. As such, the war rhetoric is incommensurable with the ethics and politics of vibrancy for which I argue in this book. Likewise, my honouring of my beloved's conative efforts to counteract the cancer should in no way be taken for an ethical or political support of transhumanist ambitions to abolish human mortality (Boström 2005). The latter endeavours remain within an elitist, human exceptionalizing onto-epistemology, and a belief in (illusory) technohuman superpowers, which have been nourished by a neoliberal technocapitalism whose darker side is an Anthropocene necropolitics (Lykke 2019b). I endorse neither of these. The ethical and political horizons opened up by *Vibrant Death* differ significantly and distinctly from the intertwined bio- and necropolitics to which conventional discourses on 'war' against cancer or virus, as well as transhumanist visions of human immortality, are inextricably linked.

As I have argued throughout, I want to reclaim death as part of a vibrant life/death continuum. This means that, in both ethical and political terms, I want to reontologize death as vibrant, in contrast to Christian and Cartesian ways of casting it as abject and gloomy, as a 'fall' into base matter, and different also from atheist and mechanistic-materialist constructions of death as nothingness. However, in addition, I also want to firmly link my reontologizing to markedly different kinds of imaginary frameworks than those that surface in war-on-cancer/virus discourses and in transhumanist dreams of abolishing human death. Through the story *Shapeshifting in Pandemic Times*, I want to recognize, honour and be true to my beloved's strong desire to live on, and the ways in which they have melted into me and our posthumous relationship, but to do so without in any way allowing this honouring to slide into a desire for the abolition of death. I consider death to be an inevitable part of both human and non-human life and, seen from the perspective of a sustainable and egalitarian planetary ecology, it needs to remain so.

With these considerations of shapeshifting, love-death and the desire to live on as my sounding board, I will now move towards the more over-arching discussions of an ethics and politics of vibrant death, with which I wish to end the book.

Orpheus/Eurydice Meets Coatlicue/Coyolxauhqui

To scale up from my own story of excessive mourning to more general ethico-political horizons to be opened up through it, I shall revisit the Orpheus/Eurydice myth as well as Chapter 6's contemplation of Anzaldua's revisiting of Aztec cosm-ontologies and philosophies – this time with a focus on her revitalizing of the Aztec myths of the goddess-pair Coatlicue/Coyolxauhqui. Shapeshifting at the threshold of life and death, which is so important in my story, figures prominently in both myth clusters,[2] and will be my key to the process of scaling up from the personal to the collective level of ethical and political considerations. A glimpse of the wider field of a-modern cosm-ontologies and philosophies to which the myth clusters of Orpheus/Eurydice, on the one hand, and Coatlicue/Coyolxauhqui, on the other, belong genealogically, will provide a pluritopic contextualization and framing of my and my beloved's personal story of shapeshifting and transgressing the thresholds of life and death. By means of this framing, I will transpose the personal story such that it becomes an invitation to imagine the life/death continuum as bound into complex processes of cyclic and rhizomatic shapeshifting. To approach this wider complexity, I want to note a cluster of links between the Orpheus/Eurydice myth, and my using it as a *leitmotif* in *Vibrant Death*, on the one hand, and, on the other, Anzaldua's reading and revitalizing of the myths of Coatlicue/Coyolxauhqui (1987, 2015).

To explain these links, I shall take a look at both myth clusters, starting with Orpheus/Eurydice. In the introduction, I have already noted that this myth is different from other romantic Western love-death myths. Even though Orpheus/Eurydice seems to resonate with common Western tales of the romantic human love couple, which end in love-death, its specific articulation of this motif sets it apart from other love-death stories cherished by Western romanticism and used in popular opera librettos. In the latter, the death of the human protagonists constitutes the dramatic finale and linear endpoint. In Orpheus/Eurydice, two central moments of the storyline make a key difference: the journey through the underworld and the ensuing events, when, after his failure to bring Eurydice back, Orpheus withdraws to deserted mountains, which eventually become covered with trees when Orpheus starts playing the lyre once more. Love-death is not the final endpoint of the story. Or, in other words, the Orpheus/Eurydice story can be interpreted as one of shapeshifting, metamorphosing and becoming-other through a journey to and from the underworld, back and forth across the threshold of the abode of the dead.

In accordance with this interpretation, it is notable that, along the way, several incidents of shapeshifting take place in the story, which all cast death as very different from a final endpoint. First, Orpheus' music causes the inhabitants of the underworld, including Eurydice, to shapeshift as they undergo an awakening from their zombielike state. Second, when Orpheus is denied entrance to the underworld for a second time, after his failure to bring Eurydice fully back, he is emptied out and becomes zombielike himself. This is his state of being when he goes to live as an excessive mourner among the deserted and barren mountains. Though, at the end of the story, he shapeshifts one final time. He changes from the desirelessness of a zombie existence to once again becoming a musician who plays passionately, ecstatically symphysizing with the earth. Through his music, he attracts an abundance of trees which vibrantly transplant themselves to the area, touching the underworld while rooting there.

This intensive travelling back and forth between the world of the living and that of the dead, and the metamorphoses and shapeshifting that occur in tandem with it, constitute key elements of the Orpheus/Eurydice story, and link it to a-modern cosm-ontologies based on the idea of cyclical renewal. According to archaeological, philological and cultural historical analyses (Graves 1955, 1972; Bachofen 1967 [1861]; Göttner-Abendroth 1980; Gimbutas 1984, 1989), the wider field of a-modern cosm-ontologies to which the Orpheus/Eurydice story belongs thrived as so-called fertility cults in early agrarian societies in the areas which today are defined as the South-Eastern parts of Europe and the Middle East. In these cultures, which have been studied as matriarchal (ibid.), death figured in markedly different ways from those in which Christianity constructed it. Death was not a point of no return in the sense of a linear teleological trajectory, launching the human subject from an earthly life to a final endpoint in heaven or hell, as depicted in Christianity. In contrast, death marked a going to the underworld in preparation for a later, cyclical return to the world of the living. These cosm-ontologies are assumed to be modelled after the life/death cycle of plants, which die during the cold seasons, and return in the warm ones. The Orpheus/Eurydice myth, as it found its way into classical European opera, via Virgil (2019 [37–30 BCE]) and Ovid (1717 [1 CE]), is genealogically linked to these cosm-ontologies, even though the stuff has been twisted and turned along the road – as has the Orpheic religion[3] which, in Hellenistic times, was built up around the figure of Orpheus.

I interpellate these wider cultural historical genealogies of the Orpheus/Eurydice myth, first, in order to, once more, emphasize its difference from other romantic love-death myths that have provided the stuff for tragic opera librettos. This is a difference which, as discussed in the introduction, leads the Orpheus/Eurydice story to resonate with the posthuman and immanence philosophical contemplation of life/death as a vibrant continuum that makes up a central frame for this book's argument. Second, however, with this wider contextualization of Orpheus/Eurydice, I not only want to make the myth perform for me as a sounding board for my and my beloved's personal story, but also to see it take part in the scaling up from the personal to the collective ethico-political level. Thus, the aim of this contextualization is to facilitate the explicit linking of the myth to the articulation of an ethico-political figuration of vibrant death, which draws attention to dimensions of shape-shifting and cyclical metamorphosing between life and death. Third – and as part of this up-scaling – I want to emphasize how Orpheus/Eurydice's embeddedness in a-modern cosm-ontologies from Europe and the Middle East makes it possible to bring the story into conversation with the indigenous cosm-ontologies and philosophies from Latin America, and the work of Anzaldua, on which I grounded the pluriversal conversations of Chapter 6. Let me now take a closer look at this latter link.

Within the framework of Anzaldua's new tribalist, and spiritual materialist revitalizing of myths and mythical figures stemming from her Aztec ancestry, she puts a lot of emphasis on the earth goddess of life and death, Coatlicue (Anzaldua 1987: 63–73; ibid. 2015: 128–34), and her daughter, the moon goddess, Coyolxauhqui (ibid. 2015: 86–9). The focus of Anzaldua's reading of these goddesses is, first of all, the ways in which the mother, Coatlicue, embodies death/going to the underworld, which leads to renewal:

> Coatlicue is rupture in our everyday world. As the Earth, she opens and swallows us, plunging us into the underworld where the soul resides, allowing us to dwell in darkness. (…) Coatlicue, the Earth, opens and plunges us into its maw, devours us. (…) Frozen in stasis, she perceives a slight movement – a thousand slithering serpent hairs, *Coatlicue*. It is activity (not immobility) at its most dynamic stage, but it is underground movement requiring all her energy. It brooks no interference from the conscious mind.
>
> 1987: 68–9

The daughter, Coyolxauhqui, is also of key importance in Anzaldua's spiritual material revisiting and reclaiming of the myth for contemporary spiritual political activism. In the ancient myth, Coyolxauhqui experiences dying/shapeshifting in the form of being cut into a thousand pieces by her baby brother, after she tries to kill her mother. While Coatlicue is the agency sending us to the underworld, Coyolxauhqui is the body being submitted to death (Anzaldua 2015: 242–3). The two goddesses are important to Anzaldua within the framework of her spiritualist materialism and activism (ibid.: 89–90). They embody what she defines as the 'Coatlicue state', a devastating, but productive journey through the underworld (1987: 63–73), and the 'Coyolxauhqui imperative', the requirement to undergo fragmentation in order to enter into an ongoing process of 'unmaking and making'

(2015: 19–20, 95–116). In this sense, for Anzaldua, the two goddesses are spiritually materializing her processes of delving into gloomy, underworld-like experiences of fragmentation. But they also embody spiritual activism, and opening oneself towards the ways in which open-minded confrontations with deep-seated pain, and serious efforts to work through it as part of a political-spiritual resistance to oppression, can lead to 'awakening, insights, understandings, realizations, courage, and the motivation to engage in concrete ways with the potential to bring us into compassionate interactions' (2015: 19).

For Anzaldua, this way of moving through painful confrontations with oppression and fragmentation towards new, spiritual material political insight is of key importance. It is framed in many ways in her work – among others through her central concept of *nepantla* (ibid.: 2–9). *Nepantla* is related to the Coatlicue state and the duality of being thrown into painful circumstances, but through hard work also gaining new insights from the experience to be used in spiritual political work for change. *Nepantla* is a Nahuatl word for being 'in the middle' and 'in between' (2015: 28, 98, 108). Anzaldua uses this word to encompass a liminal consciousness, shaped by feelings of becoming disempowered and experiencing a total loss of control due to circumstances over which the individual subject has no control, such as living in the *mestizaje* of the borderlands – or becoming critically ill (Anzaldua died from diabetes). But, at the same time, *nepantla* refers to the creativity and new, entangled ethico-political, spiritual and personal insights (*conocimiento*, 2015: 19) that can grow from liminal positions and situations. Shamanic journeying between worlds (2015: 32–3), and shapeshifting, *naguala* (2015: 105), is an important part of this process (2015: 189).

There are several affinities between the Orpheus/Eurydice myth and that of Coatlicue/Coyolxauhqui, which sustain my linking of them. First of all, affinities can be found in the motif of passing through the underworld towards renewal, which in both cases can be associated with cosm-ontologies and understandings of shapeshifting between life and death, based on cyclicity. Second, there are genealogical links insofar as the cluster of Orpheus/Eurydice myths is connected to a powerful mother/daughter goddess couple, which has cultural-historical affinities with the Coatlicue/Coyolxauhqui pair – and which in a parallel way embodies the powers of life and death, and the shapeshifting in-between them. The ancient Greek earth and life/death goddess Demeter, and her daughter Kore – also related to Persephone, the queen of the underworld, wife of Hades – are both part of the figures appearing in the wider cluster of mythical stories to which Orpheus/Eurydice belongs. Demeter has a distinct role in this wider myth cluster; among other things, she appears as a central figure in the rituals of the Orpheic religion, which merges Orpheus and Dionysus (Göttner-Abendroth 1980: 240). Moreover, there are several links between Orpheus/Eurydice and Kore/Persephone. It is, indeed, the latter who, together with Hades, is moved by Orpheus' music to let Eurydice follow him back to life in the first place. But there are even closer links than that. In some versions of the myth stories related to the Kore/Persephone figure, the daughter of Demeter, she is deemed to stay in the underworld during the winter – and then, released every spring, she is allowed to be with her mother during the summer (ibid.: 35). This seasonal movement to and from the underworld becomes notable in my context, together with another element that can be traced in the myth cluster – namely, that some versions of the Orpheus/Eurydice myth merge with that of Demeter/Kore/Persephone, making Eurydice and Kore/Persephone into one, and casting Eurydice as goddess of the underworld (ibid.: 248). In these composite versions, Eurydice as daughter of Demeter, then becomes the one who passes back and forth across the threshold to the underworld in tandem with the shifting seasons. These elements link Orpheus' attempts to bring Eurydice back to life even more closely to the previously discussed cosm-ontologies, grounded in philosophical contemplations of life/death in relation to cyclicity, and modelled on plant life. Moreover, the ways in which the Orpheus figure here becomes connected, not only to Demeter, but also to her daughter Kore/Persephone/Eurydice, means that he appears together with a mother/daughter goddess couple. In its reference to cyclic shapeshifting at the life/death threshold, this contextualizing of Orpheus as related to the mother/daughter figure of Demeter/Kore makes the genealogical affinities with the cosm-ontologies, related to the Coatlicue/Coyolxauhqui pair, stand out even more.

A third point to add to this tracing of affinities between the Orpheus/Eurydice myth and that of Coatlicue/Coyolxauhqui concerns the motif of being physically cut or torn into pieces. Coyolxauhqui is cut into a thousand pieces, but, in the wider cluster of myths in which Orpheus figures, this physically being torn apart happens to him, too. In Roman poet Virgil's version of the myth (2019 [37–30 BCE]), Orpheus is torn to pieces by Bacchantes (women followers of the god Bacchus[4]), angry with him, because, in his state of deep mourning after the second death of Eurydice, Orpheus has lost any interest in sex.[5]

An Ethico-Political Figuration of Vibrant Death

Anzaldua actualizes the Coatlicue/Coyolxauhqui myth for contemporary spiritual activist projects. I am inspired by her work, and when I scale up from my personal story to wider ethico-political horizons, and a figuration of vibrant death, this inspiration works in a dual sense. Echoing the way in which Anzaldua moves between the personal and the spiritual-political-collective levels, I claim that my autobiographical story of mourning and the ways in which I have used the myth of Orpheus/Eurydice as *leitmotif*, can be linked to wider ethical and political visions of a figuration of vibrant death. Moreover, I suggest that the genealogical links between the Orpheus/Eurydice myth and that of Coatlicue/Coyolxauhqui allow for a making the ethico-political horizons to be opened by the figuration even wider.

Before backing up this claim, I will once more underline the humble position of apprentice to which I committed myself, when discussing Anzaldua's spiritual material activism and shamanistic practices in Chapter 6. When involving Anzaldua's spiritual materialist revitalizing of the figures of Coatlicue/Coyolxauhqui in my moving from a personalized to a more over-arching ethico-political revisiting of the Orpheus/Eurydice story, I shall emphasize that I do not pretend to make any simple claims to sameness between Anzaldua and myself. I am very aware that my autobiographical story of mourning, devastation and shapeshifting is embedded in my privileged situation as a white, queerfeminist professor, my upbringing in atheist beliefs and in the coloniality of knowledge, which has rejected spiritual materialist knowledge practices, including the shamanic ones, which Anzaldua built on, as 'premodern primitivism'. All of this constitutes a decisive difference, turning me into an apprentice who needs to 'unlearn' and 'relearn' (Tlostanova and Mignolo 2012). Thus, I pay my respects to my inspirations from Anzaldua, and along the lines of my divinatory methodology, I claim diagrammatic affinities between the role played by Orpheus/Eurydice in my mourning story, and Anzaldua's way of incorporating Coatlicue/Coyolxauhqui into her own 'autohistorias' (2015: 138) of going through the *nepantla* of both *mestizaje* and bodily decomposition due to critical illness. Her take on this inspires me to understand my own spiritual material practices and shapeshifting better, and helps me to find ways to scale up from the personal to the ethico-political level. *But* to take the convergences at the personal level further than that would be to reproduce the coloniality of knowledge through an erasure of the structural power of our very different forms of geo- and corpopolitical situatedness.

With this *caveat* in mind, I summon the clusters of genealogical links and diagrammatic affinities to enable my own and Anzaldua's revitalizations of the Orpheus/Eurydice and Coatlicue/Coyolxauhqui myth clusters to help me in my effort to offer vibrant death as a pluriversally grounded, ethical and political figuration. This is a figuration which opens up critical-affirmative horizons towards thinking life/death thresholds differently than the ways in which they are predominantly ontologized, imagined and perceived in modern Western contexts. Moreover, it is a figuration which carries out this work with a methodological base in pluritopic hermeneutics and diffractive approaches that bring Anzaldua's spiritualist materialism (1987, 2015) into conversation with the vitalist materialist and immanence philosophical approaches of Deleuze and Guattari (1988), Spinoza (1996 [1677]), Braidotti (2006) and Bennett (2010). Against this backdrop, I envision the shaping of my figuration of vibrant death as embedded in a radically affirmative ethics, planetary politics and spiritual activism. It is an ethics and politics which, as Braidotti emphasizes, resists, counter-acts and contributes to transmutations of contemporary necropolitics and the pain inflicted by it not through resignation, but through 'endurance' (2016: 52). Or, as Anzaldua frames it, as an ethics and politics that is shaped by a moving through *nepantla* (2015: 28–9) towards *conocimiento* (ibid.: 19) and spiritual-political activism.

But what does it mean to figure death as vibrant in this kind of conversation between spiritualist materialist, vitalist materialist and immanence philosophical frameworks. Let me sum up some key features.

First, the figuration of vibrant death that I have come to suggest through this book's contemplations of posthuman mourning, leads towards a radical disruption of the dualist logics of Christian and Cartesian thought, which nurtures current human exceptionalism and constructs human death as different from all other deaths. The figuration also shapes spiritualist materialist and vitalist materialist alternatives to the kind of atheism, which is founded in secular mechanical materialism, which in its own way reconfirms human exceptionalism through the claim that, beyond the death of the human subject, there is only nothingness.

Second, in contrast to transhumanist dreams of immortality, the proposed figuration of vibrant death requires a recognition of mortality in terms of an ecstatic 'embracing' of death (MacCormack 2020b) – and the ways in which all forms of life are bound together with death. Moreover, framed within the immanence philosophical and vitalist materialist frameworks that are of key importance for this book, figuring death as vibrant means considering dying and living as inextricably entangled in a material and temporal sense, which, in the words of queerfeminist and posthuman biophilosopher Marietta Radomska, makes it relevant to reconceptualize life/death as 'non/living' (Radomska 2020).

Third, figuring death as vibrant is also a way of rethinking and reimagining it as inextricably linked together with life in a cyclical, continuously shapeshifting cosmic dance across spiritual material thresholds. I frame it like this with inspiration from the a-modern cosm-ontologies and philosophies which resonate both in the Orpheus/Eurydice story and in Anzaldua's revisiting of the Coatlicue/Coyolxauhqui myth cluster. Emerging from these intertwined inspirations, the figuration of vibrant death points towards revitalizations of cosm-ontological understandings of the temporalities and ecologies of the life/death threshold, that, are radically different from those dominating Western modernity. Revitalization in this sense implies a rethinking and reimagining of death with a focus on shapeshifting and passing the thresholds of life/death as embedded in non-linear – cyclical as well as *Aionic* – time, instead of remaining within the mainstream of Western modernity, fixated on chrononormative linear timelines flowing towards final endpoints. Moreover, revitalization in this context means undoing the dichotomous divides between nature/culture, human/non-human, mind/matter, living/dead which also haunt dominant Western conceptualizations and imaginings of life/death thresholds.

Fourth, however, it is to be noted that revitalization of a-modern cosm-ontologies, for which I am arguing as part of my outlining of a figuration of vibrant death, does not imply a mere 'import' of static mythical entities from the past. Such an import is unrealistic and attempts in this direction are destructive. Thus, the figuration of vibrant death that I suggest is neither endorsing inappropriate individualized appropriations of fragmented indigenous practices by superficial New Age practitioners nor identitypolitical celebrations of mythological origins of modern nation-states by right-wing nationalists or conspiracy theorists. Nor does the figuration imply approval of the neoliberal tourist industry making big business out of extracting profit from such practices. The figuration of vibrant death for which I argue is sharply distinguished from all such recolonizing ways of abusing indigenous thought and spiritual practices, as well as from all kinds of nationalistically framed mobilizing of ancient mythologies. In contrast to such abuses, revitalization, as I use it to envision my figuration of vibrant death here, means transposing relevant a-modern cosm-ontologies and philosophies in ways which enable them to perform under the radically changed conditions of present-day post/colonial capitalism and Anthropocene necropolitics. As emphasized by Anzaldua in her discussion of spiritual activism (2015: 92), revitalizing and transposing implies a maintaining of close links with struggles for collective, social and environmental justice – and with the wider networks and frameworks for thinking through contemporary political and ethical questions raised by movements that are radically concerned with anti-racist, decolonial, trans, queer, feminist, dis/ability, ecocritical and posthuman issues.

However, embedded within such contexts, figuring death as vibrant and claiming vibrant death as an ethico-political norm may, I argue, open important horizons and challenge Anthropocene – capitalist and post/colonial – necropolitics (Lykke 2019b). To insist upon death, human as well as non-human, as a vibrant event carries the potential to undo the structures that create distinctions between grievable, non-disposable bodies, on the one hand, and non-grievable, disposable ones, on the other (Butler 2004; Mbembe 2003). An ethics and politics of vibrant death will require that dying is not turned into a mechanical practice, based on normalized, unquestioned distinctions between disposable/non-disposable, grievable/non-grievable bodies, which leaves certain bodies to die while enabling others to live well. Opting for a vision of vibrant death implies that dying as being disposed of becomes deeply unethical, no matter whether the body being disposed of is human or non-human. Figuring death as vibrant leads to envisioning every critter on the planet being provided a vibrant space to unfold its potentials for a bio-and geoegalitarian shapeshifting dance on the thresholds of life and death.

What if Every Critter's Death was Vibrant?

1.
What if every critter's death was vibrant?
Uncommon, special and unique?
Anthropocene necropowers
would just crumble,
orchestrated mass-extinction
finally become undone!
Not a number in statistics,
not a 'Count the casualties'
of the common one-world mass-death.
But ecstatic vibrant endings
in the midst of the non/living
vital dance of *zoe*'s forces:
decomposing and becoming,
planetary waxing-waning,
waxing-waning,
endlessly.

2.
God in heaven?
Just forget Him!
Immortality
is fake news,
human *hubris*,
always was.
It's another way
of executing
a 'Divide and conquer,'
through a techno-fixed,
extended
life support,
reserved for
carefully selected souls,
digitally memorized,
while
their flesh is stored
in freezers.
Cryo-preservation
for eternity!
Hip hurrah,
Hallelujah.

3.
What if every critter's death was vibrant?
Ahuman,[6] rhizomatic ecstasy,
vital love-death,
Orpheus' pain
transformed to music,
and to lushly growing trees.
Coatlicue with her necklace
full of human hearts and skulls,
and her children,
Coyolxauhqui,
Eurydice,
Orpheus,
snakes and ants and stones and peat bogs,
rats and lichen,
slugs and mountains,
cats and humans,
dust and rivers
ghosts and spirits
moons and algae
cosmic black holes,

vira, cancers and bacteria,
planetary pains and pleasures.
Tricksters everywhere,
dancing to the underworld
crossing thresholds and shapeshifting,
dwelling in a zombie mode
resting, resting,
– and returning in the spring.

4.
You, my love,
enjoy the dancing,
always did,
and always will.
You were
queer and trans avant la lettre,
feminist, postsocialist.
Decolonial issues dawned on you
while, aged 16,
reading about
socialism in Iran
and the government of Mosaddegh,
overthrown in 1953,
by a coup d'état,
orchestrated by the CIA.
Later, Danish women
travelling to the UK and Poland
for abortions,
concerned you deeply,
until women's reproductive freedom
from paternalistic powers
finally was legalized
in Denmark, 1973.
Tiny little ants
in a hut in Corsica
attracted your attention
with their alien rhizomatic actions
moving back and forth to minute food spots,
while you also noticed how John Lilly's dolphins
in the books we read
while writing 'Cosmodolphins'[7]
with their clever observations
totally dismantled
how the scientists,
although in power,

most of all did stupid tricks,
letting many dolphins die
in their lab experiments
due to lack of understanding
of the fact that dolphins
cannot be anaesthetized.
What if every critter's death was vibrant?

5.
Algae slowly built the seabed,
while the water still was warm,
and volcanoes sometimes
interfered with gouts of ashes.
Dying plants
produced the dust.
Later ice rolled in
and, with its mighty geopowers,
caused the cliffs to rise
up from the ground,
while the sea
carved out the caves.
Immanence
and
spirit
matter,
let's quickly join the dance,
just embrace it
not resist it,
this is not a dance macabre,
this is
planetary
holobiont,
multispecies,
sympoetic,
symanimagenic
geo-tango,
vibrant life
in vibrant death,
vibrant death
in vibrant life.
What if every critter's death was vibrant?

Illustr. 10 What if Every Critter's Death was Vibrant? © Nina Lykke 2017.

NOTES

Overture

1 Kathleen Ferrier (1912–53) was an English opera singer, contralto (i.e. the deepest voice of female singers). Her trouser role as Orpheus in C. W. Gluck's opera *Orfeo ed Eurydice* [Orpheus and Eurydice] (2019 [1762]), was one of the peaks of her career. She performed the role several times, the last time in London in 1953, shortly before her death.

2 The aria *Che farò senza Euridice? / What is life to me without thee?*, Orpheus' lament from Gluck's opera *Orfeo ed Eurydice* (ibid.) is sung right after the failing of Orpheus' attempt to rescue his beloved Eurydice from death through a journey to the underworld to get her back to life. The aria has been translated into English a number of times with a template both in the original Italian libretto by the librettist Ranieri de Calzabigi, premiering in Vienna, 1762, and in a reworked French version of the opera by librettist Pierre-Louis Moline, premiering in Paris, 1774, and later once more reworked for the Paris Opera by the composer Hector Berlioz in 1859. The English translation, quoted here (Gluck 2021 [1762/1774]), by the translator Claude Aveling (1869–1943), is the English version which, today, is associated with opera singer Kathleen Ferrier, insofar as she sung it on a renowned recording with the London Symphony Orchestra in 1946, which still exists (at: https://www.youtube.com/watch?v=8F6JtfW5NL4, accessed 14 February 2021). Aveling's translation is a reworked version of the extended ariatext from the French libretto.

Chapter 1

1 My beloved's corpse was cremated in an ecological willow casket, and the ashes transferred into a blue urn made of dissolvable ecological materials. It was my beloved's wish to be cremated, and that her ashes should be scattered over the sea. The procedure implied that I would get the urn with the ashes, which would allow me to keep a small part of them with me, so that later, when I die, they can be mixed with mine. The mix is then to be scattered over the sea in the same place where my beloved's ashes already are scattered. Together with my rainbow kin, I chose to scatter the ashes in a fjord in the Northern part of Denmark, Limfjorden, beyond the island of Fur. I had promised my beloved to scatter her ashes in a place with many oysters, and the waters beyond the island of Fur are known for their oysters. Moreover, the area is a geologically unique place that aspires to become a UNESCO World Heritage site. Its uniqueness is related to the special seabed, and a cliff and earth formation (The Fur Formation), built out of multicoloured single-celled aquatic algae, diatoms, that fossilized fiftyfive million years ago, when a subtropical sea covered the area. There are also hundreds of layers of ashes in both the seabed and the cliffs, stemming from the significant volcanic activity that was taking place in the area at the same time. The cliffs were shaped during the Ice Age

10,000 years ago, when the ice pushed the rocklike, although very light, diatomaceous earth sediments upwards. Diatoms trace their ancestry back to the Jurassic, 150 million years ago, but living diatoms still fill the waters of the planet today, including the waters of Limfjorden. They belong to the species of phytoplankton, which, like terrestrial plants, contain chlorophyll, transforming light into chemical energy through photosynthesis, and producing oxygen. Living diatoms are today reported to generate about twenty percent of the planet's oxygen annually (Allen et al. 2011). In 2011, it was discovered that diatoms, previously considered plant-like due to their ability to photosynthesize, also have an urea cycle, enabling them to excrete nitrogen and metabolize in ways which, until then, were assumed to characterize only animals and animal-like creatures (ibid.). This alien, but very vibrant, world of living and fossilized diatoms makes up the assemblage of which my beloved's ashes have become part, and which my rainbow familiy has promised me to make sure that my ashes also will become part of, when I die.

2   When using the terms 'queering' and 'queer' in *Vibrant Death*, I follow the practice of queer theory, which underscores that they should be used open-endedly, and in acknowledgement of a broad continuum extending between the following two poles: First, 'queer' and 'queering' used to critically address open-ended processes of dismantling, deconstructing and undoing normalizing and normativities in all their forms. Queer scholar Michael Nebeling Petersen (2012) aptly used the phrase 'objectless queer theory' to indicate this end of the spectrum. It is important to note that 'objectless queer' takes off in both decolonizing and anti-racist directions (Eng and Puar 2020), as well as in posthumanizing ones (Hird and Gifney 2008), which converge, but also differ. Second, 'queer' and 'queering' related specifically to the deconstructing and undoing of heteronormativity, heteropatriarchality, binary gender and sexualities governed by reproductive biopower, what Judith Butler defined as the normative heterosexual matrix (1990). In *Vibrant Death*, I relate to both sides of this continuum.

3   There are many positions in-between Christian dualisms, on the one hand, and Cartesian dualisms, on the other. This is due to the ways in which a materialist mechanicism, which follows from Descartes' definition of bodies and matter as inert, and acting mechanically when set in motion by outside forces, merge with Christian ontologies, based on soul/matter distinctions, as well as overlap with atheist positions. The latter cast death as nothingness, against the background of a mind/matter dichotomy rather than a soul/matter dualism. However, there are convergences between these two different approaches when it comes to the casting of the corpse as base, inert matter, hierarchically subordinate to the human mind/soul.

4   Spinoza's ethics (1996 [1677]) focuses on the question of how bodies affect and become affected by each other. Bringing Spinoza's monist thought to bear on dead bodies, I imply that the capacity to affect and be affected applies to them as well.

5   Existentialist philosopher Jean-Paul Sartre's contemplation of death as nothingness (1958) resonates with the leftist atheism with which I was brought up, and in which both I and my beloved believed for many years. Throughout *Vibrant Death*, I use Sartre's version as an icon of this approach.

6   *Liebestod*, German for love-death, is iconically related to the final dramatic music in German composer Richard Wagner's opera *Tristan and Isolde* (1859). At the end of the opera, Isolde (the main female character) collapses across the dead body of her beloved Tristan. However, the motif of love-death runs throughout Western romantic opera, both before and after Wagner, from Gaetano Donizetti's *Lucia di Lammermoor* (1835) to Charles Gounod's *Romeo and Juliet* (1867), based on William Shakespeare's drama of the same name, first performed in 1597.

Interlude I

1 The poem *Tears* was, as excerpt from the back then unpublished manuscript for *Vibrant Death* (working title *Laments*), published as part of the argument in Nina Lykke, 'When death cuts apart', chapter 7 in Tuula Juvonen and Marjo Kolehmainen (eds) (2018), *Affective Inequalities in Intimate Relationships*, London and New York: Routledge, 109–25. Republished in agreement with Routledge and the Editors.

Chapter 2

1 The autobiographical story *A Normative Encounter* was, as excerpt from the back then unpublished manuscript for *Vibrant Death (*working title *Laments / Sorgsångar)*, first published in Swedish as part of the argument in Nina Lykke (2017), Sorgsångar. At bryta sorgens normer och queera döden. *Bang* 4: 22–8. Republished, according to agreement with *Bang Magazine*.
2 Cvetkovich (2012) discusses how a queer strategy of resistance, in terms of making feelings public, worked for her when she claimed depression and the right to keep 'resting in sadness' (ibid.: 14) as a public concern. Along somewhat similar lines, my work on *Vibrant Death* has been accompanied by my participation in the building of an international Network for Queer Death Studies, at https://queerdeathstudies.net/, as well as networking with other mourners. I am deeply indebted to everyone with whom I have had conversations in these contexts.
3 Cvetkovich (2012) frames her discussion of depression against the background of a queer- and affect-theoretical approach. She does not explicitly use a crip perspective. Nonetheless, her claiming of the right to remain in depressive moods in order to give them space to evolve into new insights resonates with cripqueer perspectives, as articulated by, among others, Kafer (2013).
4 In his discussion of temporalities, Deleuze (2020: 167–72) distinguishes between *Chronos* (understood as normative chronological time; the time of the now and linear progression from past towards future) and *Aion* (the time of the instant, which articulates multiple intense becomings in all directions). I found unexpected convergences with Halberstam's foregrounding of the intensity of the queer moment as an alternative to heteronormative longevity (Dinshaw et al. 2007: 182). Still, Halberstam's focus is a lifetime perspective, the living of a queer life, which, when read through Deleuze's distinction, would manifest as a sequence of 'now's, rather than as an embodiment of the *Aionic* instant.
5 My recycling of the term companionship is indebted to Haraway's (2008) way of using it in her discussion of human/dog relations. When I use the term, the undoing of human exceptionalism which is implied in Haraway's meaning-making around the term (the establishing of human/non-human relations as ethically on a par with human/human relations) is important in my context as well. What I explore in the following chapters is, among other things, how the human/human companionship that I enjoyed with my beloved evolved, through her death, and through my attempts to co-become with her inhuman remains and their new assemblages, into an intense human/non-human relation.
6 A shorter version of the autobiographical story *Sorrowful Pleasures* was, as excerpt from the back then unpublished manuscript for *Vibrant Death* (working title *Laments*), published as part of the argument in Nina Lykke, 'When death cuts apart', chapter 7 in

Tuula Juvonen and Marjo Kolehmainen (eds) (2018), *Affective Inequalities in Intimate Relationships,* London and New York: Routledge, 109–25. Republished in agreement with Routledge and the Editors.
7   The autobiographical story *To Become a Powerless Prosthesis* was, as excerpt from the back then unpublished manuscript for *Vibrant Death* (working title *Laments*), published as part of the argument in Nina Lykke, 'When death cuts apart', chapter 7 in Tuula Juvonen and Marjo Kolehmainen (eds) (2018), *Affective Inequalities in Intimate Relationships,* London and New York: Routledge, 109–25. Republished in agreement with Routledge and the Editors.
8   In phenomenological investigations of intercorporeality and concorporeality (Shildrick 2002, 2005), the former has been philosophically related to the general intertwinement, and hence interdependence, of bodies. The phenomenon of concorporation radicalizes the philosophical discussion of this interdependence and its challenges to the sovereign self, insofar as it indicates the literal physical sharing of organs or limbs by conjoined twins. When I use the term concorporation in relation to compassionate companionship, I am indicating that the bodily growing into each other that occurs through desiring symphysizing bears a resemblance to the literal physical growing together of conjoined twins, and that a philosophical reading of the two phenomena through one another can generate new insights, even though, of course, the significant differences will also have to be taken into account.

Interlude II

1   The poem *Cancerous Walks* was, as excerpt from the back then unpublished manuscript for *Vibrant Death* (working title *Laments / Sorgsångar*), first published in Swedish as part of the argument in Nina Lykke (2017), 'Sorgsångar. At bryta sorgens normer och queera döden', *Bang* 4: 22–8. Republished, according to agreement with *Bang Magazine*.
2   Gunaratnam (2013: 15).
3   The poem *You Don't Know Death* was, as excerpt from the back then unpublished manuscript for *Vibrant Death* (working title *Laments / Sorgsångar),* first published in Swedish as part of the argument in Nina Lykke (2017), 'Sorgsångar. At bryta sorgens normer och queera döden', *Bang* 4: 22–8. Republished, according to agreement with *Bang Magazine*.

Chapter 3

1   I use the category of the inhuman in accordance with Braidotti's (2013: 105–43) critically affirmative rethinking of this category. From a posthuman perspective, Braidotti radically delinks the notion of the inhuman from the negative connotations with which it has been endowed through various branches of nineteenth- and twentieth-century critical humanist modernism – from Karl Marx's way of relating the concept to the exploitation and alienation of the worker during the capitalist process of production to Giorgio Agamben's and Hanna Arendt's focus on the Nazi concentration camps' 'ultimate denial of the humanity of the other' (Braidotti 2013: 120). In stark contrast to Agamben, who uses Aristotle's category of *zoe* as equivalent to the 'bare life' of those who are denied humanity, Braidotti's posthuman feminist philosophical turns

revisit *zoe* and the inhuman from a radically different angle. Based on an immanence philosophical, vitalist materialist and Spinoza-inspired ontology, Braidotti uses the concepts of *zoe* and the inhuman to denote the immensely dynamic transcorporeal affective forces characterizing the matter that makes up the earth and the universe. These forces are to be understood as inhuman, implying that the human subject only makes up a tiny fraction of the universe, and that the immanent cosmic forces are 'supremely indifferent to humans' (ibid. 2006: 248). In this sense, the inhuman stands out as a category that critically engages with the ways in which the modern human subject has claimed supremacy over all other planetary beings. The category of the inhuman, linked to *zoe*, contributes to the undoing of the violent and exceptionalizing *hubris* involved in this human claim to superiority, and exceptionalism, mirrored by the idea of a divine entity, first and foremost preoccupied with human needs. Braidotti's *zoe*-based understanding of the inhuman, which I draw on in *Vibrant Death*, also affirmatively involves a radical bio- and geo-egalitarianism.
2 Registered partnership for same-sex couples was legalized in Denmark in 1989. My partner and I were married in 1996. I was, therefore, legally entitled to take care of the procedures related to the funeral ceremony, arranging for cremation, etc.
3 As I have related the detailed story about the days after my beloved's death in the essay *Queer Widowhood* (Lykke 2015), it became obvious to me how the systems for taking care of dead human bodies in Denmark are organized on a Christian basis, and that very active work and alertness are required from those who do not want to become enrolled in Christian regimes.
4 I have defined a methodology that combines discourse analytical and narrative approaches with new-materialist ones as postconstructionist (Lykke 2010: 120, 141). In so doing, I follow Barad's (2007) reading of Butler, which leads her to the dual claim that, on the one hand, it is pertinent to follow the lead of poststructuralism and ask how discourse comes to matter, while, on the other hand, also investigating how matter comes to matter.
5 A longer version of this autobiographical story was previously published as part of my essay Nina Lykke, 'Queer widowhood', *Lambda Nordica* 4 (2015): 85–111. Reprinted with permission from *Lambda Nordica*.
6 The collection of books in the national language was, for Karen Brahe, part of seventeenth–eighteenth-century resistance to the authoritarian and elitist powers which, through the Catholic Church, had been granted to Latin.
7 The alternative, and carefully planned, spiritual material funeral ceremony, which I arranged in collaboration with my rainbow kin, is described in detail in my essay *Queer Widowhood* (Lykke 2015).
8 The first section of this autobiographical story was previously published as part of my essay Nina Lykke: 'Queer Widowhood.' *Lambda Nordica* 4/2015: 85–111. Reprinted with permission from *Lambda Nordica*.

Interlude III

1 The poem *Fur* was, as excerpt from the back then unpublished manuscript of *Vibrant Death*, published as part of the argument in Nina Lykke (2019), 'Co-Becoming with Algae. between Posthuman Mourning and Wonder in Algae Research', *Catalyst. Feminism, Theory, Technoscience*. 5 (2). The poem was first published in Swedish, also as excerpt from the back then unpublished manuscript of *Vibrant Death* (Swedish

working title *Sorgsånger* [Laments]), as part of the argument in Nina Lykke (2017), 'Sorgsångar. At bryta sorgens normer och queera döden', *Bang* 4/2017: 22–8. Republished in agreement with *Catalyst* and *Bang Magazine*.

Chapter 4

1. As described in detail in Chapter 3 n. 1, the inhuman, understood in an immanence philosophical sense, should not be collapsed into the ways in which the concept has been used in different branches of modern humanism.
2. As observed in Chapter 2 n. 4, Deleuze distinguishes the time of *Chronos* (related to a now as distinguished from past and present along a chronological, one-directional timeline) from the time of *Aion* (the time of the instant when intense becomings happen in multiple temporal directions). According to Deleuze, the time of *Aion* is the instant that is always already in between past and future, which subdivides the present 'ad infinitum into past and future, in both directions at once' – it is 'the instant without thickness and without extension' (Deleuze 2020: 169).
3. In terms of bringing the Deleuzoguattarian understanding of becoming-imperceptible (1988: 279) to bear specifically on the vanishing of the dying human subject, it should be noted that the way in which the subject becomes a-signifying as part of becoming-imperceptible, i.e. ceases to generate signs as a human subject, does not mean that signs stop being emitted from the bodily materiality with which the subject becomes one when dying.
4. Contrasting her approach to that of Giorgio Agamben's assimilation of *zoe* 'to death in the sense of the corpse', understood within a modern humanist framework as 'bare life', i.e. the 'liminal bodily existence of a life that does not qualify as human', Braidotti (2006: 39–41) takes the understanding of *zoe* in a radically different, non-anthropocentric direction. Focusing on *zoe*'s 'generative powers' against the background of a Spinozist monist ontology and a Deleuzoguattarian immanence philosophical approach, Braidotti redefines the concept as part of a radically bio- and geo-egalitarian 'eco-philosophy of multiple belongings' (ibid.). Within this framework, *zoe* is to be understood as 'the endless vitality of life as continuous becoming', which grounds the human subject as an 'ecological entity', transversally and transcorporeally related to all other planetary existences, both human and non-human (ibid.).
5. As described in Chapter 2, I suggest that my positionality as a queer femme and my queerfeminine relationship with my partner led me to cultivate certain sensibilities which have also been important for my mourning practices. Following Dahl (2012), I define these sensibilities as a 'femmebodiment', which has facilitated an extension of the symphysizing I experienced with my beloved while she was alive, to encompass her bodily remains and their new, inhuman assemblages such as the algae sand in Limfjorden.
6. Against the background of my Spinozist belief in *conatus*, the striving of all matter to persevere (1996 [1677]), I do not claim that a desire for love-death can be totally without ambiguity. Still, I claim that the desire for love-death places the excessively mourning 'I' in a radically different position of enunciation, when speaking about death, than the sovereign 'I'.
7. Hieronymus Bosch (1450–1516) was a Dutch painter, belonging to the early Netherlandish painting school, famous for his grotesque and fantastic depictions of both the Christian Hell and Paradise.

8   In folklore, a *revenant* is a dead person who returns from the grave, often to haunt the living. The word 'revenant' is French for 'returning'. Derrida (1994) interpellates the figure of the *revenant* as part of his philosophical unfolding of a theory of hauntology, i.e. a theory about the ways in which temporal pasts act upon the present.
9   See Chapter 1 n. 1.
10 Joan Didion (born 1934) is a well known US novelist and nonfiction writer. Her two books on mourning (2005, 2012), telling the story of losing her husband, and soon afterwards her daughter, are auto-fiction. In 2005, she won the National Book Award for Nonfiction, and was a finalist for both the National Book Critics Circle Award and the Pulitzer Prize for Biography/Autobiography for *The Year of Magical Thinking* (2005). She later adapted the book into a play, which premiered on Broadway in 2007.
11 Friedrich Rückert (1788–1866) was a German Romantic poet, who wrote a comprehensive cycle of 428 poems after the deaths of two of his children from scarlet fever.
12 Hanna Hallgren (born 1972) is a Swedish poet with a PhD in Gender Studies, known for numerous poetry collections, among them one on the death of her father (2014).
13 Originally from Greenland, Naja Marie Aidt (born 1963) is a Danish poet and writer with nearly twenty works in various genres to her name. She has received numerous honours, including the Danish Critics Choice Award, The Danish Art Foundation's Award for Lifelong Service, the Nordic nations' most prestigious literary prize, the Nordic Council's Literature Prize, and the Grand Prize of the Danish Academy. Her poetic and autofictional book on mourning the death of her son has been translated into 22 languages. The English translation *When Death Takes Something from You Give it Back – Carl's Book* (Aidt 2019) was published by Quercus, London, and Coffee House Press, Minneapolis, MN. It was longlisted for the National Book Award in the US and was finalist for the Kirkus Prize.
14 Derrida's focus is the scene of spectral return at the beginning of Shakespeare's tragedy *Hamlet* (1599): Hamlet's dead father, the previous king of Denmark, haunts Hamlet, urging him to avenge his murder by killing the new king.

Chapter 5

1   Miracles have been a rather marginal topic in secular twentieth-century humanities after having figured as one of the prime targets of secular Enlightenment with its critique of theology and the political influence of the Church. However, a renewed interest in miracles has begun to re-emerge, in different ways, as part of the post-secular turn (e.g. Bensaid 2004; Santner 2005; Ricciardi 2007). The question, with which I begin Chapter 5, is tapping into this turn, insofar as it somehow echoes Germanic Studies scholar Eric Santner's (2005) article, titled 'Miracles happen'. However, I shall underline that my approach differs decisively from Santner's humanistically framed discussions of miracles. My approach is explicitly queering, posthumanizing and decolonizing. Moreover, it revisits and rethinks specific feminist versions (Braidotti 2008) of the post-secular turn, insofar as I critique not only Christianity's approach to death, but also that of mechanical materialism, which has been the foundation of much secular, leftist and feminist atheism, my own and my beloved's included. As a feminist, I also hold a strong ethico-political stake in a critical rejection of current intertwinements of post-secularism, right-wing religious fundamentalism and nationalism. However, I agree with Braidotti (2008), when she

argues that a possible way out of the dilemmas, which post-secularism poses for leftist feminists, is not to stay away from it altogether, but instead to critically-affirmatively claim radically different onto-epistemological approaches. Along these lines, I aim for my speculative autophenomenographical, and poetic-philosophical contemplation of death and mourning to reclaim the miraculous within a radical immanence philosophical, vitalist and spiritualist materialist framework.

2. The subject's self-styling of its own death (Braidotti 2006: 247–52) is central to Braidotti's rethinking of death within the framework of a life/death continuum, embedded in the generative, inhuman cosmic forces of *zoe*, and in tandem with a vital ethics of affirmation. Defining subjectivity as nomadic, Braidotti suggests 'a process ontology of auto-poiesis and self-styling' (2008: 1), which applies not only to living, but also to dying.

3. To indicate intersecting agencies (in this case of corpseness and ratness), I prefer to use Barad's (2007) concept of intra-action, which is distinguished from inter-action, in the sense that it indicates an entanglement, whereby one aspect cannot be separated from the other.

4. Diffraction (Barad 2007, 2014), understood as an (emergent) methodology, brings the notion of interference patterns from quantum physics to bear on the ways in which different bodies of thought and/or storytelling are brought together to produce new meaning, without collapsing the differences between them.

5. Trine Trier is a Danish jewellery artist whose designs are strongly inspired by themes related to the sea, available at: http://www.baerbart.dk/smykkedesignere/trine-trier/ (accessed 4 February 2021).

6. In *Cosmodolphins* (Bryld and Lykke 2000: 139–58), my beloved and I developed a theory of a-modern cosmologies as embedded in metonymical thought, bringing together inspirations from Cassirer (1922, 1987), Merchant (1980), Kristeva (1980), Irigaray (1981), Jakobson (1987) and Cixous (1992).

7. Haptic visualization is used in an experimental branch of digital technology working with ways to transfer data that explore haptics, seeing through touch, i.e. creating 'visualizations' through tactile feedback devices rather than digital images. I borrow the term here to indicate the ways in which relics, based on metonymical relations of touch and contiguity, can work as relays for the transformation of haptic information and for the establishment of haptic connections.

8. Carl Gustav Jung (1875–1961) founded analytical psychology, branching off from the psychoanalytical movement initiated by Sigmund Freud in the early twentieth century. Jung tapped into the world of a-modern cosmologies, cultivating an interest in topics such as alchemy and astrology, but used it to universalize his idea of a collective human unconscious, made up of essentialized and mystically tinged archetypes. In this sense, Jung's work is entangled in an essentialism and human exceptionalism that is out of synch with the immanence philosophical framework of *Vibrant Death*. His book on synchronicity (2008 [1955]) was originally published in England in 1955.

9. Hans Driesch (1867–1941) was a German philosopher and embryologist, known for his experimental work on embryology.

10. Wolfgang Pauli (1900–58) was an Austrian physicist and Nobel laureate, known as one of the pioneers of quantum physics.

11. Taking inspiration from Deleuze (2020) and Spinoza (1996 [1677]), I use the notion of an event to define an instantaneously actualizing coalescence of forces, speeds and intensities, occurring when assemblages of bodies affect and are being affected by each other within the flow of immanent becomings.

Interlude V

1. Camila Marambio (b. 1979) is a curator, a nomadic researcher-artist, a permaculture enthusiast, an amateur dancer, and a collaborative writer. In 2010, she founded the nomadic research practice *Ensayos* on the archipelago of Karokynka/Tierra del Fuego, at the southernmost tip of Abya Yala (The Americas). *Ensayos* brings together artists, scientists, activists, policy makers and local community to exercise speculative and emergent forms of eco-cultural ethics at the world's end. With her work, she strives to support the livelihoods of the communities, water, and lands where she researches and lives. She defines this practice as a nomadic artistic research, which is not bound to medium, or discipline, while attempting to create contributions to the fields of environmental humanities, curatorial practice, Indigenous studies, conservation biology and ecopolitics. From 2021, Camila Marambio holds a postdoc position at the Royal Institute of Art in Stockholm. She has a PhD in Curatorial Practice from Monash University, Australia (2019), a Master of Experiments in Arts and Politics from Science Po (2012) and an MA in Modern Art: Critical Studies from Columbia University (2004). Her writings have been published in Third Text, Australian Feminist Studies Journal, Discipline, The River Rail, Kerb Journal, amongst others. She is co-author of the book *Slow Down Fast, A Toda Raja* with Cecilia Vicuña (2019). Camila and I are working on an experimental story-telling monograph *Sandcastles. Cancerous Bodies and Their Necropowers* (forthcoming). The interview took place in the initial phases of our collaborative work on this book; it is published here with the permission of Camila Marambio.

Chapter 6

1. The term cosm-ontology indicates that cosmologies and ontologies are entangled.
2. Trinh T. Minh-ha (b. 1952) is a Vietnamese filmmaker, scholar, writer, composer and professor of Gender and Women's Studies and Rhetoric at the University of Berkeley, CA, internationally renowned, among other things, for her key contributions to critiques of postcoloniality from feminist perspectives, such as the seminal work *Woman, Native, Other: Writing Postcoloniality and Feminism* (1989).
3. Defining my work within a posthumanist framework, I consider it important that it should not be collapsed with transhumanism. The latter is a philosophical movement that focuses on human transformation through advanced technology, and, as far as death is concerned, envisions that technological development will enable us to pursue human immortality, i.e. in due time to abolish human death. Posthumanism, in particular feminist posthumanism (Braidotti 2022), takes into account sociotechnological transformation, but from a critical perspective, which addresses the necropowers that block the unfolding of planetwide social and environmental justice, and envisions the search for an elsewhere/otherwise (Haraway 2016) as intertwined with the ethico-political struggles for radically changed ways of inhabiting the planet.
4. In Catholicism, the Virgin of Guadalupe is associated with four apparitions of the Virgin Mary in 1531 to an indigenous, Nahuatl peasant, Juan Diego, in a place that later came to be called Villa de Guadalupe, now a suburb of Mexico City. A relic (a venerated image imprinted on a cloak), enshrined in the Basilica of Our Lady de Guadalupe in Mexico City, commemorates the event.

5 As a key concept of Barad's (2007) onto-epistemology, agential realism conceptualizes the world, against the background of a quantum-physical understanding, as made up of intra-acting phenomena. As Barad (2014) argues, there are clear affinities with Anzaldua's cosm-ontology, and its focus on the interconnectedness of everything (1987, 2015). Together with Schaeffer (2018), I argue that there are also affinities with immanence philosophical and vitalist materialist frameworks.

6 On Bennett's pathway towards defining the 'impersonal affect or material vibrancy', which she understands as immanent and not as 'a spiritual supplement or "life force" added to the matter said to house it' (2010: xiii), Bennett discusses German philosopher Emmanuel Kant's '*Bildungstrieb*' (Kant 1987 [1790]). For Kant, this is a generative force, which is different from the mechanically acting organic matter it pervades, but which still cannot be delinked from it. Bennett finds the way in which Kant uses this notion to imply a rejection of any divine intervention to be important, while she is still critical of his mechanical materialism, which leads him to propose that the '*Bildungstrieb*' is different from matter, albeit not in the sense of a divine infusion (ensoulment in a Christian sense) (Bennett 2010: 66).

7 Schaeffer (2018) critically addresses Haraway's recognition of her awkward Western relation to spirit helpers which, as Haraway contemplates (2016: 88), makes her unsuccessful at playing a video game, *Never Alone*, that 'requires players to learn Inuipiat Alaska Native peoples' world views' (Schaeffer 2018: 1012). Schaeffer recognizes Haraway's admittance of her awkwardness, but takes the discussion a step further. She asks why it is easier for radically critical Western feminist posthumanists (in casu: Haraway, but the question extends to many others, and I could, indeed, be included in the group myself) to try to engage in deeply unfamiliar 'alternative worlds with multispecies others, from orchids to coral reefs (…) than to travel with indigenous communities, including the Inuit, in their virtual journeys with spirit guides?' (ibid.: 1013–14). This is a complex question, and Haraway, too, touches upon it, while discussing the need for a rethinking and recognition of *synanimagenesis* (a self-organized co-evolving, involving mutual help at spiritual/animist levels; Haraway 2016: 88). To me, Haraway's reluctance or awkwardness around the recognition of spirit helpers seems somewhat recognizable, and perhaps in resonance with my own relationship to the 'real'/'not-real' distinction, which I have discussed earlier in Chapter 6, and which became clear to me as part of the interview in *Interlude V*. In a reading of Haraway's (ibid.) use of the adverb 'really', the philosopher Isabelle Stengers (2021) sustains this point, tracing ambiguities in Haraway's text relating to the 'real'/'not-real' distinction. For my own part, I think that my resistance to rationally, and not only intuitively, embracing the miraculous events that I had encountered together with my dying beloved, is due to ingrained epistemic habits, genealogically rooted in the enlightenment struggle to overthrow the powers of the Christian Church, which have been particularly imperative for feminists and queer people. These are habits which, as Schaeffer (2018) highlights, require radically critical attention and rethinking in pluriversal conversations with indigenous perspectives on spirituality.

8 In her analysis of Anzaldua's spiritual materialism, Schaeffer underlines the processuality that is articulated by the verb form of the term, matter: 'I use the term "spirit" in conjunction with the active verb tense "matters" to foreground the ways in which spirit materializes worlds' (2018: 1006).

9 In a study of seventeenth-century records of Jesuit missionaries taking part in the colonizing of indigenous Huron lands, the Canadian anthropologist Alexander von

Gernet (1994) traced how the Jesuits reinterpreted Huron notions of a multiplicity of spirits, aligning them with Christian understandings of 'soul'.
10 I constructed the neologism 'en-vegetated' in parallel with the word 'enfleshed', i.e. to indicate a process of becoming-vegetal.
11 Speculative ethics focuses on the modality of 'could be', implying an investigation of worlds which are not here now, but are plausible. To engage in scholarly speculations and work within a modality of 'could-be' means 'not only detecting what is there, given in a thing-gathering, but also to think what is not and what could be' (Bellacasa 2017: 59).
12 Haraway's neologism, 'response-ability' (2016: 114–16) merges the words 'responsibility' and 'ability' to indicate the ethical imperative of acting responsibly, while also unfolding sensibilities that make you able to respond adequately and sensitively.
13 *Sympoiesis* is a key term in Haraway's radical reontologizing of planetary relations as based on kinship (2016: 58–99). It takes a step further than an ontology of autopoiesis, which is used to describe self-organizing organisms. *Sympoiesis* means 'making-with' in Greek, and by using this term, Haraway emphasizes the ways in which all organisms enfold each other rather than developing independently of their 'environment'. The notion of *sympoiesis* undoes the idea of an individual and its environment as separate entities.
14 *Symanimagenic* (ibid.: 88) corresponds to *sympoiesis* (self-organized co-enfolding), but focuses on a spiritual/animistic level of self-organized co-enfolding. To sustain an argument for an intertwinement of *sympoiesis* and *symanimagenesis*, Haraway quotes a personal communication from the Chilean anthropologist Eduardo Viveiros de Castro, who emphasized that 'Animism is the only *sensible* version of materialism' (ibid.) – a statement that resonates well with my speculative contemplation of a radical, non-dualist ontology of immanent miracles.

Interlude VI

1 Microchimerism is defined as 'a small but significant presence of so-called non-self cells coexisting with a dominant population of self-cells in the same body' (Shildrick 2016: 95).
2 The poem addresses my friend and colleague, the philosopher and bioethicist Margrit Shildrick, whose research on microchimerism (Shildrick 2016) inspired me to write the first part of the poem, and whom I want to thank for many exciting conversations on the topic.
3 Refslund Christensen and Willerslev (2013).

Chapter 7

1 Synecdoche is a linguistic trope – a subcategory of the metonym. It refers to the use of a part of a whole to stand in for the whole (often also used in Latin: *pars pro toto*), or vice versa, the whole standing in for the part. An example of a synecdoche is when a literary character is characterized by a significant facial expression: 'the big smile entered the room', or when the US government is characterized as 'The White House'. In digital technology, holograms work in a synecdoche-like manner.
2 Show-don't-tell is a literary technique which implies a focus on scenes rather than the author making hir analyses explicit via descriptions and explanations. For example,

instead of the author describing a character in a novel, the character is revealed through hir actions. The Russian writer Anton Chekhov is known for a very outspoken relation to the technique. In a letter Chekhov, e.g., explained the technique like this: 'In descriptions of Nature one must seize on small details, grouping them so that when the reader closes his eyes he gets a picture. For instance, you'll have a moonlit night if you write that on the mill dam a piece of glass from a broken bottle glittered like a bright little star, and that the black shadow of a dog or a wolf rolled past like a ball.' (Yarmolinsky 1954: 14).

3   The Russian linguist Roman Jakobson (1987) studied the differences between metaphor and metonym, based on his comprehensive knowledge of Russian literature. Among others, he conducted a detailed and sophisticated analysis of the differences between the writing styles of Russian poets Boris Pasternak and Vladimir Mayakovsky, attributing a metonymical writing style to the former and a metaphorical one to the latter (ibid.: 301–17). When Lacan (1957) later adopted the distinction, and redefined it within a psychoanalytical framework as corresponding to the notions of condensation and displacement, emerging out of Freud's early work on dreams and hysteria, he was building on Jakobson's work. Jakobson's way of using the tropes, and their specific adoption into a psychoanalytical context should, however, not be collapsed. The genealogy for my discussions of metonymical relations in *Vibrant Death* is to be found in Jakobson's rather than Lacan's work.

4   The poetic format of the elegy (poetry contemplating sad and sorrowful moods) has a long literary history in Europe, stretching back to classical Greek poetry. The lament, too, has a long and diversified history, which, however, should not be confounded with that of the elegy. The elegy has even been described as an 'antidote for the sufferings of the lament' (Weisman 2010: 2). Where the elegy primarily contemplates sorrow, the lament is rather expressing suffering.

5   The storyline of the Orpheus/Eurydice myth, like all mythical stories, is told with many variations. The libretto of Gluck's opera, *Orpheo ed Eurydice [Orpheus and Eurydice]* (2019 [1762]), from which the lament quoted in the Overture to *Vibrant Death* originates, builds on the Roman poet Ovid, as discussed in Chapter 1. But while the classical myth, as poeticized by Ovid, ends with Orpheus retreating to the mountains after Eurydice's second death, the opera has a more clichéd happy ending. After Orpheus has sung the famous lament *Che farò senza Euridice? [What is life to me without thee?]* (Gluck 2021 [1762/1774]), Amor (the God of love) intervenes and revives Eurydice. As *leitmotif* for several of my poems and for *Vibrant Death* as a whole, I chose to use the classic Ovidian version of the myth (1717 [1 CE]), which resonated with my autobiographical story – my beloved was not brought back to life by a *deus ex machina*!

6   Abel aims to analyse 'the visceral response to operatic performance', underlining his way of responding to opera 'from the gut' rather than 'as a critic' (his response to spoken theatre; 1996: 10). For example, he illustrates 'operatic orgasms' through a long description of his very bodily responses to a particular trio, sung at the end of German composer Richard Strauss' (1864–1949) opera *Der Rosenkavalier* (1911). It is a highly erotic trio between Octavian (a character sung by a female singer in a trouser role), Sophie (Octavian's bride-to-be) and the Marshallin (Octavian's former lover), who now accepts the love of Octavian and Sophie and is taking leave of her lost lover). Abel vividly describes his bodily responses, while he lies on his sofa and abandons himself to the trio:

> The words are gone; the plot is gone; only the sound of the voices blending with the orchestra remains. My heart beats faster. My stomach muscles contract, my

buttocks tighten, my face contorts at each new harmonic tension. My head sways with the music; I conduct the opera with my prone body. The three sopranos reach the top of their registers. They can sing no higher, but I'm not satisfied yet. The harmonies have not resolved; the music must still go up, up. The violins take over, carrying the melody over the top, beginning to resolve the hopelessly dense harmonies. Strings and voices strain against each other, cresting on each climactic note. My back arches; it no longer touches the sofa. It stays that way through the impossibly long climax; all my muscles are taut. Finally, the complex harmonies slowly unravel themselves and find resolution.

Abel 1996: 81

7 I worked through lists such as Wikipedia (2021), and *Cyrk Music* (2021), and checked all terms with a classic dictionary of musical terms (Stainer and Barrett 1898). The terms used as titles of the *Interludes I–VII* can be found in the latter as follows: lacrimoso (ibid.: 251), lamentoso (ibid.: 251), vibrato (ibid.: 446), bruscamente (ibid.: 64), silenzio (ibid.: 397), appasionato (ibid.: 32), ardente (ibid.: 33), ondeggiante (ibid.: 318), glissando (ibid.:198), con abbandono (ibid.: 1), and con devozione (ibid.: 133).

8 Radically questioning Western modernity's self/other distinction, Shildrick (2016: 100) refers to the ways in which scientific reports on Y-chromosome-coded Human Leucocyte Antigens (HLA) in women who have never been pregnant, have led some scientists to speculate that chimerism (our carrying of non-self cells) is lifelong and the result of an 'intergenerational scenario in which each one of us – regardless of pregnancy status – could carry non-self cells from a variety of genetic relations' (ibid.). However, in order to further sustain the speculative argument that microchimerism might be 'ubiquitous', Shildrick quotes scientists who – beyond the better-known occurrence of chimerism related to 'non-irradiated blood transfusion, (...), bone marrow transplants, all types of tissue and organ transplant, pregnancy, generational genetic transfer, and human dizygotic fusion' – have 'suggested that lactation and fluid sexual exchanges can also generate microchimerism' (ibid.). Against the background of the scientific results and speculations referred to by Shildrick, it seems to be quite clear that my beloved is present as living chimeric cells in my rainbow kin (her children, grandchildren and great grandchildren), as well as in her biological siblings. However, the further speculations – among others the suggestion that 'fluid sexual exchanges' can also generate the exchange of chimeric cells – bring me to contemplate the idea that my beloved may be living as chimeric cells even in me, and that some of my chimeric cells died together with her.

9 Beyond Western sources, I have also studied the work of the Chukchi writer Yuri Rytkheu (1930–2008), some of whose novels have been translated from Russian into English, among others *A Dream in Polar Fog* (2006). Rytkheu grew up in Uelen, a village in the Chukotka region of the North-Eastern part of Siberia. In *The Chukchi Bible* (2000), Rytkheu made a great effort to recount his ancestral history, as told in myths and legends. I also watched a documentary by contemporary Chukchi film director Alexei Vakhrushev, *The Book of the Sea* (2008). Vakhrushev (born 1969) is also known for his film *Birds of Naukan* (1996), and for his research on the history, culture, spiritual and social life of the indigenous people of the far North-East of Russia. However, according to a personal communication from decolonial scholar, Professor Madina Tlostanova, thanks to whom I became aware of Vakhrushev's work, non-Western sources on the Chukchi are scarce, and have most often not been translated from Russian into English.

Interlude VII

1. The poem *Algae Chant* was, as excerpt from the back then unpublished manuscript for *Vibrant Death*, published as part of the argument in Nina Lykke (2019a), 'Co-becoming with algae: Between posthuman mourning and wonder in algae research', *Catalyst. Feminism, Theory, Technoscience* 5 (2). Republished in agreement with *Catalyst*.
2. A longer and somewhat different version of the poem *A Liver Tumour's Tale* was, as excerpt from the back then unpublished manuscript for *Vibrant Death*, published under the title *Anthropos and the Canary in the Mine* as part of the argument in Nina Lykke (2019b), 'Making live and letting die: Cancerous bodies between Anthropocene Necropolitics and Chthulucene kinship', *Environmental Humanities* 11 (1): 108–36. Republished in agreement with *Environmental Humanities*. The wider references to cancer epidemiological research, to which the poem refers, can be found in the article.

Coda

1. The methodology of scaling implies 'shifting scales and registers' (Jain and Stacey 2015: 10; Lykke 2019b: 126), i.e. a zooming in/out between a personal micro-perspective and a collective macro-perspective.
2. When speaking about myth clusters, I am referring to mythic stories that are related due to the overlapping of mythic figures and/or motifs.
3. In ancient Greece, the figure of the mythic poet-musician-hero Orpheus became the centre of a religious cult, Orphism, related to an earlier Dionysian religion.
4. Bacchus is the Roman version of the Greek god Dionysos.
5. In some versions of the myth, Orpheus' head is brought by the sea to the island of Lesbos, after he has been torn up. (Göttner-Abendroth 1980: 248; Bachofen 1967 [1861]: 201–7).
6. The term 'ahuman' refers to queerfeminist philosopher Patricia MacCormack's *Ahuman Manifesto* (2020a), which radically experiments with 'an alternate way of writing and reading' in order to 'dismantle the dominance of the human'. With the term 'ahuman', MacCormack articulates a speaking position that implies seeking 'to no longer argue like a human, with other humans' (ibid.: ix).
7. A monography that my beloved and I wrote together (Bryld and Lykke 2000).

REFERENCES

Abel, Sam (1996), *Opera in the Flesh: Sexuality in Operatic Performance*, Boulder, CL: Westview.

Acampora, Ralph R. (2006), *Corporal Compassion: Animal Ethics and Philosophy of Body*, Pittsburgh, PA: Pittsburgh University Press.

Addison, Ann (2009), 'Jung, vitalism and "the psychoid": An historical reconstruction', *Journal of Analytical Psychology*, 54: 123–42.

Afanasjew, Alexander N. (1985), *Russische Volksmärchen*, Vols 1–2, München: Deutscher Taschenbuch Verlag.

Ahmed, Sara (2010), *The Promise of Happiness*, Durham, NC, and London: Duke University Press.

Aidt, Naja Marie (2019), *When Death Takes Something from You, Give it Back – Carl's Book*, trans. D. Newman, Minneapolis, MN: Coffee House Press; trans. from Danish: *Har døden taget noget fra dig så giv det tilbage – Carls bog*, København: Gyldendal.

Allen, A. E., C. L. Dupont, M. Obornik, A. Horak, A. Nunes-Nesi, J. P. McCrow, H. Zheng, D. A. Johnson, H. Hu, A. R. Fernie and C. Bowler (2011), 'Evolution and metabolic significance of the urea cycle in photosynthetic diatoms', *Nature*, 473(7346): 203–7.

Allen-Collinson, Jacquelyn (2009), 'Sporting embodiment: Sport studies and the (continuing) promise of phenomenology', *Qualitative Research in Sport and Exercise*, 1 (3): 279–96.

Allen-Collinson, Jacquelyn (2010), 'Running embodiment, power and vulnerability: Notes towards a feminist phenomenology of female running', in E. Kennedy and P. Markula (eds), *Women and Exercise: The Body, Health and Consumerism*, 280–98, London: Routledge.

Allen-Collinson, Jacquelyn (2011), 'Intention and epoché in tension: Autophenomenography, bracketing and a novel approach to researching sporting embodiment', *Qualitative Research in Sport, Exercise and Health*, 3 (1): 48–62.

American Psychiatric Association (APA) (2013), *The Diagnostic and Statistical Manual of Mental Disorders*, DSM-5 (2013), Washington, DC: American Psychiatric Association.

Anzaldua, Gloria (1987), *Borderlands/La Frontera: The New Mestiza*, San Francisco, CA: Aunt Lute Books.

Anzaldua, Gloria E. (2015), *Light in the Dark/Luz en Lo Oscuro: Rewriting Identity, Reality, Spirituality*, Durham, NC: Duke University Press.

Arnell, Malin (2016), *Avhandling / Av_handling (Dissertation / Through_action)*. PhD dissertation. Lund: Lund University Publications.

Bachofen, Johann Jakob (1967 [1861]), *Myth, Religion and Mother Right*, trans. Ralph Manheim. Princeton, NJ: Princeton University Press.

Bakhtin, Mikhail (1984), *Problems of Dostoevsky's Poetics*, ed. and trans. Caryl Emerson, *Theory and History of Literature* 8, Minneapolis, MN, and London: University of Minnesota Press.

Barad, Karen (1998), 'Getting real: Technoscientific practices and the materialization of reality', *Differences: A Journal of Feminist Cultural Studies*, 10 (2): 87–128.

Barad, Karen (2003), 'Posthumanist performativity: Toward an understanding of how matter comes to matter', *Signs: Journal of Women in Culture and Society*, 28 (3): 801–31.
Barad, Karen (2007), *Meeting the Universe Halfway: Quantum Physics and the Entanglement of Matter and Meaning*, Durham, NC, and London: Duke University Press.
Barad, Karen (2014), 'Diffracting diffraction: Cutting together-apart', *Parallax*, 20 (3): 168–87.
Beifuss, John (2020), *Elvis' 'Sun Sessions' Guitar Sells for $1.3 Million at Auction*. Memphis, TN: Memphis Commercial appeal. Available at: https://eu.commercialappeal.com/story/news/2020/08/03/elvis-presley-sun-sessions-guitar-auction/5577897002/ (accessed 16 November 2020).
Bellacasa, Maria Puig de la (2017), *Matters of Care: Speculative Ethics in More than Human Worlds*. Minneapolis, MN: University of Minnesota Press.
Bennett, Jane (2001), *The Enchantment of Modern Life: Attachments, Crossings and Ethics*, Princeton, NJ, and Oxford: Princeton University Press.
Bennett, Jane (2010), *Vibrant Matter: A Political Ecology of Things*, Durham, NC, and London: Duke University Press.
Bensaïd, Daniel (2004), 'Alain Badiou and the Miracle of the Event', in Peter Hallward (ed.), *Think Again, Alain Badiou and the Future of Philosophy*, London and New York: Continuum.
Bird Rose, Deborah (2004), *Reports from a Wild Country: Ethics for Decolonisation*, Sydney: University of New South Wales Press.
Black, Christine F. (2018), *A Mosaic of Indigenous Legal Thought*, New York: Routledge.
Blackmer, Corinne E. and Patricia Juliana Smith (1995), *En Travesti: Women, Gender Subversion, Opera*, New York: Columbia University Press.
Boström, Nick (2005), 'A history of transhumanist thought', *Journal of Evolution and Technology*, 14 (1): 1–30. Available at: https://www.nickbostrom.com/papers/history.pdf (accessed 19 July 2020).
Braidotti, Rosi (1994), *Nomadic Subjects: Embodiment and Sexual Difference in Contemporary Feminist Theory*, New York: Columbia University Press.
Braidotti, Rosi (2002), *Metamorphoses: Towards a Materialist Theory of Becoming*, Cambridge: Polity Press.
Braidotti, Rosi (2006), *Transpositions: On Nomadic Ethics*, Cambridge: Polity Press.
Braidotti, Rosi (2008), 'In spite of the times: The postsecular turn in feminism', *Theory, Culture & Society*, 25 (6): 1–24.
Braidotti, Rosi (2011), *Nomadic Subjects: Embodiment and Sexual Difference in Contemporary Feminist Theory*, 2nd edn, New York: Columbia University Press.
Braidotti, Rosi (2013), *The Posthuman*, Cambridge: Polity Press.
Braidotti, Rosi (2016), 'Posthuman affirmative politics', in S. E. Wilmer and Audrone Zukauskaite (eds), *Resisting Biopolitics: Philosophical, Political and Performative Strategies*, 30–56, New York and London: Routledge.
Braidotti, Rosi (2018), 'A theoretical framework for the critical posthumanities', *Theory, Culture and Society*, 36 (6): 31–61.
Braidotti, Rosi (2022), *Feminist Posthumanism*, Cambridge: Polity Press.
Breton, André (1971), *Manifestos of Surrealism*, Ann Arbor, MI: University of Michigan Press.
Broglio, Ron (2019), *Romantic Self and Posthumanism*. Available at: https://criticalposthumanism.net (accessed 12 December 2020).
Bryld, Mette and Nina Lykke (2000), *Cosmodolphins: Feminist Cultural Studies of Technology, Animals and the Sacred*, London: Zed.

Butler, Judith (1990), *Gender Trouble: Feminism and the Subversion of Identity*, London and New York: Routledge.
Butler, Judith (1993), *Bodies that Matter: On the Discursive Limits of 'Sex'*, London and New York: Routledge.
Butler, Judith (2004), *Precarious Life: The Powers of Mourning and Violence*, New York: Verso.
Callon, Michael (1986), 'Some elements of a sociology of ttranslation: Domestication of the scallops and the fishermen of St Brieux Bay', in John Law (ed.), *Power, Action and Belief: A New Sociology of Knowledge?*, 196–229, London: Routledge and Kegan Paul.
Camus, Marcel and Vinicius de Moraes (1959), *Orfeu Negro*, Brazil: Tupan Filmes.
Carney, Karen (2018), *Grief, Healing and the One-to-Two Year Myth*, Psych Central Web. https://psychcentral.com/lib/grief-healing-and-the-one-to-two-year-myth/ (accessed 5 January 2020).
Cassirer, Ernst (1922), *Die Begriffsform im mythischen Denken*, Leipzig and Berlin: Teubner.
Cassirer, Ernst (1987), *Das mythische Denken. Philosophie der symbolischen Formen*, 2, Teil, Darmstadt: Wissenschaftliche Buchgesellschaft.
Cixous, Hélène (1992), 'Coming to writing', in H. Cixous, *Coming to Writing and Other Essays*, ed. Deborah Jenson, trans. Sarah Cornell, Deborah Jenson, Ann Liddle and Susan Sellers, 1–59, Cambridge, MA: Harvard University Press.
Clement, Catherine (1988), *Opera, or the Undoing of Women*, trans. Betsy Wing, Minneapolis, MN: University of Minnesota Press.
Culler, Jonathan (2017), 'Extending the theory of lyric', *Diacritics*, 45 (4): 6–14.
Cvetkovich, Ann (1995), 'Recasting receptivity: Femme sexualities', in Karla Jay (ed.), *Lesbian Erotics*, 125–46, New York: New York University Press.
Cvetkovich, Ann (2003), *An Archive of Feelings: Trauma, Sexuality, and Lesbian Public Cultures*, Durham, NC, and London: Duke University Press.
Cvetkovich, Ann (2012), *Depression: A Public Feeling*, Durham, NC, and London: Duke University Press.
Cyrk Music (2021), *Cyrk Music*. Available at: https://cyrk.dk/musik/betegnelser/ (accessed 13 February 2021).
Dahl, Ulrika (2012), 'Turning like a femme: Figuring critical femininity studies', *NORA: Nordic Journal of Feminist and Gender Research*, 20 (1): 57–64.
Dahl, Ulrika (2014), *Skamgrepp: Femme-inistiska essäer*, Stockholm: Leopard.
Deleuze, Gilles (1988), *Spinoza: Practical Philosophy*, trans. Robert Hurley, San Francisco, CA: City Lights Books.
Deleuze, Gilles (2000), *Proust and Signs: The Complete Text*, trans. Richard Howard, London and New York: Continuum.
Deleuze, Gilles (2020), *Logic of Sense*, trans. C. V. Boundas, M. Lester and C. J. Stivale, London: Bloomsbury.
Deleuze, Gilles and Felix Guattari (1988), *A Thousand Plateaus: Capitalism and Schizophrenia*, trans. Brian Massumi, New York and London: Continuum.
Deleuze, Gilles and Felix Guattari (1994), *What is Philosophy?*, trans. Graham Burchell and Hugh Tomlinson, New York: Columbia University Press.
Derrida, Jacques (1994), *Specters of Marx: The State of the Debt, the Work of Mourning and the New International*, trans. P. Kamuf, New York and London: Routledge.
Didion, Joan (2005), *The Year of Magical Thinking*, London: Fourth Estate.
Didion, Joan (2012), *Blue Nights*, London: Fourth Estate.
Dinshaw, Carolyn, Lee Edelman, Roderick A. Ferguson, Carla Freccero, Elizabeth Freeman, Judith Halberstam, Annamaria Jagose, Christopher Nealon, Nguyen Tan Hoang (2007),

'Theorizing queer temporalities. A roundtable discussion', *GLQ: A Journal of Lesbian and Gay Studies*, 13 (2–3): 177–95.

Dostoevsky, Fyodor (1993 [1880]), *The Brothers Karamazov*, trans. David McDuff, New York and London: Penguin.

Driesch, Hans (1914), *The Problem of Individuality: A Course of Four Lectures Delivered before the University of London in October 1913*, London: Macmillan.

Edwards, Erin (2018), *The Modernist Corpse: Posthumanism and the Posthumous*, Minneapolis, MN: University of Minnesota Press.

Eng, David and Puar Jasbir (2020), 'Left of queer: Introduction', *Social Text 145*, 38 (4): 1–23.

Ferrando, Francesca (2016), 'A feminist genealogy of posthuman aesthetics in the visual arts', *Palgrave Communications: Humanities and Social Sciences*, 16011: 1–12. Available at: https://www.nature.com/articles/palcomms201611 (accessed 4 January 2020).

Ferrando, Francesca (2019), *Philosophical Posthumanism*, London: Bloomsbury.

Foucault, Michel (1975), *Birth of the Clinic: An Archaeology of Medical Perception*, trans. A. M. Sheridan Smith, New York: Vintage Books.

Freeman, Elizabeth (2010), *Time Binds: Queer Temporalities, Queer Histories*, Durham, NC, and London: Duke University Press.

Freeman, Elizabeth (ed.) (2007), 'Queer temporalities: Introduction', Special Issue, *GLQ: A Journal of Lesbian and Gay Studies*, 13 (2–3): 159–76.

Freud, Anna (2018 [1936]), *The Ego and the Mechanisms of Defence*, New York: Routledge.

Freud, Sigmund (1900), *Die Traumdeutung*, Gesammelte Werke II–III, Standard Edition IV–V, Frankfurt a/M: Fischer Verlag; and London: Imago.

Freud, Sigmund (1901), Zur Psychopathologie des Alltagsleben, *Gesammelte Werke IV*, Standard Edition VI, London: Imago; and Frankfurt a/M: S. Fischer.

Freud, Sigmund (1909), 'Bemerkungen über einen Fall von Zwangsneurose', Standard Edition X, 381–463, London: Imago; and Frankfurt a/M: S. Fischer.

Freud, Sigmund (1917), 'Trauer und Melancholie', *Gesammelte Werke XII, Werke aus den Jahren 1913–1917*, 427–46, London: Imago, 1946; and Frankfurt a/M: S. Fischer.

Freud, Sigmund (1919), 'Das Unheimliche', *Gesammelte Werke, Werke aus den Jahren 1917–1920*, 229–68, Band XII, London: Imago; and Frankfurt a/M: S. Fischer, 'The Uncanny', *Standard Edition XVIII*.

Freud, Sigmund (1920), *Jenseits des Lustprinzips, Gesammelte Werke* XIII, 3–69, Frankfurt a/M and London: Imago 1940; English trans., *Beyond the Pleasure Principle: Standard Edition XVIII*, London: Hogarth Press.

Freud, Sigmund (1926), *Hemmung, Symptom, Angst, Gesammelte Werke XIV*, 113–205, Standard Edition XX, Frankfurt a/M: Fischer Verlag; and London: Imago.

Geertz, Clifford (1973), *The Interpretation of Cultures*, New York: Basic Books.

Genesis (2020), Available at: https://biblehub.com/genesis/2-24.htm (accessed 5 January 2020).

Gernet, Alexander von (1994), 'Saving the souls: Reincarnation beliefs of the seventeenth century Huron', in Antonia Mills and Richard Slobodin (eds), *Amerindian Rebirth: Reincarnation Belief among North American Indians and Inuit*, 38–55, Toronto: University of Toronto Press.

Gimbutas, Marija (1984), *The Goddesses and Gods of Old Europe: Myths and Cult Images*, London: Thames and Hudson.

Gimbutas, Marija (1989), *The Language of the Goddess*, London: Thames and Hudson.

Gluck, Christoph Willibald von (2019 [1762]), *Orfeo ed Euridice*, Libretto: Ranieri de Calzabigi, Vienna: Van Ghelen, English trans. *Orpheus and Eurydice*. Available at:

http://www.opera-guide.ch/opera.php?uilang=en&id=131#libretto (accessed 20 February, 2019).

Gluck, Christoph Willibald von (2021 [1762/1774]), *Che farò senza Euridice, What is life to me without thee*, English text, Claude Aveling. Available at: https://soundofthunder.files.wordpress.com/2012/08/imslp226346-wima-bf3c-chefar.pdf (accessed 13 April 2021).

Gómez-Barris, Marcarena (2017), *The Extractive Zone: Social Ecologies and Decolonial Perspectives*, Durham, NC, and London: Duke University Press.

González-Crussi, Frank (1993), *The Day of the Dead: And Other Mortal Reflections*. New York: Kaplan.

Górska, Magdalena (2016), *Breathing Matters: Feminist Intersectional Politics of Vulnerability*, PhD dissertation. Linköping: Linköping University Electronic Press.

Göttner-Abendroth, Heide (1980), *Die Göttin und ihr Heros: Die matriarchalen Religionen in Mythos, Märchen und Dichting*, München: Frauenoffensive.

Graves, Robert (1955), *The Greek Myths, I–II*, New York and London: Penguin.

Greimas, Algirdas Julien (1974), *Structural Semantics: An Attempt at a Method*, Lincoln, NB: University of Nebraska Press.

Grosz, Elizabeth (1994), *Volatile Bodies: Toward a Corporeal Feminism*, Bloomington, IN: Indiana University Press.

Gruppetta, Maree (2004), 'Autophenomenography? Alternative uses of autobiographically based research', in P. L. Jeffery (ed.), *Association for Active Researchers in Education (AARE) Conference Paper Abstracts – 2004*, 1–10, Sydney: AARE.

Gunaratnam, Yasmin (2013), *Death and the Migrant: Bodies, Borders and Care*, London: Bloomsbury Academic.

Halberstam, Judith (2005), *In a Queer Time and Place: Transgender Bodies, Subcultural Lives*, New York and London: New York University Press.

Hallgren, Hanna (2014), *Prolog till den litterära vetenskapsteorin*, Malmö: Pequod Press.

Haraway, Donna (1991). 'A Cyborg Manifesto: Science, technology, and socialist-feminism in the late twentieth century', in D. Haraway, *Simians, Cyborgs and Women: The Reinvention of Nature*, 149–81, London: Free Association Books.

Haraway, Donna (1992), 'The promises of monsters: A regenerative politics for inappropriate/d others', in Lawrence Grossberg, Cary Nelson and Paula A. Treichler (eds), *Cultural Studies*, 295–337, New York and London: Routledge.

Haraway, Donna (2004), *The Haraway Reader*, New York and London: Routledge.

Haraway, Donna (2008), *When Species Meet*, Minneapolis, MN: University of Minnesota Press.

Haraway, Donna (2016), *Staying with the Trouble: Making Kin in the Chthulucene*, Durham, NC, and London: Duke University Press.

Hird, Myra J. (2007), 'The corporeal generosity of maternity', *Body and Society*, 13 (1): 1–20.

Hird, Myra J. and Noreen Gifney, (2008), *Queering the Non/Human (Queer Interventions)*, Hampshire: Ashgate.

Irigaray, Luce (1981), 'And the one does not stir without the other', trans. H. V. Wenzel, *Signs*, 7 (1): 60–7.

Irigaray, Luce (1985), *Speculum of the Other Woman*, trans. Gillian C. Gill, Ithaca, NY: Cornell University Press.

Jain, Lochlann S. and Jackie Stacey (2015), 'On writing about illness: A dialogue with S. Lochlann Jain and Jackie Stacey on cancer, STS, and cultural studies.' *Catalyst. Feminism, Theory, Technoscience,* 1 (1): 1–31.

Jakobson, Roman (1987), *Language in Literature*, eds Krystyna Pomorska and Stephen Rudy, Cambridge, MA: Harvard University Press.

Jochelson, Waldemar (1908), *The Yukaghir and the Yukaghized Tungus*, ed. F. Boas, New York: American Museum of Natural History.

Jung, Carl Gustav (1991), *The Archetypes and the Collective Unconscious (Collected Works of C. G. Jung)*, London and New York: Routledge.

Jung, Carl Gustav (2008 [1955]), *Synchronicity: An Acausal Connecting Principle*, New York and London: Routledge.

Kafer, Alison (2013), *Feminist Queer Crip*, Bloomington and Indianapolis, IN: Indiana University Press.

Kant, Immanuel (1987 [1790]), *Critique of Judgement*, trans. Werner Pluhar, Indianapolis, IN: Hackett.

Kavan, Michael G. and Eugene J. Barone (2014), 'Grief and major depression: Controversy over changes in DSM-5 Diagnostic Criteria', *American Family Physician*, 90 (10): 693–4.

Kazan, Georges and Tom Higham (2019), 'Researching relics: New interdisciplinary approaches to the study of historic and religious objects', in Steffen Hope, Mikael Manøe Bjerregaard, Anne Hedeager Krag and Mads Runge (eds), *Life and Cult of Cnut the Holy: The First Royal Saint of Denmark*, 142–66, Odense: Odense Bys Museer.

Keats, John (2002), 'Letter to George and Tom Keats, 21, 27 December 1817', ed. Grant F. Scott, *Selected Letters of John Keats*, 59–64, Cambridge, MA: Harvard University Press.

Kristeva, Julia (1980), *Desire in Language: A Semiotic Approach to Literature and Art*, trans. T. Gora, A. Jardine and L. S. Roudiez, New York: Columbio University Press.

Kristeva, Julia (1982), *Powers of Horror: An Essay on Abjection*, trans. Leon S. Roudiez, New York: Columbia University Press.

Lacan, Jacques (1957), 'L'Instance de la letre de l'inconscient ou la raison depuis Freud', in *La Psychoanalyse*. Vol. 3, 47–81, Paris: Presse Universitaire de France.

Laplanche, Jean and Jean Bertrand Pontalis (1973), *Das Vokabular der Psychoanalyse*, Vols 1–2, Frankfurt a/M: Suhrkamp.

Latour, Bruno (1993), *We Have Never Been Modern*, trans. Catherine Porter, New York: Harvester Wheatsheaf.

Latour, Bruno (1996), 'On actor-network-theory: A few clarifications', *Soziale Welt* 47 (4): 369–81.

Leavy, Patricia (2016), *Fiction as Research Practice: Short Stories, Novellas, and Novels*, New York: Routledge.

Lesy, Michael (1973), *Wisconsin Death Trip*, New York: Pantheon.

Limar, Igor (2011), 'Carl G. Jung's synchronicity and quantum entanglement: Schrödinger's Cat "Wanders" between chromosomes', *NeuroQuantology*, 9 (2): 313–21.

Lorde, Audre (1980), *The Cancer Journals, Special Edition*, San Francisco, CA: Aunt Lute Books.

Lorde, Audre (1982), *Zami: A New Spelling of My Name*, Freedom, CA: Crossing Press.

Lorde, Audre (1984), Sister Outsider: Essays and Speeches, Freedom, CA: Crossing Press.

Lykke, Nina (1993), *Rotkäppchen und Ödipus. Zur einer feministischen Psychoanalyse*, Wien: Passagen Verlag.

Lykke, Nina (2010), *Feminist Studies: A Guide to Intersectional Theory, Methodology and Writing*, New York and London: Routledge.

Lykke, Nina (2015), 'Queer widowhood', *Lambda Nordica*, 20 (4): 85–111.

Lykke, Nina (2018), 'When death cuts apart: On affective difference, compassionate companionship and lesbian widowhood', in T. Juvonen and M. Kohlemainen (eds), *Affective Inequalities in Intimate Relationships*, 109–25, New York and London: Routledge.

Lykke, Nina (2019a), 'Co-becoming with algae: Between posthuman mourning and wonder in algae research', *Catalyst: Feminism, Theory, Technoscience*, 5 (2): 1–25. Available at: https://doi.org/10.28968/cftt.v5i2.31922 (accessed 6 July 2021).

Lykke, Nina (2019b), 'Making live and letting die: Cancerous bodies between Anthropocene Necropolitics and Chthulucene kinship', *Environmental Humanities*, 11 (1): 108–36.

Lykke, Nina (ed.) (2014), *Writing Academic Texts Differently: Intersectional Feminist Methodologies and the Playful Art of Writing*, New York and London: Routledge.

Lykke, Nina and Camila Marambio (2020), 'A triptych of viral tales', *Kerb* 28: 1–12.

MacCormack, Patricia (2016), *Posthuman Ethics: Embodiment and Cultural Theory*, Oxford and New York: Routledge.

MacCormack, Patricia (2020a), *The Ahuman Manifesto: Activism for the End of the Anthropocene*, London: Bloomsbury Academic.

MacCormack, Patricia (2020b), 'Embracing death: Opening the world', *Australian Feminist Studies*, 35 (104): 101–15.

MacLure, Maggie (2021), 'Inquiry as divination', *Qualitative Inquiry*, 27 (5): 502–11. Available at: https://doi.org/10.1177/1077800420939124 (accessed 6 July 2021).

Mahler, Gustav (2017 [1901–4]), *Kindertotenlieder nach Gedichten von Friedrich Rückert*, Deutsche Grammophon.

Marambio, Camila and Vicuña, Cecilia (2019), *Slow Down Fast, A Toda Raja*, Berlin: Errant Bodies Press.

Marsh, James (1999), *Wisconsin Death Trip*, film, Cinemax BBC Arena.

Massumi, Brian (2015), *Politics of Affect*, Cambridge: Polity.

Mayo Clinique (2020), *Complicated Grief*. Available at: https://www.mayoclinic.org/diseases-conditions/complicated-grief/diagnosis-treatment/drc-20360389 (accessed 5 January 2020).

Mbembe, Achille (2003), 'Necropolitics', *Public Culture*, 15 (1): 11–40.

McClary, Susan (1991), *Feminine Endings: Music, Gender and Sexuality*, Minneapolis, MN: University of Minnesota Press.

McRuer, Robert (2006), *Crip Theory: Cultural Signs of Queerness and Disability*, New York and London: New York University Press.

Melville, Herman (2016 [1853]), 'Bartleby, the Scrivener: A story of Wall Street', in Herman Melville, *Billy Budd, Bartleby and Other Stories*, 17–55, New York: Penguin Classics.

Merchant, Carolyn (1980), *The Death of Nature: Human Ecology and the Scientific Revolution*, San Francisco, CA: Harper & Row.

Merleau-Ponty, Maurice (2001), *Phenomenology of Perception*, trans. C. Smith, London: Routledge and Kegan Paul.

Merleau-Ponty, Maurice (2003), *Nature: Course Notes from the College de France*, trans. R. Vallier, Evanston, IL: Northwestern University Press.

Mills, Antonia and Richard Slobodin (eds) (1994), *Amerindian Rebirth: Reincarnation Beliefs among North American Indians and Inuit*, Toronto, Buffalo, NY, and London: University of Toronto Press.

Minh-ha, Trinh T. (1988), 'Not you/like you: Postcolonial women and the interlocking question of identity and difference', *Inscriptions: Special Issues: Feminism and the Critique of Colonial Discourse*, 3–4: 1–8. Available at: https://culturalstudies.ucsc.edu/inscriptions/volume-34/trinh-t-minh-ha/ (accessed 1 December 2020).

Minh-ha, Trinh T. (1989), *Woman, Native, Other: Writing Postcoloniality and Feminism*, Bloomington and Indianapolis IN: Indiana University Press.

Monteverdi, Claudio (1972 [1607]), *La Favola d'Orfeo*, Libretto: Alessandro Striggio; Venice: Ricciardo Amadini; and Facsimile, Fortune and Whenham, Modern Editions and Performances, 1972, 173–81.

Moraga, Cherríe and Gloria Anzaldua (eds) (1981), *This Bridge Called My Back: Writings by Radical Women of Color*, New York: Kitchen Table, Women of Color Press.

Neimanis, Astrida (2017), *Bodies of Water: Posthuman Feminist Phenomenology*, London and New York: Bloomsbury Academic.
Ovid, Publius Naso (1717 [1 CE]), 'Orpheus and Eurydice, Metamorphoses Book X', trans. John Dryden, William Congreve and others, in *Ovid's Metamorphoses in Fifteen Books*, 331–6, London: Jacob Tonson.
Pentreath, Rosie (2019), *A Lock of Beethoven's Hair has Just Been Sold at Auction – and It Went for a Whopping £35,000*, Classicfm.com: Composers: Beethoven, 12 June 2019. Available at: https://www.classicfm.com/composers/beethoven/news/lock-hair-auctioned-sothebys/ (accessed 16 November 2020).
Petersen, Michael Nebeling (2012), *Somewhere, over the Rainbow. Biopolitiske rekonfigurationer af den homoseksuelle figur*, Københavns Universitet: Centre for Gender Studies.
Pies, Ronald (2020), *How the DSM-5 Got Grief, Bereavement Right*. Psych Central Web. Available at: https://psychcentral.com/blog/how-the-dsm-5-got-grief-bereavement-right/ (accessed 5 January 2020).
Plato (2009), *Phaedo*. Oxford: Oxford World Classics.
Povinelli, Elizabeth A. (2016), *Geontologies: A Requiem to Late Liberalism*, Durham, NC: Duke University Press.
Propp, Vladimir (1971 [1928]), *Morphology of the Folktale*, trans. L. Scott, Austin, TX: University of Texas Press.
Quigley, Christine (1996), *The Corpse: A History*, Jefferson, NC: McFarland.
Radiohead (2021), *Just*. Available at: https://www.youtube.com/watch?v=oIFLtNYI3Ls (accessed 5 January 2021).
Radomska, Marietta (2020), 'Deterritorialising death: Queerfeminist biophilosophy and ecologies of the non/living', *Australian Feminist Studies*, 35 (104): 116–37.
Radomska, Marietta, Tara Mehrabi and Nina Lykke (2020), 'Queer Death Studies: Death, dying and mourning from a queerfeminist perspective', *Australian Feminist Studies* 35 (104): 81–100.
Ramey, Joshua (2012), *The Hermetic Deleuze: Philosophy and Spiritual Ordeal*, Durham, NC: Duke University Press.
Ramey, Joshua (2016), *Politics of Divination: Neoliberal Endgame and the Religion of Contingency*, London: Rowman & Littlefield International.
Refslund Christensen, Dorthe and Rane Willerslev (eds) (2013), *Taming Time, Timing Death: Social Technologies and Ritual*, Farnham: Ashgate.
Ricciardi, Alessia (2007), 'Immanent miracles: From de Sica to Hardt and Negri', *MLN*, 122 (5): 1138–65.
Richardson, Laurel (2000), 'Writing as a method of inquiry', in Norman K. Denzin and Yvonna S. Lincoln (eds), *Handbook of Qualitative Research*, 2nd edn, 923–48, London: Sage.
Rose, Nikolas (2007), *The Politics of Life Itself: Biomedicine, Power, and Subjectivity in the Twenty-First Century*, Princeton, NJ: Princeton University Press.
Rosenberg, Tiina (2000), *Byxbegär*, Stockholm: Anamma.
Rückert, Friedrich (1993 [1833–4]), 'Kindertotenlieder', in Hans Wollschläger (ed.), *Kindertotenlieder*, Frankfurt a/M: Suhrkamp, Insel Taschenbuch.
Ryle, Gilbert (1949), *The Concept of Mind*, Chicago, IL: University of Chicago Press.
Rytkheu, Yuri (2000), *The Chukchi Bible*, trans. (from Russian) Ilona Yazhbin Chavasse, Brooklyn, NY: Archipelago Books.
Rytkheu, Yuri (2006), *A Dream in Polar Fog*, trans. (from Russian) Ilona Yazhbin Chavasse, Brooklyn, NY: Archipelago Books.

Samudra, Jaida Kim (2008), 'Memory in our body: Thick participation and the translation of kinaesthetic experience', *American Ethnologist*, 35 (4): 665–81.

Sandahl, Carrie (2003), 'Queering the crip or cripping the queer? Intersections of queer and crip identities in solo autobiographical performance', *GLQ: A Journal of Lesbian and Gay Studies*, 9 (1–2): 25–56.

Santner, Eric L. (2005), 'Miracles happen: Benjamin, Rosenzweig, Freud and the matter of the neighbor', in Kenneth Reinhard, Eric L. Santner and Slavoj Žižek, *The Neighbor: Three Inquiries into Political Theology*, 76–133, Chicago, IL, and London: University of Chicago Press.

Sartre, Jean-Paul (1958), *Being and Nothingness: An Essay on Phenomenological Ontology*, trans. Hazel E. Barnes, London and New York: Routledge.

Schaeffer, Felicia Amaya (2018), 'Spirit matters: Gloria Anzaldua's cosmic becoming across human/nonhuman borderlands', *Signs: Journal of Women in Culture and Society*, 43 (4): 1005–29.

Schwartz, Margareta (2013), 'An iconography of the flesh: How corpses mean as matter', *Communication + 1*, 2 (1): 1–15. Available at: https://scholarworks.umass.edu/cgi/viewcontent.cgi?article=1012&context=cpo (accessed 9 February 2020).

Schwartz, Margareta (2016), *Dead Matter: The Meaning of Iconic Corpses*, Minneapolis, MN: University of Minnesota Press.

Shildrick, Margrit (2002), *Embodying the Monster: Encounters with the Vulnerable Self*, London: Sage.

Shildrick, Margrit (2005), 'Transgressing the law with Foucault and Derrida: Some reflections on anomalous embodiment', *Critical Quarterly*, 47 (3): 30–45.

Shildrick, Margrit (2009), *Dangerous Discourses of Disability, Subjectivity and Sexuality*, London: Palgrave Macmillan.

Shildrick, Margrit (2016), 'Chimerism and *Immunitas*: The emergence of a posthumanist biophilosophy', in S. E. Wilmer and Audrone Zukauskaite (eds), *Resisting Biopolitics: Philosophical, Political and Performative Strategies*, 95–109, New York and London: Routledge.

Shildrick, Margrit (2020), 'Queering the social imaginaries of the dead', *Australian Feminist Studies*, 35 (104): 170–85.

Spinoza, Benedict de (1996 [1677]), *Ethics*, London: Penguin.

Spinoza, Benedict de (2007 [1670]), *Theological-Political Treatise*, ed. Jonathan Israel, trans. Michael Silverstone and Jonathan Israel, Cambridge: Cambridge University Press.

St. Pierre, Elizabeth Adams (2018), 'Writing post-qualitative inquiry', *Qualitative Inquiry*, 24 (9): 603–8.

Stacey, Jackie and Janet Wolff (eds) (2013), *Writing Otherwise: Experiments in Cultural Criticism*, Manchester: Manchester University Press.

Stainer, John and William A. Barrett (eds) (1898), *A Dictionary of Musical Terms*, London: Novello, Ewer and Co.

Stengers, Isabelle (2011), 'Wondering about materialism', in L. Bryant, N. Srnicek and G. Harman (eds), *The Speculative Turn: Continental Materialism and Realism*, 368–81, Melbourne: re.press.

Stengers, Isabelle (2021), *Staying with the Troubling Words*. Available at: https://groupeconstructiviste.files.wordpress.com/2017/04/stengers_staying-with-troubling-words.pdf (accessed 9 February 2021).

Thiele, Kathrin (2021), 'Figuration and/as critique in relational matters', in A. Haas, M. Haas, H. Magauer and D. Pohl (eds), *How to Relate: Wissen, Künste, Praktiken – Knowledge, Arts, Practices*, 229–43, Bielefeld: Transcript Verlag.

Tlostanova, Madina (2015) 'Visualizing fiction, verbalizing art, or from intermediation to transculturation', *World Literature Studies*, 7 (1): 3–15.

Tlostanova, Madina and Walter Mignolo (2009), 'On pluritopic hermeneutics, transmodern thinking, and decolonial philosophy', *Encounters*, 1 (1): 11–27.

Tlostanova, Madina and Walter Mignolo (2012), *Learning to Unlearn: Decolonial Reflections from Eurasia and the Americas*, Columbus, OH: Ohio State University Press.

Todd, Zoe (2016), 'An indigenous feminist's take on the ontological turn: "Ontology" is just another word for colonialism', *Journal of Historical Sociology*, 29 (1): 4–22.

Vakhrushev, Alexei (1996), *Birds of Naukan*, Moscow: High Latitude.

Vakhrushev, Alexei (2018), *The Book of the Sea*, Moscow: High Latitude.

Vargas, Hema'ny Molina, Camila Marambio and Nina Lykke (2020), 'Decolonising mourning: World-making with the Selk'nam people of Karokynka/Tierra del Fuego', *Australian Feminist Studies*, 35 (104): 186–201.

Vendler, Helen (ed.) (2002), *Poems, Poets, Poetry: An Introduction and Anthology*, Boston, MA: Bedford/St. Martin's.

Virgil, Publius Maro (2019 [37–30 BCE]), *Orpheus and Eurydice, Book IV, Georgics, Virtue and Adversity: The Poetry of Virgil in the DA Kidd Collection*, trans. John Martin, Canterbury: University of Canterbury. Available at: https://www.canterbury.ac.nz/exhibition/virgil/georgics/orpheus-eurydice_translation.shtml (accessed 20 February 2019).

Weeks, Jeffrey, Brian Heaphy and Catherine Donovan (2001), *Same Sex Intimacies: Families of Choice and Other Life Experiments*, London and New York: Routledge.

Weisman, Karen (2010), *The Oxford Handbook of The Elegy*, Oxford: Oxford University Press.

Weiss, Gail (2009), 'Intertwined identities: Challenges to bodily autonomy', in Reneé van de Vall and Robert Zwijnenberg (eds), *The Body Within: Art, Medicine and Visualization*, 173–86, Leiden: Brill.

Weston, Kate (1991), *Families We Choose: Lesbians, Gays, Kinship*, New York: Columbia University Press.

Wikipedia (2020), *Marriage Vows*, Wikipedia. Available at: https://en.wikipedia.org/wiki/Marriage_vows (accessed 5 January 2020).

Wikipedia (2021), *Glossary of Music Terminology*, Wikipedia. Available at: https://en.wikipedia.org/wiki/Glossary_of_music_terminology (accessed 13 February 2021).

Willerslev, Rane (2007), *Soul Hunters: Hunting, Animism, and Personhood among the Siberian Yukaghirs*, Berkeley and Los Angeles, CA: University of California Press.

Willerslev, Rane (2013), 'Rebirth and the death drive: Rethinking Freud's "Mourning and Melancholia" through a Siberian time perspective', in Dorthe Refslund Christensen and Rane Willerslev (eds), *Taming Time, Timing Death: Social Technologies and Ritual*, 79–98, Farnham: Ashgate.

Yarmolinsky, Avrahm (1954), *The Unknown Chekhov: Stories and Other Writings Hitherto Untranslated*, Anton Chekhov, New York: Noonday Press.

INDEX

Abel, Sam 208-9, 266-7 n.6
abject(ed)/abjection 9, 71-2, 76-85
  see also Kristeva
Acampora, Ralph 48
  see also symphysizing
actant(s)
  and affective agencies 147, 151
  coalescing and co-becoming as
    assemblages 158-9
  conceptual genealogies 174-6
  and human/non-human
    entanglements 171, 183
  as non-human assemblages 18, 157
  see also actor-network-theory, Bennett,
    Latour, thing-power
actor-network theory 174
  see also actant(s), Latour
affect(ivity) 7, 9, 11, 14-19, 20-1,
    47-55, 80, 86-9, 106-8, 115, 124,
    126, 130, 145-54, 157-9, 171,
    182-6, 201-2, 205, 207-10, 213-15,
    218, 239, 240, 256 n.4, 282 n.11,
    264 n.6
  see also Bennett, Braidotti, Cvetkovich,
    Deleuze, Deleuze and Guattari,
    Spinoza
afterlife 78, 107, 110, 119, 121, 125,
    144, 194-7, 199-201, 205,
    213-20
agential realism 179, 264 n.5
  see also Barad
Aidt, Naja Marie 100, 119, 261 n.13
Aionic time 106, 124-5, 129, 152-3, 221,
    226, 248, 260 n.2
  vs. time of Chronos 47, 257 n.4
  see also Deleuze
aleatory elements 212, 219
  see also divining as immanent
    methodology
alienness
  and co-becoming 127-30; see also
    molecular mourning

and encounters 110, 116, 124-6, 143-5,
    213; see also spectrality and
    encounters
and the vibrant corpse 86, 88-9
Allen-Collinson, Jacquelyn 21, 200-2
  see also autophenomenography
a-modern onto-epistemologies 144, 155,
    159, 168-9, 174-6, 181-2, 235,
    242-6, 248, 262 n.6
  see also non-modern onto-epistemologies
amplification 113, 238
Anthropocene necropolitics 241, 247, 249
anti-abortion campaigns 180
Anzaldua, Gloria 7, 18-19, 115, 169-70,
    176-7, 178, 220
  auto-historias 203
  Aztec cosmologies and mythologies 19,
    176-7, 182, 184, 242-6; see also
    Coatlalopeuh, Coatlicue,
    Coatlicue/Coyolxauhqui
  indigenous-centred, queerfeminist
    philosophy 144-5, 166
  mestizaje and borderland identity 162
  new mestiza philosophy 162
  shamanistic onto-epistemology
    179-85, 216
  see also conocimiento,
    interconnectedness, naguala,
    nepantla, spiritmatter(ing), spiritual
    activism
Arnell, Malin 62, 66
atheism 71, 73-4, 77-8, 87, 113-15, 121,
    124, 143, 165, 199, 218-19, 242,
    247-8, 256 n.3
autophenomenography 21, 200-2
  see also Allen-Collinson

Barad, Karen 74, 84, 151, 169-70, 179,
    259 n.4
  see also agential realism, 'cutting
    together/apart', diffraction, matter
    'kicks back'

becoming 127–8, 257 n.4, 260 n.2, 260 n.4, 262, n.11
  becoming-corpse 69, 72–3, 83–4, 86–9
  becoming-cut-apart 47
  becoming-imperceptible 16–17, 19, 88, 103, 105–14, 124, 127–8, 152, 199, 260 n.3
  becoming-inhuman 84, 108
  becoming-intense 125, 186
  becoming-molecular 128–30
  becoming-a-mourning-assemblage 171–2
  becoming-one-flesh 48
  becoming-one-with-the-beloved's-cancersick-body 47
  becoming-one-with-the-passed-away-beloved 109
  becoming-one-with-inhuman-assemblages-of-ashes/seabed/algae/sand 126, 152, 213, 235, 236
  becoming-one-with-the-inhuman-forces-of-zoe 19, 108, 114, 127, 206
  becoming-other 86, 235, 243
  becoming-response-able 186
  becoming-sensitive 184, 186
  becoming as vibrant corpse 87
  becoming-voice-together-with-Kathleen-Ferrier 209
  becoming-widow 52, 235
  becoming-wounded 47
  see also Braidotti, Deleuze and Guattari
Bennett, Jane 7–8, 18–19, 72, 145–8, 150, 155, 170–2, 177, 179–83, 220, 247
  vibrant matter 8, 82, 89, 145, 182
  see also actant(s), soul (ensoulment), thing-power, vitalist materialism
Biblical one-flesh-image 47, 52
bio- and geoegalitarianism 175, 249, 259 n.1, 260 n.4
Blixen, Karen 100, 134
Bosch, Hieronymus 111, 260 n.7
Braidotti, Rosi 7, 105–8, 150, 182, 204, 220, 247
  cartography 55
  figuration 55, 200, 212–13
  inhuman concept 258 n.1
  philosophical potentials of mourning 108

posthuman, immanence philosophical death theory 16, 19, 72, 88, 105–8, 112–13, 146, 236, 262 n.2
posthumanism 173, 263 n.3
postsecularism and feminism 261–2 n.1
  see also self-styling one's own death, zoe
Broglio, Ron 205–6
butch/femme relationship 54

'cadaver' 77, 79, 81–2
  see also Kristeva
Camus, Marcel and Vinicius de Moraes 11
cancerdeath 2, 7, 9, 25, 27, 30, 32, 47, 49, 50, 51, 52, 53, 58–60, 64, 65, 69, 108, 122, 148, 149, 152, 164, 166, 183, 207, 228–33, 239–40, 241–2
carnal pain of mourning 47–8, 52–5, 205, 207–10
cartography 55, 145, 149
catharsis 52, 207–10
Charon 17
chrononormativity 43–6, 121, 128, 220
Chukchi people 195, 197, 214, 216–18, 219, 220, 267 n.9
Coatlalopeuh 176
Coatlicue 176, 184
Coatlicue/Coyolxauhqui 242–8, 250
co-becoming
  in Aionic time 152, 153
  of human/non-human actant assemblages 159, 171, 183
  with material remains and their new assemblages 110, 113–16, 121, 124, 126, 130, 153, 185, 202, 205, 206, 213
  miraculous 143–61
  as spectral encounter 53, 103, 111, 114, 116
  with vibrant corpse 87, 88, 103
companionship 48–56, 154, 257 n.5, 258 n.8
  compassionate 48–52
  symphysizing 52–3, 185, 199
conatus 2, 7, 8, 9, 14, 16, 18, 20, 35, 69, 72, 107, 121, 146–7, 171, 173, 182, 184, 238, 240–1, 260 n.6
  see also Spinoza

concorporation 53–5, 258 n.8
conjoined twins 27, 43, 47, 52, 53–5, 128, 258 n.8
conocimiento 184, 245, 247
  see also Anzaldua
contempt for the flesh 10, 72–3, 76–7, 83, 89
contralto 2, 13, 25, 65, 209, 255 n.1
conventional norms
  for mourning 40–1, 44, 45–6
  for relating to dead human bodies 71–6, 83–4
corpse as vibrant vs corpse as abject 71, 82, 84, 86–9
cosm-ontologies
  Aztec 19, 182
  Chukchi 216–18, 220
  of European folktales 175
  European and Middle Eastern 244
  indigenous 19, 216
  Latin American 244
  non-modern/a-modern 19, 235, 242–6, 248
cripqueer temporalities 44–6, 257 n.3
crip theory 41–3, 47
critical body theory 54
'cutting together/apart' 170
  see also Barad
Cvetkovich, Ann 220
  non-normative femininities 42
  'resting in sadness' 43, 46, 257 n.2, 257 n.3
cyborg writing 203
cyclical thought 19–20, 235, 242–6, 248

Dahl, Ulrika 42, 54, 260 n.5
Danish Ministry of Ecclesiastical Affairs 72, 135
Danish Protestant Church 71, 73
death
  as abject 76–84
  as becoming-imperceptible 16–17, 19, 67–8, 103, 105–8, 110–14, 127
  as becoming one with the molecular body, 126–30
  as becoming one with zoe 7, 126–7
  as continuum with life 7, 20, 72, 115, 146
  as cutting apart 2, 37, 47–9, 52–5, 199
  and cyclical thought 19, 242–6
  and desire 11, 54–5, 67–8, 69, 185, 235, 236–40
  distributed death vs death of the individual body 200, 213–18
  doings of dead bodies 74–5, 80–9, 148–59, 162–6
  as event beyond dualist divisions 7
  as impenetrable mystery 67–8, 69, 85–9, 218
  as inevitable part of life 11, 240–2
  as irreversible 14, 117–18, 120
  as metamorphoses 72, 191–3
  as nothingness 2, 4, 8, 10, 45, 115, 124, 143
  and phenomenology 108–10
  as transition 122
  as uncanny 74–84
  and underworld journey 3–4, 12, 235, 242–6
  as vibrancy 2, 7, 14–15, 67–8, 69, 72, 85–9, 124, 146, 220–1, 241–2, 246–52
decolonizing 10, 12, 19, 144–5, 169–70, 176–86, 201, 210, 213, 216–18, 221, 246–7, 249, 251, 256 n.2, 261 n.1
Deleuze, Gilles 20, 47, 125, 146, 172–3, 211, 217, 218–19, 257 n.4, 260 n.2, 262 n.11
  see also Aion/Chronos, event, Spinoza
Deleuze, Gilles and Guattari, Felix 16, 18, 72, 105–8, 111–12, 113, 115, 126–30, 155, 202–3, 220, 247
  see also affect, becoming-imperceptible, immanence, molecular/molar, plateau, rhizomatics
Demeter/Kore/Persephone 245–6
depression 39, 40–1, 43, 46, 136, 257 n.2
Derrida, Jacques 9, 119–21, 129, 170, 240, 261 n.8, 261 n.14
  see also ethics of hospitality, hauntology
Diagnostic and Statistical Manual of Mental Disorders of the American Psychiatric Association (DSM) 39, 44
diatoms 4, 122, 126, 149, 191, 255 n.1
  diatomaceous sand/earth/seabed/cliffs 7, 46, 116, 123–6, 199, 255 n.1

Didion, Joan 44, 99, 117–19, 121, 261 n.10
diffraction 19, 145, 148, 169–70, 175, 219, 247, 262 n.4
  see also Barad, Haraway
Dionysus/Orpheus 245, 268 n.3
divining as immanent methodology 210–13, 218–21
Dostoyevsky, Fyodor 77–9
dreams 3–4, 17, 18, 68, 92–8, 103, 124
  and Chukchi cosm-ontology 217
  as lines of flight 110–16, 119–22, 143–5
  as performative agency 114–16
  scarab dream 156–7, 159; see also Jung
  vertigo dream 238–9
Driesch, Hans 155, 262 n.9
dualist ontologies 7–8, 79–83, 87, 143–4, 150, 154–5, 170, 182, 185
  Cartesian 8, 72, 76–83, 183, 199, 212, 217–18, 247, 256 n.3
  Christian 8, 10, 48, 72, 76–83, 125, 143–4, 180, 183, 199, 212, 217–18, 247, 256 n.3

écriture feminine 203
Edwards, Erin 81–2
elegy 207, 266 n.4
elusiveness 83
  of dreams 143
  of miracles 143, 145, 153
  of spectres 129–30, 143
embalming 83–4
emergent methodologies 20–1
  see also experimental methodolgies, postqualitative methodologies
entelechy 155
entropy 107
epistemologies of ignorance 168–9, 178, 181, 183, 207, 211, 221, 233
ethics
  ethical potentials of excessive, molecular mourning 186, 233, 240
  ethics of conocimiento 247; see also Anzaldua
  ethics of hospitality 240; see also Derrida, Shildrick
  ethics of intercorporeality 42; see also Shildrick
  ethics of the miraculous 143, 145

ethics of response-ability 184; see also Haraway
hauntological ethics 121–2; see also Derrida
more-than-human planetary ethics 19, 207, 233
posthuman ethics of vibrant death 10, 19, 207, 235, 240–2, 246, 249
  and Spinoza 256 n.4
vitalist ethics of affirmation 10, 130, 247
event, see immanence
experimental methodologies 197, 200
  see also emergent methodologies, postqualitative methodologies

'fall' into abjection 79–80
Ferrier, Kathleen 2, 13, 25–6, 32, 37, 209, 255 n.1, 255 n.2
female masculinity 54
feminist posthumanism 145, 178, 180, 263 n.3
feminist science fiction 203
'femmebodiment' 54, 260 n.5
femme-inism 42, 54–5
femme invisibility 54
Ferrando, Francesca 173, 203
figuration of vibrant death 16, 19, 220–1, 236, 244, 246–9
figuring as speculative methodology 200, 210, 212–13, 218, 220–1
forensics as spectrology 9
Freeman, Elizabeth 42, 43, 208
Freud, Sigmund
  condensation/displacement 266 n.3
  dream theory 114, 115, 266 n.3
  making-undone 59, 117
  and mechanistic materialism 171
  mourning/melancholia-distinction 39, 45
  projection 171
  rats 147
  thanatos/eros-distinction 7
  the uncanny 72, 76, 79
Fur 99, 101–3, 122–3, 124–6, 128–30, 134, 139, 144, 149, 152–3, 158–9, 163–4, 184, 191–2, 199, 206, 255 n.1

genderqueer 48, 209
Gluck, Christoph Willibald 2, 11, 13, 14, 208, 255 n.1, 255 n.2, 266 n.5
Gonzalez-Crussi, Frank 76–7, 79
Górska, Magdalena 62
Greek mythology 15
Greimas, Algirdas Julien 174

Hades 14–16, 28, 245
Hallgren, Hanna 100, 119, 261 n.12
haptic visualization 152, 262 n.7
Haraway, Donna 169, 180–1, 184, 200, 203, 212, 221, 257 n.5, 264 n.7, 265 n.12, 265 n.13, 265 n.14
    see also companionship, cyborg writing, diffraction, figuring as speculative methodology, response-ability, symanimagenesis, sympoiesis
hauntology 47, 121, 240, 261 n.8
    see also Derrida, spectrality (embrace)
health-normativity 7, 41, 220
heteropatriarchality 73, 213, 214, 256 n.2
human exceptionalism 7, 8, 9, 10, 12, 20, 47, 78, 79, 82, 125–6, 130, 143, 154, 173, 176, 180, 182, 205, 241, 247–8, 259 n.1
humanist aesthetics 204
hologram 200, 211, 220, 265 n.1
    see also synecdoche

immanence
    and agency 125
    and becoming 262 n.11
    and co-becoming 157, 158, 159
    and cosmic forces 259 n.1
    and cosmic formula of becoming 127
    and divining 211–12
    and event 124
    and figuring 212–13
    and interconnectedness 176–7, 180
    and matter 173, 180, 264 n.6
    and metonymical writing styles 204
    and miracles 158, 167–86, 265 n.14
    plane of 172–3
    and postqualitative methodologies 211–13
    and shamanistic sensibilities 184
    and sign-reading 211–12, 218–19
    and spiritmattering 144, 183–5, 252
    and synchronicity phenomenon 156
    and transcorporeal assemblages 157, 175
    and vibrancy 88, 150, 182, 186
    and world's vitality 180, 183, 184
    see also Anzaldua, Bennett, Braidotti, Deleuze, Deleuze and Guattari
immanence philosophy 2, 12, 19, 48, 81, 106, 174, 179, 210
    see also Braidotti, Deleuze, Deleuze and Guattari
immortality 8–9, 125, 241, 248, 250, 263 n.3
imperceptibility 9, 17–18, 115, 125
    see also becoming-imperceptible, wall of imperceptibility
incomprehensibility 145, 162–3, 173, 183
indigenous-centered onto-epistemologies 145, 162
inhumanization process of death 11–12, 84, 127–8
intensities 89, 106, 109, 110–15, 141, 155–7, 183, 206, 208–10, 219, 262 n.11
interconnectedness of everything 176–7, 180, 182, 183–6, 264 n.5
    see also Anzaldua
intercorporeality 42–3, 48, 53–5, 84, 88, 115, 125–6, 202, 258 n.8
intersectional politics and analysis 177, 202
intra-action 129, 147, 170, 174–5, 240, 262 n.3, 264 n.5
irreversibility of death 14, 109, 117–18, 128, 241

Jakobson, Roman 151, 204, 266 n.3
    see also metonym (metaphor, writing styles)
Jung, Carl Gustav 262 n.8
    analytical psychology 115
    animus/anima 156
    archetypes 155
    collective human unconscious/world soul 155, 170–1
    human-centred mysticism 145, 154

human-centred vitalism 159
nazism 154
synchronicity 145, 154–7, 158

Kafer, Alison 41–4
Kant, Emmanuel 180–1, 264 n.6
Kore/Persephone/Eurydice 245–6
Kristeva, Julia 9, 72, 76, 79–83

lament 2–3, 20, 24, 37, 55, 199, 207–10, 255 n.2
   vs elegy 207, 266 n.4
Latour, Bruno 144, 174
life/death threshold 7, 8, 19, 55, 72, 80, 85–6, 87, 105, 191–3, 235, 236–40, 242–6
Limfjorden 7, 46, 93, 101, 122–3, 126, 134, 139, 141, 148–9, 152–3, 158–9, 163–4, 171, 191, 207, 215, 238, 255–6 n.1
lines of flight 110, 116, 128, 143
   as alien encounters 116, 121, 124–30
   as dreaming 110–16
   as spectral embraces 116–21, 124
Lorde, Audre 203
   biomythography 203
love-death 11–12, 13–20, 55, 109, 111, 114, 185, 205–7, 209, 235, 236–40, 241–2, 243–4, 250

MacCormack, Patricia
   ahuman 268 n.6
   embracing death 248
MacLure, Maggie 200, 211–12, 218–19
   see also divining as immanent methodology
magical thinking 44, 117–18, 120–1
Mahler, Gustav 99, 119
Marambio, Camila 4, 121, 162–6, 167–8, 178, 181, 201, 263 n.1
material(ist) spirituality 130, 141, 143
material remains 8, 13, 18, 46, 87–9, 105, 110, 114–16, 121, 124, 130
matter 'kicks back' 84, 88
   see also Barad
mechanic materialism 248–9, 256 n.3, 261 n.1
   and corpse 9, 77, 78, 80, 83, 146
   and material world 172, 173, 179, 180, 183, 185, 264 n.6
   vs vitalist materialism 170–2
Medical Museum of the Charité Hospital in Berlin 207, 228–32
Melville, Herman 211
   Bartleby 211–12
Merleau-Ponty, Maurice 12, 201, 204
   see also autophenomenography, phenomenology, posthuman phenomenology
metonym
   and agency 152, 157, 159, 171, 183, 210
   as affective relay 151
   and Lacanian reading of metonym/metaphor 288 n.3
   vs metaphor 151
   and relations 78, 151–3, 159, 171, 173, 177, 183, 209, 262 n.7
   and thought 262 n.6
   and writing style 203–5
   see also Jakobson
microchimerism 194–7, 214–18, 219–20, 265 n.1, 267 n.8
   see also Shildrick
Mignolo, Walter 18, 144, 168–70, 175, 185, 216, 218–19, 220, 247
   see also pluritopic hermeneutics, Tlostanova, unlearning
Minh-ha, Trinh 169–70, 263 n.2
miracles
   and agencies of more-than-human assemblages 145, 157
   and Christian colonizing 143, 144
   and co-becoming 143–59
   and divine intervention 78, 143, 172–4
   and ethics 143, 145
   and encounters 46
   and events 18, 143, 144, 145, 148–50, 154, 156, 158, 162–6
   and excess 153, 154, 155, 159
   and immanence 170–86
   and intuition 154, 167
   and limitations of scientific imaginaries 143, 144, 167–8
   and lines of flight 143
   and onto-epistemology 143, 144, 145, 153, 154, 157, 167–8, 170–86
   and phenomenality 149

and phenomenology 159
and superstition 144, 172–4
and vibrant more-than-human agency 126
and vitalist materialism 170–2
molecular/molar 18, 126–30
see also Deleuze and Guattari
monotheistic religions 71, 143, 177, 180–1
Monteverdi, Claudio 11
mourning
   and amputation 27, 43, 47–8, 52–5, 87–9, 109, 128, 195, 199, 208–9, 220
   and bodywork 205
   and carnal pain 47–55
   complicated 39
   excessive 7, 37, 44–7, 47–55
   and lamenting 207–10
   and melancholia 39
   molecular mourning vs molar mourning 18, 126–30
   and ongoing relations to the dead 18, 19, 45, 240
   and Orpheus 13–20
   and pathologizing 7, 39
   and queer eroticization 54–5
   and resignification 41–4
   and temporalities 44–7
   un/healthy 40–1
   see also posthuman phenomenology
mourning 'I' vs. sovereign 'I' 108–10
multi-genre texts 203

naguala 184, 245
   see also Anzaldua
Neimanis, Astrida 12, 201, 204–5, 220
neoliberalism
   and biopolitics 41, 212–13
   and health-normativity 7
   and multiculturalism 168
   and technocapitalism 241
   and tourist industry 248
nepantla 245, 247
   see also Anzaldua
New Age 143, 248
new materialism 178, 180
Newtonian physics 129, 155, 179
Nixon, Richard 237
non/living 148, 248, 249
   see also Radomska

non-modern onto-epistemologies 144, 155, 159, 168–9, 174–6, 181–2, 235, 242–6, 248, 262 n.6
   see also a-modern onto-epistemologies
non-normativity 41–3, 54–5

ongoingness (as relation to the dead) 18, 19, 45, 240
   see also mourning, shapeshifting
opera
   and love-death 11, 242–4, 256 n.6
   and mourning 25–7, 37, 209–10
   as posthuman body art 208–10
   and queer eroticism 2, 13, 208–10, 266 n.6
   and queer erotohistoriography 208
   see also Orpheus and Eurydice
Orpheus and Eurydice
   figuration 13–20, 28–34, 37, 208–9, 246–7
   myth 11–12, 235, 242–8, 268 n.3, 266 n.5
   opera 2–3, 11, 25–7, 37, 208–9, 255 n.1, 255 n.2, 266 n.5
   poem 11, 13–20, 208–9
Ovid, Publius Naso 11, 208

Pauli, Wolfgang 155, 262 n.10
Persephone 14–16, 245–6
phantom pain 55, 128, 195
phenomenality
   and afterlife 205
   and agency 145
   and incorporation 238–9
   and memories 46
   and metonymical relations 149–54
   and miracles 148–9, 167
   and ongoing relations to the dead 240
   and the revenant 119–21, 125, 129
   and spectrality 9, 12, 13, 18, 53, 105, 120, 129, 206
phenomenology, see autophenomenography, Merleau-Ponty, posthuman phenomenology
planetary ethics 19, 207, 233, 235
   and existence 212–13
   and interconnectedness 176, 186
   and kinship 196, 213–14, 265 n.13
   and politics 247
   and sustainable egalitarian ecology 242

plateau 110–14
   see also Deleuze and Guattari
Plato 10
pluritopic hermeneutics 168–9, 216,
   218–19, 242, 247
pluriversalism
   and conversation 18–19, 168–9,
      170–83, 235, 244, 264 n.7
   and onto-epistemology 144, 168–9,
      176, 182, 183, 247
position of enunciation 10, 12, 21, 108–10,
      120–1, 169, 206–7, 233, 260 n.6
positivism
   onto-epistemology 109, 119 120,
      143–5, 167, 173
   reality principle 45, 117–18, 120–1, 162, 169
postconstructionism 83–4, 259 n.4
posthuman
   aesthetics 21, 203–10
   performativity 84
   poetics 21, 203–10
   posthumanizing 8, 11–12, 41–3, 81,
      130, 144, 200, 201, 207–8, 210, 213,
      256 n.2, 261 n.1
   sensibilities 186
   see also posthuman phenomenology
posthumanist philosophy 10, 81, 145, 168,
      173, 178–81, 204, 212, 214, 263 n.3,
      264 n.7
   see also new materialism
posthuman phenomenology
   and abjectable matter 82, 86
   and intercorporeality 53–5
   and mourning 7, 10–13, 18, 20, 42, 47,
      52, 145, 148, 154, 203, 204–5, 209,
      220, 235
   and queer femme widowhood 53–5
   and vibrant matter 82, 86–9
   see also autophenomenography,
      Merleau-Ponty, phenomenology
postqualitative methodologies 20–1, 200,
      202, 210–12
   see also emergent methodologies,
      experimental methodologies
postsecularism 261 n.5
'premodern/modern' 144, 168, 174, 176,
      177, 221, 247
   see also a-modern onto-epistemologies,
      non-modern onto-epistemologies

Propp, Vladimir 174–5
   see also actant(s), Russian folktales
psychological projection 87, 153, 163,
      170–2, 183

quantum physics 155, 169–70, 179,
      262 n.4, 262 n.10, 264 n.5
queer
   queerfeminine 13, 42, 53–5, 109, 201,
      208–9, 219, 260 n.5
   queerfeminist 2, 7, 135, 176–7, 247–8
   queer femme 13, 42, 43, 53–5, 108–9,
      185, 235, 260 n.5
   queer femme-inism 42, 54–5
   queering 8, 10, 11, 12, 41–3, 46,
      144, 200–1, 208, 210, 213,
      256 n.2
   queermasculine 13, 53–5, 128, 209
   queer theory 41–3
Quigley, Christine 76–7

Radiohead 211–12
Radomska, Marietta 248
Ramey, Joshua 155, 200, 211, 218–19
real/not-real-distinction 120, 168, 179,
      239, 264 n.7
relic theory 151
response-ability 184, 265 n.12
   see also Haraway
'resting in sadness' 43, 46, 257 n.2
   see also Cvetkovich
revenant 112, 114, 119, 129, 261 n.8
rhizomatics 45, 105, 106, 109, 110–16,
      121, 124, 144–9, 154–5, 159, 167,
      173, 184, 195, 235, 242
   see also Deleuze and Guattari
Russian folktales 174–6
   see also Propp
Rückert, Friedrich 99–100, 119, 261 n.11
Rytkheu, Yury 214, 217, 267 n.9

Sartre, Jean-Paul 10, 44–5, 107, 113, 115,
      200, 256 n.5
scaling up 235–6, 242, 244, 268 n.1
Schaeffer, Felicia Amaya 144, 178–83,
      264 n.5, 264 n.7, 264 n.8
self-styling one's own death 146, 236–7,
      262 n.2
   see also Braidotti

sexual difference theory 55
Shakespeare, William 11, 120, 170, 256 n.6, 261 n.14
shamanism 176, 178, 179, 181, 184, 185, 216, 246
   see also Anzaldua
shapeshifting 20, 182, 235, 236–52
Shildrick, Margrit 42, 54, 121, 194–5, 214–18, 240, 258 n.8, 265 n.1, 265 n.2, 267 n.8
   see also concorporation, conjoined twins, critical body theory, ethics of hospitality, intercorporeality, microchimerism
show-don't-tell 202, 265 n.1
soul
   and agency 179
   Christian colonizing of 'soul' 181–2, 264–5 n.9
   ensoulment 175, 179–82, 264 n.6; *see also* Bennett
   immortal 8–9, 78, 125, 250
   and indigenous philosophy 181–2, 214–6, 244
   and moral ladder 216
   soul/body dualism 10, 12, 80, 83, 87, 146, 182–3, 185, 215, 256 n.3
   soul vitalism 180–2; *see also* Bennett
   world soul 155, 157, 170–1; *see also* Jung
sovereign 'I', *see* mourning 'I' vs sovereign 'I'
spectrality
   and phenomenality 9, 12, 13, 18, 53, 105, 119–21, 125, 129, 206
   and embrace 121, 124–30, 152, 240
   and encounters 46, 110, 114–16, 120–30, 152
   and hauntology 47, 121, 240, 261 n.8; *see also* Derrida
speculation
   and ethics 265 n.11
   and fabulation 203
   as philosophical methodology 18, 159, 168–86, 267 n.8
Spinoza
   bodies affecting bodies 15, 16 18, 256 n.4
   conatus 2, 7, 8, 35, 240

de-authorizing of religious institutions 180
miracles 172–4, 180
monism 16, 146
'what can bodies do?' 115, 145
   see also affect(ivity)
spiritmatter(ing) 4, 89, 206, 220–1
   and non-modern/a-modern cosm-ontologies 177, 182–6
   vs Christian ensoulment 181
   and immanence philosophy 144, 182–6
   and indigenous philosophies 144, 177, 180, 181–6, 201, 214, 216–18, 219;
      see also Anzaldua, Schaeffer
   and vitalist materialism 144, 182–6
spiritual activism 176–7, 185, 245, 247, 249
   see also Anzaldua
spiritual(ist) materialism 8, 143, 145, 166, 168, 178–9, 244, 247–8, 264 n.8
   see also Anzaldua, material(ist) spirituality, Schaeffer
split reality 118
strange temporalities of mourning 44–7
surrealism 115, 203
Styx 17
symanimagenesis 185, 262, 265 n.14
symphysizing 48–55, 82, 84, 87, 109, 185, 199, 201–2, 209, 218–19, 238–40, 241, 243, 258 n.8, 260 n.5
sympoiesis 185, 226, 265 n.13
synchronicity 145, 154–7, 158
   see also Jung
synecdoche 200, 211, 219, 265 n.1

Tchaikovsky, Pyotr Ilyich 237
temporalities
   Aionic time 106, 124–5, 129, 152–3, 221, 226, 248, 260 n.2
   arrow of time 45
   chrononormative time 43–6, 106, 120–1, 124, 125, 128, 220, 248
   cripqueer time 43–4
   cyclical time 216–18, 235, 243–4, 246, 248; *see also* shapeshifting
   strange temporalities of mourning 44–7
thing-power 145, 146–54, 171, 174–5
   see also actant(s), Bennett

Tlostanova, Madina 18, 144, 168–70, 175, 185, 216, 218–19, 220, 247
  see also Mignolo, pluritopic hermeneutics, unlearning
Todd, Zoe 178, 181
transhumanism 241–2, 248
  vs critical posthumanism 173, 263 n.3
Trier, Trine 149, 262 n.5
triptych 1, 92, 111, 211
trouser role 2, 13, 209, 255 n.1, 266 n.6

underworld journey 2, 3–4, 12, 14–20, 28, 235, 236–40, 242–6, 251, 255 n.2
unlearning 53, 130, 162, 168–9, 178, 185–6, 221
unscripting 47–8, 52
'until-death-do-us-part' 47–8

Vakhrushev, Alexei 217, 267n.9
vibrant corpse 85–9
vibrant death as figuration 16, 19, 220–1, 236, 244, 246–52
  see also death as vibrancy
vibrant matter 8, 82, 89, 145, 182
  see also Bennett
Virgen de Guadalupe 176–7, 182, 184
Virgil, Publius Maro 11, 243, 246
vitalist materialism 7, 18–19, 145, 148–50, 154–9, 171, 180–2, 247–8
  and ethics of affirmation 130
  and immanence philosophy 18–19, 145, 148, 150, 154–9, 172, 174, 247–8
  and ontology 171
  and mechanic materialism 170–2
  and planetary commitment 235
  and posthuman frameworks 145, 150, 154, 171

and spiritualist materialism 18–19, 168, 177–82, 247–8
  see also spiritual(ist) materialism

wall of imperceptibility 17–18, 46, 52, 55, 125, 192
wall of silence 17–18, 46, 103, 105–6, 114–16, 121–30, 199–201, 220–1, 236
'war on cancer' 242
Western imaginaries 76, 80, 143, 213, 248
Western modernity 7, 11–12, 41, 72, 74, 76, 83, 109–10, 120, 126, 144, 168–9, 179, 183, 185, 220, 221, 248
Western onto-epistemologies 72, 162, 168–70, 174–7, 181
Western philosophy 10–11, 18, 174, 182
Western romantic lyrics 205–6
Wisconsin Death Trip 83
wonder
  and miracles 163–4
  'phenomenology of wonder' 206;
    see also Broglio
Woolf, Virginia 4, 136, 236
writing as a method of inquiry 200–2

zoe
  and alien encounters 125
  and Braidotti's death theory 19, 107–8, 182, 258–9 n.1, 260 n.4, 262 n.2
  and co-becoming 114
  concept 7, 16, 150, 258–9 n.1, 260 n.4
  corpse as vibrant zoe body 72, 88–9, 103
  and dreams 115
  dying as becoming-one-with-zoe 107–9, 113, 125–8, 152
  and indifferent inhuman agency 108